AMERICAN JEWS

A READER

Edited, with introductions and notes,
by MARSHALL SKLARE

Center for Modern Jewish Studies
Brandeis University

Library of Jewish Studies

EDITOR

Neal Kozodoy

ADVISORY COMMITTEE

Emil L. Fackenheim
Judah Goldin
Isadore Twersky

BEHRMAN HOUSE, INC. | PUBLISHERS | NEW YORK

ACKNOWLEDGMENTS

The author and publisher thank the following for permission to reprint:

American Behavioral Scientist for Chaim I. Waxman, "The Threadbare Canopy: The Vicissitudes of the Jewish Family in Modern American Society." ©1980 by Sage Publications.

The American Jewish Committee for Daniel J. Elazar, "Decision-Making in the American Jewish Community." © 1973 the American Jewish Committee.

The American Jewish Committee and Jewish Publication Society for Sidney Goldstein, "Jews in the United States: Perspectives from Demography": Charles S. Liebman, "Orthodoxy in American Jewish Life." © 1965, 1979, 1980 by the American Jewish Committee and The Jewish Publication Society of America.

Commentary for David Singer, "Living with Intermarriage." © 1979 by *Commentary*.

The Jewish Publication Society of America for selections from Charles S. Liebman, *The Ambivalent American Jew.* © 1973 by The Jewish Publication Society of America.

The Macmillan Company for Herbert J. Gans, "The Origin and Growth of a Jewish Community in the Suburbs: A Study of the Jews of Park Forest." © 1958 by The Free Press.

Teachers College Press for selections from Lloyd P. Gartner, ed. *Jewish Education in the United States.* © 1969 by Teachers College, Columbia University.

The Theodor Herzl Foundation for selections from Ben Halpern, *The American Jew.* © 1956 by The Theodor Herzl Foundation.

The Theodor Herzl Foundation and *Midstream* for Marshall Sklare, "Lakeville and Israel/The Six-Day War and its Aftermath." © 1968 by Marshall Sklare.

UNESCO for Lloyd P. Gartner, "Immigration and the Formation of American Jewry, 1840–1925." © 1968 by UNESCO. This article has also been published in H. H. Ben-Sasson and S. Ettinger, ed., *Jewish Society Through the Ages* (New York: Shocken, London: Vallentine Mitchell, 1971).

The Union of American Hebrew Congregations for selections from Leonard J. Fein, Robert Chin, Jack Dauber, Bernard Reisman, and Herzl Spiro, *Reform is a Verb: Notes on Reform and Reforming Jews.* © 1972 by the Union of American Hebrew Congregations.

The University of Chicago Press for selections from Marshall Sklare and Joseph Greenblum, *Jewish Identity on the Suburban Frontier: A Study of Group Survival in the Open Society.* 2nd ed. © 1979 The University of Chicago Press.

Library of Congress Cataloging in Publication Data
Sklare, Marshall. comp.
American Jews/A Reader.
  (Library of Jewish Studies)
  Includes bibliographical references.
  1. Jews—United States—Social conditions—
Addresses, essays, lectures. 2. Judaism—United
States—Addresses, essays, lectures. 3. United
States—Ethnic relations—Addresses, essays,
lectures. I. Sklare, Marshall, 1921–
II. Series.
E184.J5A614   1982   305.8'924'073   82-9742
ISBN 0-87441-348-6
© Copyright 1983 by Marshall Sklare
Published by Behrman House, Inc., 1261 Broadway, New York, N.Y. 10001
Manufactured in the United States of America

10 9 8 7 6 5 4 3 2

CONTENTS

PREFACE

THE PRESENT VOLUME replaces, and partially incorporates, two texts which are now out of print in the Library of Jewish Studies published by Behrman House: *The Jew in American Society* and *The Jewish Community in America*. While this volume represents something of a departure from the original, in general its organization follows the chapter headings of my book *America's Jews*, and can therefore be used as a reader in conjunction with that work.

I am grateful to colleagues who have given me the benefit of their classroom experience with the previous, two-volume edition. They include Abraham J. Karp of the University of Rochester and Bruce Phillips of Hebrew Union College-Jewish Institute of Religion, Los Angeles. I have also benefited from the observations of Gerald Showstack, who has served with distinction as my teaching assistant.

This work would not have been possible in its present form without the support of the Center for Modern Jewish Studies of Brandeis University, established with the aid of the Charles H. Revson Foundation. The statements made and views expressed, however, are solely the responsibility of the authors.

I appreciate the encouragement of Marvin Fox, the Director of the Lown School of Near Eastern and Judaic Studies at Brandeis. I am also indebted to Neal Kozodoy, editor of the Library of Jewish Studies. Finally I am grateful to the authors and publishers who have permitted their works to be utilized in this volume.

Marshall Sklare
Waltham, Massachusetts

AMERICAN JEWRY / SOCIAL HISTORY AND GROUP IDENTITY

IMMIGRATION AND THE FORMATION OF AMERICAN JEWRY, 1840–1925
by LLOYD P. GARTNER

INTRODUCTION

JEWISH IMMIGRATION from the colonial period to the 1920's is generally divided into three periods: the Sephardic, the German, and the East European. The division does not always correspond to the actual facts of immigration but rather indicates which group set its cultural stamp upon the Jewish community at a given period.

The understandable tendency of present-day American Jews is to endow their immigrant ancestors with a higher status than they actually attained. The religious piety of these ancestors is also frequently exaggerated. The persistent tendency to change the shape of the past to conform with present needs can be noticed in a variety of different contexts. Thus, individuals who are active in Jewish affairs frequently deplore what they consider a lack of solidarity in the contemporary community. Implicit in their criticism is the belief that at an earlier period in American Jewish history there was strong cohesion within the Jewish community. However, in reality there was a measure of friction between Sephardic and German Jews and at a later period there was serious confrontation and conflict between German and East European Jews. Conflict existed side by side with cohesion—conflict was related to cohesion inasmuch as the established community saw itself as responsible for the newcomers.

3

In the nineteenth century important groups within the established Jewish community felt that America had reached its absorptive capacity and that prospective Jewish immigrants should be influenced instead to settle in other parts of the globe, or even to remain in Europe. Rather than viewing the newcomers as brothers who would fortify the Jewish community and improve its chances for survival, the established element tended to look upon the immigrants as paupers lacking in the desire to improve themselves, as beggars who would constitute a permanent drain upon the resources of the established group, and as foreigners incapable of understanding American ways or of adapting themselves to the American environment. In reality, the East European immigrants proved exactly the opposite: they eagerly sought self-improvement, they made heroic efforts to be self-sustaining, they were strongly attracted by American culture. The behavior of the established community can only be explained by the fact that despite their patriotism and seeming confidence in the country, they harbored deep doubts about the underlying sentiment of Gentile America toward the Jew. On the one hand, the established element affirmed its confidence in American fair-mindedness but, on the other hand, it was afraid to put the nation to the test.

Lloyd P. Gartner is widely admired for his penetrating writing on American and English-Jewish history. In the present essay, Gartner highlights the way in which American Jewry has been shaped by the traditions of both Western and Eastern European Jews. Furthermore, by stressing the impact of the Kishinev pogrom on the German Jew, as well as the fact that many leading German Jews eventually came to defend the right of free immigration to America, Gartner makes possible a more sophisticated understanding of the complicated relationship between Germans and East Europeans in the Jewish community. Finally, in his treatment of the colonial period, Gartner analyzes the contrast between the position of the Jew in American law and public life and the situation in Europe; the contrast is essential for understanding the character of American Jewish life. The ramifications of this crucial theme are analyzed in the article by Ben Halpern.

M. S.

THE JEWS of the United States form today the largest Jewish group of any country in the world, as they have since the break up of Czarist Russia in 1918. Their number is estimated at 6,060,000 persons.[1] Although they have lived since the mid-seventeenth century in the territories which now compose the United States, only since approximately 1880 has the Jewish population attained great size. Historians generally accept that perhaps 2,000 Jews lived in the Thirteen Colonies at the time of the American Revolution, and fifty years later, about 1825, the number was still no higher than about 6,000. Sharp increase began from then, however, for in 1840 there were about 15,000 Jews, and at the outbreak of the American Civil War in 1861 an estimated 150,000 lived there.[2] When the first rudimentary survey of American Jewry was undertaken in 1877 by the Board of Delegates of American Israelites, the total was put at 280,000.[3] From this point, the Jewish population multiplied with astonishing rapidity, owing almost entirely to mass immigration from Eastern Europe. Contemporaries estimated that 1,000,000 Jews dwelled in the United States in 1900, 3,000,000 in 1915, and 4,500,000 in 1925, when drastic immigration laws took effect.[4] The rate of Jewish population increase between 1840 and 1925 was thus far higher than that for the United States as a whole. While the

---

[1]*American Jewish Year Book,* 1972, ed. Morris Fine and Milton Himmelfarb (New York and Philadelphia, 1972), pp. 386–87 (abbrev. *AJYB*). The statistics of American Jewish population for all periods are unreliable. For the earliest known head count of an American Jewish community, taken by a Milwaukee rabbi in 1875, see Louis J. Swichkow and Lloyd P. Gartner, *A History of the Jews of Milwaukee* (Philadelphia, 1963), pp. 65–67. There have been, however, numerous quite exact population surveys of local communities during recent decades, based on careful sampling rather than actual count.

[2]Salo W. Baron and Joseph L. Blau, eds., *The Jews of the United States 1790–1840: A Documentary History,* 3 vols. (New York, Philadelphia, London, 1963), I, pp. 85–86, 255 n. 1; Bertram W. Korn, *American Jewry and the Civil War* (Philadelphia, 1951), p. 1.

[3]David Sulzberger, "The Growth of Jewish Population in the United States," *Publication of the American Jewish Historical Society* (abbrev. *PAJHS*), VI (1897), pp. 141–149.

[4]The growth may be seen from the annual estimates in the *AJYB,* "Statistics of Jews" section.

country's 11,000,000 inhabitants multiplied over tenfold to 115,000,000 during this period, the Jews increased more than three hundred times over. Since 1925, however, Jewish population growth has been reversed. With 206,000,000 persons now (November, 1972) living in the United States—an increase of 91,000,000 since 1925—the Jewish increment has been a reatively small 1,560,000. This disproportionately small growth has occurred notwithstanding the fact, that despite immigration laws, American Jewry has received a proportionately greater accession to its numbers since 1925 from foreign immigration than has the general American population.[5]

Between 1825 and 1925, therefore, the increase in American Jewry was owing to immigration from abroad. Since 1925, the relatively small increase seems due to the great decrease in that immigration.

These immigrants became transformed into Americans in culture, language, and loyalties, yet the vast majority also remained distinctly Jewish in consciousness, by desire, and in formal affiliation. It is of great interest, therefore, to examine the sources and character of Jewish immigration, and its adaptation to American life.

Well before substantial Jewish immigration began to flow, the highly favorable terms by which Jews, and others, could enter and accommodate themselves in American life were fixed. Early America was a land of Protestant Christians, whose bugbear in religion was not the near-legendary Jews but recognizable Catholics—a bitter heritage of Reformation struggles. Gradually, however, religion in America was permeated during the eighteenth century with philanthropy and humanitarianism, the belief that the truest Christianity was man's fulfillment of his purpose to do good on earth. These ideas tended to slice through Protestant denominational walls, and very slowly to flatten them. The denigration of the historic dogmas of Christianity opened the chance that the ancient "synagogue of Satan" might be granted rights nearly equal with the church of Christ on American soil. Moreover, the emphasis upon

---

[5]United States Department of Commerce, Bureau of the Census, *Historical Statistics of the United States: Colonial Times to 1957* (Washington, D.C., 1963), Series A 1–3, p. 7; Series C 88–114, p. 56; Mark Wischnitzer, *To Dwell in Safety: The Story of Jewish Migration since 1800* (Philadelphia, 1948), p. 289; the *AJYB* contains an annual report on Jewish immigration to the United States.

good works was to have very far-reaching consequences for the character of Judaism in America during the nineteenth century.[6]

Thinking about religion during the eighteenth century also helped to produce a change of fundamental character in the relations between Church and State. Most Protestant sects in America stressed the utterly individual nature of human sin and conversion and salvation, and vigorously opposed any coercive ecclesiastical intervention, particularly the Church linked to the State. Members of state churches in Europe, such as Lutherans and Catholics, were generally small, little loved minorities in Colonial America which also became accustomed to maintaining their religious institutions unaided and unhampered.

The power of the Protestant left thus combined with its spiritual opposite, the secular, anti-clerical bias of Enlightenment thinking, to bring about the separation of Church and State. Religious tests and sectarian oaths of office were abolished and prohibited, and the First Amendment to the federal constitution virtually completed the process by forbidding Congress to establish or support any religion. State constitutions made similar provisions.

These momentous developments during the latter half of the eighteenth century were of invaluable importance for the Jews who were destined to come to America. Except for an occasional religious qualification for public office in a few State constitutions, all of which were presently removed, the Jews enjoyed full civil, religious, and political equality with other religions from the time of American independence. This was full emancipation in the European sense, and it was acquired with barely any reference to the Jews as such, but rather as a matter of broad principle.[7] The separation of Church and State also meant that no one was required to profess religious belief or maintain religious affiliation; churches, and religious societies generally, were private associations which

---

[6]H. Shelton Smith, Robert T. Handy, Lefferts A. Loetscher, *American Christianity: An Historical Interpretation with Representative Documents*, 2 vols. (New York, 1960), pp. 374–414.

[7]Alan Heimert, *Religion and the American Mind from the Great Awakening to the Revolution* (Cambridge, Mass., 1966), pp. 128–129, 136–137, 524–527, 537–539; Anson Phelps Stokes, *Church and State in the United States*, 3 vols. (New York, 1950), I, pp. 133–149, 240–253, 519–552, 731–744, 744–767; for the exceptions to the generalities, see *ibid.*, pp. 428–432 (New Hampshire), 865–878 (Maryland). A useful review is Abram Vossen Goodman, *American Overture: Jewish Rights in Colonial Times* (Philadelphia, 1947).

established rules as they wished. Religious sects and insitutions could be established at will; schismatics enjoyed unlimited freedom alongside orthodox communicants. How deeply Judaism was affected by this pattern may be judged from the fact that most Jewish religious institutions in the United States are synagogues which have deviated more or less from the Jewish canon, and nearly nothing could be done by traditionalists to restrain them. While the constitutional deliberations were in progress, the Jews seem to have remained indifferent to them. They were mainly interested in the abolition of religious tests and oaths,[8] not in the separation of Church and State. But then, these Jews were newcomers, and probably still retained the historic Jewish wariness of intruding into the political affairs of the Gentile world.

Thus, even before European Jewry began its historic struggle for emancipation, which was not consummated until the end of World War I, the entire question was settled quite casually in America. The issue of the enfranchisement of Jews specifically, and the terms of Jewish entry into the general society, never existed here. Jewish immigrants also found that no formal, legally established Jewish community existed here with its traditions, controls, and taxes. They could be or not be Jews, as they pleased, and if they preferred not they did not have to become Christians—an act repugnant to most reluctant Jews. They could occupy the neutral ground of enlightened secular humanism or religious indifferentism. The possibilities of Judaism and Jewish life in America under the regime of free option, state aloofness, and automatic emancipation were to be explored by every generation of Jews who came to America. Such a regime had no precedent in the entire millennial history of the Jews.

The first Jews in America were Sefardim, descendants of Spanish and Portuguese Jews. It has long been known that many of these pioneers were not actually of Spanish culture. By the eighteenth century, formally Sefardi congregations consisted mainly of Ashkenazi (Central and East European) congregants, who accepted the strange liturgy and customs of what was then the single synagogue in the town.[9] In fact, the Philadelphia synagogue,

---

[8]Stokes, op. cit., pp. 286–290, 528–529; Edwin Wolf 2nd and Maxwell Whiteman, The History of the Jews of Philadelphia from Colonial Times to the Age of Jackson (Philadelphia, 1957), pp. 147–149.

[9]David de Sola Pool, An Old Faith in the New World (New York, 1955), pp. 437, 461.

founded only a few years after the first recorded appearance of Jews in that city in 1735, had no Sefardi members, yet adopted the Sefardi rite.[10] The continuance of the Sefardi form of worship, despite the minority of Spanish and Portuguese Jews in the little Colonial communities, was assisted by the characteristically Sefardi rule of prohibiting the separate local congregations which proliferated among Ashkenazim, and of centralizing local Jewish affairs in the *Mahamad* (executive) of the single established synagogue.

Colonial Jews who were not Sefardim were mainly recently arrived Central Europeans. The differences between them and the Sefardim lay deeper than in ritual. The latter were for centuries naturalized in Iberian culture, spoke Spanish or Portuguese, and had fused their Judaism with Spanish culture. To that extent they could be called modern Jews. Their Judaism was not learned or passionate, but polite and urbane. The comparative success of this combination of contemporary culture and Jewish tradition, although it was rather superficial, suggests the principal reason why no Sefardi synagogue abandoned Orthodoxy for Reform Judaism during the nineteenth century. On the other hand, the Central European Jewish majority consisted largely of Jews of traditional culture. They were not learned or wealthy stock, nor had they moved in the small circles of German Jews which were reaching out ultimately to create the memorable synthesis of German culture and Judaism. These Bavarian, Posen, or Silesian Jews came to America from the villages and small towns of their native land, generally knew and observed the rudiments of Judaism and little more, and spoke and wrote Yiddish rather than German. In their great majority they were tradesmen, ranging from country peddlers to merchant shippers, and many were independent craftsmen. Apprentices and indentured servants could be found, and rarely a physician, a lawyer, or a leisured gentleman.[11] The main cities were New York City, Philadelphia, and Charleston, South Carolina, with outlying settlements in inland or "fall line" towns like Lancaster, Pennsylvania, Albany, New York, and Richmond, Virginia.

[10]Wolf and Whiteman, *op. cit.*, pp. 7, 32, 41–42, 122, 228; correspondence was conducted in Yiddish (p. 226).

[11]Jacob R. Marcus, *Early American Jewry*, 2 vols. (Philadelphia, 1951–1953), II, pp. 395–428; Wolf and Whiteman, *op. cit.*, pp. 165–186; Leo Hershkowitz, *Wills of Early New York Jews, 1704–1799* (New York, 1967), supplies unique, fresh data.

The 6,000 Jews of 1826 began to increase rapidly from that year. The impulse to emigrate was strongly felt in German Jewry, which by the 1830's and 1840's was more different from its eighteenth-century ancestors than those ancestors had been from sixteenth-century German Jews. Young Jews of the day uniformly received a German education, and even university study was not uncommon. Great political events also had their influence. During the Napoleonic years bright hopes for emancipation and full entry into German society soared, as Prussia and other duchies and cities freed their Jews from venerable restrictions on marriage, settlement, occupation, and from special taxes. But the period of political reaction and economic depression after 1815 brought the deepest disappointments to expectant Jews. Political restrictions were reinstituted, and the restored powers of Christian guilds denied access to some occupations for skilled Jews. The Christian State theories by which these measures were justified were subscribed to by influential politicians and intellectuals, and increased the Jews' sense of deprivation and exclusion. Apostasy was one escape from the predicament, and emigration was another. If the German homeland would not have them as faithful subjects, a new homeland could be found in free America. Land hunger, which drove millions of Germans across the Atlantic, played no role in Jewish emigration.[12]

German Jews had known and idealized America during the eighteenth century. The Constitutional Convention of 1787 received a puzzling but ardent petition from anonymous German Jews about settling in America, and periodic talk of the New World was not rare.[13] To the economic and psychological background of immigration could be added the steady improvement in the safety,

---

[12]Mack Walker, *Germany and the Emigration 1816–1885* (Cambridge, Mass., 1964), pp. 42–102; Marcus L. Hansen, *The Atlantic Migration 1607–1860* (new ed., New York, 1961), pp. 120–171; Selma Stern-Taeubler, "The Motivation of the German-Jewish Emigration to America in the Post-Mendelssohnian Era," *Essays in American Jewish History* (Cincinnati, 1958), pp. 247–262; Rudolf Glanz, "The Immigration of German Jews up to 1880," *YIVO Annual of Jewish Social Science* (abbrev. *YAJSS*), II/III (1948), pp. 81–99; *idem*, "Source Materials for the History of Jewish Immigration to the United States 1800–1880," *YAJSS*, VI (1951), pp. 73–156 (invaluable gathering of sources, mostly from German-Jewish press).

[13]Baron and Blau, *op. cit.*, III, pp. 891–893; Morris U. Schappes, *A Documentary History of the Jews in the United States 1654–1875* (2nd ed., New York, 1953), pp. 159–160.

speed, and regularity of trans-Atlantic travel. Between the 1820's and 1870's perhaps 150,000 Jews from German lands came to the United States, mainly from Bavarian towns and villages, German Poland, Bohemia, and Hungary.[14] Their geographic diffusion in America was wider than any Jewish immigrant group of earlier or later times. During these mid-nineteenth century decades of newly founded western frontier cities, California gold, and the peak of the southern cotton economy, German Jews scattered throughout the United States. Probably the majority settled in the Northeast, but a large number made their way to newly opened California, centering in San Francisco; a string of Jewish settlements appeared at the ports down the length of the Mississippi River; numerous Jewish communities arose in the cities along the Ohio River and the Great Lakes, centers of commerce and heavy industry; in dozens of small towns in the South, Jewish merchants kept store and traded in the freshly picked cotton.[15]

Jews from German lands took pride in their German culture. They were pillars of American Germandom, contributing and participating heavily in the advancement of German in the United States. They maintained German social and charitable societies, were subscribers to and writers for German newspapers, singers and instrumentalists in German musical societies, impresarios, performers and faithful patrons in the German theaters. It appears also that Jews enjoyed access to the Turnverein athletic societies and German social clubs in many cities. German fraternal orders included many Jewish members. Indeed, Jews were included among the American Germans who articulated the idea that they had the

[14]Rudolf Glanz, "The Immigration of German Jews . . . ," loc. cit.; idem, "The 'Bayer' and the 'Pollack' in America," Jewish Social Studies, XVII, 1 (January 1955), pp. 27–42; Guido Kisch, In Search of Freedom: A History of American Jews from Czechoslovakia (London, 1949), pp. 13–58.

[15]Allan Tarshish, "The Economic Life of the American Jew in the Middle Nineteenth Century," Essays . . . ," pp. 263–293; Rudolf Glanz, The Jews of California from the Discovery of Gold until 1880 (New York, 1960), pp. 18–91, 106–109; Harris Newmark, Sixty Years in Southern California 1853–1913 (3rd ed., Boston and New York, 1930); Jacob R. Marcus, Memoirs of American Jews 1775–1865 (3 vols., Philadelphia, 1955), contains dozens of useful and interesting autobiographical statements, typically by immigrant businessmen of the times; Swichkow and Gartner, op. cit., pp. 12–18, 93–110; W. Gunther Plaut, The Jews of Minnesota: The First Seventy-Five Years (New York, 1959), pp. 9–30, 61–68; Stephen Birmingham, "Our Crowd": The Great Jewish Families of New York (New York, 1967), is a gossipy social chronicle occasionally useful.

mission of diffusing a higher, philosophic culture among the Yankees.[16]

For some German Jews, the German milieu in America was so fully satisfying that they more or less abandoned their ancestral Judaism. One might mention in this connection Abraham Jacobi (1830–1919), the father of American pediatrics, the socialist leader Victor Berger (1860–1929), or Oswald Ottendorfer (1826–1900), who published the leading German newspaper in New York. The great majority, however, remained within Judaism and created a version satisfying to their desire for a religion which harmonized intellectually with contemporary liberalism, rationalism, and historical scholarship. This was Reform Judaism. On the surface, it meant that the old informality and intensity of Jewish worship was replaced by a liturgical model suggestive of Protestantism, housed in a temple which often imitated intentionally the "Golden Age" architecture of Spanish Jewry. All Jewish laws and customs which enforced a social gulf between Jews and Christians were abrogated, with the single, critical exception of Jewish-Christian marriages. The transition from inherited Orthodoxy to new-style Reform took place with astonishing speed. After a false beginning in Charleston during the 1820's, Reform actually began about 1850. By 1890 nearly every synagogue founded by German Jews had overturned the traditions of centuries and taken up the new way. The Orthodox and proto-Conservatives survived as small groups, individual rabbis, and a few congregations.[17]

In any of dozens of American Jewish local communities during the 1880's and 1890's, the typical scene was a representative

---

[16]Rudolf Glanz, *Jews in Relation to the Cultural Milieu of the Germans in America up to the Eighteen-Eighties* (New York, 1947); Swichkow and Gartner, *op. cit.*, pp. 13–27; John A. Hawgood, *The Tragedy of German-America* (New York and London, 1940), is a penetrating analysis.

[17]David Philipson, *The Reform Movement in Judaism* (new ed., New York, 1967), (originally published in 1907 and somewhat revised in 1931; this rather partisan work is quite antiquated but has not been superseded as a whole); James G. Heller, *Isaac M. Wise: His Life, Work and Thought* (New York, 1965), (a voluminous, compendious biography of the most important leader); Swichkow and Gartner, *op. cit.*, pp. 32–51, 171–192; Morris A. Gutstein, *A Priceless Heritage: The Epic Growth of Nineteenth Century Chicago Jewry* (New York, 1953), pp. 57–92, 139–208 (these studies exemplify local developments); Moshe Davis, *The Emergence of Conservative Judaism: The Historical School in 19th Century America* (Philadelphia, 1963), pp. 149–228 (on the opposition to Reform); the *Dictionary of American Biography* includes Berger, Jacobi, and Ottendorfer, as well as most major nineteenth-century Jewish religious figures.

leadership of prosperous merchants, sometimes bankers and lawyers. By coming to America, they had not left a bitter for a gentler exile, where they would await messianic redemption; the Messiah was the millennium of all mankind, and their own future lay entirely in America. To these Jews, "Jew" meant only to profess the Jewish religion. All that was suggestive of "ghetto" had to be discarded, now that the physical ghetto was a thing of the past and Jews no longer wished to live in segregation. Their Judaism contained nothing mystical or contemplative; it was formulated as an optimistic, reasonable American religion, with happiness and salvation attainable by human effort. The essence of Judaism was only moral and ethical, while the externals of the traditional way of life were classified among changeable outward observances and consequently abandoned. Yet persons who did not practice or believe in any Jewish religious principles were still regarded as Jews. The ethnic basis of Judaism remained alive among the German Jews, but subdued, until vigorously thrust forward by the new arrivals from Eastern Europe.[18]

Germanic Judaism declined in America from the 1880's. The Second Reich founded by Bismarck disappointed the liberal traditions cherished by '48-ers and hastened their American assimilation, while the anti-Semitic trends in Imperial Germany did not encourage Jews.[19] Germanness in the United States was preserved longest not among urban German liberals, but in the conservative, rural, and small-city German Lutheran churches. Yet it was inevitable that children and grandchildren finally ceased to speak and study German and finally forgot it. The close, comfortable association of Germanness with Judaism ended when East European Jewish immigrants inundated the 280,000 Jews of 1880. Although German was still spoken in the privacy of many families, the German age was past at the close of the nineteenth century.

Once again, numbers tell much of the story which began in the 1880's. By 1900, there were 1,000,000 Jews in the United States, and about 3,000,000 in 1915. When free immigration to America ended in 1925, there were probably 4,500,000 Jews; this was the point when

[18]This paraphrases Swichkow and Gartner, op. cit., pp. 169–170.

[19]Glanz, Jews in Relation to the Cultural Milieu . . . , pp. 34–37; Swichkow and Gartner, op. cit., pp. 133–136; Carl F. Wittke, Refugees of Revolution: The German Forty-Eighters in America (Philadelphia, 1952), pp. 344–373; two small tales recounted in Birmingham, op. cit., pp. 159, 191–192; Hawgood, op. cit.

Jews reached their highest proportion in the American population—about four percent. The climactic years of East European immigration came after the pogroms of 1881, again in 1890 and 1891, and above all during the years of war, revolution, and reaction in Russia which began for Jews with the notorious Kishinev pogrom of 1903. From 1904 through 1908, 642,000 Jews entered the United States.[20]

It would be an error to take pogroms as the main cause of emigration. Galicia, with its Jews emancipated from 1867 and without pogroms, showed perhaps the highest proportion of emigration from Eastern Europe. It was the fivefold increase of East European Jewry during the nineteenth century and the failure of the economy to keep pace with this multiplication, which must be considered the most deeply rooted cause. Repressive Russian laws restricted economic opportunities still further, and drove Jews to a feeling of hopelessness about their future in Russia. With railroads and steamships fully developed into instruments of migration, there were widely advertised and regularly scheduled departures of emigrant ships from such major ports as Hamburg, Bremen, Rotterdam, and Liverpool. Human movement could proceed in massive proportions. Russia also took a passive attitude toward emigration, by unofficially permitting hundreds of thousands of Jews to cross its border. After 1905, the Jewish Colonization Association was permitted to maintain emigrant offices in several cities. Above all, entrance into the United States continued to be nearly unhindered, although immigrants feared the examination at the port of entry (usually Ellis Island, in New York harbor) which disqualified for entry perhaps one percent of arrivals.[21]

Between East European and Germanic Jews there are marked contrasts. The newer arrivals were almost exclusively of traditional Jewish culture. They had no Polish or Russian education—although the Galicians had been required to attend a government school— and few knew the languages of Eastern Europe. A significant

[20]On East European Jewish immigration, in addition to sources cited supra, note 5, see Samuel Joseph, *Jewish Immigration to the United States 1881–1910* (New York, 1914), (useful for statistics) and the massive collective work: Walter F. Willcox, ed., *International Migrations*, 2 vols. (New York, 1929, 1931), which contains a useful conspectus on the Jews by L. Hersch (II, pp. 471–521). Lloyd P. Gartner, *The Jewish Immigrant in England 1870–1914* (London and Detroit, 1960), may serve for comparative purposes.

[21]John Higham, *Strangers in the Land: Patterns of American Nativism 1860–1925* (New Brunswick, N.J., 1951), pp. 87–105.

illustration is furnished by the Russian Jewish revolutionary refugees who came to America especially in 1882 and during the post-revolutionary reaction in 1906, 1907, and 1908. Before they could assume leadership in the Jewish labor movement, they had to learn or relearn Yiddish. East European Jewry was undergoing a period of extraordinary ideological development, but most immigrants came from the small towns and villages, far from the centers of thought and agitation. Their ideological experiences were to take place in huge urban colonies in America.

The earlier Jewish immigrants had not much intellectual dynamic. They developed a Judaism which they found suitable and believable, and then tended to hold to it with little change. Well-conceived philanthropy was their strongest urge as Jews. The East Europeans, on the other hand, tended to be intellectually mobile and innovative, in keeping with their regional traditions of intense piety and arduous, sharp-witted Talmudic study. This intellectuality had a pervasiveness rarely equaled in Jewish history. Even quite simple Jews lay under the spell of these traditions, and those who broke with them to pursue newer causes—Zionism, Russian revolutionism, Hebrew or Yiddish revival, entry into Russian, Polish, or American culture—rarely lost the quality of intensity and mobility.

There is a third important contrast. Germanic Jews had spread pretty thinly across the United States, although, like their Christian neighbors, they later left the smaller towns for large cities. The vast majority of East European Jews settled at once in the largest cities, above all New York, and Chicago, Philadelphia, Boston, Baltimore, and Cleveland. If seven or eight smaller metropoli are added, over ninety percent of East European Jews are accounted for.[22]

American Jewry has been shaped by the numbers and traditions and aspirations, and also the envies, jealousies, and mutual dependence, of Germanic and East European Jewries. This will not deny the awareness of their common Jewishness, nor the overwhelming force and attraction of American life in shaping a

[22]Moses Rischin, *The Promised City: New York's Jews 1870–1914* (Cambridge, Mass., 1962), pp. 19–47; Elias Tcherikower, *Geshikhte fun der Yiddisher Arbeter Bavegung in der Faraynikte Shtatn*, 2 vols. (New York, 1943), of which Volume I contains invaluable material on this background (there has been an unsuccessful English translation, abridgment, and revision: Elias Tcherikower and Aaron Antonovsky, *The Early Jewish Labor Movement in the United States* [New York, 1961], pp. 3–74).

Jewish group different from any previously known. How old and new American Jews encountered each other merits closer notice:

> My dear Russian brethren, who have done so much to cast a stigma on the Jewish name, are now adding this new sin to their long list of offenses which we are asked to stand responsible for.[23]

Thus a Reform rabbi in the Middle West; the sin on this occasion was the founding of a Jewish political club for Bryan in 1896. Nine years earlier, Benjamin F. Peixotto addressed a New York City audience:

> I would say here to those who say "send them back, let them stay at home, we don't want them here," I would say you might as well attempt to keep the waves of the old ocean from rushing on our shores, as to keep those from seeking the refuge which this country offers.[24]

The speaker had spent five years in Rumania during the 1870's. Few, if any American Jews had seen Jewish immigrants in their lands of birth or better appreciated why they sought to quit them. Fifteen years, more or less, passed before American Jews—themselves near immigrant origins—appreciated Peixotto's insistence that a high proportion of the 5,000,000 to 6,000,000 Jews of Eastern Europe was bound to leave for America. Since the emancipation and modernization of German Jewry beginning in the eighteenth century, there had been a scornful or condescending attitude to backward, impoverished, persecuted Polish and Russian Jews. For their part, Polish and Russian Jews admired and envied their German fellow-Jews and, like other intelligentsia of their time, some acquired German language and culture at a distance. But there were also many who feared and deprecated the de-Judaization of these favored brethren.[25] All of these heritages were brought to

---

[23]Swichkow and Gartner, op. cit., p. 151.

[24]Benjamin F. Peixotto, What Shall We Do With Our Immigrants? (New York, Young Men's Hebrew Association, 1887), pp. 3–4, quoted in Zosa Szajkowski, "The Attitude of American Jews to East European Jewish Immigration (1881–1893)," PAJHS, XL, 3 (March 1951), p. 235.

[25]Cf. S. Adler-Rudel, Ostjuden in Deutschland 1880–1940. (Tübingen, 1959), pp. 1–33. The attitudes of some German Jews to first encountering Jews in Eastern Europe are suggestive; e.g., Franz Rosenzweig, Briefe (Berlin, 1935), pp. 320–322; Alexander Carlebach, "A German Rabbi goes East," Leo Baeck Institute Yearbook, VI (1961), pp. 60–121.

America. Now, German and East European Jews found themselves living next to each other, inhaling and exhaling, one may say, each other's attitudes.

Through the voluminous literature of the decades of large-scale Jewish immigration from the 1880's into the 1920's, several motifs are to be easily discerned in the "uptown" and "downtown" views of each other. To Russian immigrants, the German Jew was hardly a Jew, but a "yahudi," a "deitshuk." His Reform Judaism was a sham as Judaism, little more than a superficial aping of Christianity meant to curry Christian favor. Not only the minority of unswervingly Orthodox among immigrants thought so, but also the much larger mass which failed to recognize anything but old-time Orthodoxy as real Judaism. Probably more damning than the Reform Judaism of the German Jews was the seeming absence among them of folk-feeling, that sense of mutuality, of common fate and kinship, so well developed among poor, oppressed Jews. The immigrants were acutely conscious of the native American Jews' social distance from them, and of their haughtiness and condescension. Even their vaunted charities were cold and impersonal, miscalled "scientific," vacant of sympathy and kindness. It grated them that Jews should hold aloof from other Jews. Among Jewish socialists, this feeling was expressed in the detestation of the Jewish uptowners as capitalist oppressors, although one has the impression that the immigrant Jewish socialists really disliked a much closer target—the climbers to fortune among their own Russian and Polish Jews.[26]

The native German-American Jews had perceptions of their own. The new immigrants were primitive and clannish, unwilling to take on American ways, insistent on maintaining "Asiatic" and "medieval" forms of religion and social life. "Culture" and "refinement" could not be found among them. They demanded charity as a matter of right without any appreciation for what they received. They were unduly aggressive and assertive, and embarrassed the painfully acquired good name of the American Jew. They had a disturbing penchant for unsound ways of thought, especially political radicalism, atheism, Zionism, and held to a form of speech

[26]Rischin, op. cit., pp. 95–111; Harold M. Silver, "The Russian Jew Looks at Charity—A Study of the Attitudes of Russian Jewish Immigrants Toward Organized Jewish Charitable Agencies in the United States in 1890–1900," Jewish Social Service Quarterly, IV, 2 (December 1927), pp. 129–144; Arthur Gorenstein (Goren), "The Commissioner and the Community: A Study of the Beginnings of the New York City 'Kehillah'," YAJSS, XIII (1965), pp. 187–212.

which could not be called a language.[27] Only slowly did it come to be understood why they were coming en masse, and that pleas to stay home were fruitless. Well into the 1890's, Western—not only American—Jewry pleaded for Russian, Polish, Rumanian, Galician Jews to stay home and await the better times which would surely come in an age of inevitable human progress.[28] Benjamin F. Peixotto was nearly isolated. The few natives who welcomed immigration seem mostly to have been traditionalists who expected reinforcement of their small numbers by Jews arriving from the East European reservoir of religious piety.[29] For those who did come, the policy preferred by native Jews was to develop a class of respectable workingmen. Skilled manual trades in the city and farming on the countryside were to replace peddling and tailoring.[30] How remote this was from the explicit as well as the buried hopes of the immigrants may be seen from the widely known outlines of their social history during the last fifty years.

The real change in the native Jews' attitude occurred around 1903. The Kishinev pogrom of that year, in which high Czarist officials were notoriously implicated, followed by the Russo-Japanese War, the Revolution of 1905 and the pogrom-ridden counterrevolution, proved that the condition of Russian Jews would only deteriorate, not improve. Reluctant American Jewish sympathy replaced the earlier dislike as greater numbers of immigrants than ever poured into the United States during the decade before World War I.[31]

---

[27]Szajkowski, op. cit., pp. 221–293; Irving A. Mandel, "The Attitude of the American Jewish Community toward East-European Immigration as Reflected in the Anglo-Jewish Press (1880–1890)," American Jewish Archives, III, 1 (June 1950), pp. 11–36; Heller, op. cit., pp. 583–586; David Philipson, "Strangers to a Strange Land," American Jewish Archives, XVIII, 2 (November 1966), pp. 133–138 (excerpts from his diary); Selig Adler and Thomas E. Connolly, From Ararat to Suburbia: The History of the Jewish Community of Buffalo (Philadelphia, 1960), pp. 227–231.

[28]This theme is treated in Zosa Szajkowski, "Emigration to America or Reconstruction in Europe," PAJHS, XLII, 2 (December 1952), pp. 157–188.

[29]Davis, op. cit., pp. 261–268.

[30]Herman Frank, "Jewish Farming in the United States," The Jewish People: Past and Present, 4 vols. (New York, 1948–1955), II, 68–77; Moses Klein, Migdal Zophim (Philadelphia, 1889).

[31]Higham, op. cit., pp. 106–123; Zosa Szajkowski, "Paul Nathan, Lucien Wolf, Jacob H. Schiff and the Jewish Revolutionary Movement in Eastern Europe (1903–1917)," Jewish Social Studies, XXIX, 1 and 2 (January and April 1967), pp. 3–26, 75–91; Morton Rosenstock, Louis Marshall, Defender of Jewish Rights (Detroit, 1965), pp. 79–89.

This decade also marks the coming of Jews to the political and intellectual forefront among the defenders of free immigration. Of course, other immigrant groups also staunchly defended the right of their families and countrymen to come to America, but of the more recent immigrant stocks the Jews had the best established native element which would press the case effectively. Behind the political and communal leaders were a group of intellectuals both demonstrating and advocating the anthropological and intellectual equality of Jewish and all other newcomers—Israel Zangwill, Mary Antin, Israel Friedlander, Franz Boas, Horace M. Kallen, and others. Moreover, immigrants at the ballot box were now effectively enforcing the doctrines of human equality expounded by these intellectuals.[32] The most favored and seemingly innocuous aid to immigrants remained the dispensing of charity. The old-time charitable societies founded during the 1850's and 1860's–dozens of them named "Hebrew Relief Society" and "Hebrew Ladies Benevolent Society"—took on masses of new clients. How bread and coal and warm clothing developed around the 1920's into family budgets, mental health, and vocational guidance is a story vaguely but widely known in its barest outlines. Again, how the disparate relief societies, orphanges, homes for the aged, and the like united their fund raising and then began to spend and plan in unison, is another story of wide significance. These forward-looking "scientific" institutions were not at all the first resort of the distressed immigrant, who had his own "home town" societies, mutual aid groups, and "lodges" in the hundreds. The tendency to resent charitable patronage was one of the reasons which brought immigrants to found separate institutions. It was stressed that only in their own hospitals and orphanages and homes for the aged was kosher diet and an intimately Jewish atmosphere fostered. Yet it is revealing how "downtown" unconsciously flattered "uptown" by accepting the institutional network founded by the natives and attempting to rival it.[33]

The evolution of other, much more sophisticated institutions is

---

[32]Higham, op. cit., pp. 123–130, 304–305; Arthur Gorenstein (Goren), "A Portrait of Ethnic Politics: The Socialists and the 1908 and 1910 Congressional Elections on the East Side," PAJHS, L, 3 (March 1961), pp. 202–238.

[33]A useful historical anthology is Robert Morris and Michael Freund, Trends and Issues in Jewish Social Welfare in the United States 1899–1952 (Philadelphia, 1966); Swichkow and Gartner, op.cit., pp. 53–54, 211–212, 215–234; Plaut, op. cit., pp. 140–146; Gutstein, op. cit., pp. 334–360.

instructive. The Educational Alliance was built on New York's Lower East Side in 1889. During its first years, no Yiddish or immigrant cultural expression was permitted within its walls, and the regime was one of an often artificially imposed English culture. By 1914, however, it had become a cultural and social center where young artists and musicians, as well as athletes, trained, where Yiddish was publicly used, and where even youthful Hebraists practiced the reviving language.[34]

The case of the Jewish Theological Seminary suggests still more subtle problems. Jewish natives worried over the young people who rejected the religion of their fathers in favor of radical social doctrines or militant atheism, or drifted into hedonism and seemed criminally inclined. It was virtually postulated that Jewish immigrants would not take to Reform Judaism (actually some of the younger ones became interested in Ethical Culture). In the eyes of native leaders, a traditional but modern form of Judaism for immigrant or immigrants' children was needed, and so the moribund Jewish Theological Seminary was refounded to train "American" rabbis at an institution of higher Jewish learning. A substantial building, considerable endowment, and an outstanding library and faculty were quickly brought together. Yet tensions were never absent between the eminent Solomon Schechter, head of the Seminary, who desired before anything else an institution of learning, and some of the board who seemed to want religiously inspired "Americanization."[35] A suggestive contrast is furnished by the immigrants' yeshiva on New York's East Side. With very meager resources, it was solely a full-time non-professional school for advanced Talmudic study by young men. Long controversy within Yeshivat Rabbenu Yizhak Elhanan preceded the introduction of very modest secular studies. But before 1920, however, the Yeshiva provided full secular secondary training within its own walls, and later established Yeshiva College. This was much to the displeasure of most native Jews, who considered general education under Jewish auspices "ghettoizing." On the other hand, the modernist Jewish scholarship fostered by Schechter at the Jewish Theological Seminary was religiously unacceptable to the Yeshiva's contempo-

---

[34]Rischin, op. cit., pp. 101–103; In the Time of Harvest: Essays in Honor of Abba Hillel Silver, ed. Daniel Jeremy Silver (New York, 1963), p. 3.

[35]Norman Bentwich, Solomon Schechter (Philadelphia, 1938), pp. 187–197; Louis Marshall: Champion of Liberty, ed. Charles Reznikoff, 2 vols. (Philadelphia, 1956), II, pp. 859–894.

rary leaders. Secular study could be taken in and by some welcomed, but not the modernized, historical study of the sacred tradition.[36]

Immigrant Jews began to acquire uptown esteem. For one, they exhibited an intellectual élan and interest in ideas—especially unconventional ideas—which younger members of staid society found exhilarating. For some Jewish members of proper society the Jewish immigrants seemed to show a more authentic, passionate, somehow appealing way to be a Jew. A second source of esteem derived from the immigrants' greatest short-term achievement, the Jewish labor movement. After a full generation of unsuccessful fits and starts, the movement's surge of vitality and success attracted bourgeois liberals, and drew wide respect and attention. Native Jews repeatedly attempted to mediate strikes of Jewish workers against Jewish employers, on the grounds that they washed Jewish linen in public. The Jewish labor leaders, generally committed to revolutionary rhetoric, refused to regard the strikes as an internal Jewish quarrel but quite often accepted "uptown" mediators anyhow.[37]

World War I was an intense, even decisive experience for both the old and new Jewish stock. Immigrants or their sons wore military uniforms in large numbers, and Army egalitarianism and patriotic fervor proved a superlative "Americanizing" experience. Native Jews were more vigilant than ever in defending immigrants at a time of patriotic xenophobia, against the imputations of disloyalty to which they were vulnerable on account of revolutions and political complexities in their lands of origin and widespread Socialist anti-war sentiment among them. But during World War I also, native Jews became persuaded and in turn became advocates of causes once distasteful to them. Thus they took up the cudgels for Jewish national minority rights in Eastern Europe, toning it down to "group rights" as a more palatable term. The Jewish National Home promised in Great Britain's Balfour Declaration was the other cause. The relief poured out for European Jewry came

[36]*Ibid.*, II, pp. 888–894; Gilbert Klaperman, *The Story of Yeshiva University* (New York, 1968).

[37]Rischin, *op. cit.*, pp. 236–257; Louis Levine (Lorwin), *The Women's Garment Workers: A History of the International Ladies Garment Workers Union* (New York, 1924), pp. 360–381; Hyman Berman, "The Cloakmakers' Strike of 1910," *Essays in Jewish Life and Thought Presented in Honor of Salo Wittmayer Baron* (New York, 1959), pp. 63–94. The slowly rising interest in Yiddish literature may be seen through Morris Rosenfeld, *Briv*, ed. E. Lifschutz (Buenos Aires, 1955), pp. 34–105.

from "uptown" and "downtown," and was distributed mostly by the well-named American Jewish Joint Distribution Committee.[38]

The problems of the 1920's lie beyond the scope of this essay. By that time, the influence of the two segments upon each other was, or should have been, long evident. The old stock's staid conception and practice of Judaism was outmatched and altered by the newcomers' intellectual vigor in that and in other spheres. Indeed, two generations of native Jews, gradually joined en masse by acculturated and prospering immigrant families, focused practically the whole of their communal life and concerns upon the East European immigrant and his transformation. It was the older Jewish stock which long and effectively defended the Jewish newcomers, while chastising them not too privately, and above all helped to keep immigration virtually free before 1925.[39] For the East European immigrants, the example of their predecessors provided a model—for many *the* model—of the way to be an American and a Jew. Adaptation and change were extensive, but those who came first showed those who came later this most significant of lessons. The still sizable numbers of Jews who came after 1925, especially from Germany and Austria during the 1930's, and after 1945 as survivors of the European Jewish Holocaust, found a fully formed American Jewry. Their limited influence on American Jewish life, with the possible exception of its Orthodox religious sector, also shows that the formative years had ended.

---

[38]Oscar I. Janowsky, *The Jews and Minority Rights 1898–1919* (New York, 1933), pp. 161–190, 264–320; Rosenstock, *op. cit.*, pp. 98–127; Zosa Szajkowski, "Jewish Relief in Eastern Europe 1914–1917," Leo Baeck Institute *Yearbook*, X (1965), pp. 24–56; Naomi W. Cohen, "An American Jew at the Paris Peace Conference: Excerpts from the Diary of Oscar S. Straus," *Essays . . . Baron*, pp. 159–168; for a view of World War I on the local Jewish scene, see Swichkow and Gartner, *op. cit.*, pp. 268–285; see also E. Lifschutz, "The Pogroms in Polland of 1918–1919, the Morgenthau Committee and the American State Department" (Hebrew with English summaries), *Zion*, XXIII–XXIV, 1–2 and 3–4 (1958–1959), pp. 66–97, 194–211.

[39]Higham, *op. cit.*, pp. 264–330; Rosenstock, *op. cit.*, pp. 214–233.

AMERICA IS DIFFERENT

by BEN HALPERN

INTRODUCTION

JEWISH IMMIGRANTS knew that America was different from their communities of origin, but it was not immediately apparent why this was so. Ben Halpern's analysis supplies the answer. The fact that American Jewry was formed in the post-Emancipation era, means there was no need for a European-style national debate over whether Jews should be emancipated. Furthermore, the absence of this kind of debate ensured that American anti-Semitism would necessarily have a special character. While European anti-Semitism in the modern period was an integral part of an ideology dedicated to the restoration of a previous era in national history, American anti-Semitism was free of such beliefs.

The post-Emancipation character of American Jewry has affected not only the national ethos in respect to Jews but the internal aspects of American-Jewish life as well. Inasmuch as their own emancipation had never really been questioned, American Jews never felt the need to develop a serious ideological response to the phenomenon of anti-Semitism. European Zionism not only took anti-Semitism seriously, it propounded a specifically Jewish response to the malady; the Zionism which developed on American soil, by contrast, regarded anti-Semitism as more of a Gentile problem than a Jewish one. Similarly, because of their historical situation, American Jews have been uniquely free to determine how extensively they wish to participate in the larger society. Thus "assimilationism" in the United States differs from its European counterpart both in extent and in character. According to Halpern, while the larger society assumes that American ethnic groups will ultimately disappear, it brings only minimal pressure upon them to assimilate. They are free to remain in their ethnic enclaves if they wish to do so.

The value of Halpern's perspectives becomes apparent when the American reaction to Jewish participation in the life of the larger society is contrasted with the European reaction. As Halpern points out, in Europe nationalistic elements viewed such participation " . . . as an illegitimate intrusion, or even [as] a plot by the enemies of the people to corrupt its national spirit." However, in the United States participation in the life of the larger society has generally been welcomed. Such participation is viewed as a tacit acknowledgment of the cultural authority of the dominant group, encouraging evidence of a healthy desire to leave the ethnic enclave in favor of participation in the cultural mainstream. It is not viewed as an illegitimate intrusion or as a corruption of the national spirit.

M. S.

JEWS IN AMERICA at their three-hundred-year mark have their own very strong reasons to underscore the theme that "America is different," and when they orchestrate this music, it is to a counterpoint of peculiarly Jewish *motifs*. America is different —because no Hitler calamity is going to happen here. America is different—because it has no long-established majority ethnic culture, but is still evolving a composite culture to which Jews, too, are privileged to make their characteristic contributions. America is different—it is not Exile, and whatever may be the case with other Jewries, the open doors of the State of Israel do not beckon. With such a rich choice of harmonies, is it any wonder that the tercentenary celebrations [in 1954] of the American Jews swelled to a powerful chorus, elaborately enunciating the single theme, "America is different!"

It seems, however, that the crucial respect in which American Jewry is different was missed altogether in the tercentenary celebrations. That is not surprising, because if this difference were stressed it could have made the whole occasion seem artificial and contrived. American Jewry *is* different from other Jewries. It is younger than any other significant Jewry—with the exception of the State of Israel. In terms of *real*, effective history it is far from being three hundred years old. There is good sense in Croce's contention that only the history of free, rational, creative effort is real history, and that the chronicle of events in which man is passive is a different kind of thing altogether. At any rate, if American Jewry has a truly distinct and individual character, giving it a destiny different from that of other Jewries, there is only one way it can have acquired it: only by freely, rationally, and creatively grappling with the specific problems of its existence, and then handing down its distinctive working hypotheses for elaboration by succeeding generations. American Jewry has had nothing like three hundred years of this sort of history. If there are any native American Jewish institutions that were initiated before the Eastern European immigration of the 1880's, then most of these, too, are creations of the middle nineteenth century. The earliest idea evolved and perpetuated to this day in American Jewry can be nothing younger than the Reform movement, which goes back in this country to 1824. The characteristic American Jewish type today is a second- or third-generation American.

This is, then, one of the youngest of Jewries, one of the youngest even of the surviving Jewries. Its real history begins *after* the "solution" in America of the most critical problem that faced other Jewries in modern times—the problem of the Emancipation of the Jews. This was the problem that other Jewries had to grapple with when they entered the modern world, and the various solutions that they freely, rationally, and creatively evolved for it gave them each their individual character. French Jewry dealt with the issues and problems of Emancipation differently from German Jewry, German Jewry differently from Austro-Hungarian or from Russian Jewry; but all of them had to deal with the problem, and there was a continuity and connection among the solutions they found. What is characteristic of American Jewry, and what makes it different from all of these together, is that it began its real history as a post-Emancipation Jewry. Emancipation was never an issue among American Jews: they never argued the problems it presented in America, nor did they ever develop rival ideologies about it and build their institutions with reference to them.

Because of this, the continuity of European-Jewish ideologies is broken in America. American Jews never had ardent groups of partisans who saw in Emancipation the whole solution of the Jewish problem. In Europe the Zionist movement arose in opposition to this thesis, and proposed "Auto-Emancipation" instead of "Emancipation" as the solution. The theory of "Diaspora nationalism"—the advocacy of minority rights as an answer to the Jewish problem—likewise opposed to the Emancipation principle of individual enfranchisement the view that the Jews must be granted autonomy as a group, as an ethnic entity. All these theories existed in America only as pale copies of the European originals.

There is in America a small group who vociferously defend Emancipation, the American Council for Judaism. The pointlessness of their propaganda is obvious to anyone who asks himself who among the American Jews is opposed to Emancipation. There is no such group or person, for no one proposes to undo what has been the accepted basis of life here since *before* American Jews made any effort to shape their history. Nor does the American Council defend Emancipation as a *solution* for the Jewish problem. Their view would be more accurately expressed by a classic statement of Abraham Cahan's, who declared in 1890:

> We have no Jewish question in America. The only question we recognize is the question of how to prevent the emergence of "Jewish questions" here.[1]

As for the opponents of this view, they, too, do not think in terms of a Jewish question which America has been vainly seeking to solve by the emancipation of the Jews, and for which alternative solutions other than Emancipation must be sought. We are only beginning to see what the Jewish question actually is in America.

Anti-Semitism and Assimilation

From a Jewish point of view, two elements are inseparable from any discussion of the Jewish problem: anti-Semitism and assimilation. For to a Jew the problem essentially is this: how can the Jewish people survive in the face of hostility which threatens to destroy it, and, on the other hand, in the face of a friendliness which threatens to dissolve group ties and submerge Jews, as a whole, by absorbing them individually? Both phases of the Jewish problem are different in America than in Europe, and in both cases the reason is the same: in most countries of modern Europe the questions of anti-Semitism and the Emancipation and assimilation of the Jews were essentially connected with revolutionary crises in their national affairs, while no such connection existed in American history.

All we need do is consider what the Emancipation of the Negroes meant in American political and social history in order to measure the difference between a status that was never really contested, like that of the Jews, and one that it took a civil war to establish. Thus, when we think of anti-Semitism in such countries as France and Germany, Russia and Poland, we must remember that the great revolutions and revolutionary movements in those

---

[1] Cited in C. Bezalel Sherman's article, "Nationalism, Secularism, and Religion in the Jewish Labor Movement," *Judaism*, Fall 1954 (Tercentenary Issue), p. 355. The statement occurs in a manifesto issued by "Abraham Cahan, Organizer," on behalf of the Hebrew Federation of Labor of the United States and Canada, which was published in *Die Arbeiter Zeitung* (New York), 5 December 1890, two months after the Federation's founding convention. The full text is reproduced in E. Tcherikower's *Geshikhte fun der Yidisher arbeter-bavegung in die Fareynikte Shtatn* (New York, 1945), Vol. II, pp. 499–502.

countries, at critical moments in their national history, placed the emancipation of the Jews upon their agenda for basic reform. Whatever has become part of the program of a national revolution not only divides the people at the first shock, but continues to divide them in the cycles of counterrevolution that always attend such upheavals in a nation's life. Hence, as Jewish Emancipation was an issue raised by the Revolution, so anti-Semitism had a natural place in the programs of European counterrevolutionary parties.

How different it was in America is quite clear. If the American Jews never had to divide ideologically over the issue of Emancipation, ·one of the reasons is that Emancipation of the Jews never became a revolutionary issue dividing the American people generally. For that matter in the history of America, the Revolution itself did not become a real (rather than academic) issue permanently dividing the people, since it was a revolution against outsiders—and the Loyalists remained in emigration. In England, on the other hand, the Cromwellian revolution was a crux in British history which still serves to determine opposed political attitudes. But at the time of that Glorious Rebellion there were practically no Jews in England. Consequently, at a later time, after the Jews had begun to arrive, the question of their Emancipation was debated in England (just as in America) in a relatively unimpassioned, desultory way. Whatever minor political struggles took place in spelling out the equal rights of the Jews had no inherent connection with, or essential place in, the major upheavals recorded in the national history. To be an anti-Semite in England, as in America, had no obvious, symbolic affinity with a counterrevolutionary ideology opposing the Glorious Rebellion or the American Revolution.

If one examines the American anti-Semitic movements, one cannot fail to appreciate how different they are from their European counterparts. Only in England do we find so anemic, so insignificant an anti-Semitic movement, a movement so unmistakably belonging to the "lunatic fringe."

The anti-Semitic movements of France and Germany, Poland and Russia may also have been fit subjects for psychopathological investigation; but no one will deny that they occupied a place in the forefront of the political affairs of their countries, and moved in (whether with or against) the mainstream of their national history. Far from being "fringe" phenomena, they had political power, or a reasonable chance to attain it. What we have in America in comparison is nothing but an aimless hate-mongering. The kind of anti-Semitism common in America is, and always has been, endemic throughout the Diaspora. It may be found in every social condition and in every political persuasion, from extreme right to extreme left. It is an anti-Semitism of impulse: the most characteristic thing about it is that it is not really organized on the basis of a clearly enunciated program providing what ought to be done about the Jews if the anti-Semites had their way.[2] This is

[2]When American anti-Semites avail themselves of election periods in order to conduct their propaganda, they do, of course, formulate "programs." The provisions relating to Jews in these documents are usually more vituperative than programmatic in character, and they combine obvious, though rather feeble, imitations of European models with some specific American features, reflecting animosity against American Jewish organizations. I owe the following typical examples to the courtesy of Jack Baker of the Anti-Defamation League. "The New Emancipation Proclamation—The Silver Shirt Program" appeared in Pelley's Silver Shirt Weekly of 5 September 1934. It proposed "racial quotas on the political and economic structure" in order to prevent Jewish office-holding "in excess of the ratio of (Jews) . . . in the body politic." All Jews, and all foreign-born persons not "completely naturalized," were to be registered, under severe penalties for evasion. All Jews were to be compelled to "forswear forever . . . Jewish allegiance," and any Jew apprehended in giving support to Jewish nationalism was to be criminally prosecuted for sedition. (Quoted in Gustavus Myers, History of Bigotry in the United States [New York, 1943], pp. 405–406).

The 1948 election platform of Gerald L. K. Smith's Christian Nationalist Party called for "the immediate deportation of all supporters of the political Zionist movement" and the outlawry of "this international machine and all its activity." Such "Jewish Gestapo organizations" as "the so-called Anti-Defamation League, the American Jewish Congress, the so-called Non-Sectarian Anti-Nazi League, the self-styled Friends of Democracy" were to be dissolved. Immigration of "Asiatics, including Jews, and members of the colored races" was to be stopped. The partition of Palestine was opposed. The party program published by Smith in 1952, however, had no such specific references to Jews.

The nine point "Program of the National Renaissance Party" (published in the National Renaissance Bulletin, October 1953, pp. 3 and 4) proposed, under point 1, to "repudiate the operetta-State of Israel"; in point 2, "to enforce a strict policy of racial segregation in America"; and in point 3 "to bring about a gradual deportation of unassimilable elements . . ." viz., the "Puerto Ricans, Negroes, Jews and Asiatics"; in point 4, to bar Jews "from all political and professional posts" and to forbid marriage between Jews and "members of the dominant White Race"; and in point 6, to base American foreign policy upon a "German-American alliance in Europe; a Moslem-American alliance in the Middle East; and a Japanese-American alliance in Asia" (reproduced in the U.S. House of Representatives, Committee on Un-American Activities, Preliminary Report on Neo-Fascist and Hate Groups, Washington, 17 December 1954, pp. 21–22).

See also Richard Hofstadter's comment on the tendency of the political attitudes of the "new American right" to express themselves "more in vindictiveness, in sour memories, in the search for scapegoats, than in realistic proposals for action" ("The Pseudo-Conservative Revolt" in The New American Right, Daniel Bell, ed. [New York, 1955], p. 44, and note similar observations in other sources referred to by Hofstadter (Ibid., p. 54, note 7).

something quite different from an anti-Semitism that was primarily political in vision. Modern European anti-Semitism was character-ized from the beginning by large and active political aims, and it included, among other far-reaching social revisions proposed in its counterrevolutionary program, precise provisions for making the Jews second-class citizens, expelling them, or exterminating them. In comparison with these movements, American anti-Semitism (and, for the most part, British) has never reached the level of an historic, politically effective movement. It has remained, so to speak, a merely sociological or "cultural" phenomenon.

The question of assimilation also looks different in America, because the Jews never had an established status here other than that of so-called Emancipation: there never were enough Jews here before the nineteenth century to warrant a special, institutionally established status. In Europe, on the other hand, Emancipation came as an effort to alter a hoary, time-honored status in which Jewish communities lived long before the Revolution.

The Emancipation seemed to promise the Jews that the difference between them and the Gentiles would be reduced to the private realm of religion. All public relations with the Gentiles would be carried on in the neutral area of citizenship, where Jews were guaranteed equality. Jews assumed that the public realm was identical with the whole social realm of intercourse between them and the Gentiles, and that in all other than purely Jewish religious affairs they would have full and free contact and equal status with Christians. This they soon found to be a delusion, for in all countries they discovered that Jewishness was a barrier and a disability in a wide range of social relations and that citizenship opened far fewer doors than they had imagined.

In most European countries the areas closed to Jews had been elaborated by centuries of custom and usage. When one had explored the precise extent of new freedoms opened to the Jews by the new status of citizenship, the barred contacts remained clearly and decisively, in fact often quite formally, defined. The army, the higher government service, the magistracy, and the universities were all careers closed to Jews which, by quite explicit understand-ing, became open immediately upon baptism.

In all of Europe, Jews soon found that even after Emancipation actual relations in society continued to be governed by a series of restrictions taken from the religiously grounded stratifications of the *ancien régime.* To protests that all this was contrary to the new doctrine of citizenship, purporting to open all careers to talent and all doors of social intercourse to individual merit, an answer was soon provided: a still newer doctrine, the doctrine of romantic, organic nationalism, superseded the principle of citizenship. The national idea gave a new justification and pumped new life into practices which had theretofore survived as stubborn relics of feudalism and now all at once became grafted onto the modern idea of democracy. Fixed social positions, traditional folkways and culture, inheritance of privileges and obligations—all that had once been grounded in the divine will—now gained an organic sanction in the national history. The Jews found their assimilation even more rigidly opposed than under the purely religious criterion. If inheritance (that is, ethnic origin) became the key to admission into society and the license for participation in culture, then even the formal step of conversion was of no avail to the Jew.

In the beginning of the present century the actual social conditions that faced the Jew seeking to be part of his European nationality represented a shifting balance between divergent tendencies. One tendency was that of the Revolution, whose principle was to treat the Jew as an individual no different from all the rest. Actual social relations conformed to this principle only to the extent that the Revolution itself, or other forces, had succeeded in atomizing society. The Industrial Revolution and the development of trade allowed Jews to find new opportunities in business and thereby brought them into a new relation of equality with Gentiles. The Revolution succeeded in imposing its own principles in all political relationships except the bureaucracy. But the Jews could not simply move into these new positions unaltered. The grant of equality imposed its conditions and demanded its price. The "clannish" solidarity of the Jews had to be given up so that they could enter the body of citizens as individuals. They could keep their religion as a private cult, but not necessarily the kind of religion that was traditional among them. Jewish tradition was too organic in its own way, it incorporated too much historic distinctiveness and ethnic character, for the rigid individualism of radical revolutionary doctrine. Not that anyone expected to see the full consequences of egalitarian theory rigorously applied to Gentile society. But the revolutionary ardor to liberate the Jews had roots of its own in the anti-Semitism that is endemic in all Gentile society and expresses itself in all its divisions. The Jews might not get all they expected out of Emancipation, but the Emancipators were disposed to watch with a jealous eye how the Jews went about paying its price.[3]

The nobility, the army, the universities, all the corporate embodiments of privilege bearing upon them the stamp of consecration and tradition escaped the leveling influence of Revolution. As Jews rose in society through other channels they found their ultimate elevation blocked at these points. Some fought their way through to these positions as Jews, but most found that access to their goal, otherwise blocked, became magically open through a relatively simple and (in most cases) quite perfunctory operation. So they acquired new "convictions" and became baptized.[4] To the other Jews, this renegadism, as they regarded it, was their first great shocking disillusionment with the Emancipation, the first disclosure of the human degradation which is the price of assimilation.

The most serious strain upon Jewish-Gentile relations was the rise of counterrevolutionary anti-Semitism, which absorbed into an ethnic pattern the basic attitudes to the Jews implied in their old feudal, religiously determined status. Conservative anti-Semitism in an officially liberal society had contented itself with excluding Jews from those areas of corporate traditionalism which the Revolution had not succeeded in atomizing. But now nationalistic counter-revolution, seeking to turn the clock back, opposed the penetration Jews had already made into areas opened up by liberalism. Economic boycotts of the Jews were resorted to in order to bring industry and commerce "back" into the hands of the Germans or the Poles, or whatever the ethnic majority might be.

Particularly did the nationalists resent the great participation of Jews in all cultural activities. The organic doctrine of nationalism sought to overcome a cleavage between culture and tradition that had existed in Europe since the Renaissance. Modern culture had become a secular realm parallel to the traditional beliefs, art forms,

---

[3]See Graetz's narrative of the "Synhedrion" in Paris and the events leading up to it, *History of the Jews* (Jewish Publication Society translation, Philadelphia, 1895), Vol. V, pp. 474–509.

[4]The quip of the famous Orientalist Chwolsohn—that he was converted out of conviction, the conviction that it was better to be a professor in Petersburg than a tutor in Shnipishok—is only one of a long line of cynical anecdotes (going back at least as far as Heine), which illustrate the psychology of many such conversions.

ceremonials, and etiquette still grounded in religion. The social framework of culture, the *Gelehrtenrepublik*, as the eighteenth-century Germans called it, was a liberal, international, individualistic, and secular intercourse among free spirits, which, even before the Revolution, existed side by side with the corporate social structures where the religious, feudal tradition was fostered. The Revolution was the signal that gave the Jews entrée into this world. It was a liberty that they eagerly embraced, shut out as they were on other sides from assimilation and its rewards. But it was a main object of counterrevolutionary nationalism to bring all culture back into an organic coherence based on the national tradition, even if both the religious and the secular were adulterated as a result. This meant imposing upon all forms of creative expression the same corporate principles and ethnic criteria that regulated participation in the religiously grounded forms. The participation of Jews in any cultural form was henceforth regarded as an illegitimate intrusion, or even a plot by the enemies of the people to corrupt its national spirit.

Thus there were forces in European society determinedly striving to undo even the amount of assimilation Jews had achieved. They were opposed not only to the integration of the Jew into such social relations as were governed by liberal principles but also to the admission of the Jewish convert into social relations still governed by corporate, religiously grounded criteria.

How different was the situation here in America! Here the bare conditions of geography and social statistics made liberalism the dominant principle of social organization. It was not so much revolution against an old regime that opened the door to assimilation for the Jews; it was the large extent of sheer formlessness in American society which allowed Jews and many other heterogeneous groups to live side by side, with the forms of their readjustment to each other to be determined.

Free entry into American society, of course, had its price and also its restrictions, just as did the assimilation of the European Jews after Emancipation. The price of the freedom to let the ultimate forms of mutual relationship between immigrant Jews (like all immigrants) and the whole American community remain for the future to determine was the willingness of the immigrant to give up old inherited forms. Just as settled America was willing, within limits, to be elastic, so it demanded of immigrants wishing to be naturalized that they first of all be elastic and accommodating. Not that there was any haste about the scrapping of outworn Old World customs. America was large enough to set aside "ghettos" in its cities or even whole regions in its broad lands where immigrants could live undisturbed more or less as they had been accustomed to live in the Old Country. But this was a provisional form of living, in effect outside the real America, which everyone expected to be superseded as the forms of true American living were worked out by immigrant and native Americans in a continuing process of give and take.

The willingness to relinquish Old World habits was the *price* of assimilation in America. Its *limits* were defined by the established prerogatives of the older settlers. It is true that the ultimate forms of American life remained—as they still remain—in principle undetermined, and our assumption is that the cultural contributions of all America's components are equally welcome. Yet it is both implicitly and explicitly assumed that those who came here first are entitled to preserve and impose such forms of living as they have already made part of the American way. America is not only in essence free and democratic; it is also, in its established pattern, Anglo-Saxon, religiously multi-denominational, and dominated by the mentality of white, Protestant, middle-class, native Americans. However, this social dominance and cultural predominance are maintained not by delimiting any areas of social life under traditional, religiously grounded, and formally elaborated codes of exclusion which reserve them for particular families or religions, as in Europe. American history has not been long enough for that, perhaps, and in any case it has from the start consecrated the principles of complete social mobility, denying in theory all exclusions. But the claims and privileges of the older settlers are maintained by informal, almost tacit social covenants, which only rarely (as in anti-immigration laws) need to be openly voiced.

Thus if liberal principles fail to be actually observed in America, just as in Europe, and if assimilation stops short at the barriers set up to protect inherited privilege, there is at least this difference: in Europe, the initial status is the historical, quasi-feudal status, and liberalism rules only those areas which it specifically conquers; in America, the initial status is that of freedom, and only experience proves what areas privilege has successfully reserved for itself. Those in America who nurse a nostalgia for historically rooted social status have not been able to swim in the midcurrent of an American counterrevolutionary movement. The American Revolution is the very beginning of real American history, and there is no one who more proudly flaunts it as his symbol than the American conservative. The self-conscious American opponent of the liberal revolution has no real alternative but to become an expatriate.

The result has been that while the history of American Jewish assimilation, too, has been full of disappointment and unanticipated checks, it has run a characteristically different course from the European experience. At the very outset of the European Emancipation, Jews were brusquely confronted with the price they must pay: for freedom of the individual, virtual dissolution of the group. The immigrant to these shores, too, found that the prize of Americanization was to be won at a price: by unreserved elasticity in discarding everything which America might find foreign. In both cases, only religion was reserved as a sanctuary of Jewish tradition. But there were these differences: in Europe, there was a fixed pattern that Jews were expected to adopt in discarding their own customs; in America, the ultimate American way of life was still in principle to be determined, taking into account what of their own immigrants might succeed in "selling" to the whole public. Besides, the demands of the European Emancipation upon the Jews were peremptory, they had to be conceded at once, and even through a formal declaration such as Napoleon extracted from the French Jews. In America, there was no urgency about the procedure. The Jews, like other immigrants, could make their way into the real American community as swiftly or as slowly as they themselves chose. They could, if they preferred, remain in their ghetto seclusion indefinitely.

In Europe, then, the stick; in America, the carrot. A parallel difference existed when the Jews came up against the unexpected barriers to assimilation, the reserved areas not governed by liberal principles. In Europe, the principle of exclusion was clear-cut, traditional—and quite simply overcome, if you wished, by conversion. There was no such clear choice in America. Established privileges were no less alien to this country than an established church. It was neither the accepted practice to demand conversion for specific social promotions, nor to grant them upon conversion. Thus, if American Jews went over to Christianity, it was no such concerted wave as arose in Germany, in the first eagerness to overleap the unexpected sectarian barrier to full assimilation. It

was rather a final seal, in individual cases, upon an assimilation
otherwise complete.

The Patterns of Modern Jewish Thought

It is clear, then, that the typical situation faced by the American Jew
was not the same as that characteristic of the European Continent.
The differences apply to both major aspects of the Jewish problem,
to anti-Semitism and to assimilation. But modern Zionism, and
indeed all modern Jewish ideologies, arose when Jews began to
confront, to take account of, and to understand—or try to "reach an
understanding" with—the typical situation of Continental Europe.
The characteristic American Jewish situation had hardly even
begun to be faced—until the establishment of the Jewish State
abruptly forced the issue. It need not be surprising, then, if at
precisely this time we witness a feverish effort to create a new
American Zionism and new American Jewish ideologies generally;
nor that these forced-draught efforts should in the beginning often
bring more confusion than enlightenment.

What was the historical situation of Continental Jewry in the
late nineteenth century, when the modern Jewish ideologies arose?
As we have seen, it was characteristically a period of post-revolutionary or, if we may say so, neo-traditionalist nationalism, a period
with a living memory of an *ancien régime,* a revolutionary
movement, and a wave of post- or even counterrevolutionary
reactions. Moreover, the Jewish problem was intimately involved
with every phase of that living tradition.

The spirit of that time was critical of the Enlightenment and
the Revolution, of rationalism, capitalism, and social relationships
based on the undifferentiated equality of citizenship. For the
modern European, the Jew became a symbolic embodiment of all
these discredited traits. The out-and-out anti-Semites (but not only
they) regarded the Jew as the head and fount of everything they
despised in the liberal revolution—its rationalism, capitalism, and
principle of civic equality. Similarly, of course, the eighteenth-century rebels against the *ancien régime* had seen in the ghetto a
symbol of the medievalism they were determined to uproot. And
just as the Revolution had proposed the assimilation of the Jews in
all respects except as a reformed religious sect, so, by a reversal of
history, the critics of the Revolution wanted to solve their Jewish
problem by halting or annulling the assimilation that had already
taken place and eliminating Jews and Jewish influence from the new
order they hoped to set up.

What made one a modern Jew in the late eighteenth century was to understand and accept the attitude of Gentile contemporaries to social problems, and to the Jewish problem among them. The modern Jews of that time accepted the demands of the Enlightenment to change their habits and customs—those relics of medievalism—in order to enter a new enfranchised status; on the other hand, they could not understand or accept the exclusions still practiced against them after they had paid this entry fee. But the modern Jew of the late nineteenth century "understood" fundamentally, however much it may have pained him, why it was that he was not assimilated into full fellowship in his country. He shared with the modern Gentile the feeling that European society had not yet become what it should be, or that it had even gone quite astray from its true path. Thus, integration into society on the basis of the liberal principles of the Revolution no longer seemed to be the solution of his Jewish problem. In fact, the degree to which that integration had already taken place, in culture, in economic pursuits, and even in political participation, began to constitute for him, as for the Gentile, the very crux of the Jewish problem, the false position in which both danger and self-denial dwelled. He, like the Gentile, began to see or foresee other solutions of the Jewish problem as part of a new revolution of the whole structure of European society, in the course of which Jews would either disappear entirely as an entity or regroup in a new segregation from the Gentiles. "Modern" Jews hoped either for a radical revision of the liberal revolution, leading to Socialism and the disappearance of Judaism together with all other religions, or for a new nationalist era in which Jews would live as a distinct national entity, in the places where they then lived or in a new national territory. In other words, either total assimilation in a new, millennial secular society, without the eighteenth-century reservation of freedom to maintain a reformed Jewish religious community, or the total rejection of assimilation and an attempt to establish a new Jewish ethnic independence, in the several countries of Europe or in a new territory to be colonized by Jews.

The rejection of assimilation was a doctrine shared by Zionists with other ethnic autonomists. The failure of Emancipation, from this point of view, demonstrated that there had been a breach of faith by the Gentile Emancipators and an historical error on the part of the Jews; for after the latter had practically reformed themselves out of existence as an historic group, Gentile society had failed to keep its part of the bargain by assimilating the Jews individually. Zionism, however, viewed not only eighteenth-century Gentile liberalism with a disenchanted eye. It also had its reservations concerning those Gentile movements which, like itself, were critical of existing society and hoped to reconstruct it. In this respect, Zionism differed sharply from other modern Jewish movements. Jewish Marxism, regarding the Jewish problem as an expression of capitalism that would disappear in the classless society, implied faith that one's Gentile fellow-Socialists would not break their covenant as had the Gentile liberals. The advocates of national autonomy for minorities in Europe similarly trusted that Gentiles would abide by the covenants that were to embody this principle. Zionism had no faith in the willingness of the Gentiles to extend a welcome to Jews, under any definition, as free and equal brethren in the same land. It was a disillusionment built upon the experience that it was possible for revolutionists to regard Jewish blood spilled in pogroms as merely "grease on the wheels of the revolution."[5]

Zionism took anti-Semitism seriously and expected it to persist. This is the specific way in which it differed from other modern Jewish ideologies. The Socialists, who expected to submerge the Jews in a classless, cosmopolitan society, the Diaspora nationalists, who planned for minority rights—none could hope to succeed unless anti-Semitism vanished. The Zionist (and territorialist) solution of the Jewish problem, contemplating the removal of the Jews from Europe, remained intrinsically possible even if one were pessimistic or prudent enough to reckon with the persistence of anti-Semitism among the Gentiles.

Zionism, like other modern Jewish ideologies, felt it understood the critics of European liberalism (among them, the anti-Semites)

[5]David Shub (in *The Jewish Daily Forward*, New York, 15 May 1955) says that this sentiment was attributed by Zionists to the Jewish Socialist leader Vladimir Medem (1879-1923), and was always denied by Medem and his associates. Whatever the origin of the quotation, which I have not been able to check further, it became a popular byword succinctly expressing an attitude of which Russian and Polish Jews had had several striking evidences among revolutionaries.

A pamphlet inciting to pogroms was issued by the revolutionary *Narodnaya Volya* group, and though it was withdrawn subsequently, there was a continuing discussion of the advisability of using anti-Semitism to foster a revolutionary atmosphere. The shock effect of this event on the Russian Jewish intelligentsia is described in Abraham Liessin's "Episodes," in the Yiddish Scientific Institute's *Historishe Shriften*, Vol. III (Vilna-Paris, 1939), pp. 196-200. It was from this same time that we date the reaction of a significant group of Russian Jewish intellectuals against the ideal of Emancipation and the rise of the counter-ideal of auto-Emancipation.

and their disapproval of the liberal solution of the Jewish problem. Accepting, as they did, the organic, ethnic views of history and nationality, they felt it was a betrayal both of the Gentile and the Jewish national destiny for Jews to make themselves the protagonists of Gentile culture, for example, instead of fostering their own. Moreover, they appreciated that if it were the aim of a group to use all sources of power in a given territory for the preservation and propagation of its distinct national values, its traditional style of life and culture, its own ethnic variant of Christian culture, then it was bound to be resented when political and economic power came into the hands of Jews. Such an attitude left only one possibility for a compact between Jews and Gentiles that the two distinct groups could loyally uphold: those Jews who could not or would not assimilate must have a country of their own where they would be separate and independent.

Two things are characteristic of American Jewish ideologies. The first is that American Jews never faced directly the whole historic complex of problems, centering around Emancipation as a traumatic event, from which modern Jewish ideologies arose. The second is that only in our own time, actually in the years since World War II, has American Jewry been compelled to face its own peculiar situation and to create its own history. One could conclude, then, that American Jewish ideological development may still not really have begun.

Whatever truth there may be in such a conclusion, it need not mean that there have been no differences of opinion, no debates until now. That is obviously untrue, for whatever ideology existed in Europe has had its adherents, few or many, here. Thus American Zionism, for example, arose by understanding and sharing in the typical attitudes, problems, and situation of Zionism in Europe—especially in the degree that American Zionists continued to live the life of the Old Country in America.

Now it was quite generally characteristic not only of American Zionism, or of American Jewry, or even of all immigrants, but of America itself to share and understand the life and thoughts, the trends of modern culture and politics in the Old World. Those newcomers who lived in the immigrant ghettos (at least, the cultural elite among them) shared the life of the Old World most directly and most specifically. Those older settlers (again, the cultural elite among them) who were establishing the permanent forms of American life also continued to live in the current of European political and cultural development, though with greater detachment and in a more general form. It was a more international European culture, and not so specifically a particular national culture, in which they shared. As for the culture arising in America itself, the specific "culture" native to the immigrant ghettos was based not only on an obviously transitory experience but also on an experience of suffering rather than of creation; "permanent" American culture remained intrinsically open and partially unformed, constituting, in a way, a set of defensible hypotheses rather than a body of axioms and absolute values.

It is important to note that only in our own time has the characteristic American Jewish type come to be the native-born American Jew. American Zionism, product of an earlier generation, was to a large extent a movement of the American immigrant ghetto.[6] Thus, intellectually, it shared in and understood the Zionism of the nineteenth-century "modern" European Jew, just as the other immigrant ghettos shared in and understood the social and intellectual movements of the Old Country they came from. The immigrant intellectuals who dominated American Zionism had a more direct and more specific understanding of the situation, problems, and attitudes of the modern European Jew than is possible for the native American Jew. Yet even for them European Zionism was a *vicarious* experience.

It was natural, therefore, that even for the immigrants, new American experiences—the experience of the American immigrant ghetto, and the unfolding experience of the new American society in formation—began to color their Zionism. This tendency was heightened by the influence of native American leaders who were active in American Zionism from the very beginning. The nuances by which American Zionism was touched through its naturalization

[6]See, however, Judd L. Teller's article, "America's Two Zionist Traditions," in *Commentary*, October 1955, pp. 343–352. This article emphasizes the existence of a pre-Herzlian Zionist "tradition" in America, represented by Mordecai Emanuel Noah and Emma Lazarus. It also highlights the difference in attitude between some native-born (or American-educated) early Zionists, like Louis D. Brandeis and Julian W. Mack, and the Eastern European outlook of immigrant Zionism. In common with many writers during the recent Tercentenary celebrations of American Jewry, Teller strains the data perceptibly in an effort to make episodes add up to a native American Jewish tradition; but the differences he emphasizes between the Zionism of the immigrant ghetto and the Zionism of "uptown" Jews is a significant one, in view of the similarity of the latter to the neo-Zionist mood of today. . . .

in America have now, in a time when American Jewry is largely native-born and remains as the major surviving Diaspora, become the dominant coloration of a new American Zionism.

The two major divisions of the Jewish problem, assimilation and anti-Semitism, look different against an American environment. The theory of assimilation as a solution of the Jewish problem was a revolt against an old-established historic status of the Jews in Europe, into which they had sunk vast creative energies. The "ghetto" in Europe was not only an oppression the Jews suffered but a way of life they clung to. And when the reaction against assimilationism came in European Jewry, it paralleled, in a way, the post-revolutionary movements among the Gentiles: it saw itself as the synthetic conclusion of a Hegelian dialectical process. The Emancipation had been an antithesis of an original thesis, the ghetto; and Zionism (like other modern Jewish movements), in transcending the Emancipation, intended to absorb what was valuable not only in the liberal revolution but in the primary status—the ghetto—which assimilationism had rejected.

"Assimilationism" in America was a rejection of life in the immigrant ghetto. But life in the tenements had never been filled with any creative significance, no historic values had been placed upon it and institutionalized through it, it contained no unfulfilled promises, no high demands spontaneously arising from its own context to give historic dimensions to its past and historic perspectives to its future. The immigrant ghetto from the beginning was entered into only to be abandoned. For the Jewish immigrants it represented either the collapse and bereavement of the old values of the true, historic, European ghetto—or, if they had already emancipated themselves from the historic Jewish values, it was a "melting pot," a grimy anteroom to the real America, a sordid extension of Ellis Island.

The generation that entered the immigrant ghetto was confronted by one overwhelming task: to get out, or enable the next generation to get out. This task they accomplished. But the generation that accomplished it had, in a way, stepped out of the frame of history, for history consists in whatever continues over a span of successive generations. The immigrant ghetto was not a continuation of the context of European-Jewish life, whether ghetto or emancipated; it was an interruption of that continuity, a break with that context. Nor did it, nor was it ever intended to, continue into the life of the next generation. It was a specific experience outside the frame of history and hence outside the frame of culture, at least insofar as culture is essentially historic.

There was nonetheless a very active cultural life and a vivid sense of history in the Jewish immigrant ghetto. That generation, in fact, reached an unsurpassed peak of historical awareness as Jews. And, concomitantly, it led a life of high cultural intensity. But the historical movements and cultural trends in which American Jews participated were European-Jewish history and European-Jewish culture, relevant to the situations and problems and expressing the values of European Jewry. The social reality of American Jewry was the one-generation experience of the immigrant ghetto, known from its very inception to be out of the frame of history and culture. Of course, American Jewry could never accept a merely vicarious participation in history and a merely nostalgic participation in culture, however intense these might be. The immigrant generation felt itself to be as much (if not more) a new beginning as a final chapter in the historic and cultural continuity of the Jews. They looked to the day when the threads of vicarious history and cultural nostalgia would weave into a new American pattern of continuity. But every American Jew, whatever his ideological sympathy—religious or secular, Zionist or non-Zionist, "survivalist" or "assimilationist"—knew beyond any question that the new hoped-for continuity that would transmit the American Jewish experience into history and culture must necessarily begin beyond the threshold of the immigrant ghetto.

If, then, "assimilationism" means radically to reject the "institutions" of the ghetto—in America, of the *immigrant* ghetto—then every American Jew, whatever his ideology, is an "assimilationist." And, in fact, the actual process of "assimilation" in the United States *is* the absorption of immigrants out of the immigrant ghettos. This is a movement in social relationships which it is common ground for every American Jew to accept. When "assimilation" served as an issue dividing American Jews it was not the actual process of assimilation out of the immigrant ghetto into the real American society about which they were debating; their argument was about assimilation as it occurred in Europe.

The differences of opinion native to the American Jewish experience are only now beginning to be defined. They arise after assimilation out of the immigrant ghetto has not only been tacitly accepted in principle but carried out in practice. Assimilation can only become an issue, in terms of the actual experience dividing the

American Jews, after the liquidation of the immigrant ghetto. At that point, when he is an "integrated" member of American society, the American Jew—now typically native-born—discovers that he still has a problem of assimilation. The problem is a totally new one, it presents the first challenge whose creative mastery might establish a continuous American Jewish historic tradition. If we may speak in terms of the Hegelian dialectic at all in America, then we are only at the point of establishing a thesis, not, as in Europe, capping an historic antithesis with its synthetic resolution.

In view of this fact it should not be surprising if American Jews are unwilling to begin their history with the disillusioned conclusion that they can come to no satisfactory terms with the Gentiles for the creative survival of the Jewish people in America. Nor should it be surprising that in looking backward for its supports in history, no portion of American Jewry seeks to recapture any values institutionalized and expressed in the characteristic experience of the immigrant ghetto. Nor, finally, should it be surprising—however little gratifying we may find it—that the first attempts to set up American Jewish ideologies are based on a rather empty, almost defiant optimism about Jewish survival in the Diaspora and a somewhat boastful confidence in the values Diaspora Jews will yet produce.

The question of anti-Semitism also looks different when viewed from an American perspective. In the past, to be sure, American Zionists and anti-Zionists have divided ideologically in their reactions to anti-Semitism almost entirely in relation to the nationalistic anti-Semitic movement of Europe. The anti-Zionist view was that, even if the Jewish status of Emancipation liberalism was inadequate, Jewish ideology must have as its premise the full confidence that anti-Semitism must and will disappear in a new Gentile society. The Zionist premise was that modern nationalistic anti-Semitism would not disappear, and that where it had once appeared Jewish life would increasingly become intolerable.

But the characteristic fact about America was that modern nationalistic anti-Semitism had not really appeared here. Moreover, the usual historic grounds for its appearance were lacking. The Jews in America did not come out of a medieval ghetto through an act of emancipation, to find that, as a bourgeois people, they aroused nationalistic anti-Semitism. They filtered out of an immigrant ghetto not as a people but individually. They encountered anti-Semitism in America, but it was not based on a nationalistic reaction, rejecting the emancipation of the Jews. The native American anti-Semitism encountered here was the old perennial anti-Semitism in which Herzl discriminated the elements of "cruel sport, of common commercial rivalry, of inherited prejudice, or religious intolerance." This was a kind of anti-Semitism which neither Zionism nor any other modern Jewish movement could or would understand. It was the type of anti-Semitism with which only the medieval ghetto had provided a certain established basis of understanding.

It is true, on the other hand—and very significant—that European anti-Semitism was able to extend its influence across the Atlantic and demonstrate, on numerous critical occasions, that the fate and destiny of American Jewry were intimately connected with the fate and destiny of European Jewry. But at other times, the global threat to the Jews having subsided, the American Jews who busied themselves with the matter were faced with the problem of their own, specifically American anti-Semitism.

This problem never really became an ideological issue between Zionists and non-Zionists in America any more than did the problem of American assimilation. At most there was a difference in the degree of concern about native anti-Semitism between Zionists and non-Zionists, a sort of temperamental difference rooted quite remotely in differences of ideas. The Zionist attitude, at bottom, assumes anti-Semitism to be ineradicable. With nationalistic secularist anti-Semitism, Zionism once hoped for an understanding through divorce. But where anti-Semitism remains theological, demanding perpetuation of the Jewish Exile until the Second Advent and the subjugation of Jews to Christians in the meantime, Zionism has no understanding to propose. Thus the characteristic attitude of American Zionism to this problem—that is to say, to native American anti-Semitism—is not to take it too seriously, to feel that it is essentially a Gentile, not a Jewish, problem. On the other hand, it is characteristic of non-Zionism to take precisely this problem seriously. Non-Zionists are inclined to turn a blind eye to the seriousness of nationalistic anti-Semitism such as we saw in Europe, rejecting the notion that Jews should attempt any "understanding" with Gentiles through emigration. The basis for this attitude is an underlying belief that anti-Semitism is not really a "modern" movement, with more vitality and contemporaneity than the Emancipation of the Jews, but only a medieval survival that should expire with the inevitable increase of rationality. Among the "missions" which non-Zionism has proposed for the Jewish Diaspora, one taken up with great earnestness in every country, and in America as well, is to cure the Gentiles of their vestigial anti-Semitism and so to consummate fully the Jewish Emancipation. But whether this is at all conceivable, assuming that Jews remain a distinct entity in the Diaspora, is a problem the non-Zionist ideologists still have to face.

The crucial difference which has been brought about in the Jewish problem in the past generation is not only the rise of the State of Israel, but perhaps even more the destruction of European Jewry. This is a factor whose significance is likely to be overlooked because it is a negative factor —and one, of course, which it is anything but pleasant to remember. Without European Jewry, the face of the Jewish problem as it appears to American Jews is radically altered, and in a way simplified. Hitherto, views on the Jewish problem, in its two aspects of assimilation and anti-Semitism, were based on European traditions and, no less, upon involvement with the European-Jewish situation. But now American Jews live in a Jewish world where, essentially, they see only two main constitutents: themselves—American Jewry—and the State of Israel. In Israel, the Jewish problem of assimilation and anti-Semitism does not exist, or only in the most indirect and transmuted forms. It continues to exist in America. But the problems of assimilation and anti-Semitism must now be approached in the forms native to America, without the overtones of significance previously lent them by their involvement with the developments in Europe. That simplifies the situation considerably.

We cannot say as confidently that it clarifies it as well. The nature of the Jewish problem characteristic of America has not yet been considered with the degree of rigor and incisiveness that were typical of European-Jewish ideologies. That was natural so long as the American situation was regarded as an atypical and not too significant variant of the Jewish problem. It now becomes the major exemplification of that problem in our times. That fact requires, as it is beginning to produce, a new focus in the direction of Jewish thought.

SOCIAL CHARACTERISTICS OF AMERICAN JEWS

JEWS IN THE UNITED STATES: PERSPECTIVES FROM DEMOGRAPHY
by SIDNEY GOLDSTEIN

INTRODUCTION

SIDNEY GOLDSTEIN PRESENTS *a concise but thoughtful analysis of the demographic situation of American Jewry. His focus is on how demographic change affects the Jewish community, especially the implications of such change for Jewish identity.*

In recent years articles in various periodicals have emphasized the prospects for an alarming reduction in the size of American Jewry. Goldstein proceeds quite differently, recognizing unfavorable developments but stressing the gradualness of demographic change. He begins with a consideration of the factors which directly affect the size of the Jewish community, such as migration, fertility, intermarriage, and assimilation. He highlights the fact that American Jewry has never been large in size if considered as a proportion of the total U.S. population. Still, sensitive to the implications of changes in population size, he emphasizes in this connection the importance of fertility as well as of intermarriage—there are some who place almost exclusive emphasis on intermarriage. Furthermore, Goldstein attempts to study the impact of intermarriage without preconceptions. Utilizing all of the available evidence, he avoids the extreme position of those who see intermarriage as dooming American Jewry, but at the same time disagrees with those who minimize its impact and tend to highlight positive factors in the type of intermarriage found in the present-day Jewish community.

Goldstein is particularly helpful in pointing out implications and connections which are frequently neglected. While the interest of Jews in secular education is well known, Goldstein demonstrates how the rising level of secular education is connected with patterns of internal migration. A move to a new community may have serious consequences for Jewish identity, despite the size of the Jewish population of the new area. Whether the community is large or small there is the need to establish new bonds. Highly motivated individuals will establish such bonds without difficulty, but for others migration may serve to weaken traditional loyalties and patterns of affiliation. The implication of Goldstein's analysis is that the Jewish community cannot rely upon factors which worked in the past and were responsible for "automatic" affiliation. Jewish communal leaders, confronted with an increasingly transient population, must plan accordingly.

The rising level of secular education brings other problems as well. Not only does it increase internal migration but it may have the effect of reducing family solidarity, which may in turn produce weakened group identity. Higher education may also help raise the rate of intermarriage. And it may mean the pursuit of occupations which lack continuity with historic Jewish experience. The individual may pursue an occupation which involves people drawn from a wide variety of religious and ethnic groups, who come together in a new kind of quasi-community. Ironically, the individual may become alienated from the same Jewish community whose culture initially impelled him to pursue educational attainment.

A low birth rate—in combination with other factors—inevitably produces an older population. A community with a high proportion of aged will tend to have a substantial proportion of individuals in financial distress, or at least in reduced circumstances. This may mean that the Jewish community will experience greater difficulties meeting its local commitments as well as its obligations to world Jewry and more especially to Israel. However, the financial problems of an aging community are only one dimension of the problem; the psychological implications may be even more serious. Nothing makes for greater optimism about Jewish life than the presence of young people, particularly if they give promise of continuing the "chain of tradition"; conversely, the absence of large numbers of young people may give rise to a certain pessimism.

A demographer of American Jewry must work with a wide vari-

ety of sources of varying quality. He must be judicious in evaluating studies and resourceful in utilizing evidence drawn from many different research projects. Sidney Goldstein's judicious and resourceful article alerts the reader to fundamental changes which have important implications for the future of American Jewry.

M.S.

ℰ◇ℬ

AT A TIME WHEN THE demographic, social, and perhaps even economic structure of the American Jewish community is undergoing rapid change, there is a crucial need for a continuous monitoring of the situation and an assessment of its implications for the future. Changes in size, composition, and distribution, as well as in the patterns and levels of births and deaths, have tremendous significance on both the local and national levels. Knowledge of demographic factors is clearly essential for purposes of planning whether a community should provide certain services, where facilities should be located, how they should be staffed, and who should bear the funding burden. Moreover, the demographic structure of the Jewish community greatly affects its social, cultural, and religious viability, whether this is judged by the ability to support an educational system, to organize religious life, or to provide sufficient density of population to insure a sense of community. Because the socio-demographic structure of the Jewish community, like that of the larger American community, is both a product and a cause of change, we clearly need to have current data available. Unfortunately, however, such data are often lacking.[1]

The absence of a question on religion in the United States decennial census precludes tapping the wealth of information that would otherwise be available from that source on the religious characteristics of local populations. The need for comprehensive data on religious identification is indicated by the fact that perhaps the best single source of information available on the size and composition of Jews and other religious groups remains that collected by the Bureau of the Census in the 1957 Current Population Survey.[2] Because answers were voluntary, the survey was able to include a question on religion. But 1957 is long past, and much has happened

---

[1]An excellent review of the varied efforts undertaken between 1818 and 1977 to gather and assess statistics on the American Jewish community appears in Jack Diamond, "A Reader in the Demography of American Jews," *American Jewish Year Book,* Vol. 77 (1977), pp. 251–317.

[2]U.S. Bureau of the Census, "Religion Reported by the Civilian Population of the United States, March 1957," *Current Population Reports,* Series P-20, No. 79 (1958).

to the American population and to American Jewry since then. The 1957 data, therefore, relatively rich though they are, can serve only as a bench mark against which changes can be measured, rather than as an indication of the current situation. Unfortunately, we have few new sets of comprehensive data.

The National Jewish Population Study (NJPS) was an important and promising attempt to conduct a nationwide survey representative of the United States Jewish population. As a report in the 1973 *American Jewish Year Book (AJYB)* indicates: "The study, sponsored by the Council of Jewish Federations and Welfare Funds, now has completed data collection and other tasks prerequisite to analysis, and constitutes a repository of information that will require 'mining' and interpretation for many years to come."[3] The NJPS remains largely just that—to date only a few published reports on the number and basic characteristics of the Jewish population have appeared. This overview will make use of the limited information that is available, but in the absence of a comprehensive evaluation of the NJPS data, such information must be used with caution.

Other nationwide demographic statistics containing information on religious identification are available from various surveys undertaken by public opinion polls and other organizations.[4] Some of these surveys have been used to gain insights on American Jewish fertility,[5] but because they include a very small number of Jews, detailed analysis for general purposes is greatly restricted.

Aside from the 1957 Current Population Survey and the data from the NJPS, locally sponsored community surveys still provide the best sets of data on the characteristics of American Jews. These studies differ considerably in quality, depending in particular on the manner in which the sample populations were selected, but also on the quality of the interviewers, the response rates, and the sophisti-

---

[3]Fred Massarik and Alvin Chenkin, "United States National Jewish Population Study: A First Report," *AJYB*, Vol. 74 (1973), p. 264.

[4]As, for example, the annual General Social Survey conducted by the National Opinion Research Corporation (NORC).

[5]Ronald Freedman, Pascal K. Whelpton, and Arthur A. Campbell, *Family Planning, Sterility, and Population Growth* (New York, 1959); Norman B. Ryder and Charles F. Westoff, *Reproduction in the United States, 1965* (Princeton, 1971); Charles F. Westoff, Robert Potter, Jr., and Philip Sagi, *The Third Child* (Princeton, 1963); Charles F. Westoff, Robert Potter, Jr., Philip Sagi, and Eliot Mishler, *Family Growth in Metropolitan America* (Princeton, 1961); Pascal K. Whelpton, Arthur A. Campbell, and John E. Patterson, *Fertility and Family Planning in the United States* (Princeton, 1966).

cation of the analyses. Since some of the surveys rely exclusively on lists of families available to the local federations, serious doubts are raised about the representativeness of the samples covered; they are usually strongly biased in favor of individuals and families who contribute to fund-raising efforts. In some communities, the federations have made concerted efforts before undertaking surveys to insure coverage of donors and non-donors, as well as of both affiliated and non-affiliated families. The success of such attempts varies both with community size and with the ease of identifying non-affiliated households. In the limited instances where these efforts have been successful, the resulting samples provide a good basis for studying the entire population; in other cases, the findings about the extent and nature of Jewish identification, intermarriage, and demographic characteristics and behavior are probably seriously biased.

Beyond these concerns the findings from community surveys must be used with great caution for generalizing to the national community, since other considerations affect how representative the local sample will be for such broader purposes. Most of the surveys conducted in local communities have been for moderate-sized Jewish populations of 25,000 or less; Boston, Los Angeles, Washington, Detroit, Baltimore, and San Francisco are exceptions. Legitimate questions must be raised about the extent to which findings based on moderate-sized communities are typical of the total American Jewish population. Yet, these studies appear to display impressively similar patterns for the varied locations that have been surveyed.[6] Variations can generally be explained by the nature of the communities themselves, that is, whether they are older communities or newer suburban areas, and in which region of the country they are located. The relatively high degree of homogeneity that characterizes the patterns of these communities suggests that the underlying demographic profile of American Jewry as a whole probably does not deviate significantly from that depicted by already existing sources, incomplete as they are. The fact that the findings which are available to date from the NJPS also conform to the general patterns, provides some additional basis for confidence in both the community studies and in the NJPS itself.

In undertaking this review, the focus, within the limits of

---

[6]Sidney Goldstein, "American Jewry, 1970: A Demographic Profile," *AJYB*, Vol. 72 (1971), pp. 17–19.

available information, will be on the major areas of concern to demographers—size, composition, distribution, and the components of change (fertility, mortality, and migration). The presentation would not be complete, however, without some attention to intermarriage. Throughout the discussion, the implications of the current situation for future patterns of growth and identification will be explored.

POPULATION GROWTH

At no time in American history has there been a complete enumeration of the nation's Jewish population. Whether referring to the population in 1790 or in the 1970's, the statistic is an estimate, and therefore subject to question. For example, in 1972 the AJYB[7] reported a total Jewish population of 6,115,320, while in 1974 it cited a considerably lower figure of 5,732,000. The drop reflected the findings of the NJPS, and particularly the reassessment of Greater New York's population, which had been reported by the AJYB at 2,381,000 between 1962 and 1973, but which was estimated by the NJPS to be only 1,998,000 as of 1971.[8] As the latest AJYB stressed, at least two factors continue to make even the most recent estimates problematic—the difficulty in documenting the extent of the shift to the "sunbelt" states, and continuing doubts as to the accuracy of the New York City estimate, which may still be too high.[9]

Even the NJPS estimate of a 5,800,000 total American Jewish population in 1971 needs qualification. The statistic refers to individuals residing in Jewish households, exclusive of the institutional population, and as such includes both Jews and non-Jews. If non-Jews are excluded, again based on information gathered in the NJPS, the total number of Jewish residents in households is 5,370,000. If added to that estimate is an estimated 50,000 Jews in institutions, the total population in 1971 would be 5,420,000, still

---

[7] The U.S. Jewish population estimates which appear in the AJYB are prepared by staff members of the Council of Jewish Federations and Welfare Funds.

[8] Cf., Alvin Chenkin, "Jewish Population in the United States, 1972," AJYB, Vol. 74 (1973), pp. 307–309, and Alvin Chenkin, "Jewish Population in the United States, 1974," AJYB, Vol. 76 (1976), pp. 229–236.

[9] Alvin Chenkin and Maynard Miran, "Jewish Population in the United States, 1979," AJYB, Vol. 80 (1980), p. 159.

some half million less (a 10 percent differential) than the previous estimates cited by the *AJYB*. This is far too great a range of difference to allow strong confidence in the estimates which have been provided.[10]

A set of annual estimates by Ira Rosenwaike of the American Jewish population for the period 1940 to 1975, based on use of the 1957 Bureau of the Census estimates, indicates that the U.S. Jewish population in 1970 was 5,550,000—very close to the estimate emanating from the NJPS. Rosenwaike estimated a 1975 population of 5,619,000, only 69,000 greater than in 1970.[11] This estimate takes account of levels of fertility, mortality, and immigration, but does not incorporate estimates of losses resulting from intermarriage and assimilation. While all estimates are subject to question, the close correspondence between Rosenwaike's 1970 estimate and the NJPS figure, and the small growth since then, point to the strong likelihood that the total population in 1970 was well below the 6 million mark, and that it has remained so. The *AJYB* estimate that the 1979 Jewish population totaled 5,860,900 conforms to this expectation.[12]

The Jewish population of the United States has clearly experienced tremendous growth between the time of the formation of the United States and the 1970's. From a community estimated to number only slightly above 1,000 in 1790, the Jewish population had passed the 1 million mark by the end of the next century. Over three-quarters of that growth occurred, however, in the last two decades of the century, reflecting the onset of massive immigration

---

[10]Given the nature of the sampling procedures employed in the NJPS and resulting potential biases, the "official" NJPS estimate of the U.S. Jewish population of 5,780,000 is actually the middle of three estimates that range from a low of 5,560,000 to a high of 6,000,000. Each of these statistics has its own standard error, so that the 95 percent confidence limit for the respective estimates would be

High	6,000,000 ±	1,175,000
Medium	5,780,000 ±	884,000
Low	5,560,000 ±	763,000

The wide range encompassed by these estimates, especially when their sampling errors are taken into account, provides further evidence of the absence of exact statistics describing the Jewish population. See Bernard Lazerwitz, "An Estimate of a Rare Population Group: The U.S. Jewish Population," *Demography* (August 1978), pp. 389–394.

[11]Ira Rosenwaike, "A Synthetic Estimate of American Jewish Population Movement Over the Last Three Decades," paper presented at the Seventh World Congress of Jewish Studies, Jerusalem, August 1977.

[12]Chenkin and Miran, *op. cit.*, p. 162.

from Eastern Europe in the 1880's. Between 1881 and 1902 almost 800,000 Jews entered the United States. By the beginning of the twentieth century, Jews constituted 1.4 percent of the total American population (Table 1). Immigration continued to augment the Jewish population even more substantially in the first decades of the twentieth century; between 1902 and 1924 over 1.5 million Jews immigrated, and all but a small percentage remained in the United States, in contrast to high return rates among other ethnic groups. By 1927 Jews were estimated to number 4.2 million persons. The fourfold increase in an interval of less than three decades was far greater than the increase of the total population of the United States; during the same interval the American population grew by about only 60 percent. Reflecting this differential rate of growth, Jews more than doubled their proportion of the total population—from 1.4 percent in 1900 to 3.6 percent in 1927.

Thereafter, the imposition of immigration quotas slowed the rate of growth. What is often overlooked, however, is that between 1925 and World War II about 250,000 Jews immigrated to the United States, and that another 320,000 did so between the end of the war and 1975. Despite its reduced volume compared to the 1881–1924 peak period, immigration has therefore continued to be an important component of growth. Without it, the American Jewish population today would be substantially smaller in size, particularly given the low rates of natural increase, losses through intermarriage and assimilation, and a small loss through emigration, especially to Israel and Canada.[13] What is interesting is that despite this immigration, only one-half million persons are estimated to have been added overall to the Jewish population between 1927 and 1937, and only one-quarter million more by 1950. Such slow growth, with comparatively minor exception, has persisted to the present, and the Jewish population has increased at a much slower rate than the population as a whole. Whereas the total U.S. population increased by just over three-fourths in the 50 years between

---

[13] Simon Kuznets, "Immigration of Russian Jews to the United States: Background and Structure," *Perspectives in American History* (1975), pp. 35–124; Jacob Lestchinsky, "Jewish Migrations, 1840–1956," in Louis Finkelstein, (ed.), *The Jews* (New York, 1960), pp. 1536–1596; Calvin Goldscheider, "The Demography of Jewish Americans: Research Findings, Issues, and Challenges," paper presented at Brandeis University Planning Conference for Modern Jewish Studies, Waltham, October 21–24, 1979.

TABLE 1

Jewish population growth, United States, 1790–1979

Year	Number	Percent of total U.S. population
1790[b]	1,200	0.03
1818[a]	3,000	0.03
1826	6,000	0.06
1840	15,000	0.1
1848	50,000	0.2
1880	230,000	0.5
1888	400,000	0.6
1897	938,000	1.3
1900	1,058,000	1.4
1907[b]	1,777,000	2.0
1917	3,389,000	3.3
1927	4,228,000	3.6
1937	4,771,000	3.7
1950[c]	5,000,000	3.5
1960	5,531,000	3.1
1970	5,870,000	2.9
1975	5,732,000	2.7
1979	5,860,900	2.7

[a]Estimates for 1818–1899 are based on "Jewish Statistics," *AJYB*, Vol. 1, (1900), p. 623.
[b]Estimates for 1790 and 1907–1937 are from Nathan Goldberg, "The Jewish Population in the United States," *The Jewish People, Past and Present*, Vol. 2 (New York, 1955), p. 25.
[c]The 1950–1979 estimates are taken from *AJYB*, Vols. 70–80, (1969–1980).

1930 and 1980, the Jewish population grew by about only one-third in the same interval.

Estimates[14] of the net effects of international migration on the growth of the Jewish population in the 1970's suggest that net immigration has contributed about 8,000 persons per year. If estimates of the near-equal number of births and deaths during this period are correct, net immigration may thus have accounted for as much as 60 percent of the small growth of the American Jewish population

---

[14]Rosenwaike, *op. cit.*, pp. 6–7.

between 1970 and 1975. By contrast, in the early 1950's net immigration is estimated to have accounted for only one-fifth of total growth. With the increase in the influx of Russian Jews in the 1970's, amounting to approximately 58,700 persons between 1975 and 1979,[15] supplemented by what may be a substantial immigration of Israelis, immigration undoubtedly has persisted as the most important component of growth.

Reflecting the long-term reversal in rates of growth between the Jewish and the total population, the proportion of Jews in the total population, after peaking at 3.7 percent in 1937, has undergone a steady decline to 2.7 percent in 1979—about the same percentage as around 1910. Given the low Jewish birthrate, the losses sustained through intermarriage and assimilation, and what may well be higher levels of mortality due to the aging of the population, there seems little prospect of a reversal in the slower rates of growth that have come to characterize recent years. If anything, the growth rate is likely to continue to decline, and may even become negative in the not too distant future.

Consideration of the joint impact of the above factors has led to dire predictions about the virtual extinction of the American Jewish population within the next 100 years. One forecast suggests that "when the United States celebrates its tricentennial in 2076, the American Jewish community is likely to number no more than 944,000 persons and conceivably as few as 10,420."[16] While this prediction is overly pessimistic, in the absence of a drastic reversal in ongoing patterns, a decline does seem probable; the projections by Lieberman and Weinfeld of a Jewish population of 3–4 million by the end of the twenty-first century seem much more likely.[17]

The decline in relative numbers may not be very significant in view of the fact that Jews have never constituted a numerically large segment of the American population. Despite their small numbers, Jews are generally considered the third *major* religious group in the country. There seems little reason to expect that this situation will change, even should the Jewish percentage of the total population

---

[15]Personal communication from HIAS, March 11, 1980. The number includes only those Russian immigrants who were assisted by HIAS.

[16]Elihu Bergman, "The American Jewish Population Erosion," *Midstream* (October 1977), p. 9.

[17]Samuel S. Lieberman and Morton Weinfeld, "Demographic Trends and Jewish Survival," *Midstream* (November 1978), pp. 9–19.

decline further. As long as Jews, both as a group and individually, continue to play significant roles in the cultural, educational, political, and economic life of the country, more important factors than sheer numbers may influence the position of the Jewish community within the total American community. These factors include changes in Jewish geographical concentration, as well as in Jewish representation in selected socioeconomic strata of the population. Only when the change in total numbers is accompanied by significant changes in distribution and composition which are deleterious to the prominent role Jews have played on the American scene will the change in numbers itself take on a new significance.

MORTALITY

Better health and longer life have characterized the Jewish population in the Western world since at least the mid-seventeenth century.[18] Factors contributing to this favorable differential have included the positive effect of religious observance on health conditions; the relatively longer exposure which Jews have had to "civilized" environments and urban settings, resulting in higher levels of immunity against certain contagious diseases; and the higher-than-average socioeconomic status which Jews have enjoyed, permitting them thereby to obtain more and better medical attention, and to live in a better environment. Because of the low mortality levels and the generally good health conditions which have characterized American society in recent years, minimum attention has been paid by Jewish scholars to the mortality experience of the American Jewish population. In part this also reflects the difficulty of obtaining the necessary data in the absence of direct information on religion on death certificates. No study on Jewish mortality levels appears to have been conducted since 1970. The few studies undertaken before 1970 were limited both because of their restriction to a small number of communities, and because they were cross-sectional and did not, therefore, provide trend data that might be useful for projections.

---

[18] Salo Baron, A Social and Religious History of the Jews, Vol. II (New York, 1937), p. 169.

Although the specific findings differ somewhat among communities, the general conclusion seems warranted that as recently as the 1960's some differences existed between Jews and the total white population in age specific death rates, life expectancy, and survival patterns—generally more so for males than for females.[19] Jewish age specific death rates were below those of the white population at younger ages, possibly because of a combination of the conditions already outlined which have lowered the susceptibility of Jews to contagious diseases. The particularly lower mortality among Jewish babies under one lends support to this interpretation. Older Jews have a higher mortality than the total white population, which may reflect the possibility that, given the better medical attention they receive at earlier ages and their better ability to survive contagious diseases, more Jews with physically impaired lives survive until later years, when the effects of chronic diseases produce higher death tolls. Data for Providence, Rhode Island, by cause of death, support such an interpretation.[20]

Again, it is necessary to use caution in interpreting these data, because of their limited coverage of the American Jewish population, as well as their outdated character. It is especially important to recognize that the cross-sectional character of the data provides no basis for projecting future patterns, particularly about the mortality experience of older persons. In the United States in general, minimal changes in mortality are expected. The fact that relatively small differences already existed between Jews and non-Jews in the 1960's, and that these have most likely diminished still further as the socioeconomic environment of Jews and non-Jews and their utilization of health services have become more similar, probably means that future mortality will be even more similar than that observed here. Certainly, the differences observed for the 1960's are not large enough to account for the overall differences in the rate of natural increase of the Jewish population compared to the total population. At the same time, the aging of the Jewish population means that the number of Jewish deaths is likely to rise. To the extent that this happens, the rate of natural increase is likely to decline in the absence of a corresponding rise in births, all the more so if the birthrate should decline. Given these patterns, whatever differential

---

[19]Goldstein, op. cit., pp. 12–15.

[20]Sidney Goldstein, "Jewish Mortality and Survival Patterns: Providence, Rhode Island, 1962–1964," Eugenics Quarterly (March 1966), pp. 48–61.

in natural growth characterizes Jews and non-Jews in the future will be largely attributable to variations in levels of fertility.

FERTILITY

The available evidence clearly indicates that throughout American history Jews have had a lower birthrate than non-Jews. Yet, only in very recent years has lower fertility become an openly discussed concern of the Jewish community. In part, this reflects the fact that Jewish fertility, like that of the larger society, has recently declined to a point where continuation at its current levels would lead to zero population growth (ZPG) or possibly even negative population growth (NPG)—reflecting situations wherein births are either equal to or below the number of deaths, thereby leading to stability or decline in population size in the absence of reenforcement from international migration. For Jews this threat of population decline is particularly serious, since it can be exacerbated by losses resulting from intermarriage and assimilation.

Despite the Biblical injunction to be fruitful and multiply, Jews have had the smallest families of virtually all ethnic and religious groups. As early as the late nineteenth century, available evidence pointed to a Jewish birthrate which was lower than that of the non-Jewish population; this differential, although narrowing, has persisted to the present.

In the Rhode Island census of 1905, the only state census that obtained information on religion and related it to family size, the average family size of native-born Jewish women was 2.3, compared to an average of 3.2 for native-born Catholics, and 2.5 for native-born Protestants.[21] Studies in the 1930's found Jews to have not only lower fertility, but also higher proportions using contraceptives, planning pregnancies, and relying on more efficient methods to achieve that goal.[22] The 1941 Indianapolis fertility study, a milestone in demographic research in the United States, found the fertility of Jews, controlling for age differences, to be 25 percent

---

[21]Calculated from *Rhode Island Census of 1905*, "Conjugal Conditions, Maternity Tables," Bulletin IV, part one of the annual report for 1907, Table VII, p. 551.

[22]R. K. Stix and Frank Notestein, *Controlled Fertility* (Baltimore: 1940), p. 29; Raymond Pearl, *The Natural History of Population* (New York, 1939), pp. 241–242.

lower than that of Protestants, whereas that of Catholics was about 15 percent higher.[23]

The results of the 1957 population survey conducted by the United States Bureau of the Census also confirmed the lower fertility of Jews.[24] The cumulative fertility rate (children ever born) of Jewish women 45 years of age and over was 2.2, compared to 3.1 for Catholic women and 2.8 for Protestant women. Lower fertility also characterized Jewish women at younger ages. Moreover, controlling for area of residence, the fertility rate for Jewish women in urban areas was 14 percent below that of all urban women.

Beginning in the 1950's, a series of surveys was undertaken to investigate the fertility behavior of the American population. Although Jews constituted only a small portion of each of the samples in these surveys, the data clearly pointed to lower Jewish fertility. The 1965 Growth of American Families study showed that the average number of children born by that year to women under age 44 was 2.3 for Protestants and 2.8 for Catholics, compared to only 2.1 for Jews.[25] By the end of childbearing, Jews also expected to have a smaller total number of children (2.9) than either Protestants (3.0) or Catholics (3.9). The similarity between the Protestant and Jewish expected averages is particularly noteworthy in view of earlier observed differences, but expectations may not be fully realized. In a 1970 study, Westoff and Ryder found that among women 35–44 years of age, those at the end of the reproduction period, sharp religious differentials existed.[26] Restricting the comparison to white women, Catholics averaged 3.6 children compared to only 2.9 for Protestants and 2.1 for Jews—a level equivalent to ZPG. The authors also made a distinction between wanted and unwanted children. Only 3 percent of the Jewish children were reported as unwanted, by far the lowest percentage for all religious groups—a fact that reflects successful fertility control.

Although focusing on a somewhat different population, and using a follow-up approach to their original sample rather than an independent cross-section of the population in successive rounds of

---

[23]Pascal K. Whelpton and Clyde V. Kiser, "Differential Fertility Among Native White Couples in Indianapolis," *Social and Psychological Factors Affecting Fertility, I, Milbank Memorial Fund Quarterly* (July 1943), pp. 226–271.

[24]U.S. Bureau of the Census, *op. cit.*

[25]Ryder and Westoff, *op. cit.*

[26]Charles F. Westoff and Norman B. Ryder, *The Contraceptive Revolution* (Princeton, 1977).

interviews, the Princeton Fertility Studies of 1957 and 1960 reached the same conclusions as those reported by GAF.[27] Jews, when compared to Protestants and Catholics, desired fewer children and more successfully planned their pregnancies.

Since the late 1960's, a new set of statistics allows national comparison of the current fertility of Jews and non-Jews.[28] The data collected in the National Natality Surveys of 1967, 1968, and 1969 by the National Center for Health Statistics are based on follow-up interviews with samples of mothers of legitimate births reported on birth certificates in those three years. By combining the data from the three years, it was possible to assemble a sample of 167 Jewish women who gave birth during that period; they constituted 2 percent of the total sample. Omitted are all childless married women, all mothers of illegitimate children, and all women who did not have a child during 1967–1969. The latter restriction means that the respondents are younger than all married women and that they probably average somewhat more children than the total married.

Use of these data does have the advantage of allowing assessment of current fertility, whereas most of the surveys focus on cumulative fertility. In conjunction with the estimates of Jewish women by age from the NJPS, a variety of basic fertility measures could be computed; these were, in turn, compared with those of the U.S. white population. It must be stressed that the fertility rates calculated represent only very crude estimates, since they are subject to wide sampling errors. However, even when these sampling errors are taken into account, the evidence clearly documents the low fertility of Jews.

During 1967–1969, the crude birthrate for total U.S. whites was 16.8, but only 9.6 for the Jewish population (middle estimates will be used throughout the discussion). Because the age composition of the Jewish and total population is quite different, a better comparison of Jewish and total fertility can be made if age is controlled. As the data in Table 2 show, with the exception of the 25–29 age group, Jewish fertility is consistently below that of the total white population, and usually substantially so. Probably reflecting the later age of marriage of Jewish women, related in part to their tendency to stay in school longer, the birthrate of Jewish women

---

[27]Westoff, Potter, and Sagi, op. cit., p. 89; Westoff, Potter, Sagi, and Mishler, op. cit., pp. 72–92.

[28]Sidney Goldstein, "Jewish Fertility in Contemporary America," in Paul Ritterband, (ed.), Modern Jewish Fertility (Leiden, 1979).

aged 15–19 is only 7.2 per thousand, compared to 59.9 per thousand for the total white population. This differential narrows in the next age group, but the birthrate remains very low for Jewish women. Because of the delay in marriage and consequent delay in fertility, the age specific fertility rate for Jewish women in the 25–29 year age group is actually slightly above that of the total white population. About half of all Jewish births occur to women aged 25–29, and almost three-quarters of total fertility is completed by age 29. Corresponding percentages for the total white population are only 25 and 63 percent, respectively. The Jewish fertility rate drops precipitously for women aged 30–34, and continues the decline for higher aged groups.

The cumulative effect of these age differences leads to an estimate of an average of 1,468 children per thousand Jewish women at the end of their reproductive cycle, assuming that the 1967–1969 age specific patterns persisted. This contrasts to 2,388 for the total white group. To the extent that 2.1 is the average number of births per woman required for replacement level, these data make it very clear that, unless there are drastic errors in either the birth data or the base population data, Jewish fertility levels were already below replacement during the early 1960's, whereas those for the total whites in those years were still above replacement level. The tremendous differential between the two, approaching the ratio of 2 to 1, is substantial enough to confirm that the difference in the crude rate is not strictly a matter of age composition, but also reflects a very real difference in fertility behavior between Jews and the total population.

Replacements can be measured more clearly through use of the net reproduction rate, which shows the number of daughters who would be born to a thousand women passing through their reproductive years, subject to both current age specific fertility rates and current mortality patterns. In general, a net reproduction rate of a thousand indicates that the women will produce enough daughters to exactly replace themselves; a rate below a thousand is indicative of inadequate replacement. Based on the assumption that Jewish mortality and that of the U.S. white population are quite similar, the net reproduction rate for Jews is shown to be between 668 and 722 per thousand, compared to 1,144 per thousand for the total white population. The net reproduction rate thus confirms what has already been indicated by the other measures, i.e., that the replacement level of Jews is far below that of the total white popula-

TABLE 2

Comparative measures of fertility, Jewish and total white
United States populations, 1967–1969

	Jewish population*			
	Low population base	Medium population base	High population base	U.S. white population
Crude birthrate	9.9	9.6	9.2	16.8
General fertility rate	48.1	46.2	44.5	82.3
Total fertility rate	1,527.5	1,467.5	1,412.5	2,388.0
Net reproduction rate	722.5	694.2	668.2	1,143.6
Age specific birthrates				
15–19	7.5	7.2	6.9	55.9
20–24	63.2	60.8	58.4	164.1
25–29	153.0	147.0	141.5	141.0
30–34	60.3	57.9	55.8	73.7
35–39	17.5	16.8	16.2	34.0
40–44	4.0	3.8	3.7	8.9

*Based on population estimates from National Jewish Population Study, 1970–1971, and on fertility estimates from the 1967–1969 National Natality Surveys.

Low Population Estimate	=	5,550,000
Medium Population Estimate	=	5,775,000
High Population Estimate	=	6,000,000

tion, and also considerably below the level needed to insure growth if 1967–1969 rates persist.

The restriction of the National Natality Survey data to women actually having children during the specified years argues for the exploitation of complementary data which allow assessment of cumulative fertility. Some limited insights into this can be obtained from data available from the National Opinion Research Census (NORC) annual surveys. By combining the data from the 1972 through 1975 surveys, it was possible to obtain 89 ever married

Jewish women in all age groups over 18.[29] These women had averaged 2.0 children up to the time of the survey, compared to 2.7 for
both Protestants and Catholics. Among women aged 40–49, the age
group at the end of childbearing, corresponding averages were 2.4,
3.4, and 3.6 for Jews, Protestants, and Catholics, respectively. The
pattern of lower Jewish fertility is reflected dramatically in the parity
data. About equal percentages of all religious groups were childless,
but 70 percent of the Jewish women had two or fewer children,
compared to only 53 percent of the Protestants and 52 percent of the
Catholics. By contrast, 16 and 17 percent, respectively, of Protestant
and Catholic women had five or more children, compared to only 1
percent of the Jews. Regardless of the index used, therefore, the
NORC data, which reflect cumulative fertility behavior rather than
current performance or expected future levels, point to consistently
lower Jewish fertility compared to that of non-Jews.

The evidence available from 15 Jewish community studies
encompassing the period 1953–1976 also points to lower Jewish
fertility (Table 3). These data measure fertility by comparing the
number of children under 5 years of age per 1,000 women aged
20–44. Particularly noteworthy is the observation that five of the
seven communities which took surveys before 1960 reported
child-woman ratios above 500, whereas none of the surveys taken
since 1960 have done so; and the ratios for three of the four communities surveyed in the 1970's display the lowest of all, below 400,
and in the case of Greater Kansas City only 231. That this low
fertility is typical of the national scene is indicated by the NJPS data
for 1970–1971 which reveal a child-woman ratio for Jews of only
352, some 27 percent below the 1970 national average of 485 for the
white 1970 urban population.

Also using data from the NJPS, Della Pergola has undertaken
what constitutes one of the most comprehensive assessments yet
completed of fertility patterns among the Jewish population of the
United States as a whole.[30] The large sample size, consisting of
5,303 ever married females age 15 and over, allows much more
in-depth study, despite some concern about the coverage of the
NJPS, than any other national sample. The exploitation of the

---

[29]General Social Surveys, 1972 through 1975, conducted by National Opinion
Research Center, Roper Research Center, Inc., Williamstown, Mass.
[30]Sergio Della Pergola, "Patterns of American Jewish Fertility," mimeographed
paper, Jerusalem, 1979.

TABLE 3

Jewish child-woman ratio: Number of children under age 5 to number of women aged 20–44, selected communities

Community	Year	Fertility ratio
New Orleans, La.	1953	496
Lynn, Mass.	1955	528
Canton, Ohio	1955	469
Des Moines, Iowa	1956	596
Worcester, Mass.	1957	525
New Orleans, La.	1958	510
Los Angeles, Calif.	1959	560
South Bend, Ind.	1961	494
Rochester, N.Y.	1961	489
Providence, R.I.	1963	450
Camden, N.J.	1964	480
Springfield, Mass.	1966	418
Columbus, Ohio	1969	444
Dallas, Texas	1972	304
Minneapolis, Minn.	1972	436
Houston, Texas	1975	342
Greater Kansas City	1976	231
National Jewish Population Study	1971	352
U.S. white urban population	1960	635
U.S. white urban population	1970	485
U.S. white metropolitan population	1975	360

Sources: Sidney Goldstein, "American Jewry, 1970: A Demographic Profile," *AJYB*, Vol. 72 (1971).
Betty J. Maynard, *The Dallas Jewish Community Study* (Dallas, 1974).
Judith B. Erickson and Mitchel J. Lazarus, *The Jewish Community of Greater Minneapolis* (Minneapolis, 1973).
Sam Shulman, David Gottlieb, and Sheila Sheinberg, *A Sociological and Demographic Survey of the Jewish Community of Houston, Texas* (Houston, 1976).
The Jewish Population Study of the Greater Kansas City Area (Kansas City, 1977).

retrospective fertility history information collected in the survey enhances the richness of the analysis undertaken. The findings of the analysis basically confirm the insights gained in other studies.

Throughout the period covered by the analysis, Jewish fertility was consistently lower than among total whites, varying from a ratio of 69 Jewish births per 100 white births in about 1930, to a high of 87 in 1945, and declining thereafter to only 68 in 1965, when the total Jewish fertility rate was again below replacement level. As Della Pergola notes, "Jewish fertility levels basically followed over time the general fluctuations of the total whites, but patterns of response to period societal change were relatively earlier, sharper, and faster as appropriate to a nearly perfectly contracepting population."[31] The most recent cohorts were unmistakably directed towards increasingly lower fertility, even though young ever married women indicate an expectation to slightly surpasss replacement levels; these expectations seem unrealistically high, given other patterns observed.

Della Pergola also notes considerable variation in fertility levels of different marriage and birth cohorts, but these generally occur within the boundaries of lower fertility. He also suggests, however, that there may be a "minimum" level below which families are unwilling to lower their fertility, providing societal circumstances are not too exacting. What seems to vary more among cohorts than the absolute differences in average number of children born (which generally varies within a range of one child) is the tempo of childbearing which is affected by age of woman at marriage, duration of marriage, and societal circumstances.

The detailed analysis leads Della Pergola to conclude that "long-term American cycles of socio-demographic change stimulated a multi-faceted Jewish demographic response. This included, during the more adverse years, non-marriage, later marriage, more frequent childlessness, fewer children per mother, longer birth intervals, and later termination of childbearing. After World War II, trends were quite similarly reversed for the different components of Jewish family formation, although relatively late marriage and low fertility generally characterize the entire period."[32]

A final set of data, whose major attractivenes is its currency and national coverage, but which includes only a small number of Jews, is the National Survey of Family Growth sponsored by the federal

---

[31]*Ibid.*, p. 18.
[32]*Ibid.*, pp. 13–14.

government.[33] The results of the first survey, conducted in 1973–1974, showed that for the white population of the United States the number of children ever born was 2,180, but the average for Jews was only 1,914 (Table 4). If the comparison is in terms of total children expected, the Jewish average of 2,356 per thousand was 15 percent below the total white average of 2,783. Perhaps more significantly, Jewish women aged 20–24 expected to have 1,569 children per thousand women, a number 32 percent below the 2,313 expected by all white women, and well below replacement level. Only among women aged 35 and older was the average number of children expected above replacement level; yet even these averages were only 0.4 to 0.6 children above replacement level, and well below the averages of the total population.

Lower Jewish fertility is also reflected by the fact that only 15 percent of all Jewish women aged 15–29 were pregnant, seeking to become pregnant, or in a post-partum status at the time of the survey, compared to 23 and 26 percent, respectively, of the white Protestant and Catholic married women in the same age range.[34] These data indicate, too, the high levels of fertility control characterizing Jews: 91 percent of all currently married Jewish women 15–44 years of age were practicing contraception or were sterilized at the time of the 1973 survey. This level contrasted to 79 percent of the white Protestant women and 73 percent of the white Catholic women.

The low levels of Jewish fertility observed in these various studies strongly suggest that Jews continue to have highly favorable attitudes toward family planning, and to be highly successful in the use of contraceptives. In a period of generally declining fertility, the fertility of Jews may be lower still. Goldscheider and Uhlenberg have argued that the "characteristics" approach, which attempts to explain the lower Jewish fertility by the social and economic characteristics that distinguish Jews from non-Jews, falls short of supplying a full explanation for the differential.[35] They maintain that attention

---

[33]Gordon Scott Bonham, "Expected Size of Completed Family Among Currently Married Women 15–44 Years of Age: United States, 1973," *Advancedata* (August 1977).

[34]Kathleen Ford, "Contraceptive Use in the United States, 1973," *Vital and Health Statistics*, Series 23 (forthcoming).

[35]Calvin Goldscheider and Peter R. Uhlenberg, "Minority Group Status and Fertility," *American Journal of Sociology* (January 1969), pp. 361–372.

TABLE 4

*Total number of children ever born and total births
expected per 1,000 currently married women aged 15–44,
by age and religion: United States, 1973*

Religion	15–19	20–24	25–29	30–34	35–39	40–44	All Ages
			Children Ever Born				
Protestant	482	928	1,670	2,548	2,993	3,169	2,158
Catholic	471	888	1,773	2,727	3,273	3,546	2,359
Jewish	*	*	994	2,058	2,510	2,733	1,914
Other, none	*	1,035	1,025	2,103	2,471	2,510	1,467
All women	479	921	1,651	2,575	3,054	3,251	2,180
			Births Expected				
Protestant	2,246	2,260	2,402	2,798	3,088	3,198	2,710
Catholic	2,790	2,514	2,650	3,138	3,476	3,632	3,057
Jewish	*	1,569	2,094	2,058	2,583	2,771	2,356
Other, none	2,020	2,117	2,002	2,553	2,680	2,586	2,257
All women	2,376	2,313	2,445	2,879	3,183	3,297	2,783

*Figure does not meet standards of reliability.
Source: Gordon Scott Bonham, "Expected Size of Completed Family Among Currently Married Women 15–44 Years of Age: United States, 1973," *Advancedata* (August, 1977).

must also be given to the minority position of Jews and to the cross-culturally shared Jewish values that have helped to account for lower Jewish fertility in the past and in widely different societies. Perceptions of discrimination, feelings of insecurity, and values particularly conducive to fewer children may continue to contribute to lower Jewish fertility.

Thus, although Jewish fertility may foreshadow the patterns of other groups as we move into the era of the perfect contraceptive population, Jews may still continue to be characterized by lower levels of fertility because of other social-psychological factors associated with the still unique position of Jews in the larger society. That the already low Jewish fertility levels have evidently declined even further as part of the national pattern suggests that the motives for small families reflect a complex combination of factors involving both conditions unique to the Jews and those shared with the larger population. Even though Jewish community leaders have spoken out against ZPG and in favor of higher Jewish fertility in order to compensate for losses through intermarriage and to avoid declines in aggregate numbers, American Jews have shown little evidence of reversing their exceptionally low fertility levels.

At the same time, it seems apparent that, as among the general population, the number of Jewish singles has increased in recent years. In part this reflects higher levels of enrollment in college and graduate school, later age at marriage, changes in life style that involve more frequent sharing of households while unmarried, and higher divorce rates. This comparatively new development has implications both for fertility levels and for the vitality of the Jewish family, which has been a mainstay of the community's strength and survival. To date, the community and its institutions continue to experiment with various methods by which to insure maintenance of Jewish identification on the part of this segment of the population.[36]

It will be interesting to observe, if general fertility levels should rise in the next decade as some experts predict,[37] whether Jews participate in the upward swing. Past patterns suggest that, if they do, it will not be to the same extent as the general population. As Cohen has recently suggested, the factors helping to explain the low Jewish birthrate—including higher divorce and separation rates, later age at marriage and possible rises in levels of celibacy, increased extra-familial activity, higher education levels, greater secularism, and higher rates of intermarriage—should serve to reenforce low fertility levels.[38]

For the immediate future, and most likely for the longer run as well, therefore, available evidence points to birth levels among Jews which are inadequate to insure growth, especially when viewed in

---

[36]Cf., New York *Times*, (April 2, 1976).

[37]Ronald Lee, "Demographic Forecasting and the Easterlin Hypothesis," *Population and Development Review* (1976), p. 459.

[38]Steven Cohen, "Renascence or Oblivion," paper presented at meeting of Task Force on Jewish Population, New York, September 19, 1977.

conjunction with possible losses through intermarriage and assimilation. There seems little prospect that the total Jewish population of the United States will rise above 6 million in the foreseeable future. The chances are much more likely that it will stabilize or move toward 5 million, and possibly go even lower. Moreover, the losses in population resulting from ZPG or NPG take on added significance because they will also produce changes in the age composition of the Jewish population, reducing the percentage of youths and increasing that of the aged. Before turning to questions of composition, however, attention needs to be given to the other components of change: intermarriage, assimilation, and migration.

INTERMARRIAGE

In contrast to the recentness of concern about the levels of Jewish fertility, interest in the levels and impact of intermarriage has a much longer history. Particular importance was attached to intermarriage, not so much because it was seen as a threat to the demographic maintenance of American Jewry, but because it was viewed as an index of the loss of Jewish identification, and as a threat to the social and religious cohesiveness of the community. Yet, if martial assimilation takes place at a high rate, the Jewish group faces demographic losses both through the assimilation of the Jewish partner in the marriage and through the loss of children born to such a marriage. Thus, it is not surprising (particularly in the face of earlier evidence that Jews had been remarkably successful, compared to other groups, in maintaining religious endogamy) that a variety of evidence suggesting an increasing rate of intermarriage has set off alarm bells in the Jewish community.

Regrettably, the quality of the information that we have on the rates of intermarriage and its impact on identity is still poor; we lack a clear picture of the overall situation. The evidence suggests that the level of intermarriage and its impact vary considerably depending on community size, location, and social cohesiveness. Complications are also introduced by the manner in which intermarriage is measured. Studies relying exclusively on current religious identification of marriage partners run the risk of undercounting intermarriages, since those partners to a mixed marriage who have changed their religion in conjunction with the marriage would not be identified as having intermarried. This problem can be compounded by fairly loose definitions of who is regarded as a Jew. At the other extreme, the rate of intermarriage may be inflated if the criterion for religious identification is the ancestry of individuals rather than their personal life histories.

Despite these measurement problems, the evidence clearly points to an increased rate of Jewish intermarriage. A number of communities surveyed in the late 1950's and 1960's showed levels of intermarriage between 5 and 10 percent—levels which differed only minimally from those observed in communities surveyed in the 1930's. The March 1957 sample survey conducted by the Bureau of the Census found that only 3.8 percent of married persons reporting themselves as Jews were married to non-Jews, and that 7.2 percent of all marriages in which at least one partner was Jewish were intermarriages.[39] Both of these statistics are probably somewhat low, since no information was collected on the earlier religion of the marriage partners. Yet the 1950's and 1960's also produced studies that revealed intermarriage rates as high as 17 percent in New York City, 37 percent in Marin County, California, and 54 percent in Iowa.[40]

Erich Rosenthal's analysis of intermarriage among the Jewish population of Washington, D.C. in 1956 aroused serious anxiety concerning the threat which intermarriage posed to the demographic survival of the Jewish population.[41] This anxiety grew out of his observation that the rate of intermarriage increased from 1.4 percent among foreign-born husbands, to 10.2 percent among second-generation men, and up to 17.9 percent among husbands of third- and higher-order generation status. The possibility that these generation differentials reflected a trend toward rising levels of intermarriage was reinforced by data emanating from other community studies, such as Providence and Springfield,[42] even though the levels of intermarriage were lower than those for Washington. The

---

[39]U.S. Bureau of the Census, *op. cit.*

[40]Goldstein, "American Jewry, 1970," p. 28.

[41]Erich Rosenthal, "Studies of Jewish Intermarriages in the United States," *AJYB*, Vol. 64 (1963), pp. 34–51.

[42]Sidney Goldstein, *The Greater Providence Jewish Community: A Population Survey* (Providence, 1964); Sidney Goldstein, *A Population Survey of the Greater Springfield Jewish Community* (Springfield, 1968).

1965 Boston survey also suggested a sharp rise in the level of inter-marriage among the very youngest segment of the population; in contrast to a 3 percent level of intermarriage among couples in which the age of the husband was 51 and over, 20 percent of the couples in which the husband was 30 years old or younger were intermarried.[43] Interestingly, the 1975 Boston survey also found 3 percent of couples in which the age of the husband was 50 and over to have been intermarried; but the rate had risen to 26 percent of those under 30 years of age.[44] The sharpest increase occurred in the intermediary age groups. In contrast to 7 percent of those with the husband between ages 31 and 50 who were intermarried in 1965, 22 percent of those in the 30–49 age range in 1975 were intermarried. The lesser rise for the youngest age group may reflect the high percentage in that age group who are still unmarried, and that intermarriage occurs somewhat later.

The NJPS provided the first nationwide set of comprehensive data on Jewish intermarriage patterns.[45] Since it ascertained the religious identity of the marriage partners at the time they met, it allowed fuller assessment of intermarriage than did the census data. The NJPS found that 9.2 percent of all Jewish persons married at the time of the survey were intermarried. This level was not unusu-ally high; what was "shocking" about the NJPS findings was the analysis of intermarriage in terms of marriage cohorts. This analysis determined that the level of intermarriage rose from 2 percent of those individuals who had married between 1900 and 1920, to 6 percent of those marrying between 1940 and 1960, and increased precipitously thereafter to 17 percent of the 1960–1965 marriage cohort and 32 percent of those marrying in the five years preceding the survey.

In the absence of a full evaluation of the NJPS data and of supporting evidence from independent sources attesting to the va-lidity of this very high level of intermarriage, its exactness must be questioned. There seems little doubt, however, that the finding does justify the conclusion, based on reports by rabbis, newspapers, and

---

[43]Morris Axelrod, Floyd J. Fowler, and Arnold Gurin, A Community Survey for Long Range Planning: A Study of the Jewish Population of Greater Boston (Boston, 1967).

[44]Floyd J. Fowler, 1975 Community Survey: A Study of the Jewish Populations of Greater Boston (Boston, 1977), pp. 66–67.

[45]Massarik and Chenkin, op. cit., pp. 292–306.

other sources, that the level of intermarriage has risen very substantially in recent years. This is undoubtedly related to the increasing proportion of the population that is now third-generation, and has moved away from older areas of dense Jewish population to newly developed, more integrated areas within both the cities and suburbs; to the very high proportion of Jewish youth enrolled in colleges and universities; to the entrance of Jews into occupations and social groups which earlier had been closed to them; to the generally greater freedom and integration which Jews have enjoyed in American society in recent years; and to the increasing secularization and weakening of tradition among younger Jews. Whether these conditions will lead to still further increases in intermarriage, or whether a plateau may have been reached, has not been ascertained. To answer this question, comparative data of the type emanating from the Boston study are needed.

Whether the effects of intermarriage on demographic growth are serious may largely be determined by the extent of conversion to Judaism on the part of the non-Jewish partner to such marriages, as well as by the extent to which children born to such marriages are raised as Jews. Obviously, counts such as this for purposes of measuring the demographic outcome may not do justice to the effect of intermarriage on Jewish identification and religiosity per se, which constitute other significant dimensions of the intermarriage question. Considerable evidence does exist, however, suggesting that a substantial part of the threat of high levels of intermarriage to demographic survival is reduced by comparatively high rates of conversion to Judaism and of children being raised as Jews.

When attention was given to these questions as part of the 1963 Providence survey, for example, it was found that of all the intermarried couples, 42 percent had experienced the conversion of one partner to Judaism, thereby creating religious homogeneity within the family unit.[46] Even more significantly, perhaps, the proportion of persons converting increased with decreasing age, a finding consistent with that of many other studies. The 1975 Boston survey did not find as high a level of conversion; those data indicate that only about 10 percent of all the intermarriages of males 30–49 years of age at the time of the survey resulted in a conversion of the non-Jewish partner.[47] The NJPS found that in 27 percent of the inter-

---

[46]Goldstein, *The Greater Providence Jewish Community*, pp. 186–187.
[47]Fowler, *op. cit.*

marriages in which the husband was originally Jewish, the wife converted; however, among those couples in which it was the wife who was originally Jewish, only 2.5 percent of the husbands converted.[48] An interesting finding of the NJPS is that a very substantial percentage of non-Jewish partners in intermarriages identify themselves as Jews even though they have not officially converted. This was true of 46 percent of the non-Jewish wives and 44 percent of the non-Jewish husbands.

The same questions can be raised from the point of view of the religion in which the children of intermarriages are reared. According to the 1963 Providence survey, 78 percent of the 280 children born to intermarried couples were being raised as Jews. This contrasted very sharply to the 70 percent of the children of mixed marriages being raised as non-Jews according to Rosenthal's Washington survey. The NJPS found a high proportion of children of intermarriage being raised as Jews: 63 percent of the children of Jewish fathers and 98 percent of those of Jewish mothers.

Overall, therefore, the evidence suggests that although the rate of intermarriage has increased sharply, a substantial proportion of these intermarriages result in the conversion of the non-Jewish spouse to Judaism, while an even larger number result in the non-Jewish spouse identifying as Jewish. Moreover, the rate of conversion seems to be higher among the very groups having a higher intermarriage rate. Furthermore, a significant proportion of children from such marriages are evidently being raised as Jews. Finally, evidence from several studies indicates that the fertility patterns of intermarried couples are coming to reflect those of the nonintermarried, whereas older groups had a much stronger tendency to have significantly lower fertility.[49] Taken together, these changes suggest that the net effects of intermarriage on the overall size of the Jewish population may not be as serious as the rates of intermarriage themselves suggest. The effect of intermarriage on Jewish identification and religiosity may be a different matter, and these concerns can certainly have long run implications for the demographic variables.

Reflecting the continuing concern with the impact of intermarriage on Jewish demography and identity, the American Jewish

---

[48] Massarik and Chenkin, *op. cit.*, pp. 296–297.

[49] Sidney Goldstein and Calvin Goldscheider, *Jewish Americans: Three Generations in a Jewish Community* (Englewood Cliffs, 1968), pp. 168–169.

Committee in 1976–1977 sponsored an eight-city study focusing on Intermarriage and the Jewish Future, directed by Egon Mayer.[50] Defining intermarriage broadly as a marriage between any individual born Jewish and one who was not, the study population encompassed 446 intermarried couples in Cleveland, Dallas, Long Island, Los Angeles, New York City, Philadelphia, San Francisco, and Westchester. Given the ad hoc character of the selection of the respondent couples (largely through reliance on local informants) and high rates of non-response, the results cannot be regarded as representative of all intermarried couples. Furthermore, the absence of any control groups of Jewish homogamous marriages precludes direct comparisons with the characteristics of the non-intermarried as well as calculation of rates of intermarriage.

Typical of previous findings, two-thirds of the intermarried consisted of a Jewish man and a non-Jewish woman. Interestingly, the ratio was lower in the younger age group, suggesting that higher rates of intermarriage may come to characterize women as their educational and occupational patterns more closely resemble those of men. The effect of the women's liberation movement, and the deficits in potential Jewish husbands under conditions of high intermarriage rates, may also lead to a closer balance in the ratio of male and female intermarriage rates. If this does not happen, it could well lead to a growing proportion of Jewish women who remain unmarried due to the lack of available Jewish spouses.

In this population study, just over one-quarter of the not-born-Jewish respondents had converted to Judaism, whereas only 3 percent of the Jews had converted out. The finding that rates of conversion were highest in the youngest age group (one-third of those aged 20–29 compared to one-fourth of those aged 30–49, and only one-fifth of those aged 50–59) again lends support to earlier evidence that higher rates of conversion prevail among groups with the highest intermarriage rates. About 80 percent of the Jewish spouses in marriages in which the other spouse had converted considered their children Jewish, compared to about one-third of the Jewish spouses in mixed marriages.

Overall, the study concludes that intermarriage represents a threat to Jewish continuity, as evidenced by the low conversion rate, the low level of Jewish conduct and practice in mixed marriages, the

---

[50]Egon Mayer, "Patterns of Intermarriage Among American Jews: Varieties, Uniformities, Dilemmas, and Prospects," mimeographed report, New York, 1978.

low proportion of children regarded as Jewish, and the fact that most of the children are not socialized as Jews. Strong stress is therefore placed on the need for outreach programs designed to provide more formal and informal opportunities to enhance the Jewish content of the family life of the intermarried, and especially to strengthen the likelihood that children will identify as Jews. Most provocative is Mayer's suggestion that a new category of "naturalized" Jews be established to allow those who have not converted to identify more formally with the Jewish people and thereby confer a sense of legitimacy to the non-converted spouse as a way of strengthening the Jewish identity of the family.

Together, the results of the varied studies reviewed here confirm that the problem of intermarriage warrants considerable concern on both the policy and research levels. That it is receiving such attention is evidenced by recent calls by such community leaders as Rabbi Alexander Schindler of the Reform movement to reverse the practice of centuries and begin a drive to convert the unchurched to Judaism.[51] He especially argues for conversion of the non-Jewish partner in an impending marriage and for removal of the "not-wanted signs" that make non-Jewish spouses feel alienated. It needs to be stressed, however, that from a demographic perspective, attention to intermarriage certainly should not exclude concern about the impact of fertility and population redistribution on the size of Jewish population and on the quality of Jewish identification. Concurrently, the Jewish community needs to take heed of the words of Marshall Sklare:

> A more realistic confrontation is necessary, and that requires a much larger body of research than we now possess on the current rate of intermarriage in the country as a whole. It also requires much more information about the Jews who intermarry and about the causes and consequences of their doing so. So, too, there is a need for studies to evaluate the various methods in use to combat intermarriage, particularly those involving Jewish education. And demographic research will have to be done at regular intervals so that a reliable trend-line can be established.[52]

---

[51]Providence *Sunday Journal* (December 3, 1978).
[52]Marshall Sklare, "Intermarriage and the Jewish Future," *Commentary* (April 1964), p. 52.

ASSIMILATION

If attempts to assess the demographic consequences of intermarriage on Jews are difficult, attempts to evaluate the impact of assimilation are almost impossible. To some extent, the problem is illustrated by the experience of the NJPS. To qualify a household for inclusion in the NJPS at least one person within it was required to be "Jewish." By intent, a broad definition of Jewish was used;[53] the respondent had to provide an affirmative reply, for himself or for one or more household members, to at least one of the following questions: 1) was person born Jewish? 2) is person Jewish now? 3) was person's father born Jewish? 4) was person's mother born Jewish? Clearly, a more narrow or halakhic definition would exclude certain households, some of whose members may, however, satisfy sociological (ideological and/or behavioral) definitions of Jewishness. It was on the basis of a broad definition of a Jewish household as one including one or more Jewish persons that the NJPS reached the estimate of 5,800,000 Jews in 1971. But as was noted earlier, if non-Jewish persons in such households (including non-Jewish spouses and children not being raised as Jews) are excluded, the total number of Jewish residents in households is reduced to 5,370,000, almost a 10 percent reduction.

The use of a loose definition of Jewishness has particular implications for the study of intermarriage. In his assessment of intermarriage, using NJPS data, Massarik distinguishes between "typical intermarriage" (in which either the husband or the wife was Jewish at the time the couple met) and "marginal intermarriage" (in which one or both partners expressed no preference concerning religious viewpoint at the time of initial meeting, noted the existence of some Jewish familial or ancestral roots, but affirmed either only vague relatedness to Jewishness or none at all).[54] Massarik's analysis does not indicate the numerical division between these groups, but it could well be that the high rates of intermarriage he noted are partially a function of the inclusion of "marginal intermarriages" in the total.

The problems encountered by the NJPS and comparable surveys clearly document the difficulties in determining for survey

---

[53]National Jewish Population Study, *National and Regional Population Counts* (New York, 1974), p. 6.

[54]Massarik and Chenkin, *op. cit.*

purposes who constitutes a Jew. The halakhic definition is too simple for the sociologist and demographer, particularly for analysis of assimilation. Yet, the possibility is very limited of identifying clearly those individuals who were born Jews but who do not identify themselves as such; even the NJPS may not have succeeded in identifying a representative sample of such persons in its survey, despite the wide net that was thrown out.

Some limited insights about assimilation have come from studies of college students who have "dropped out" from Judaism. A study of Jewish seniors in 1961 found that about 13 percent had apostatized, while in 1969, 21 percent of the graduates reported no religious preference. Comparison of freshmen in 1965 and 1972 surveys shows a rise in the number who expressed no religious preference from 13 to 18 percent. However, it is not at all clear whether such individuals, if approached in a general population survey, would or would not report themselves as Jewish; therefore these data have only very limited value. All that one can conclude is that the same general conditions in society which have led to a rise in intermarriage also probably lead to substantial rates of dropouts; there is little basis for believing that the rate will decline in the foreseeable future.[55]

A study designed to assess assimilation was recently undertaken in Los Angeles.[56] Based on 413 respondents selected from a canvas of 5,000 households, the analysis concludes that intermarriage, a reduced birthrate, and the decline of Jewish neighborhoods are contributing to the assimilation of the nearly half-million Jews of Los Angeles. This was compounded by declining rates of affiliation and involvement in Jewish religious and secular organizations. The authors also find that "at the same time, the picture that emerges from the survey is of a vibrant people whose closest personal associations are with other Jews in their family, friendship, and occupational groupings." They further note that "one of the most significant changes in Jewish life in the last generation is the way in which Jews act out their Jewishness. Whereas only 18 percent see being Jewish as primarily religious, 61 percent perceive of Jews as an ethnic-cultural group." This was seen as "a dramatic shift from formal religious involvement to ethnic and cultural commitment."

---

[55]Cohen, *op. cit.*

[56]Neil C. Sandberg and Gene N. Levine, as summarized in *News from the Committee*, American Jewish Committee, (November 21, 1979).

As a result, the challenge for Jewish leaders is seen as the need to adapt their institutions to the increasingly informal expressions that are becoming more common.

Overall, one can raise the questions whether assimilation is, in fact, an especially new phenomenon in Jewish history. We know that crusades, inquisitions, and pogroms all took a heavy toll of the Jewish population, but these occurrences in themselves were probably inadequate to account for the tremendous loss in numbers that must have occurred if only 16.7 million Jews were alive just before the Holocaust. Many, quite clearly, were also lost through assimilation and intermarriage. Yet then, as now, any attempt to approximate the losses sustained through "dropouts" would be sheer guesswork. It is likely to remain so for many years to come.

MIGRATION AND POPULATION REDISTRIBUTION

Jewish history might easily be written in terms of migration and resettlement, from the days of Abraham's move to Canaan to the recent exodus of Jews from the Soviet Union. Yet, in the United States the large majority of immigrants arriving between 1880 and 1924 tended to be quite stable geographically. They settled in communities, often ports of entry, where there was a need for their labor in various industries. Subsequently many immigrants went into business for themselves, but while socially and economically mobile, they and often their children remained in the same city all their lives. This pattern now seems to be undergoing significant change. Because Jews are increasingly third- and fourth-generation residents of the United States, and are more highly educated than ever before, they enjoy the widest possible range of occupational choices. But the kinds of education which Jews are seeking, and the kinds of jobs for which their high education qualifies them, very often require geographic dispersion—movement away from family and out of centers of Jewish population concentration. The problem is exacerbated by the fact that many high-level jobs require repeated movement, so that individuals and families have no opportunity to plant deep roots in any single Jewish community.

Regional Distribution

Estimates indicate that in 1900, 57 percent of American Jewry lived in the Northeast, in contrast to 28 percent of the total American population; and virtually all of the Jews in the Northeast were in New York, Pennsylvania, and New Jersey (Table 5). New York alone accounted for about 40 percent of the national total. The North Central region accounted for the next largest number of Jews— about one-fourth—with most concentrated in Illinois, Ohio, Indiana, Wisconsin, and Michigan. By contrast, one-third of the total U.S. population lived in this region in 1900. Compared to the general population, Jews were also underrepresented in the South, where 14 percent were located, largely in Maryland. Florida at that time had only 3,000 Jews. The proportion of Jews in the West in 1900 was identical to that of the general population, just over 5 percent.

The continued mass immigration from Eastern Europe during the first decades of the twentieth century resulted in a fourfold increase in the Jewish population of the country between 1900 and 1930; and it became even more concentrated in the large cities of the Northeast, especially New York. By 1930 the Northeast region contained 68 percent of the American Jewish population and most of it lived in New York. The other regions of the country all contained smaller proportions of the Jewish population than they had in 1900, with the sharpest change occurring in the South. The Far West continued to be the region with the smallest percentage of Jews, although the proportion of the total American population living in the Western states doubled between 1900 and 1930. Jews had clearly not yet joined the Western movement on the same scale as had the rest of the population.

By 1979 the pattern had changed considerably, reflecting both the cutoff in large-scale immigration and increasing internal mobility. Jews in large measure seem to have followed the pattern of redistribution characterizing the population as a whole; in fact, they may have been doing so to an exaggerated degree. For example, between 1930 and 1979, the percentage of Jews living in the Northeast declined from 68 to 58 percent. This was a larger percentage decrease in absolute points than those characterizing the general population (see Table 5). The drop was even more substantial for the North Central states, where Jews decreased from 20 percent of the national total in 1930 to only 12 percent in 1979. In contrast, both the South and the West contained growing proportions of the total U.S. Jewish population, reflecting the strong participation of Jews in the shift to the Sun Belt and to the Western states. Between 1930 and 1979, the South's share more than doubled, and that of the West tripled. The growth of the Jewish population in the South is illustrated by the experience of the Orlando metropolitan area. In 1966 it included only 600 Jews; by 1977 the Jewish population of Orlando had reached 11,000, and it is projected to rise to over 20,000 by 1985.[57] Although the South and the West continued to contain proportionally fewer Jews than it did members of the general population, the differences in distribution had considerably narrowed.

Thus, by 1979 the greater mobility of the Jews had resulted in patterns of distribution throughout the country that resembled somewhat more closely those of the general population. These similarities are likely to become accentuated in the future, as Jews increasingly enter occupations requiring mobility because of the limited opportunities available in particular areas, as family ties become less important for third-generation Jews than they had been for the first- and second-generation, and as more Jews no longer feel it necessary to live in areas of high Jewish density. In an ecological sense, therefore, the population will become a more truly "American population," with all this implies in terms of assimilation and numerical visibility.

At the same time, the Middle Atlantic subregion, and the New York area in particular, remains a very large and obviously dynamic center of American Jewry. Over half of the American Jewish population was still concentrated in the Middle Atlantic states in 1979, and two out of these three million persons lived in Greater New York. Yet even here changes were occurring: the estimates of Jewish population prepared for the AJYB show a decline in the Jewish population of Greater New York from 2.38 million in 1972 to just under 2.00 million in 1979.[58] In part this may reflect an artifact of the system of estimating the population; but it may also reflect the impact of changing rates of natural increase and out-migration from the New York area. The AJYB statistics show a decline in the Jewish population of New York City from 1.84 million in 1972 to 1.23

---

[57]*Rhode Island Herald* (September 1, 1977).

[58]Alvin Chenkin, "Jewish Population in the United States, 1974," *AJYB*, Vol. 76 (1976), pp. 232–236.

TABLE 5

Distribution of total United States and Jewish population, by regions, 1900, 1930, 1968, and 1979

Region	1900		1930[c]		1968[d]		1979[e]	
	Jewish[a]	United States[b]	Jewish	United States	Jewish	United States	Jewish	United States
Northeast	56.6	27.7	68.3	27.9	64.0	24.2	57.9	22.5
New England	7.4	7.5	8.4	6.6	6.8	5.7	6.6	5.6
Middle Atlantic	49.2	20.3	59.9	21.3	57.1	18.5	51.3	16.9
North Central	23.7	34.6	19.6	31.4	12.5	27.8	11.9	26.7
East North Central	18.3	21.0	15.7	20.5	10.2	19.8	9.6	18.9
West North Central	5.4	13.6	3.9	10.9	2.3	8.0	2.3	7.8

South	14.2	32.2	7.6	30.7	10.3	31.2	15.8	32.4
South Atlantic	8.0	13.7	4.3	12.8	8.1	15.0	13.5	15.9
East South Central	3.3	9.9	1.4	8.0	0.7	6.6	0.7	6.4
West South Central	2.9	8.6	1.9	9.9	1.5	9.6	1.7	10.1
West	5.5	5.4	4.6	10.0	13.2	16.8	14.3	18.4
Mountain	2.3	2.2	1.0	3.0	0.9	4.0	1.8	4.7
Pacific	3.2	3.2	3.6	7.0	12.2	12.8	12.5	13.7
Total United States								
Percent	100.0	100.0	100.0	100.0	100.0	100.0	100.0	100.0
Number (in 1,000s)	1,058	75,994	4,228	123,203	5,869	199,861	5,861	218,059

a"Jewish Statistics," AJYB, Vol. 1 (1900), pp. 623–624.

bU.S. Bureau of the Census, 1960 Census of Population, Vol. 1, Characteristics of the Population (Washington, D.C., 1961), pp. 1–16.

cH. S. Linfield, "Statistics of Jews," AJYB, Vol. 33 (1931), p. 276.

dAlvin Chenkin, "Jewish Population in the United States," AJYB, Vol. 70 (1969), p. 266.

eAlvin Chenkin and Maynard Miran, "Jewish Population in the United States, 1979," AJYB, Vol. 80 (1980), p. 163.

million in 1979, and even this is considered an overestimate, with 1 million probably being a more realistic statistic. This decline reflects both the change in enumeration procedures, partly related to the estimates derived from the NJPS, and the impact of changing distribution patterns. There seems little doubt, however, that the concentration of Jews in the Northeast corridor focusing on New York is likely to undergo substantial change in future years as increasing numbers of Jews leave this section of the country.

This process of dispersal is documented by an analysis of the changing geographic distribution of American Jews between 1952 and 1971, based on data from the *AJYB*.[59] The heavy residential concentration of the Jewish population is demonstrated by the fact that only 504 of the 3,073 populated counties of the continental United States contain at least 100 Jews; most of these are metropolitan counties and most are in the Northeast. More interesting, however, is the fact that the highest growth in Jewish population between 1952 and 1971 occurred in counties other than those of traditional residence. In all, 77 counties were added to the list of those containing 100 or more Jews; 37 of these are in what the authors refer to as "new areas," and 10 more are in California and Florida. On the other hand, areas of high concentration in 1952 displayed moderate or low growth. Concurrently, therefore, the changes point to higher rates of dispersal and continued growth associated with urbanization and metropolitanization. Overall, while Jews still remain highly concentrated compared to other religious groups, the evidence on changing residence patterns leads to the conclusion that they locate in counties with high degrees of denominational pluralism, regardless of the size of the Jewish community. This suggests that Jews "feel accepted in America and are less concerned about venturing out into more traditionally conservative culturally homogeneous enclaves."[60]

Suburbanization

The redistribution of population is occurring concurrently on a number of levels, including regional changes as well as shifts within

---

[59]William M. Newman and Peter L. Halvorson, "American Jews: Patterns of Geographic Distribution and Change, 1952–1971," *Journal for the Scientific Study of Religion* (June 1979), pp. 183–193.

[60]*Ibid.*, p. 192.

and between metropolitan and non-metropolitan areas. Throughout American history the Jewish population has been overwhelmingly concentrated in urban places. At the time of the 1957 census survey, about nine out of every ten Jews lived in urbanized areas of 250,000 or more persons.[61]

Within the urban and metropolitan areas, Jews tended to live in a limited number of neighborhoods, but this pattern is also undergoing change. For example, between 1923 and 1970 radical shifts in distribution occurred in New York City alone.[62] Although very approximate estimates, these data illustrate the pattern of development that has probably characterized other areas of Jewish concentration. In 1923, 39 percent of the 1.9 million Jews living in New York City resided in Brooklyn, and 37 percent lived in Manhattan; less than 3 percent lived in Queens. By 1970 Manhattan's share of the New York City Jewish population had declined to only 14 percent, that of Queens had risen to 31 percent, while Brooklyn increased its dominance to 42 percent. Concurrently, the proportion of the total living in the Bronx declined from 20 to 12 percent. Even more significantly, the percentage of Jews in the Greater New York area living in the city proper, in contrast to the suburban counties, declined from 82 percent of the total in 1957 to 64 percent by 1970. By 1979 the AJYB estimated that only 61 percent of Greater New York's Jewish population was living in the city proper, and the real figure may be 50 percent or less.[63]

Similar patterns emerge from the limited data available for such metropolises as Chicago and Detroit; and the same pattern characterizes moderate sized communities. In 1970, for example, only 17 percent of the Jews of Greater Providence, Rhode Island, were living in the old urban areas of the central city, in contrast to 45 percent in 1951; and the proportion living in the suburbs had grown from 11 to 36 percent.[64] The comparative data from the Boston 1965 and 1975 surveys show similar patterns.[65] Both the city and the older suburbs experienced population decline while the

---

[61] U.S. Bureau of the Census, op. cit.

[62] Goldstein, "American Jewry, 1970," pp. 39–41.

[63] Jack Diamond, "How Many Jews in New York City?" Congress Monthly (January 1978), pp. 8–10.

[64] Goldstein, "American Jewry, 1970," p. 42.

[65] Axelrod, Fowler, and Gurin, op. cit.; Fowler, op. cit., pp. 28–33.

newer outer suburbs gained, resulting in an increased dispersal of the population. Suburbanization is also clearly evidenced in Minneapolis. In 1957, 66 percent of the population was found to be living in the city and 34 percent in the suburbs. By 1971 the pattern had been more than reversed, with 23 percent in the city and 77 percent in the suburbs.[66]

Overall, therefore, the developing pattern seems to be one of ever greater dispersion and a more general integration. As a result, Jewish institutions may become located at quite widely separated points within a metropolitan area, and many communities find it increasingly difficult to decide on a central location for those institutions serving the community as a whole. In the past, residential clustering has been an important variable in helping to perpetuate Jewish values and the institutions important to the functioning of the community. In metropolitan areas with large Jewish populations, such clustering undoubtedly will continue, both within the central cities and in some of the suburbs. But greater dispersal and integration seem likely to become more common in the future, effecting greater changes in the extent and character of ties to Judaism, and making it increasingly difficult, from both a financial and an organizational perspective, to provide services to the total population. The impact of both suburbanization and more general dispersal of the population throughout the United States on the assimilation process needs to be fully recognized. In particular, much more research is necessary to ascertain how communal orientation varies among Jews living in cities and suburbs of differing Jewish density and size, and what significance the various activities available to Jews and the patterns of interaction and experience of Jews with non-Jews have for the larger question of Jewish identification and survival.

Small-Town Jewry

Because the vast majority of America's Jews live in large metropolitan areas, until recently little attention has been given to the situation of Jews in those small towns where the Jewish community itself typically numbers no more than a few thousand families, and often less. Since World War II many of these small communities have

---

[66]Judith B. Erickson and Mitchel J. Lazarus, *The Jewish Community of Greater Minneapolis* (Minneapolis, 1973).

had great difficulty retaining their population, Jewish and non-Jewish. Like their neighbors, Jews have left to seek better educational, occupational, and social opportunities in larger cities. Many of those who remained small-town residents tended to minimize their Jewishness, and often assimilated or intermarried. On the whole, small-town life was generally viewed as isolating the Jew both from his coreligionists and from the non-Jewish community in which he was often regarded as a "stranger."[67]

Yet, beginning with the 1970's (and consonant with what seems to be an emerging trend among the American population as a whole of movement from metropolitan areas to small towns and rural places, including locations which had earlier lost population) a number of small Jewish communities have been once again gaining population. Some Jews are now seeking the tranquility and slower pace of small-town life, and at the same time seem to be developing a more active identification with Judaism in their new surroundings. Jewish life in small towns is beginning to be viewed as having positive as well as negative effects on its members. Despite the limited communal services that are available in such places, the strong desire of many small-town Jews to maintain their identification may result in "more Judaism per square Jew in the small town than in the big city."[68]

Although levels of identification are not easily measured, the demographic effects of both the old trend away from small Jewish communities and the more recent trend toward them are evident in communities such as Charleston, West Virginia.[69] In 1959 the city included 1,626 Jews; by 1975 the Jewish population had declined to 1,118, of which only 703 persons had been in Charleston 16 years earlier. The decline in population resulted from both an excess of deaths over births and more out-migrants than in-migrants; it was further compounded by a high rate of intermarriage. By 1977, despite continuing high intermarriage rates, the community's migration losses had been reversed and it was gaining population.

The 1977 *Annual Report on Charleston's Jewish Population,*

---

[67]Eugen Schoenfeld, "Problems and Potentials," in Abraham D. Lavender, (ed.), *A Coat of Many Colors: Jewish Subcommunities in the United States* (Westport, 1977), pp. 71–72.

[68]Rabbi Benjamin M. Kahn, quoted in *New York Times* (November 25, 1973).

[69]See, *The Jewish Population of Charleston, W. Va.,* annual reports of 1959 through 1977, Charleston.

the 19th in this unique series, was one of the most optimistic to appear. Its introduction states:

> In our report of a year ago we stated that there were indications, however slight, 'that we are on our way upward (demographically) instead of downward. . . .' We are pleased to report that this year's study reveals that Charleston's Jewish population is definitely on its way upward. In this past year more newcomers (90) moved to our community than in any year since 1959, when we began these studies. Our losses through moving (49) were less than in any of the past 18 years. The good news, then, is that fewer are leaving and more are coming.[70]

The importance of such a reversal is further evidenced in the fact that the gain through migration was more than enough to compensate for losses through a surplus of deaths over births and through intermarriages, accounting for all of the increase experienced in the community's total size from 1,121 to 1,151 during 1976–1977.

The reports on Charleston issued since 1977 have been less optimistic. The 1978 report shows a gain of only two persons, and the 1979 analysis recorded a resumption of the decline in total population size, from 1,158 to 1,086.[71] This reversal reflected in part the continuing excess of deaths over births; it also resulted from the removal from the 1979 population count of those individuals who had been counted for a number of years even though they had left the community. Nonetheless, despite this record cleaning operation, in both 1978 and 1979 Charleston gained Jews through migration. Such in-migration is probably being experienced by a number of small communities and could be crucial in either maintaining or creating the critical mass requisite to initiation and maintenance of the institutional facilities essential for continued Jewish identification. Migration may thus constitute the "blood transfusion" which greatly improves the chances of small community survival.

Internal Migration

We know little about the extent and character of Jewish migration within the United States. For such an analysis national data are

---

[70]*Ibid.*, 19th annual report, p. 1.

[71]*Ibid.*, 20th and 21st annual reports.

essential; however, except for the recent information available from the NJPS, no such data exist. Our insights on Jewish migration patterns have, therefore, been largely restricted to what can be gleaned from local Jewish community surveys.

Judged both by the percentage of population born outside the community of residence and the length of time that individuals have resided in the area in which they were enumerated in community surveys, high levels of population mobility have come to characterize American Jews. The 1963 Detroit study found that only one-third of the total Jewish population of Detroit was born in the city; 28 percent were foreign-born; and 36 percent had moved to Detroit from other places in the United States, half from other locations in Michigan.[72] A similar picture emerged for Camden, New Jersey, where one-third of the residents had been born in the Camden area, and as many as 60 percent had moved from other places in the United States (probably reflecting the younger age of the Camden population).[73]

The 1975 Boston survey found that only 30 percent of the respondents living in Boston in 1975 had also been living in the city in 1965.[74] Although the 1965 survey provided no basis for anticipating the decline of Newton and Brookline, both those older suburbs experienced heavy out-migrations and Jewish population decline. Of those Jews who lived in the city of Boston in 1965 and still resided in the Boston area in 1975, more than half remained in the city itself. However, this stable core was supplemented by a considerable influx from outside the Boston area, and there was some shifting in residence within the area by those living in it in both 1965 and 1975.

In Dallas, the 1972 survey found that only 35 percent of the population were born in Dallas, and a high percentage of these were children.[75] Over half the Jewish population had moved to Dallas from other parts of the United States, and an additional 14 percent were foreign-born. Consistent with the patterns of regional redistribution noted earlier, 23 percent of the U.S.-born migrants to Dallas had originated in the Northeast, and 27 percent in the North Central states. Similarly, the 1976 Greater Kansas City survey found

[72]Albert J. Mayer, *The Detroit Jewish Community Geographic Mobility: 1963–1965 and Fertility—A Projection of Future Births* (Detroit, 1966).

[73]Charles F. Westoff, *A Population Survey* (Cherry Hill, 1964).

[74]Fowler, *op. cit.*, p. 29.

[75]Betty J. Maynard, *The Dallas Jewish Community Study* (Dallas, 1974).

that "not only are the majority of the household heads not born in Kansas City, but there is little tendency for this proportion to increase among the younger people."[76]

Given these illustrative data, it is not surprising that the NJPS found that only 62 percent of the Jewish population aged 20 and over in 1970 were still living in the city in which they resided in 1965.[77] One out of every five adult Jews had changed city or town of residence while remaining in the same county or metropolitan area; an additional 3 percent had changed areas within the same state; while 10 percent of the total adult population had actually moved to a different state within the five-year interval. These high mobility levels are even more dramatic for Jews in the peak migration ages of 25–39 years. As the data in Table 6 show, just under half of persons aged 25–29 and 35–39 resided in the same city in 1970 as 1965; and only four out of every ten persons aged 30–34 did so. Moreover, for the 25–29 age group, interstate migration accounted for the largest number of mobile persons—almost one out of four. Even for those aged 30–34, almost one in five moved between states. The higher percentage in this age group moving within the same county or metropolitan area is related to their life-cycle stage of family formation and expansion.

Residential stability rises quite dramatically above age 40 and peaks for ages 55–64; three-fourths of those among the latter group reported themselves as living in the same city in 1970 as they had in 1965; a large proportion who moved did so only within the same general area. For persons aged 65 and over the stability rate remains comparatively high, although declining somewhat as a result of retirement, the breakup of families through the death of one of the spouses, or the departure of children from home. Yet the fact that 30 percent or more of the persons 65 and over had made some kind of residential move within a five-year period indicates that geographic mobility must be incorporated into community planning processes. The need to do so is especially crucial for the younger age groups, among whom much more movement occurs, and more of it involving longer distances requiring clear breaks with former communities and integration into new ones.

---

[76]*The Jewish Population Study of the Greater Kansas City Area* (Kansas City, 1979), p. 12.

[77]National Jewish Population Study, *Mobility*, New York, 1974.

TABLE 6

Mobility: Current residence by place of residence in 1965, by age (total for each age group = 100 percent)

Age group	Same city as 1965	Different city, same general area in 1965*	Different area, same state as 1965	Different state from 1965	In foreign country in 1965
20–24	60.2	28.3	1.3	8.0	1.7
25–29	48.0	21.3	2.6	22.8	4.2
30–34	41.6	30.8	2.9	18.8	4.5
35–39	48.6	28.7	11.7	7.1	3.5
40–44	62.2	22.1	1.6	12.0	1.5
45–49	66.8	16.6	1.3	11.9	1.0
50–54	67.2	17.7	3.0	6.5	5.1
55–59	75.3	13.6	2.0	3.4	5.4
60–64	76.1	12.4	1.7	4.8	1.5
65–69	70.1	14.8	0.7	10.9	2.6
70–74	70.2	17.5	0.7	8.2	2.3
75–79	69.9	17.6	3.7	4.0	2.7
80 & over	62.7	24.6	1.5	5.2	2.6
Total**	61.6	20.0	3.1	8.9	2.5

Note: Horizontal details may not add to 100 because of "no answer."
*Same county or same Standard Metropolitan Statistical Area.
**Includes 6 percent persons under 19 for whom no detailed data are shown above.
Source: National Jewish Population Study, Mobility (New York, 1974).

The continuation of a large degree of movement is apparent from preliminary tabulations of the NJPS data based on questions about plans to move.[78] Of the total population, 16 percent indicated plans to move within at least five years. Again, sharp age differentials characterize this aspect of mobility: 61 percent of those 25–29 years of age indicated they planned to move, and 11 percent expected to do so immediately; 47 percent among those aged 20–24 years also planned to move. These mobility intentions are related to the family formation and career stages of persons in these age groups. The greater stability of older ages is evidenced by the sharp decline in the percentage (29) planning to move among those aged 30–34, a further decline to only 19 percent among those aged 35–39, and a percentage varying within a 15–19 percent range through age 70, following which even greater stability seems to set in.

Further evidence of changing Jewish mobility patterns is available through surveys of family units conducted so as to permit comparison of place of residence of children with that of their parents. Lenski has noted that one of the best indicators of the decreasing importance attached to family and kin groups by modern Americans is their willingness to leave their native community and migrate elsewhere.[79] Since most migration is motivated by economic or vocational factors, he suggests migration serves as an indicator of the strength of economic motives as compared to kinship ties. In modern society the removal of economic rewards out of the hands of kinship and extended family groups lessens the dominance of Jewish families over the economic placement of its young. The change in kinship relations, coupled with more fluid labor markets, thus contributes to higher mobility rates.

If this interpretation is correct, data available for both Providence and northern New Jersey suggest that kinship ties among Jews have been weakening. In the 1963 Providence survey only one-third of sons aged 40 years and over were living outside Rhode Island, compared to just over half of the sons aged 20–39.[80] Moreover, a higher proportion of the younger group were living further away. Accentuation of this trend is suggested by the fact that almost two-thirds of sons under age 20 living away from their parental home

---

[78]*Ibid.*, pp. 5–6.

[79]Gerhard Lenski, *The Religious Factor* (Garden City, 1963), p. 214.

[80]Goldstein, "American Jewry, 1970," pp. 51–52.

resided outside the state. Although fewer daughters lived away from their parental community, the basic age pattern was the same as for the males. In northern New Jersey, about one-fourth of both sons and daughters living outside of their parental home remained in the same general area, and an additional quarter were living in other parts of New Jersey.[81] But about 25 percent were living in parts of the United States outside of New Jersey, New York, and Pennsylvania, pointing to a fairly substantial dispersal of family members.

Together, these data support the assumption that the American Jewish community is increasingly mobile, and that such mobility must be taken into account in any evaluation of Jewish life in the United States. Such mobility affects not only the size of a particular community but also the characteristics of its residents if the migration process is selective of age, education, occupation, and income. At the same time, migration may have an important effect on the migrants, as well as on community institutions. To the extent that community ties within the Jewish population are expressed through membership in synagogues and temples, enrollment of children in educational programs, and participation in local organizations and philanthropic activities, the high degree of population movement may disrupt patterns of participation or weaken the loyalties they generate. More seriously, they may result in the failure of families and individuals to identify with organized life in the local community. Sociological research has suggested, for example, that recent migrants to a community are much less active in its formal structure than are long-term residents.[82] Although their participation eventually increases, the adjustment has been shown to take five years, and migrants may never reach the same level of participation as persons who grew up in the community. If a significant proportion of migrants know in advance that their residence in a community is not likely to be permanent, the stimulus for active participation and affiliation may be even weaker.

Mobility is not a new facet of Jewish life, and at a number of points in Jewish history it may have served to strengthen the Jewish community and indeed to insure its very survival. Such mobility may still perform a positive function in selected situations. Small

---

[81]Mervin F. Verbit, *Characteristics of a Jewish Community: The Demographic and Judaic Profiles of the Jews in the Area Served by the Jewish Federation of North Jersey* (Paterson, 1971), p. 13.

[82]Basil Zimmer, "Participation of Migrants in Urban Structures," *American Sociological Review* (1955), pp. 218–224.

Jewish communities may benefit considerably from the influx of other Jews who are attracted by nearby universities or new economic opportunities.

More often, migration may have a deleterious effect on the community and the migrant. Especially when repeated movement occurs, the individual's ties to Judaism and the Jewish community may be weakened. This, in turn, may affect the strength of the formal community structure as an increasing proportion of individuals fail to develop strong loyalties to local institutions. For all too long, local Jewish communities have assumed that most Jews remain residentially stable for a lifetime, and that they are therefore willing and obligated to support local organizations. This may no longer be true for many Jews. An increasing number may be reluctant to affiliate with the local community, not so much because they do not identify with Judaism, but because they anticipate that they will not remain in the local area long enough to justify the financial and other investments required. The situation is further complicated by the dispersed residential patterns which Jews adopt and by their high degree of social integration into religiously heterogeneous groups. All of this suggests the need for greater concern with the role of migration in the future of American Judaism. Indeed, the rising rates of intermarriage may largely be only a by-product, along with other undesirable consequences, of increased mobility and weaker ties to both the family and the community. Given high mobility rates, there is a pressing need to view the Jewish community from a national as well as a local perspective, so that the official affiliation of individual Jews to Jewish institutions can be easily transferred from one community to another, thereby facilitating maintenance of Jewish identity.

SOCIO-DEMOGRAPHIC COMPOSITION OF THE POPULATION

While size and density are crucial variables in the strength and vitality of any segment of the population, a wide range of demographic, social, and economic variables also significantly affects the group's current vitality and future survival. To the extent, for example, that generation status affects the strength of ties to traditional Judaism, the changing proportion of native- and foreign-born individuals in the Jewish community takes on great relevance. Rising levels of education and changing patterns of occupational careers also have direct effects on the levels of population movement, the degree of integration into the social and residential structures of the larger community, and the likelihood of intermarriage. Age structure is a crucial variable, because the socio-demographic structure of the population as well as the processes of birth, death, and migration are closely affected by it. In the growing attention, both in research and planning, that has been given to the Jewish population, the size of the total population and the dynamics of change have received priority. Too little attention has been given to composition and the impact of its changes. The discussion which follows attempts briefly to review the major composition variables with a view to describing the present socio-demographic characteristics of the American Jewish population, likely changes in the future, and the implications that such changes may have.

Generation Status

Of all the demographic characteristics of the Jewish population, the one with perhaps the greatest relevance for its future is the changing generation status, that is, how many are foreign-born, how many are children of foreign-born, and how many are third- or higher-generation Americans. In the past, a major factor in the continued vitality of the American Jewish community has been the massive immigration of Jews from Eastern Europe. Now, for the first time in the community's history, third-generation Jews face the American scene without massive outside reinforcement. At the same time, Jews enjoy much greater freedom than ever before, so that in several respects the Jewish community in the United States is increasingly an American Jewish community. Although this emergent pattern has been somewhat modified by the influx of Jews from both the Soviet Union and Israel, the full extent to which the upsurge in this immigration affects the demographic composition and particularly the sociological character of American Jewry, especially of the populations in those communities where they are settling, remains to be documented.

Every community study which has collected data on generation status documents the diminishing proportion of foreign-born and the rise in third-generation Jews. These studies show the percentage of American-born Jews as well above 70 percent and becoming increasingly higher.[83] In Boston, for example, between the

---

[83]Goldstein, "American Jewry, 1970," pp. 53–57.

1965 and 1975 surveys, the percentage of foreign-born declined from 22 to 12 percent of the total.[84] By contrast, those with American-born parents rose from 20 to 49 percent. Evidence of change is even sharper when judged by the generation composition of different age groups. Over 80 percent of those under age 40 in Boston were born of American-born parents, but this was true of only 2 percent of those aged 65 and over.

The same general pattern emerges from the NJPS, which found 23 percent of household heads in the Jewish population to be foreign-born, and one out of every five already third-generation.[85] The distribution would favor American-born individuals much more strongly if the NJPS data referred to the population as a whole.

Assessment of the demographic, social, economic, and religious characteristics of three generations in the Jewish community suggests that the community's future depends to a great degree on how its members, now increasingly third-generation, react to the freedom to work for integration into the American social structure. Whether they are reversing or accelerating certain trends toward assimilation, initiated by their second-generation parents or by the small number of older third-generation Jews, needs careful monitoring.

Research has suggested that the geographic dispersal and deconcentration of the Jewish population marked for many not only a physical break from the foreign-born, but also symbolized the more dramatic disassociation of American-born Jews from the ethnic ties and experiences that had served as unifying forces for the earlier generation.[86] The degree of identification with Judaism of the third-generation Jews who participate in this dispersal has become a key issue. The residential changes are taking place concurrently with sharp increases in the amount of secular education and with an opening up to Jews of career opportunities in the professions and at high executive levels of business. All of these factors increase the amount of interaction between Jews and non-Jews, and contribute to high intermarriage rates and to redirections of the religious system.

Yet, these trends toward assimilation have been counterbal-

---

[84]Fowler, op. cit., p. 16.

[85]Massarik and Chenkin, op. cit., p. 276.

[86]Goldstein and Goldscheider, op. cit.

anced by a tendency toward increased Jewish education for the young, as well as by increases in certain religious observances which are seen as better fitting into the American scene. The religious change among three generations of Jews is undoubtedly a complex process involving the abandonment of traditional forms and the development of new forms of identity and expression which are seen by many Jews as more congruent with the broader American way of life. Analysis of the Providence community in 1963 suggested that, evolving out of the process of generational adjustment, the freedom to choose the degree of assimilation has been exercised in the direction of Jewish identification.[87] Whether that pattern holds for the nation as a whole and whether it has changed since the Providence survey are major questions that argue strongly for fuller exploitation of existing data and collection of new information on the interactions among generation change, demographic variables, and Jewish identity.

Age Composition

Of all demographic variables, age is regarded as the most basic. The significant impact of age on the generation status of the Jewish population, as well as on fertility and migration, has already been noted. Age composition also has obvious implications for communal institutions. Until the NJPS, the only source of information on the age composition of Jews nationally was the 1957 Census Survey. It clearly indicated that the Jewish population was, on the average, older than the general white population of the United States. The median age of the Jewish group was 36.7 years, compared to 30.6 for the total white population. This substantial differential results from sharp differences in the proportion under 14 years of age and in the 45–64 age category. The youngest group constituted only 23 percent of the Jewish population, compared to 28 percent of the total white population; this reflected lower Jewish fertility. By contrast, only 21 percent of the total white population, but 28 percent of the Jews, were between 45 and 64 years of age in 1957 (Table 7). Both the Jewish and the total white populations had quite similar proportions in the 65 and over category, 10 and 9

---

[87]*Ibid.*, pp. 171–231.

TABLE 7

Percent distribution of Jewish population by age, selected communities and United States

Community	Date of study	Age Distribution				
		Under 15	15–24	25–44	45–64	65 and over
Washington, D.C.	1956	30	9	38	18	5
Worcester, Mass.	1957	27	11	26	26	10
Los Angeles, Calif.	1959	27	12	25	28	8
Rochester, N.Y.	1961	25	12	24	26	13
St. Joseph, Ind.	1961	30	14	24	24	8
Pittsburgh, Pa.	1963	27	14	25	26	8
Providence, R.I.	1963	25	14	24	27	10
Detroit, Mich.	1963	31	11	25	25	8
Milwaukee, Wis.	1964	24	15	23	28	10
Camden, N.J.	1964	30	13	23	28	6
Springfield, Mass.	1966	24	16	21	27	12
Boston, Mass.	1966	23	17	25	24	11
Flint, Mich.	1967	29	10	30	23	8
Columbus, Ohio	1969	27	13	23	28	9
Houston, Texas	1976	25	14	30	22	9
Greater Kansas City	1976	15	15	22	29	19
U.S. Jews	1957[a]	23	12	28	28	10
U.S. whites	1957[a]	28	14	28	21	9
U.S. Jews	1971	23	18	22	25	11
U.S. whites	1970	28	17	24	21	10

[a]For United States, lowest age categories are "under 14" and "14–24."

Sources: Sidney Goldstein, "American Jewry, 1970: A Demographic Profile," *AJYB*, Vol. 72 (1971).

Fred Massarik and Alvin Chenkin, "United States National Jewish Population Study: A First Report," *AJYB*, Vol. 74 (1973), p. 271.

1970 U.S. Census of Population.

percent, respectively. On the whole, data on age structure available from individual communities confirm the older age of the Jewish group compared to that of the total population.

The data from the 1971 NJPS indicate that Jews continue to differ from the general population in age composition. Whereas 28 percent of the national population were under age 15 in 1970, only 23 percent of the Jewish population were in this age category—virtually identical to the 1957 differential which refers to those under age 14. By 1970 both the Jewish and the general population had more persons aged 65 and over, 11 and 10 percent, respectively; but this differential is understated, since the Jewish institutional population was not covered directly in the NJPS. If they are included, the proportion of Jewish aged rises to 12 percent. The effects of the declining birthrate are clearly evidenced in the decreasing percentage of Jewish children in the youngest age groups. Whereas 20 percent of the Jewish population in 1970 were aged 10–19, only 12 percent were under 10 years old. If these data are accurate, they point to a very substantial reduction in the absolute number of youngsters in the population and in their proportion of the total. Such changes have serious implications for future growth, for educational program needs, and for the size of a future "reservoir" from which adult support and leadership can be drawn.

The dramatic changes occurring in age composition are illustrated on the community level by comparative data from surveys taken in the same community. For example, the 1958 survey of New Orleans found 11 percent of the population to be under age 5 and 15 percent to be age 65 and over.[88] Reflecting, in part, the effect of lower fertility and, in part, the cumulative effects of migration and lengthening of life, the 1973 survey found only 6 percent of the population to be under six years (six was used instead of five as the cutoff in 1973) but 21 percent to be 65 and over. Clearly, there has been a substantial aging of the community in the fifteen-year interval.

As demonstrated, the American Jewish community already has an older age structure than the total U.S. white population; over time, because of its lower fertility and its higher proportion of individuals in the middle age group, the Jewish population can be expected to become even older. The United States as a whole is already facing serious problems associated with an aging population; but during the next few decades these problems may become even more serious for the Jewish community. We can look forward to a rise in the percentage of older Jews from the 11 percent observed in

---

[88]*Opinions and Attitudes of the New Orleans Jewish Community* (New Orleans, 1973).

1971 to over 15 percent by the early 1990's.[89] This implies a 40 percent increase in the number of aged over the 1971 count. Concurrently, the number of children under 15 will be lower, reflecting the low birthrates noted earlier. Changes will also occur in the middle range of the age hierarchy, as the reduced number of persons born during the depression years move into the upper middle-age range. This change may initially create some serious problems for the community, as the pool of persons to whom it can turn for leadership and financial contributions is somewhat reduced.

In short, Jewish communities need to reevaluate and reorganize their services to deal with the changing age composition. Equally important, continuous monitoring of the changing age composition must be maintained. The past fluctuations in fertility will manifest themselves in the magnitude of differing age cohorts as they pass through the life cycle, and may lead to temporary rises or declines in the need for services catering to particular segments of the community. While recognizing the general trend toward an aging population, and its associated problems of housing, financial restrictions, and health impairments, there must also be an awareness that changes are taking place in other key points of the age hierarchy and that the need for schools, playgrounds, camps, and teenage programs will also change as the overall age profile varies. Even if the size of the population were to remain constant, the shifting age composition would undoubtedly call for drastic changes in services, and affect residential distribution patterns and the ability of the community to provide the resources needed for strong leadership.

One of the more serious consequences of changes in the age structure and the resulting higher proportion of Jewish aged may be increasing problems of poverty. Lulled by the general affluence of America's Jews, the Jewish community paid little heed to its poor until the publication in 1971 of Ann Wolfe's "The Invisible Jewish Poor."[90] As a result of her findings and the ensuing controversy over the actual number of Jewish poor in America, communal institutions in a number of cities initiated efforts to deal with the problem, and new research programs were undertaken to document the subject.

Regardless of whether the number of Jewish poor in the United

---

[89] National Jewish Population Study, *The Jewish Aging*, New York (1973), p. 1.

[90] Ann G. Wolfe, "The Invisible Jewish Poor," in Lavender, *op. cit.*, pp. 137–144.

States is estimated at 264,000[91] or 700,000–800,000[92] persons, those concerned with the issue generally agree that a large majority of the poverty-stricken are over age 60. Descriptions of the Jews who have retired to South Beach in Miami[93] or of those still left in the tenements of the Lower East Side in New York[94] serve as poignant examples. If, as Bertram Gold states, "most of the Jewish poor are poor because of special circumstances—isolated old age, cultural separateness, maladjustment, death of the breadwinner,"[95] the problems may well become more severe in the near future. Larger numbers of older persons, coupled with the loosening of family ties and the greater mobility among American Jews, would help to create the conditions which foster poverty. The Jewish community may thus have one more dimension to add to the services it will be called on to provide. At the very least, it is an area which should be closely monitored, with an eye to alleviating the situation before it becomes more acute.

Education

Of all the Jews who immigrated to America in the late 1800's and early 1900's, a large majority came because of the supposedly equal opportunities for social and economic mobility. But lacking secular education, adequate facility in English, and technical training, rapid advancement proved an unrealistic goal for many. For others, both education and occupational achievement were made difficult, if not impossible, by factors related to their foreign-born status and/or their identification as Jews. Frustrated in their own efforts to achieve significant mobility, many Jews transferred their aspirations to their children. First-generation American Jews recognized the special importance of education as a key to occupational mobility and made considerable effort to provide their children with a good secular education. Reflecting the great value placed on education, both as a way of life and as a means of mobility, the Jews of America have compiled an extraordinary record of educational achievement.

---

[91]Kaplan, "Comment: The Invisible Jewish Poor, I," in Lavender, *op. cit.*, p. 149.

[92]Wolfe, *op. cit.*, p. 143.

[93]Elinor Horwitz, "Jewish Poverty Hurts in South Beach," in Lavender, *op. cit.*, pp. 160–166.

[94]Mark Effron, "Left Behind, Left Alone," in Lavender, *op. cit.*, pp. 167–179.

[95]As quoted in *Rhode Island Herald* (February 4, 1972).

The limited data available for the period around 1950 show the education of Jews was higher than that of the white population, averaging about 12 and 10 years, respectively.[96] This differential was confirmed on the national level by the 1957 Census Survey.[97] For the population 25 years old and over, the median number of school years completed by Jews was 12.3, compared to 10.6 for the general population. Yet, even sharper differences than those conveyed by these statistics distinguished the educational achievements of Jews from those of the general population: 17 percent of the adult Jews were college graduates, compared to only 7 percent of the general population. At the other extreme of the educational hierarchy, 29 percent of all adult Jews had received only an elementary school education, compared to 40 percent of the total population. Various community studies lent further weight to the strength of the differential, and pointed particularly to the rising levels of education among younger Jews, both male and female.[98] That an estimated 80 percent of those in the college age group were enrolled in college emphasized the very high value placed by Jews on college education. In fact, within the Jewish population the important educational differential in younger groups is between those who had only some college education and those who went on to postgraduate work. This was further confirmed by studies of educational expectation among school-age children. In 1965, 86 percent of the Jewish students planned to attend college, compared to only 53 percent of the general student body.

The NJPS lends further support to the conclusions based on these earlier sets of data (Table 8). Among the male Jewish population aged 25 and over, only 15.2 percent had not graduated high school. By contrast, 60 percent had had some college education. Of those aged 30–39 (age specific data not shown in Table 8), who constitute the youngest age cohort likely to have completed their education, only 4 percent had no high school education and 83 percent had some college education. In fact, at least 70 percent had graduated college, and 45 percent of all the males aged 30–39 had done some graduate work. Although sex differentials are appar-

---

[96]Ben Seligman and Aaron Antonovsky, "Some Aspects of Jewish Demography," in Marshall Sklare, (ed.), *The Jews* (Glencoe, 1958), p. 54.

[97]Sidney Goldstein, "Socioeconomic Differentials Among Religious Groups in the United States," *American Journal of Sociology*, (May 1969), pp. 612–631.

[98]Goldstein, "American Jewry, 1970," pp. 63–65.

ent among Jews, as they are for the total population, Jews value extensive education for women, particularly among the younger cohorts. Like the men, very few women (16 percent) had less than a high school degree, but many more had restricted their education to a high school level; and just over half reported some college education. Sharp age differentials are evident, however. Among women aged 30–39, only 2.4 percent had less than a high school degree, and as many as 75 percent had some college education. The sharpest difference between men and women appears with respect to graduate work. Of women 30–39 years of age, only 15 percent reported a graduate or professional degree. The trend data suggested by age differentials point clearly, however, to rising levels of graduate work among the younger women.

Comparison in Table 8 of the levels of education completed by Jews with those reported in the 1970 U.S. census for the total white population documents the persistence of sharp educational differentials. Just over half of the Jews, but only 22 percent of the non-Jews, had some college education; the widest difference characterized those with some graduate studies: 18 percent of the Jews compared to 5 percent of all whites. At the other extreme, only 16 percent of the Jews had less than twelve years of schooling, compared to 46 percent of all whites. Clearly, Jews continue to be characterized by distinctively higher levels of educational achievement, and, as the data in Table 8 shows, this holds for both men and women.

These data on the changing educational achievements within the Jewish population and the differentials between the Jews and the larger American population have a number of implications for the various demographic developments reviewed in this assessment. First, they clearly confirm the exceptionally high level of education that has come to characterize the Jewish population. Although the differentials between Jews and non-Jews will diminish, particularly if current emphasis on recruitment of minority group members and underprivileged students persists, it will still be some time before college attendance levels among the non-Jewish population reach those achieved by the Jews. As a result, some of the educational differences can be expected to persist for a number of decades, and indirectly to continue to affect occupation and income differentials. The growing enrollment of women in graduate work and the implications that this has for their developing independent careers have particular significance for both marriage rates and fertility, as well as for family stability.

To the extent that education is highly correlated with occupation, the continuing high percentage of college graduates in the Jewish population will affect its occupational composition, provided, of course, that the opportunities for employment exist which utilize skills developed through education. In the future even more Jews will likely be engaged in intellectual pursuits and in occupations requiring a high degree of technical skill. Concommitantly, there will probably also be a reduction in the number of self-employed, both because small, private business will not provide an adequate intellectual challenge and because patterns of discrimination which thus far have held back Jews in large corporations are likely to continue to weaken.

As before, and perhaps increasingly so, the impact of higher education will go beyond occupation. In order to obtain a college

TABLE 8

Percent distribution of years of school completed by persons aged 25 and over, Jewish and total United States white population, by sex, 1970

Years of School Completed	Males		Females		Both Sexes	
	Jewish	Total White	Jewish	Total White	Jewish	Total White
Less than 12 years	15.2	46.1	16.0	44.9	15.6	45.5
12 years	22.5	28.5	35.3	35.5	29.2	32.1
College:						
1–3 years	17.3	11.1	21.0	11.1	19.2	11.1
4 years	14.9	7.2	13.6	5.7	14.2	6.4
5 or more years	26.5	7.1	10.6	2.8	18.2	4.9
Unknown	3.5	—	3.5	—	3.5	—
Total percent	100.0	100.0	100.0	100.0	100.0	100.0

Sources: For the Jewish population: Fred Massarik and Alvin Chenkin, "United States National Jewish Population Study: A First Report," *AJYB*, Vol. 74 (1973), p. 280.
For the United States white population: U.S. Bureau of the Census, *1970 U.S. Census of Population: General Social and Economic Characteristics*, PC(1)-C1, (Washington, 1972), p. 386.
Note: Since the differentials between the Jewish and the total white population change only minimally when age is controlled, the non-standardized data are presented here.

education, particularly at the postgraduate level, a large proportion of young Jews must leave home. As a result, their ties to both family and community will weaken. Moreover, many of these college-educated Jews will not return permanently to the communities in which their families live and in which they were raised.

A 1973 study undertaken in Savannah, Georgia, for example, has shown that from 1954 to 1958 half of Savannah's Jewish college graduates settled in the city.[99] From 1965 to 1969 only one in five returned; the Jewish community was losing its college graduates for lack of job opportunities. Thus education serves as an important catalyst for geographic mobility which eventually leads many individuals to take up residence in communities with small Jewish populations, to live in highly integrated neighborhoods, and to work and socialize in largely non-Jewish circles. The extent of such a development needs to be assessed and future patterns need to be monitored.

Finally, Jews with higher education may have significantly higher rates of intermarriage and become more alienated from the Jewish community. This development involves not only the possible impact of physical separation from home and the weakening of parental control in dating and courtship patterns, but also the general liberalizing effect a college education may have on religious values and Jewish identity. It would be ironic if the very strong positive value which Jews have traditionally placed on education, and that now has manifested itself in a very high proportion of Jewish youths attending college, turns out to be an important factor in the general weakening of the individual's ties to the Jewish community.

Whether the high levels of enrollment in colleges and in graduate work will persist remains an open question. If the Jewish population becomes more generally dispersed and tendencies toward migration increase, a much higher proportion of Jewish youth may be raised in neighborhoods and attend schools that are less densely Jewish. Some evidence suggests that in such a situation the motivation for higher education is less strong.[100] If so, a somewhat lower proportion of Jewish youth may plan to go to college in the future. Still another factor that may affect enrollment levels is the

---

[99]*Rhode Island Herald* (September 1, 1977).
[100]A. Lewis Rhodes and Charles B. Nam, "The Religious Context of Educational Expectations," *American Sociological Review* (April 1970), pp. 253–267.

perceived employment opportunity open to college students. If the job market is such that students are discouraged from continuing their college and graduate studies, Jews may well be affected more than other segments of the population, especially if this situation is coupled with emphasis on minority group selection in admission to universities and in the hiring practice of large firms. We need studies to document whether the college dropout rate has risen for Jews and whether the more recent Jewish high school graduates are, in fact, continuing their education. It seems less likely now than it did one or two decades ago that a college education will become virtually universal for Jewish youth. More likely, levels of educational achievement will plateau at the very high level they have already reached or slightly below it.

Occupational Composition

Reflecting in part their high levels of education, Jews are disproportionately concentrated in the upper ranks of the occupational structure. As part of his analysis of the social characteristics of American Jews prepared in 1954 for the tercentenary celebration of Jewish settlement in the United States, Nathan Glazer observed that, outside of New York City, the homogeneous character of the occupational structure of Jewish communities was beyond dispute.[101] Basing his conclusions on a number of local Jewish community surveys conducted between 1948 and 1953, he noted that the proportion of Jews in the nonmanual occupations ranged from 75 to 96 percent, compared to 38 percent for the American population as a whole. Even in New York City, where greater heterogeneity would have been expected, as many as two-thirds of the employed Jews were engaged in nonmanual work. Glazer further noted a general tendency for the ethnic concentration in a single occupation to suffer dilution as the native-born generation became better educated and more familiar with occupational opportunities. In the case of Jews, however, "this dilution upward becomes a concentration, for the Jews began to reach the upper limit of occupational mobility relatively early."[102] For Jews to reflect the general occupational structure of the United States would, in fact, require downward mobility for many, and Glazer concluded that, since this will not happen,

---

[101] Nathan Glazer, "The American Jew and the Attainment of Middle-Class Rank: Some Trends and Explanations," in Sklare, *op. cit.*, p. 138.

[102] *Ibid.*, p. 146.

"we may expect the Jewish community to become more homogeneous in the future as the number of first-generation workers and the culture they established declines."[103]

The data from the fairly large number of community studies conducted in the 1950's and 1960's, as well as those from the 1957 Census Survey, support Glazer's thesis of an upward shift in Jewish occupational affiliations. The census survey, in particular, has special significance because of its national coverage. It found that three-fourths of all Jewish, employed males were in white collar positions, compared to only 35 percent of the total white male population.[104] To a very great extent, this large difference is attributable to the much greater concentration of Jewish men in professional and managerial positions. Compared with men, women in the labor force were much more concentrated in white collar positions, and therefore the differentials between Jewish women and all women were less marked than those for men. Just over four out of every five Jewish women were in white collar jobs, compared to just over half of the total female labor force.

The sharp generation changes in occupational affiliation reflected in the 1957 data are attested to by a 1964 B'nai B'rith Vocational Service report.[105] It found that three-fourths of all Jewish high school youths hoped to enter professional and technical jobs, whereas only one in five of their fathers actually held such jobs. By contrast, only 3 percent hoped to be business proprietors, compared to 27 percent whose fathers owned businesses.

The 1965 and 1975 Boston surveys have particular value in documenting recent changes in occupational composition, although some of the changes may reflect selective in- and out-migration and changing opportunities in the Boston area.[106] In 1965 one-third of the employed Jewish males in Boston were professionals; by 1975 this proportion had risen to 40 percent. The percentage engaged in clerical and sales work also rose from 15 to 21 percent. As might be expected on the basis of developments noted earlier, the proportion engaged in managerial activities declined from 37 to only 27 percent of the total in 1975. In all, therefore, the percentage

---

[103]*Ibid.*

[104]Goldstein, "Socioeconomic Differentials."

[105]*New York Times* (June 25, 1972).

[106]Axelrod, Fowler, and Gurin, *op. cit.*; Fowler, *op. cit.*, pp. 46–47.

of males making their living in white collar work rose, but the distribution by specific types of occupations shifted.

Jewish women followed a somewhat different pattern, with increasing percentages engaged in both professional and managerial activities. These changes relate to the rising educational levels of women and their greater participation in the labor force. In both 1965 and 1975 in the Boston area, over 90 percent of all women were in white collar jobs, contrasted with 70 percent for the non-Jewish employed women, with most of the differential being attributable to fewer non-Jews in professional and managerial positions.

Similar patterns of occupational distribution were found by the NJPS (Table 9). Almost 90 percent of all males and females were employed in white collar positions, and those in the younger ages were much more heavily concentrated in professional activities. Only a very small proportion were engaged in manual work. Data from the various community surveys also point to a continuing increase in the proportion of Jews engaged in white collar work, but within the white collar group there appears to be a shift toward more professionals; either stability or decline characterizes the managerial and proprietor group. With the decrease in small businesses, an increasing proportion of Jewish men may be turning to executive positions in larger corporations, instead of operating their own firms as did many of their parents and grandparents.

Simon Kuznets, in his analysis of the trends in the economic structure of U.S. Jewry, assessed the various constraints affecting the occupational choices of American Jews. He concluded that it is evident that changes in these constraints have contributed toward greater concentration of Jews in professional and technical pursuits; an increase in employees rather than employers among officials, managers, and within the professional-technical group; a decline in the share of industrial blue collar jobs; and a lesser concentration in trade, particularly small proprietorships.[107] The reasons he cites are similar to those mentioned earlier in this analysis.

Change also characterizes the non-Jewish population. Between the 1957 census survey and the 1970 decennial census, the occupational differentials between Jews and non-Jews seemed to have narrowed somewhat, as a result of the noticeable increase in the per-

---

[107]Simon Kuznets, *Economic Structure of U.S. Jewry: Recent Trends* (Jerusalem, 1972), pp. 17–18.

TABLE 9

Occupational distribution of the Jewish and total United States
white population,[a] by sex, 1970

Occupation	Males		Females		Both Sexes	
	Jewish	Total white	Jewish	Total white	Jewish	Total white
Professional and technical	29.3	15.0	23.8	16.3	27.4	15.5
Managers, administrators	40.7	12.0	15.5	3.9	32.2	9.0
Clerical	3.2	7.6	41.7	8.1	16.2	18.4
Sales	14.2	7.4	8.3	36.8	12.2	7.7
Crafts	5.6	21.8	1.5	1.9	4.2	14.4
Operatives	3.9	18.7	2.3	14.0	3.4	17.0
Service	1.2	7.3	3.6	17.4	2.0	11.0
Laborers	0.3	5.7	0.2	0.9	0.3	3.9
Agriculture[b]	—	4.5	—	0.7	—	3.1
Unknown	1.7	—	3.1	—	2.2	—
Total percent	100.0	100.0	100.0	100.0	100.0	100.0

[a]The Jewish population includes persons aged 25 and over; the total white population includes persons aged 16 and over.
[b]No separate category for agriculture was included in the NJPS data.
Source: For the Jewish population: Fred Massarik and Alvin Chenkin, "United States National Jewish Population Study: A First Report," AJYB, Vol. 74, 1973, pp. 284–285.
  For the United States white population: U.S. Bureau of the Census, 1970 U.S. Census of Population: General Social and Economic Characteristics, PC(1)-C1, (Washington, 1972) p. 392.
Note: Since the differentials between the Jewish and the total white population change only minimally when age is controlled, the non-standardized data are presented here.

centage of non-Jews in white collar jobs. Three-fourths of all Jewish males 14 and over were already in white collar work in 1957, compared to only 35 percent of all the white males; by 1970 this was true of 87 percent of the Jewish males aged 25 and over covered by the NJPS and 42 percent of all white males aged 16 and over in the 1970 census. For females the data also suggest some narrowing.

Whereas 83 percent of Jewish women were in white collar work in 1957, and 89 percent in 1970, among all white women the percentage rose from 55 to 65 percent. More importantly, perhaps, sharp differences persisted despite the narrowing. For example, among men twice as large a proportion of Jews as of all white males were in the professional and technical group. Only 11 percent of Jewish men were engaged in manual work, compared to 58 percent of all white men; for women the difference was almost as great—8 percent of Jewish women, compared to 35 percent of all white women.

As differentials between Jews and non-Jews with respect to educational level diminish, and as discriminatory restrictions on occupational choice weaken, it seems likely that occupational differentials generally, and within white collar occupations specifically, will decline. The major question, as with education, revolves about the specific direction in which the youngest generation will move as they face career decisions. How many of them, motivated by different values and attracted by new life styles, will forego college and attempt to make a living through manual work or lower white collar positions? How many of those who are trained for higher positions, but who are frustrated by their inability to obtain such work, will opt for blue collar jobs or seek employment in clerical or sales positions?

A 1972 assessment of employment prospects for Jewish youth stressed that Jewish young men and women faced "relatively greater" job-hunting difficulties in the near future, and should therefore give more consideration to nonprofessional jobs than they had in the past, due to the projected slower rise in professional and technical jobs between 1970 and 1980.[108] In his review, Herbert Bienstock called for more emphasis on vocational guidance and placement, and on "attitudinal reconditioning, particularly in terms of value structures relating to nonprofessional job opportunities,"[109] especially as the latter became more attractive in pay and security than in the past. Although predicting that a majority of Jews entering the job market would continue to seek white collar jobs, Bienstock, a labor force expert, also suggested that young Jews might turn in increasing numbers to self-employment, not in the old-style shop or small store, but in new areas where demands for services were likely to grow.

---

[108]New York Times (June 25, 1972).
[109]As quoted in Ibid.

Only repeated surveys of the kind that have been undertaken in Boston, but preferably on a more frequent basis, and more intensive monitoring of changes occurring both at the attitudinal and behavioral levels, will provide the opportunities to fully assess the very significant reversals in the trends of the past that may be occurring at present or that are likely to occur in the near future. At the same time, research is needed to ascertain whether the changing occupational affiliations of Jews, and particularly their entrance into new types of professional and managerial responsibilities, lead to increased channeling of self-identification through professional or intellectual sub-societies rather than through the Jewish community. We also need to know more about the ways in which occupational mobility is related to geographic mobility. The two together may well provide the organized community with one of its major challenges.

THE CURRENT AND FUTURE DEMOGRAPHIC SITUATION

An assessment of the demographic situation of American Jewry in 1970[110] pointed to a number of challenges which the American Jewish community would have to face in the closing decades of the twentieth century as a result of the demographic changes that were then taking place. The low level of Jewish fertility, coupled with some losses from intermarriage, pointed at best to maintenance of the slow growth rate characterizing the Jewish population in the second and third quarters of the twentieth century, and possibly to still slower growth. Concurrently, increasing Americanization seemed likely to continue, as judged by greater geographic dispersion, a higher percentage of third- and fourth-generation Americans, and narrowing of such key socioeconomic differentials as education, occupation, and income. All these changes pointed to the potential for greater behavioral convergence between Jews and non-Jews, and corresponding losses in Jewish identity. However, it was also suggested that structural separation and the continuity of Jewish identity would persist as American Jews continued their efforts to find a meaningful balance between Jewishness and Americanism.

---

[110]Goldstein, "American Jewry, 1970."

Since the 1970 assessment was undertaken, many of the patterns that were then emerging have become further accentuated. By 1977 the Jewish population constituted only 2.7 percent of the American population, in contrast to the peak of 3.7 percent reached in the mid-1930's. Jewish fertility levels seem to have declined even further as part of the national pattern in the 1970's. If the fertility rates of Jews persist at the low levels reached in the 1970's, the American Jewish population is quite certain to decline in actual numbers (unless there continue to be compensating additions through immigration). Even should fertility remain at near the replacement level, the losses resulting from intermarriage and assimilation will compound the effects of either very low natural increase or negative growth resulting from an excess of deaths over births.

Recent estimates of the Jewish population suggest that although the American Jewish population had approached the 6 million mark in the late 1970's, it has not yet passed that milestone and, given the recent pattern of demographic growth, is not likely to do so. A realistic assessment suggests that the Jewish population of America will remain at approximately its present size, between 5.5 and 5.8 million, through the end of the century. In the absence of significant reversals in fertility behavior or in rates of intermarriage, a decline will set in during the first decades of the twenty-first century that could well lead to a reduction of one to two million by the time of the tricentennial. Most of the social and economic changes characterizing the United States in general, in combination with the unique characteristics of the Jewish population itself, are likely to reinforce the low growth rates or decline. These include high rates of divorce and separation, later age at marriage and possible rises in levels of non-marriage, increased extrafamilial activity on the part of women, higher education levels, greater secularism, growing concern about overpopulation, and rising costs of living. Many of these very same factors are likely to lead to continued high levels of intermarriage. Although its effects on population size are compensated to a degree by conversions to Judaism and the rearing of many of the children of intermarriages as Jews, maintenance of the high levels of intermarriage reported in recent years would undoubtedly compound the impact of low fertility on the rate of population growth.

Jews have already become widely dispersed throughout the United States, and this trend is likely to continue in the future. The available evidence suggests that as a result of continuously higher education and changing occupations, lower levels of self-employment, weakening family ties, and reduced discrimination, Jews have begun to migrate in increasing numbers away from the major centers of Jewish population. Even while distinct areas of Jewish concentration remain, and while Jews continue to be highly concentrated in the metropolitan areas, the emerging patterns of redistribution point to fewer Jews in the Northeast, substantial decreases in central cities, and possibly even some reduction in the suburban population as Jews join the movement to non-metropolitan areas, smaller urban places, and even rural locations. Regardless of which particular stream becomes more popular, the net result is likely to be a much more geographically dispersed Jewish population in the decades ahead.

Such greater dispersal means that factors other than religion will provide an increasingly important basis for selecting areas and neighborhoods of residence. In turn, the lower Jewish density will provide the seeds for still greater acculturation and assimilation. Moreover, to the extent that Jews increasingly participate in the pattern of repeated population movement which characterizes the American scene, additional dangers to the strength of community ties loom on the horizon.

The decline in relative or even total numbers may not be very significant in the next few decades, since Jews have never constituted a numerically large segment of the American population. What may be more crucial is the vitality of individual Jewish communities, and this may be much more influenced by the size of such communities and their socioeconomic composition. Only when the change in total numbers is accompanied by significant changes in distribution and composition which are deleterious to both the ability to maintain a vital Jewish community and to foster individual Jewish identification will the change in numbers itself take on a new significance. Because population movement has special significance for these concerns, any substantial change in the pattern of residential distribution of Jews and in their ability to maintain close identity with a Jewish community takes on special importance.

Operating partly as a cause and partly as an effect of these changing patterns of growth, distribution, and intermarriage are the underlying changes in population composition characterizing American Jewry. Perhaps the most striking compositional change has been the reduction in the percentage of foreign-born. Indeed, as already noted in 1970, even the proportion of second-generation American Jews has begun to diminish as third- and fourth-generation persons become an ever larger proportion of the Jewish population. The pace of change would be even faster were it not for the low levels of Jewish fertility, which, in addition to contributing to the low rate of population growth, result in a reduced number of young persons in the population and an increasing proportion of aged.

Given the ZPG levels of fertility which the Jewish population seems to have reached, the average age of the Jewish population is likely to rise still further and to remain substantially above the average of the general population. Thus, a major challenge for the Jewish community in the future will be the comparatively large numbers of older persons, a considerable portion of whom will be widows.

Jews remain unique, despite some evidence of narrowing differentials, in having a heavy concentration of members who are highly educated, who hold white collar positions, and who have large incomes. It is the large proportion of Jews who obtain specialized university training—with their tendency to move out of small family businesses into salaried employment, and their increasing willingness to seek and take positions away from their community of current residence—that helps to explain the growing residential dispersal of the Jewish population. The same factor undoubtedly also contributes to the high rates of intermarriage, the low level of fertility, and the growing tendency toward assimilation.

In combination, the current pattern of very low fertility, high levels of intermarriage, and lower residential density through population redistribution may all serve to weaken the demographic base of the Jewish population in the United States. Yet, to the extent that Jews retain a comparatively close-knit, ethnic-religious identification within the total society, the potential for continued vitality remains. Stability of numbers or even declining numbers need not constitute a fundamental threat to the maintenance of a strong Jewish community and to high levels of individual Jewish identity. The risk that this may happen is obviously present, but this was also true in the past when larger numbers obtained. Although maintenance of numbers is certainly desirable in the interest of providing a strong base for insuring Jewish identity and vitality, whether or not the community as a whole should or can do anything to control the changing fertility levels or the patterns of redistribution is debatable.

To the extent that mobility and fertility behavior represent reactions to a wide and complex range of social, economic, and normative changes in the larger American society, they are probably well beyond the direct and even indirect control of the organized Jewish community. What is perhaps more important is that the community undertake and maintain fuller assessments of the implications of these developments, and that it be prepared, on the basis of such assessments, to develop new institutional forms designed, at a minimum, to mitigate the negative effects of population decline and dispersal. Ideally, these efforts should also increase opportunities for Jewish self-identification and for greater participation of individuals in organized Jewish life. By taking these steps, the community will help insure that the changes that do occur still allow for a meaningful balance between being Jewish and being American.

FAMILY AND IDENTITY

THE THREADBARE CANOPY:
THE VICISSITUDES OF THE JEWISH FAMILY
IN MODERN AMERICAN SOCIETY
by CHAIM I. WAXMAN

INTRODUCTION

WHILE FICTIONAL PORTRAYALS of the Jewish family are so numerous as to tax the endurance of even the most omnivorous reader, social science treatments of the subject are comparatively few in number. This is troubling not least because there is no reliable way to measure the fidelity of art to life in this highly charged area of experience.

It is evident that many Jews feel that all is not well with the Jewish family. In response to this sentiment, Jewish organizations and institutions, both local and national, have held meetings and conferences to discuss the present state of the Jewish family and its prospects for the future. Part of the concern is accounted for by the fact that changes in family life may have serious repercussions for Jewish survival. Then too, changes in family life can have serious consequences for individuals, bringing unhappiness, confusion, anxiety, and depression.

Another component of general concern is the growing necessity for relinquishing the image of Jewish family life as beautiful and fulfilling. The traditional notion was that whatever might happen in the outside world to diminish the Jews's self-esteem and make his life difficult or even dangerous, the family circle remained undisturbed. And whatever the example provided by the larger society, the way of life of the Jewish family continued in its accustomed path of tranquility. Whether these traditional images were real or idealized is irrelevant; the point is that Jews regarded their mode of family life as both distinctive and superior to that found in the general society.

Current discussions about the shortcomings of the Jewish family do not generally take as their starting point the fact that Jewish distinctiveness (and hence Jewish superiority) is on the wane, yet the tone of these discussions suggests a tacit acknowledgment that this is so. Although it should come as no surprise that Jewish family life has come to reflect many of the patterns now found in more sophisticated precincts of the general culture, this conclusion is no consolation to many Jews who have felt, perhaps privately, that it was possible to enjoy the best of both worlds.

Indeed, for a time it did seem possible. Second-generation American Jews modified the time-honored pattern of early marriage in the interest of occupational mobility, educational attainment, and the need to free themselves from ways of life which were incongruent with modernity. But even though delayed, an extraordinarily high proportion of second-generation American Jews did marry—a much higher proportion than would have been expected, statistically, given the avoidance of early marriage. In recent years, however, the single state has gained respectability in the culture at large, and third- and fourth-generation Jews are not immune to it; in fact, the pattern of late marriage may make them especially vulnerable. Some younger Jews have also adopted the no longer uncommon pattern of living with a partner while postponing marriage for an indefinite period.

In the article which follows, Chaim Waxman examines the Jewish family in respect to five factors: age and frequency of marriage, divorce, fertility, intermarriage, and extended familism. Some of these same matters are treated elsewhere in this volume, but Waxman's perspective is that of a specialist in the family rather than a demographer. Waxman views the traditional Jewish family as essential to defining and transmitting Jewish identity to the next generation, and he regards change in family life as threatening Jewish survival and continuity. Others have contended that new family forms hold out possibilities for continued Jewish identity. In any case, Waxman's analysis is worthy of serious consideration. It may well be that classical patterns of assimilation are not as relevant today as they were in previous periods, and that changes in family life and structure may come to constitute a major influence on Jewish survival and continuity.

M.S.

ᕭᕉᕼ

ONE OF THE MAJOR SOCIAL issues which was widely debated during the 1970's was the future of the family in modern society. The issue was probed from a variety of perspectives and involved spokespersons from such fields as sociology, social welfare, social history, religion, and politics; indeed, Sussman has suggested that the 1970's may well come to be known as the decade of "The Great Family Debate."[1] The sources of that debate and an evaluation of the various prognoses will not be offered herein. For the purposes of this article it is sufficient to point out that within the American Jewish community, as well, there was (and is) widespread concern over the future of the American Jewish family. However, whereas regarding the larger societal issue of the future of the family, there were those who were not overly concerned about the implications of the decline of the family, within the Jewish community, there has been a virtual consensus that the decline of the American Jewish family presents a serious challenge to the future of the American Jewish community. It should be emphasized that the focus of concern has been upon individuals as members of the American Jewish community and the implications for the continuity of that community, and not solely upon the well-being of individuals qua individuals. Why is American Jewry so uniquely concerned about the future of the American Jewish family? This article will attempt to explain this concern by, first, pointing to the role of the family in Jewish socialization and continuity, and then by analyzing the empirical data with respect to the contemporary American Jewish family.

Despite the alleged acceptance of the ideology of cultural pluralism in American society since the late 1960's, self-conscious ethnic minorities must exert determined efforts to retain members within the group, in order to resist the pervasive and powerful forces of assimilation and Anglo-conformity. American Jews, as an ethno-religious minority, have created a wide variety of institutional networks to protect and enhance the physical and social well-being of

---

[1] M. B. Sussman, "The Family Today: Is It an Endangered Species?" *Children Today* (March–April, 1978), pp. 32–37, 45.

their members;[2,3] and the organizational leadership of American Jewry has adopted a more distinct "survivalist" perspective and stance since the late 1960's.[4] Within this perspective, the well-being of the Jewish family is a primary concern because it plays a central, if not the central, role in defining and transmitting Jewish identity and identification. There is a vast body of literature which describes and explains the socialization of children by the family, the more relevant parts of which have been reviewed elsewhere.[5] Certainly within the history and tradition of Jews, the family has been the most prominent institution involved in ethno-religious identity-formation and the transmission of ethno-religious norms and values. (For a detailed, though idealized, description of the role of the Jewish family in eastern European small towns and villages, see Zborowski and Herzog.)[6] It is, thus, no coincidence that the home and the synagogue are the two, and the only two, institutions in Jewish life that are referred to in traditional Jewish literature as "*mikdash me'at*" or "sanctuary in miniature." The family and the synagogue, which historically was not solely a "house of worship," but equally the center for education, study, and learning, were the two major institutions through which both Judaism and "Jewishness" were transmitted.[7] The family has been, in addition, the stage, if not the focal point, for much of Jewish religious tradition. Both historically and among a number of contemporary observers, the family has been viewed as the institution responsible for Jewish continuity.[8]

Having established that the family has long been perceived as playing a central role in Jewish continuity, we will now examine the contemporary condition of the American Jewish family, followed by

---

[2]D. Elazar, *Community and Polity* (Philadelphia, 1976).

[3]C. S. Liebman, "Leadership and Decision-Making in a Jewish Federation: The New York Federation of Jewish Philanthropies." *American Jewish Year Book*, Vol. 79 (1979), pp. 3–76.

[4]N. Glazer, *American Judaism* (Chicago, 1972).

[5]C. I. Waxman, "The Centrality of the Family in Defining Jewish Identity and Identification," *Journal of Jewish Communal Service* (June, 1979), pp. 353–359.

[6]M. Zborowski and E. Herzog, *Life Is With People: The Jewish Little Town of Eastern Europe* (New York, 1962), pp. 269–380.

[7]Glazer, *op. cit.*

[8]P. C. Vitz, *Psychology as Religion* (Grand Rapids, 1977), p. 89.

a consideration of the implications of this condition for the future of the American Jewish community. The focus of this part of the analysis will be upon five structural variables: marriage, divorce, fertility, intermarriage, and extended familism.

One basic problem in attempting to determine these and other demographic features of America's Jews is the difficulty of obtaining reliable empirical data. The doctrine of separation of church and state has been interpreted to preclude asking questions with respect to religious affiliation on the surveys conducted by the Bureau of the Census. In the mid-1950's, the Bureau of the Census did conduct a special survey of about 35,000 households, in which respondents were able to voluntarily answer a question on religion, and a brief report of that survey was published.[9] This report and two later studies subsequently derived from the data upon which it was based were, for many years, virtually the only sources of national information on the characteristics of the American population by religion. However, given the many shifts and changes in American society and culture during the past twenty years, it is highly doubtful that these data can be effectively used to indicate anything about the religious characteristics of the American population in general and America's Jews in particular at the dawn of the 1980's.

For more or less current characteristics of the Jewish population in the United States, there are two main sources. The most widely used and quoted, and probably most reliable for the decade of the 1970's, is the National Jewish Population Study, sponsored by the Council of Jewish Federations and Welfare Funds. This study, which is the nearest to a national census of American Jewry ever conducted in the United States, did provide a wealth of information previously unavailable. However, a complete report of the findings was never published. For a variety of reasons, only a series of brief reports which summarized data relating to about a half dozen issues of concern to those involved in community planning within local Jewish federations, was issued. Also, at this time there is some question as to the appropriateness of the data, since they were collected during the late 1960's and the very early 1970's. Again, it seems reasonable to assume that not insignificant changes have taken place in the characteristics of American Jewry during the 1970's.

---

[9]United States Bureau of the Census, "Religion by Civilian Population of the United States." *Current Population Reports*, Series P-20, No. 79 (February, 1958).

Another resource of information about the American Jewish population is community surveys conducted periodically by local Jewish federations. Since they frequently survey only Jews affiliated with local Jewish institutions, the quality of these surveys, in terms of scientific social research techniques, varies widely, and the degree of representativeness, even for the local community, has been questioned in many cases. In addition, questions have been raised as to the degree to which a particular community is representative of American Jewry as a whole. Nevertheless, with respect to this latter question, Goldstein reports that his review of the community surveys revealed rather surprisingly uniform patterns.[10]

An additional source of information is in the limited number of specialized studies conducted by social scientists and most frequently reported in social scientific journals. Many of the criticisms raised with respect to the community surveys are applicable here as well. Given all of the limitations noted with respect to reliable data, the following discussion of family patterns of America's Jews should be taken as tentative and based upon "guestimates." Regretfully, the current situation is not much better than it was almost a decade ago when Marshall Sklare bemoaned "the paucity of substantial research studies on the American-Jewish family."[11] And yet, since the data do come from a variety of sources and, in most cases, the findings are more or less similar, there is reason to assume that the picture which emerges does approximate reality.

Jews and Judaism have traditionally placed a high priority on marriage as an intrinsic value, and the available data indicate that a high proportion of America's Jews are married, and that the vast majority marry at least once. In their study of Providence, Rhode Island, Goldstein and Goldscheider found that Jews had a higher rate of marriage than non-Jews.[12] In a more recent study of Rhode Island, Kobrin and Goldscheider found marriage to be virtually universal among Jewish men and women, with the proportion of ever-married increasing over the years.[13] That these findings are

---

[10]S. Goldstein, "American Jewry: 1970," *American Jewish Year Book*, Vol. 72 (1971), pp. 3–88.

[11]M. Sklare, *America's Jews* (New York, 1971), p. 73.

[12]S. Goldstein and C. Goldscheider, *Jewish Americans* (Englewood Cliffs, NJ, 1969), pp. 102–103.

[13]F. E. Kobrin and C. Goldscheider, *The Ethnic Factor in Family Structure and Mobility* (Cambridge, MA, 1978), p. 38.

fairly representative is evident when they are compared with figures reported from the National Jewish Population Study (NJPS). In the table showing "Percent Distribution of Households Age of Head, by Marital Status, U.S. Jewish Population—1971," less than 5 percent of the respondents aged 30 years and older are single. More than 95 percent are listed as married, separated or divorced, or widowed.[14]

However, Andrew Greeley reported rather different findings in data derived from seven NORC surveys. He found that, "Among the three major religious bodies, the Jews (at least if they are eastern European and Other) are rather surprisingly less likely to be married than the Catholics, and the Catholics are less likely to be married than the Protestants."[15] His figures showed a somewhat higher rate of never-marrieds than those reported by Chenkin. Without specifying age cohort, Greeley found that for American Jews of German background, 3.2 percent were never married, for those of eastern European background the percentage rose to 11.3, and for "Other" American Jews, 15.7 percent were never married.[16] The discrepancy between the NORC and NJPS data cannot be explained at this point. Nevertheless, it should be noted that Greeley's data are somewhat more commensurate with the perceptions of many observers of American Jewry that the rate of marriage is now considerably lower than that reported in pre-1970's studies.[17]

One source of information which contains relatively recent data and also provides for a comparison of data collected a decade earlier, is the study of the Boston Jewish population, sponsored by the Combined Jewish Philanthropies of Greater Boston.[18] Despite the fact that the Jewish population of Boston is, to no small degree, atypical of American Jewry as a whole, in that the Boston population has a disproportionally high number of Jews involved in academia, its trends may, nevertheless, be indicative of patterns which will spread to other American Jewish communities, in due

---

[14]A. Chenkin, "Demographic Highlights: Facts for Planning," in *National Jewish Population Study* (New York, 1972), p. 16.

[15]A. M. Greeley, *Ethnicity in the United States* (New York, 1974), p. 450.

[16]*Ibid.*, p. 46, Table 6.

[17]C. Goldscheider, "Demography and American Jewish Survival," in M. Himmelfarb and V. Baras (eds.), *Zero Population Growth* (Westport, CT, 1978) pp. 119–147.

[18]F. J. Fowler, Jr., *1975 Community Survey: A Study of the Jewish Population of Greater Boston* (Boston, 1977).

time. A number of the changes in family patterns from the mid-1960's to the mid-1970's are significant. Whereas in 1965, 73 percent of the adult Jewish population of greater Boston was married, by 1975, this figure had declined to 56 percent. More specifically, in the 21–29 year age cohort the percentage of those married dropped from 58 percent in 1965 to 42 percent in 1975. Overall, the percentage of the Jewish population which is single, that is, never married, rose from 14 percent in 1965 to 32 percent in 1975, and the percentage of those currently divorced or separated rose from 1 percent in 1965 to 4 percent in 1975.

As far as age at first marriage is concerned, most of the evidence suggests that Jews marry later than their non-Jewish neighbors. Thus, Kobrin and Goldscheider found "that only a very small proportion of Jewish males marry at ages 20 or younger compared to Protestants and Catholics" and that "Jewish women marry at older ages on average than Protestants and Catholics in both age cohorts."[19] Sklare cites a study conducted in New York City during 1963–1964 from which he concludes that "native-born Jews marry later than their peers but when they reach what they consider an appropriate age they outdistance all others."[20] While this finding is borne out by every study of American Jews, Greeley's studies of American Catholics produced somewhat different findings. He reports data which show that "Catholics are much less likely than either Protestants or Jews to be married before their twenty-first birthday."[21] Since he does not provide precise information on the source of his data and the number of Jews in his sample, it is difficult to reconcile Greeley's findings with the majority of studies which uniformly report later marriages for Jews than for non-Jews.

Despite the high priority on marriage in the Jewish tradition, Judaism has never viewed marriage as an absolutely permanent and interminable bond. Though betrothal is defined as a sacred bond, the Hebrew term of which is *kidushin*, from the term *kodesh*, which translates as sacred, Judaism does provide for an institutionalized ceremony through which people can dissolve that bond when they perceive remaining together as an intolerable state. In considering divorce rates, and especially when analyzing the comparative rates

---

[19] Kobrin and Goldscheider, *op. cit.*, pp. 78, 83.

[20] Sklare, *op. cit.*, p. 75.

[21] A. M. Greeley, *The American Catholic* (New York, 1977), p. 187.

of different groups, we must emphasize that the absence or infrequency of divorce is not necessarily an indication of strong and positive relationships between spouses. As Goldberg points out in his survey of Jewish and non-Jewish divorce rates in Europe since the nineteenth century, parts of Africa and Asia, including Israel, and the United States and Canada, attitudes toward divorce vary from society to society and group to group, and in those societies where Jews had a larger percentage of divorces than non-Jews, it was frequently the product of the Jewish emphasis on human dignity, rather than the marital bliss of the non-Jewish population.[22] In examining the data from those communities in the United States from which they were available, he found that "separation and divorce are less prevalent among Jews than among the general white population" (p. 68). Similarly, in his Detroit sample, Lenski[23] found a lower divorce rate for Jews than for Protestants and Catholics, as did Goldstein and Goldscheider[24] and Kobrin and Goldscheider[25] in their studies of Providence, Rhode Island. Among Jews themselves, Goldstein and Goldscheider found the divorce rate to be higher among those born in the United States than among those born elsewhere, and higher among Reform than among Conservative and Orthodox Jews (p. 113). In contrast to a number of studies which indicate that, among the general American population, the more educated have lower divorce rates, Goldstein and Goldscheider found divorce and separation to be more common among more highly educated Jews. They suggested that this may be attributed to the fact that the more highly educated Jews are more secularized and acculturated, and that their rates would, therefore, be more similar to those of non-Jews. If their data were representative of national Jewish patterns, one could have predicted a growing divorce rate among America's Jews. In fact, while there are no reliable data on current divorce rates among American Jews, there is virtual consensus among rabbis and other Jewish communal workers that the American Jewish divorce rate has risen dramatically in recent years. Some have gone so far as to claim that the American Jewish divorce ráte is virtually identical to the general American

---

[22]N. Goldberg, "The Jewish Attitude Toward Divorce," in J. Freid (ed.), *Jews and Divorce* (New York, 1968), pp. 44–76.

[23]G. Lenski, *The Religious Factor* (Garden City, NY, 1961), p. 198.

[24]*Op. cit.*

[25]*Op. cit.*

divorce rate.[26,27] When pressed for reliable evidence, most will admit that their allegation is based upon intuition and personal observation, rather than upon reliable empirical data.

Furthermore, while it has been an article of faith, until recently, that the Orthodox Jewish divorce rate is very low, not only relatively, but absolutely as well, that too, it is claimed, is rapidly changing. For example, for three consecutive years, 1977–1979, the leaders of the largest Orthodox rabbinic organization, the Rabbinical Council of America, highlighted the issue of the rapidly increasing Orthodox Jewish divorce rate at the organization's annual conventions.[28] Again, these reports are based upon intuition and personal observation, with no reliable supportive data available.[29] Virtually the sole item approximating empirical data is the report by Kranzler of a large girl's high school in Boro Park, Brooklyn, the largest Orthodox Jewish neighborhood in the United States, whose guidance counselor estimated that about 8 percent of the approximately one thousand girls came from homes in which the parents were divorced.[30] Given that this is a very traditional Orthodox school in an intensely Orthodox neighborhood, the 8 percent figure might come as a surprise. Moreover, since these relate to cases of divorce in which there are high-school-aged children, it seems reasonable to assume that if younger and/or childless divorced Orthodox Jews were included in a sample, the percentage would be even higher.

A directly related aspect of American Jewish family life, which has recently become an issue of concern to survivalists within the community, is that of single-parent families.[31] Again, there are no solid data on the number of such families, or on the rate of increase. Nevertheless, there are indices of significant increases in particular within the larger American middle class, which strongly suggest that

---

[26]B. Smolar, "Easy Marriages Bring Easy Splits, Jews in the 1 in 3 Divorce Scene," *New Brunswick Jewish Journal* (March 8, 1979).

[27]B. Postal, "Postal Card," *Jewish Week* (March 11, 1979).

[28]*Jewish Week* (Jan. 30, 1977), p. 4; (Feb. 5, 1978), p. 17; (June 24, 1979), p. 22.

[29]See the exchange of letters on this subject between Mayer and Waxman, *Jewish Week* (July 1, 1979), p. 38; (July 15, 1979), p. 22.

[30]G. Kranzler, "The Changing Orthodox Jewish Family," *Jewish Life* (Summer/Fall, 1978), pp. 23–26

[31]C. I. Waxman, "American Jewish Single-Parent Families: Individual and Communal Concerns," *Pertinent Papers* (New York, 1979).

there has been a significant increase in the number of American Jewish single-parent families within the decade of the 1970's.

From the standpoint of the group, the causes for concern lie in the challenge to the central role which the family, in its two-parent form, has played in socializing Jews and from evidence of disaffiliation and sense of alienation from community among many American-Jewish single parents. Concerned as they are about the rate of increase, leaders of institutionally affiliated American Jewry have not yet resolved the dilemma of successfully integrating single-parent families into a two-parent family-centered communal life. There are both structural and cultural elements to this dilemma. The structural components of Jewish communal life are two-parent family oriented, and there is a dialectical relationship between the structure and the religio-cultural value of the centrality of that form of family. The perception of alienation on the part of many single parents derives from the structure which implicitly excludes single parents, the religio-cultural values which do likewise, and from the explicit rejection of the demand by some single parents that the Jewish community not only accept and integrate them as individuals but legitimate single parenthood as an equal and viable alternative to the two-parent form. With the increasing numbers of Jewish single-parent families, it may be anticipated that there will be increasing pressures upon the organized Jewish community to take cognizance of the needs of those families and to accommodate itself to them.

Presumably, all self-conscious minority groups are concerned about group size, since it is anticipated that the larger the size of the group, the greater are its chances for survival as a group in the dominant-minority situation. Among America's Jews, the areas where this is most clearly articulated are fertility and intermarriage. That both of these facets of Jewish family life are perceived by some as determining the very survival of the Jewish community in the United States is even evident from the very titles of many of the most-quoted writings on the subjects, e.g., "The Vanishing American Jew,"[32] "Intermarriage and the Jewish Future,"[33] and "The American Jewish Population Erosion."[34] Indeed, a former president

[32]L. B. Morgan, "The Vanishing American Jew," *Look* (May 5, 1964), pp. 42ff.

[33]M. Sklare, "Intermarriage and the Jewish Future," *Commentary* (April, 1964), pp. 46–52.

[34]E. Bergman, "The American Jewish Population Erosion," *Midstream* (October, 1977), pp. 9–19.

of the New York Board of Rabbis is quoted as having urged the American Jewish community to exempt itself from the nationwide trend toward zero population growth and instead increase its population. Otherwise, "it will grow weaker and will face a threat to its existence." "Three children should be the minimum number for Jewish families," he asserted, "but the larger the better."[35]

Most demographers would probably view this perception as alarmist, if not downright paranoid.[36,37] There is, however, another approach within which the fears about the decline of the American Jewish population are well founded. Goldscheider has perceptively summarized the two contrasting perspectives on the issue:

> To an outsider, the concern about the disappearance of American Jewry or the vanishing American Jew appears exaggerated or alarmist, if not ludicrous. At best the issue appears rhetorical or artificially created, to be rejected with the obvious retorts about the strength of American Jewish life. One does not have to go beyond a regular reading of the press to know that Jews are conspicuously present in a wide range of political and social activities. . . . An insider who knows the strength and weaknesses of the Jewish community goes beyond the superficial indicators and below the surface, however. Other signs appear, more powerful and challenging, subtle and destructive, which provide an alternative perspective.[38]

A look at a number of the demographic variables of American Jewry provides substance to the "insider" perspective.

According to the current *American Jewish Year Book* the size of the American Jewish population is 5,781,000, or about 2.67 percent of the total population of the United States.[39] When these figures are compared with those of the past, the 1930's for example, when Jews were 3.7 percent of the total population, it can be readily seen that American Jewry is becoming an increasingly smaller part

---

[35]L. Spiegel, "Rabbi Deplores Small Families," *New York Times* (January 24, 1974), p. 40.

[36]F. S. Jaffe, "Alarums, Excursions and Delusions of Grandeur," in M. Himmelfarb and V. Baras (eds.), *Zero Population Growth* (Westport, CT, 1978), p. 26–40

[37]B. Berelson, "Ethnicity and Fertility," in M. Himmelfarb and V. Baras (eds.), *Zero Population Growth* (Westport, CT, 1978), pp. 74–118.

[38]Goldscheider, "Demography and Jewish Survival," *op. cit.*, pp. 121, 123.

[39]A. Chenkin and M. Miran, "Jewish Population in the United States, 1978," *American Jewish Year Book*, Vol. 79 (1979), pp. 177–189.

of the overall American population. However, this does not necessarily mean that American Jewry is shrinking. Rather, these figures may be reflective of the traditional pattern of Jews maintaining a lower birthrate than their non-Jewish counterparts. As Goldscheider has demonstrated, the lower birthrate of Jews is not only characteristic of contemporary American Jewry but has been the pattern since the nineteenth century, in Europe, as well.[39a] Goldstein puts it rather succinctly:

> Already in the late nineteenth century, the Jewish birthrate was lower than that of the non-Jewish population. This differential has persisted to the present. Jews marry later than the average, desire and expect to have the smallest families, have had the most favorable attitudes toward the use of contraceptives, have used birth control to a greater extent than other groups, and have been among its most efficient users.[40]

Closer inspection, however, reveals that American Jewry is not only becoming an increasingly smaller percentage of the total population, but that the American Jewish birthrate is virtually at, and quite possibly below, the generally accepted replacement level of an average of 2.1 children per family. Thus, for America's Jews, the issue is not that of zero population growth (ZPG), but negative population growth (NPG). Studies of the fertility expectations of women of childbearing age, which suggest a narrowing of the gap between the birthrates of Jewish and non-Jewish women, leave no room for optimism with respect to the Jewish birthrate, because the projected decline in the differential is not due to a rise in the Jewish birthrate, but, rather, to the anticipated decline in the non-Jewish birthrate.[41,42] Moreover, if current trends of religious intermarriage continue, as will be discussed below, the rate of Jewish fertility seems likely to decline even more significantly, since, as Goldstein indicates, couples in which one of the spouses is Jewish have significantly fewer children than do couples in which both spouses are

---

[39a]C. Goldscheider, "Fertility of the Jews," *Demography* 4 (1967), pp. 196–209.

[40]S. Goldstein, "Jewish Fertility in Contemporary America," in P. Ritterband (ed.), *Modern Jewish Fertility* (Leiden, 1979).

[41]*Ibid.*

[42]S. M. Cohen and P. Ritterband, "Why Contemporary American Jews Want Small Families," in P. Ritterband (ed.), *Modern Jewish Fertility* (Leiden, 1979).

Jewish. For Jewish women married to Jewish husbands, the average is 2.1 children, whereas for Jewish women married to non-Jewish husbands the average is 1.6. Similar patterns prevail with Jewish husbands married to non-Jewish wives. The reasons for this differential are beyond the scope of this article. Within this context, the significant issue is that the differential exists and the intermarriage rate is rising.

It must be emphasized that there are a number of qualifications to these projections. First, there are limitations inherent in the discipline of demography itself which, at times, make it appear that the accuracy of forecasting in demography is not much better than in meteorology. Secondly, as most demographers of American Jewry caution, the limitations of studies whose samples are significantly Jewish, and the small number of Jews represented in virtually all national surveys, make for an even greater risk factor in predicting Jewish demographic patterns. A third limitation is the fact that there is a serious bias in samples in all of the surveys and studies upon which the predictions are based. There are groups of American Jews, such as Hasidim and other highly traditional Orthodox Jews, who live not only in Brooklyn, but in sections of practically every large city in the United States, who for a variety of reasons are not represented in the samples. Because they are very modest and, therefore, not likely to talk to anyone about their private family matters, because they live in extremely insular communities and are even less likely to discuss such matters with strangers, because they have a greater tendency to remain within their own primary groups, their chances of being queried as respondents and interviewees for demographic studies are extremely remote, if not nil. But the demographic patterns of these groups may well be radically different from those of the mainstream, and may be sufficiently so to offset the trends of the majority. For example, it has been suggested that families with more than a half dozen children are quite common among these groups. If that continues to be the case, their high birthrate could feasibly compensate for the low birthrate of the majority and, thus, curtail the American Jewish population decline.

As is the case with virtually all social groups, Jews reserve one of the most severe group sanctions, intense ostracism, for members of the group who reject and deny the group. Apostasy has, therefore, historically been deemed to be an even more serious affront than the violation of religious codes. The former is perceived as a rejection of both the religion and the group, whereas the latter only involves at most rejection of the religion.

Until relatively recently, intermarriage, that is, the marriage of a Jew to a non-Jew, was considered an act of rejection and was severely sanctioned. Among traditionalists, not only was the marriage not condoned, but the Jewish spouse was considered, for all purposes, dead and his or her family actually observed many of the traditional rites of mourning. Even in the minority of cases where the non-Jewish spouse converted to Judaism, there was strong disapproval from the Jewish community. The community feared that the conversion was religiously insincere, and that while such a couple might not have explicitly rejected the Jewish community, its children would surely be lost to the Jewish community. It was inconceivable that the offspring of such parents would be socialized as Jews. Intermarriage, even when involving conversion, was perceived as harmful to the Jewish people and the Jewish feeling of corporate identity.

With the advent of the modern era, the socioeconomic position of Jews in the United States and urban centers of Europe improved. Along with rising political and social equality, there were increased informal social contacts and interpersonal relationships. Predictably, the intermarriage rate of Jews increased somewhat,[43] but the group as a whole remained highly endogamous. However, in his review of studies of Jewish intermarriage, Rosenthal reported that data from a study of Washington, D.C. by Stanley Bigman in 1956 indicated an overall Jewish intermarriage rate of 13.1 percent with that rate rising to about 18 percent for third-generation American Jews. Moreover, "the Washington data revealed that the children in at least 70 percent of mixed families are lost to the Jewish group" (p. 32).[44] By 1965, the National Jewish Population Study estimated the intermarriage rate to be 29.1 percent and rising. As of 1972, it estimated that the rate of intermarriage had risen to 48.1 percent.[45]

As evidence of rising intermarriage rates mounted during the 1960's, the public expressions of concern for the Jewish future of the intermarried couples and their children grew louder. In 1964, Mar-

---

[43] M. C. Barron, *People Who Intermarry* (Syracuse, 1946), pp. 177–189.

[44] E. Rosenthal, "Studies of Jewish Intermarriage in the United States," *American Jewish Year Book*, Vol. 64, (1963), pp. 3–53.

[45] F. Massarik, "Intermarriage: Facts for Planning," in *National Jewish Population Study* (New York, 1973), p. 11.
The rates cited here are based upon percentages of Jewish marriages. Those rates cited by Goldstein are based upon percentages of Jewish people intermarrying.

shall Sklare, widely regarded as the foremost authority on the
sociology of American Jewry, decried the "Jewish complacency
about the rate of intermarriage."[46] Contrary to the prevalent arguments citing questionable studies suggesting that intermarriage is
symptomatic of individuals with psychological maladies and invariably leads to marital instability, Sklare asserted that, "It is precisely
the 'healthy' modern intermarriages which raise the most troubling
questions of all to the Jewish community" (p. 51). He warned that
the rising intermarriage rate posed a most formidable threat to "the
Jewish future." In 1970 he reiterated his warning and asserted that it
is a threat which overshadows all of the recent positive developments in the American Jewish community. "It strikes," he argued,
"at the very core of Jewish group existence."[47]

However, despite the stern warnings and dire predictions of
Sklare and many others, no strategy for dealing with the issue has
emerged on the Jewish communal agenda. What appears to have
developed is an attitude that it is inevitable, and the community will
have to reconcile itself to "living with intermarriage" and making
the best of it.[48] In an attempt to resolve the tensions of the resulting
"cognitive dissonance" a number of students of Jewish intermarriage
now argue that what had heretofore appeared as a threat may actually be a blessing in disguise.[49] Fred Massarik, who was the Scientific Director of the National Jewish Population Study, has reconsidered the data, and suggests that the issue for Jewish survival is not
really intermarriage, per se, but fertility, and that "the net effect of
intermarriage may be an increase in Jewish population rather than a
decrease."[50] While not arriving at an unequivocal conclusion, Massarik argues that the issue of intermarriage as it affects the Jewish
future is more complex than was previously evident. It is only one
variable which itself has many variable features, such as those in
which the originally non-Jewish spouse converted and those in

---

[46]Sklare, "Intermarriage and the Jewish Future," p. 48.

[47]M. Sklare, "Intermarriage and Jewish Survival," *Commentary*, (March, 1970),
pp. 51—58.

[48]D. Singer, "Living with Intermarriage," *Commentary*, (July, 1979), pp. 48—53.
48—53.

[49]L. Festinger, *Theory of Cognitive Dissonance* (New York, 1957).

[50]F. Massarik, "Rethinking the Intermarriage Crisis," *Moment* (June, 1978), pp.
29—33.

which he or she did not, and those in which the Jewish spouse is male and those in which she is female. Each of these variants has a differential impact upon the future identification and involvement of the intermarried couple and its children with the Jewish community and Jewish religio-cultural life.

Similarly, in their summary report of a national study[51] sponsored by the American Jewish Committee on "Intermarriage and the Jewish Future," Mayer and Sheingold[52] argue that since the rate of Jewish intermarriage will, doubtlessly, continue to increase "in the foreseeable future," and since the study confirmed the earlier findings of Lazerwitz[53] that what they term "conversionary marriages," in which the previously non-Jewish spouse converts to Judaism, compare favorably in terms of religious affiliation and observance, not only with "mixed marriages," in which the non-Jewish spouse does not convert, but also with endogamous Jewish marriages, "The Jewish community would do well to examine what steps it can take to encourage . . . conversion."[54] However, while they accept the inevitability of an increasing rate of intermarriage, and call for steps to encourage conversion, they do not go so far as to say that intermarriage is not a threat. On the contrary, they conclude that the data "tend to reinforce the fear that intermarriage represents a threat to Jewish continuity," primarily because "most non-Jewish spouses do not convert to Judaism; the level of Jewish content and practice in mixed marriages is low; only about one-third of the Jewish partners in such marriages view their children as Jewish; and most such children are exposed to little by way of Jewish culture or religion."[55]

In two subsequent publications, the author of the A.J.C.-sponsored study, Egon Mayer, elaborates upon his outreach proposal. In the lengthier of the two, written for the National Jewish Conference Center,[56] he urges that the Jewish community change its

---

[51]E. Mayer, *Patterns of Intermarriage Among American Jews* (New York, 1978).

[52]E. Mayer and C. Sheingold, *Intermarriage and the Jewish Future* (New York, 1979).

[53]B. Lazerwitz, "Intermarriage and Conversion: A Guide for Future Research," *Jewish Journal of Sociology* (June, 1971), pp. 41–63.

[54]Mayer and Sheingold, *op. cit.*, p. 32.

[55]*Ibid.*, p. 30.

[56]E. Mayer, "Intermarriage Among American Jews: Consequences, Prospects and Policies," *Policy Studies '79* (New York, February 15, 1979).

traditional discouraging stance toward prospective converts, and establish "conversion outreach centers" which "should bridge the gap between the religious Jewish community and the potential convert" (p. 7). However, he maintains, the great majority of mixed marriage spouses are probably not receptive to conversion in any case, and therefore there is virtually no chance that the non-Jewish ones will ever become wholly integrated into the Jewish community. Moreover, their Jewish spouses, who may serve as their Jewish role models, rarely, if ever, manifest any religious behavior. To the extent that they are Jewishly active they are so within secular rather than religious Jewish frameworks. Mayer maintains that there are many non-Jewish spouses in mixed marriages who "identify" as Jews, in that they have positive feelings toward Jewry and participate in secular Jewish activities, such as on the committees of Jewish community centers, the boards of local Hadassah chapters, and in U.J.A.-federation fund-raising functions. Given this growing group in mixed marriages of spouses who, according to Jewish religious law, *halachah*, are not Jewish, but who do feel themselves to be somewhat Jewish, in a secular, perhaps ethnic sense, Mayer recommends that a new category of Jew be created, namely, those who are members of the "people" but not of the "faith" (p. 7). In a second article on this subject,[57] Mayer is even more explicit in calling for "a kind of 'ethnic conversion,' which will respond to the desire of many of the mixed-married to see themselves as Jews and to be seen as Jews, but without religious conviction" (p. 64). Motivated by a desire to improve the demographic outlook, Mayer sees hope in the minority of spouses in mixed marriages who, he claims, "are Jews through the alchemy of sociology, not of *halachah*."

Whether or not he is correct in his estimate of the number of potential sociological Jews who would respond to outreach efforts aimed at "ethnic conversion," is, for now, a moot point. For better or for worse, the organized Jewish community is not quite harking to Mayer's urgings; it is not embarking on an organized outreach campaign, but neither has it developed any strategy for stemming the rising intermarriage rate. While the community no longer perceives intermarriage as the curse that it had been, neither does it perceive it as a blessing. Essentially, the community has come to begrudgingly accept intermarriage with the implicit faith that this

---

[57]E. Mayer, "A Cure for Intermarriage?" *Moment* (June, 1979), pp. 62–64.

can be successfully endured. Empirical research on the next generation may reveal the degree to which that faith is warranted.

With respect to the patterns of kinship relationships, "the ideal household of the American Jew, like that of the middle class generally, consists of parents and their minor children"[58] in contrast to the three-generation household which was typical among Jews in eastern Europe. However, the American Jewish family does appear to be relatively unique with respect to the maintenance of strong kinship ties. This characteristic is so out of line with what one would have predicted on the basis of the group's socioeconomic status, that Berman has pointed to it as "an inconsistency in theory."[59] Nevertheless, with the increasing rate of intermarriage, it remains to be seen to what extent the extended familism of American Jews will prevail and, more significantly, to what extent this kind of extended family will serve to reinforce and transmit Jewish identity and identification.

It was argued at the beginning of this article that an examination of the contemporary American Jewish family is warranted, particularly because of the central role which the Jewish family plays in defining and transmitting Jewish identity and identification. The foregoing examination indicates that though certain unique family patterns persist, the American Jewish family has changed significantly from the traditional Jewish patterns, and is increasingly manifesting the same patterns as the general American middle-class family. If that is the case, it would be appropriate to raise the question of the probability of Jewish group survival in American society. In fact, developments within the American Jewish community during the last decade appear to suggest that the prognosis for the survival of American Jewry is more positive, not less, than it appeared in the early 1960's. For example, in his assessment of recent changes in the suburban Jewish community of Lakeville,[60]

---

[58] Sklare, America's Jews, p. 94.

[59] G. S. Berman, "The Adaptable American Jewish Family," Jewish Journal of Sociology (June, 1976), pp. 5–16. Also see J. Balswick, "Are American Jewish Families Close Knit?" Jewish Social Studies (July, 1966), pp. 159–169; J. Westerman, "Note on Balswick's Article: A Response," Jewish Social Studies 29 (October, 1967), pp. 241–244; R. F. Winch, S. Greer, R. I. Blumberg, "Ethnicity and Familism in an Upper Middle Class Suburb," Amer. Soc. Rev. 32 (April, 1967), pp. 265–272; M. Sklare, America's Jews, p. 95. For a study of the interesting development of family clubs and cousins clubs among Jews in New York City, see W. E. Mitchell, Mishpokhe, (The Hague, 1978).

[60] M. Sklare and J. Greenblum, Jewish Identity on the Suburban Frontier (Chicago, 1979), pp. 333–405.

Sklare points to "many positive signs of Jewish survivalism," which, he implies, might mitigate against the "negative signs, most obviously the rise in intermarriage" (p. 404).

Do such findings support the argument of those, such as Kutzik, that the family actually plays a subsidiary role in Jewish identification, and that the communal institutions, such as the synagogue and the various social welfare institutions, play the more basic role?[61] And, if so, is the scarcity of empirical data on the contemporary American Jewish family justified by its secondary nature? Our response to both of these questions is in the negative. To begin with, we have argued that although the family plays a central role in Jewish identity formation and transmission, it cannot be viewed in a vacuum, as functioning alone, without the support of the other, more formal, institutions of the Jewish community.[62] On this matter Kutzik agrees.[63] Therefore, his position on the primacy of the communal institutions and secondary nature of the family is based, in a large part, on his view of "the limited . . . role of the contemporary American family in . . . enculturation or sociocultural identification." The contemporary family, "whether Jewish or not," he asserts, "is structurally incapable of carrying out enculturation on its own."[64] Here Kutzik is echoing Rosenberg and Humphrey, who assert "the secondary nature of primary groups." They argue:

> Agencies of socialization transmit culture; they do not necessarily create it. Primary groups may be the nursery of a human nature whose shapes and contours they do not determine. A sacred society will use its neighborhoods in one way, a secular society in another. The child must always be socialized within a small group, but the norms it is obliged to "interiorize" have another and a larger locus. The child is plastic, and he is molded to a large extent by his family, his play group, and his neighbors, but all these take their essential character from courses external to them.[65]

---

[61] A. J. Kutzik, "The Roles of the Jewish Community and Family in Jewish Identification." Prepared for the American Jewish Committee, Jewish Communal Affairs Dept. (1977).

[62] C. I. Waxman, "Perspectives on the Family and Jewish Identity in America," (New York, 1977), pp. 5, 7.

[63] Kutzik, op. cit., p. 35.

[64] Ibid., p. 11.

[65] B. Rosenberg and N. D. Humphrey, "The Secondary Nature of Primary Groups," Social Research 22 (Spring, 1955), pp. 25–38.

While, as indicated, there is no disagreement as to the family's inability to function in this manner "on its own," Kutzik underestimates the significant degree to which the family, of the past and of the present, Jewish or not, is involved in identity formation. The family is not only a "haven in a heartless world"[66]; it is a "small world"[67] in which the self emerges and in which the individual acquires a stable sense of identity and reality.

In terms of Jewish identity and identification, likewise, the family plays the central role in primary socialization and provides the foundation for the complementary roles of the formal community institutions. This, obviously, does not mean that strong traditional family ties will necessarily provide that foundation. Obviously, those who are not self-consciously Jewish will not. As Rosenberg and Humphrey point out in their analogy of the primary group and the conveyor belt, "The belt is *eo ipso* a neutral object, which must be adjusted to work norms and end products impersonally thrust upon it."[68] We are, of course, dealing with families which are self-consciously Jewish and the central role which the family plays in defining and transmitting that consciousness to the next generation.

The communal institutions are certainly important in providing the structural context for realizing and living out that identity, and for reinforcing it, but they are still secondary to the primary role of the family. It is, thus, no coincidence that recent studies by Cohen indicate that those who live in "alternate families" are considerably less Jewishly active than those who live in traditional normative families.[69] Apparently, nontraditional forms of family are not able to provide the framework within which the individual would acquire a stable sense of *Jewish* identity and *Jewish* reality, and therefore do not seek out structural contexts within which Jewish identity is operationalized.

If, as the evidence suggests, the changes in the American Jewish family have been most dramatic within the past two decades,

---

[66]C. Lasch, *Haven in a Heartless World* (New York, 1977).

[67]B. Luckmann, "The Small Worlds of Modern Man," *Social Research* (Winter, 1970), pp. 580–596.

[68]Rosenberg and Humphrey, *op. cit.*, p. 27.

[69]S. M. Cohen, "Will Jews Keep Giving: Prospects for the Jewish Charitable Community," paper delivered at the Tenth Annual Conference of the Association for Jewish Studies, Boston, December 18, 1978.

it may be premature to take solace from the recent positive signs of Jewish survivalism which Sklare and others have found. They may be but short-term patterns resulting from a number of events which took place both within the Jewish and general American communities during the late 1960's and early 1970's.[70] But their staying power may be limited, especially as both the American cultural milieu and the American Jewish family have changed.

Furthermore, those positive signs are found in the American Jewish community but not necessarily among all American Jews. This is not the contradiction it appears to be. There is a basic difference between being an American Jew and being a member of the American Jewish community. The latter refers to those who are affiliated with the communal structure of American Jewry; the former refers to those who are nominally Jewish but who may be unaffiliated with the organized community. While it is obviously difficult to get precise figures, indications are that the unaffiliated comprise a rather large portion of the American Jewish population. For example, Elazar has divided the American Jewish population into seven groups, represented as a series of seven uneven concentric circles, ranging from the hard core, "Integral Jews," to those whose Jewish status is least clear, "Quasi-Jews."[71] If we add up his estimates of those who are "Peripherals" and beyond, we find that 25 to 30 percent of the American Jewish population is completely uninvolved in Jewish life. And another group, "Contributors and Consumers," who "clearly identify as Jews, but are minimally associated with the Jewish community as such," comprise "about 25 to 30 percent of all American Jews." The condition of contemporary American Jewry is, thus, one in which there is a "shrinking middle." That is, there is a polarization taking place with respect to Jewish commitment. Clearly the positive signs discussed by Sklare are manifested only within that approximately 50 percent of the American Jewish population which is affiliated with the American Jewish community. The weakening commitment of the other 50 percent, the unaffiliated, however, has distinct implication for the qualitative survival and well-being of the whole.

Those concerned with Jewish survival in the United States

---

[70]Glazer, op. cit., pp. 151–186.

[71]Elazar, op. cit., pp. 70–74.

would be advised to give careful attention to the state of the American Jewish family—and this means supporting and engaging in reliable social scientific research, and developing communal policies and programs for supporting and strengthening it in its traditional form and character.

COMMUNITY AND IDENTITY

THE ORIGIN OF A JEWISH COMMUNITY
IN THE SUBURBS
by HERBERT J. GANS

INTRODUCTION

*P*ARK FOREST, ILLINOIS—one of the largest of the post-World-War II housing developments—happens to be located within easy commuting distance of the University of Chicago and as a result has been intensively investigated by social scientists. Herbert J. Gans, a leading urbanologist, was a graduate student at the university when Park Forest was founded and he took on the task of studying Jewish life in the new community.

Since the outward direction of Chicago Jewry was almost entirely to the northern and northwest suburbs, for a time it seemed unlikely that there would be anything worth studying in Park Forest. However, despite its location southwest of the city, Park Forest did succeed in attracting some Jewish families for several possible reasons: Park Forest was itself developed by Jews who were widely known in the Jewish community, it offered housing at a time of critical shortage, its private dwellings and apartments cost less than comparable housing in suburbs which were attracting large numbers of Jews, and for some breadwinners transportation from Park Forest to their jobs was more convenient than from the northern suburbs.

The Jews who were attracted to Park Forest tended to be

somewhat marginal to the Jewish community.* Their marginality was compounded by the fact that there was no preexistent Jewish community—or for that matter, any real community at all—in Park Forest to which they might attach themselves. Thus in theory, and perhaps in reality as well, the Jews who settled in Park Forest had the option of integrating themselves into the life of the newly forming general community and, if not themselves assimilating, at least encouraging their children to do so. The other available option was to pursue group survival by seeking to establish a Jewish community in the inhospitable territory of the southwestern suburbs.

The predominant response was to pursue the goal of group survival, and a Jewish community soon came to be established in Park Forest. While some Jews did very little to advance the cause, the activists were sufficiently numerous and influential to achieve their goal. (In any case there was no organized group dedicated to preventing the emergence of a Jewish community; given the pluralism and permissiveness of American social structure, it would have been difficult to organize one.) To be sure, the kind of community which emerged in Park Forest was far from tradition-al—it accorded instead with the patterns of Jewish culture and identity practiced by members of the community themselves. No mikvah was built in Park Forest, and indeed the early pioneers of the community were in no hurry even to establish a synagogue, the one institution which symbolized Jewish affirmation in so many other suburban communities. But despite the indifference to a mikvah and the hesitancy to form a synagogue, very soon after the first Jewish residents arrived it was clear that the question of whether there was to be a Jewish community had been resolved in the affirmative.

What did the Jewish pioneers of Park Forest establish? Gans discovered that the community consisted of two layers—what he calls the informal community and the formal community. The formal community was established second—indeed it was made possible by the existence of an informal community and was erected on its foundation. At the outset the formal community was rudimentary in structure and consisted of little more than a single

*It is quite possible that one of Park Forest's attractions was that it would not become a Skokie—a northwestern suburb of Chicago which was transformed in a relatively few years from an all-Gentile community to a thickly populated Jewish area.

organization for men and another organization for women. (When Gans returned to Park Forest in the mid-1950's he found the formal community to be much more elaborate; for example, it had come to include a synagogue much like those in other communities settled by highly acculturated Jews after World War II.)

That the organized Jewish community in general might rest on the base of an informal community had escaped most observers, who as a rule saw a community well after its establishment and whose attention was drawn to the formal structure: the synagogues, the offices of Jewish organizations, the Jewish community centers, the hospitals. Since the clique structure which undergirded the formal community (and which itself was undergirded by a Jewish kinship network) was invisible, the eye naturally focused on the formal aspects of the community. Gans, however, had the good fortune to witness the Park Forest Jewish community at its birth and being an unusually gifted field observer he not only detected the significance of the informal community but came to understand how its existence led to the establishment of a formal community.

Gans distinguishes four stages in the organization of the informal community: contact, recognition, acquaintance, and friendship. Since movement from stage to stage was exceedingly rapid in Park Forest we must draw the conclusion that ethnic identity has salience even for marginally situated Jews. The cycle from contact to friendship is particularly impressive if we remember that the Jews of Park Forest were not only a minuscule group but were scattered throughout the sprawling development—in the early days of Park Forest there was no one area with a concentration of Jewish population. In addition, whether because they were detached from Jewish tradition or because they were unwilling to distinguish themselves publicly from their neighbors, the Jews of Park Forest did not "advertise" their Jewishness: Gans does not mention a single instance of a mezuzah being fastened to a door frame. Nevertheless the initial 150 Jewish families (out of a total of 1,800 families then in Park Forest) speedily discovered each other; the devices they used are delineated by Gans with particular clarity. The process, which began with contact, culminated in the formation of an informal Jewish community—cliques that were all or predominantly Jewish in composition.

As Gans points out, even individuals who maintained the irrelevancy of the Jewish-Gentile distinction in choosing their friends came to belong to predominantly Jewish cliques. The informal Jewish community thus consisted of Jews who varied in the level and type of their Jewish identity. Although in the earliest days of Park Forest these differences were not reflected in the formal community, as that community became more elaborate they did come to take on public significance.

M. S.

. . . PARK FOREST, ILLINOIS, the scene of the study described here, is not an ordinary suburb but rather a partially planned garden city.[1] Located thirty miles south of Chicago's Loop, it was envisioned both as a dormitory for Chicago white-collar workers (which it is), and a partially self-sufficient community with its own industries (which it still hopes to be). The plan called for 3,000 rental garden apartments, for 4,500 single-family homes available for sale, as well as for shopping centers, schools, churches, playgrounds, and other community facilities.[2] The conversion of

[1] The garden-city movement—founded by Ebenezer Howard in England at the turn of the century—advocated the building of small communities with their own industries, to combine what were considered to be the social and psychological advantages of small-town living with the requirements of an urban economy (see Howard's book, *Garden Cities of Tomorrow*, [London: 1902]). Leaders of this movement were instrumental in the construction of two garden cities in England. They have influenced, either directly or indirectly, the new towns built near London after World War II, the U.S. government's greenbelt towns built during the 1930's, and private developments such as Radburn (New Jersey), Park Forest, the Levittowns, and several industry-built communities. Some of these are analyzed in Clarence Stein, *Towards New Towns for America* (Chicago: 1951).

[2] The plans for Park Forest (which were revised during construction) are described in "American Community Builders," *The Architectural Forum*, August 1948, pp. 70–74, and by H. Henderson and S. Shaw, "City to Order," *Collier's*, 14 February 1948. Many other articles on the community have appeared in various architectural journals and general magazines since that time. The best report on life in Park Forest is an insightful journalistic-sociological study by William H. Whyte, Jr., "The Transients," *Fortune*, May-August 1953. See also, Herbert J. Gans, "Planning and Political Participation," *Journal of the American Institute of Planners*, Winter 1953, pp. 1–9, and "Political Participation and Apathy," unpublished M.A. thesis, Division of the Social Sciences, University of Chicago, June 1950.

For studies of English communities similar to Park Forest, see Ruth Durant, *Watling* (London: 1939); Harold Orlans, *Utopia Limited* (New Haven: 1953), and Leo Kuper *et. al.*, *Living in Towns* (London: 1953). For studies of American communities, see Robert K. Merton, "Social Psychology of Housing," in Wayne Dennis (ed.), *Current Trends in Social Psychology* (Pittsburgh: 1948), pp. 163–217, and his forthcoming *Patterns of Social Life: Explorations in the Sociology and Social Psychology of Housing*, with P. S. West, and M. Jahoda; William Form, "Status Stratification in Low and Middle Income Housing Areas," in "Social Policy and Social Research in Housing," *Journal of Social Issues*, Issues 1 and 2, 1951, pp. 109–131, and "Status Stratification in a Planned Community," *American Sociological Review*, October 1945, pp. 605–613. Two as yet unpublished studies of the Levittowns are Marie Jahoda *et. al.*, *Community Influences on Psychological Health* (tentative title), and John Liell, "Levittown: A Study in Community Development and Planning,"Ph.D. dissertation, Department of Sociology, Yale University, 1952.

the golf course and farmland which were to be the site of the new town began in 1947, and the first tenants moved in on August 30, 1948. By April 1949, the community had been incorporated as a village.

Like other postwar suburbs, Park Forest first attracted the people most sorely pressed for shelter—young couples with one or two children of preschool age.[3] In 1949, the median age of the men was thirty-two, of the women somewhat less; anyone over forty was generally considered old. Many of the men were beginning their careers, and most of them were in professional, sales, or administrative and other business fields. . . . It seemed probable that the village was attracting the socially and geographically more mobile members of the generation of returning veterans.

In November 1949, when the interviewing for this study was completed, about 1,800 families were living in the village. About 25 percent of them were Catholic. The Jewish community then numbered just under 150 families. Of these, about twenty (fifteen of them mixed marriages) rejected all relationships with the formal Jewish community.[4] Another thirty families had not been in Park Forest long enough to have made contact with the established Jewish community. We interviewed a sample which consisted of forty-four of the remaining group of 100 families.[5] This sample was subdivided into families of people who had been *active* in the formation of Jewish organizations or were now in leadership positions, and those *inactive*, whether or not they were members of organizations.[6] Within the total sample, the median age of heads of

[3]This description of the residents of Park Forest is based on participant observation as well as some fifty interviews with residents chosen at random (though not from a statistically designed random sample), for a study of political participation.

[4]The total number of known "mixed marriages" was estimated at twenty-four, or 17 percent of the Jewish population. Despite the efficiency of the community grapevine, this estimate is probably conservative. Of the twenty-four couples, about a third participated in the Jewish community.

[5]This group of one hundred also included twenty who said they were not interested in the Jewish community. However, they had Jewish friends and were at least part of the communication network of the Jewish group.

The data presented here are based on about six months of observation in the village, including attendance at many meetings, on conversations with Jewish residents, and on full interviews with one person in each of forty-four Jewish families and partial ones with ten more. . . .

[6]The sample on which the data presented in this section is based was stratified between a group of leaders and actives selected from all factions of the community for the analysis of community processes, and a group of residents most of whom were

households was thirty-five, and of their wives, thirty. Some 43 percent of the families had one or more school-age children, while 57 percent had only younger children or were still childless. Although there were no age differences between the actives and the inactives, the former had a slightly higher proportion of older children. . . .

About 90 percent of the men in the sample had some college training. Some 57 percent had graduated from college, and 32 percent held graduate or professional degrees. . . . Some 36 percent of the sample were professionals. A total of 48 percent were in business and industry, though only 14 percent were owners.

Eighty-eight percent of the adults in the sample were native-born. Most of the parents of this group were foreign-born. Overwhelmingly, the families came from Eastern Europe. All but a few of our interviewees were brought up in large cities (60 percent of them in Chicago); they came primarily from working-class or lower-middle-class areas of second settlement. While Park Foresters are mainly "second generation," they are the children of later immigrants or of immigrants who themselves came to America as children, and must be distinguished from second-generation descendants of Jews in the first waves of Eastern European immigration (before 1900) whose own children (third generation) are already adolescents or young adults. . . .[7]

In summary, the Jewish sample can be described as a group of young, highly educated, second-generation Jews of Eastern European parentage, most of whom have already achieved—or are likely to achieve—upper-middle-class income status, given con-

known not to be leaders, chosen at random from the mailing list. In the original sample, actives were overrepresented; but with a knowledge of the proportion of actives and inactives in the total community (based on the judgments of a number of informants), this sample was brought closer to representativeness, *post facto*, by the random elimination of some interviews with actives.

[7]The generational analysis using formal genealogical categories is complicated by the fact that Jewish immigration from Eastern Europe lasted over two generations. Furthermore, the immigrants were themselves of two generations, being either children or adults. Also, since Eastern European Jewry was then already acculturating in the wake of urban-industrial change and Western cultural influences, immigrants may have been of two or more *cultural generations* (i.e., "generations" defined in terms of deviation from the traditional culture). Consequently, an analytically meaningful concept of generation would have to include several factors, and a generational description of a second generation Jew would not be complete without an analysis of his parents' age at arrival and their cultural orientation at the time of his upbringing. Such an analysis of the Park Forest material remains to be done.

tinued prosperity. The active members of the community rate somewhat higher on socio-economic characteristics than do the inactives.

Turning to the problem of cultural distinctiveness, it is apparent that many of the Jewish residents could not easily be distinguished from other Park Foresters. Although many of them could be said to "look Jewish," they wore the same fashions, ate the same dishes (except on special occasions), and participated with other Park Foresters in the ubiquitous American class- and leisure-culture of the "young moderns." They observed few of the old cultural and religious traditions. The village's isolation from synagogues and kosher butcher shops discouraged observant Jews from becoming tenants, and brought problems to those who did.

Not only did Park Forest Jews live like other Park Foresters; they lived *with* them. Whereas most American cities have neighborhoods which are predominantly Jewish (if not always in numbers, at least in atmosphere and institutions), such was not the case with Park Forest. The Jewish families were scattered at random, and only rarely were two Jewish families to be found in adjacent houses. The tenants, Jewish and non-Jewish, lived in so-called "courts"—*cul-de-sac* parking bays encircled by twenty to forty two-story garden apartments, built together in rows of five to seven, and renting in 1949 for $75–$100 per month.[8]

The occupants of the courts described themselves as living in a goldfish bowl in which privacy was at a minimum. Depending on the makeup of the group, this court life ranged from that of "one big happy family" to a tense collection of unwilling neighbors, although with the passing of time people learned how to find privacy in a high-density world of picture windows. For many of the non-Jewish Park Foresters, the court was almost an independent social unit in which they found most, if not all, their friends, and from which they ventured only rarely, at least during the first year or two.[9]

[8]Some of the Jewish families showed a decided preference for end-units, which were slightly more expensive. The extent to which this choice was due to desire for isolation rather than the need for an extra bedroom for older children or the ability to pay higher rents, was not studied. The homeowners who came later live on a more traditional but curved street plan. For a highly generalized description of the court life see William H. Whyte, Jr., "How the New Suburbia Socializes," *Fortune*, August 1953, pp. 120–122, 186–190. For a rigorous study of certain limited aspects of the social life of a housing project, see Leon Festinger, Stanley Schachter, and Kurt Back, *Social Pressures in Informal Groups* (New York: 1950).

[9]A systematic stratification analysis would probably show that those with upper-middle-class aspirations tended to find friends outside the court; this in part also explains the behavior of the Jewish residents.

The Formation of the Jewish Community

The Jews who came to Park Forest were impelled by the same need for housing, and a desire for a suburban environment in which to raise their children, as were their neighbors.[10] (Some of them also came to learn how to live in the suburbs before buying a house.) Soon after they arrived, they aligned themselves into a number of cliques. In a remarkably short period these formed an interrelated network by which news, gossip, and rumor could be communicated. Out of this informal community there developed a formal community of voluntary associations and religious organizations.

A. *Evolution of the Informal Community.* The developmental processes of this informal community can be described in four stages: *contact, recognition, acquaintance,* and *friendship.*

Contact is the opportunity for face-to-face meeting. In order for interaction to develop beyond this point, there had to be the mutual recognition of each other's Jewishness and status position. *As an ethnic group, the Jews form a cohesive ingroup and tend to behave differently toward a member of the ingroup than toward a non-Jew, in many cases reserving the intimacy of friendship for the former.* Thus, before two persons can act in terms of the more personal ingroup norm, they must have a sign that identifies them to each other as fellow ingroup members. Without this recognition there can be no progress toward the formation of acquaintance and the regular interaction of an intimate nature (i.e., the exchange of personal facts, attitudes, and feelings which we call friendship).

Due to the fact that most of the officers of American Community Builders, Inc. (A.C.B.), the corporation that built Park Forest, are Jewish, and the further fact that several have long been active in Jewish affairs, a Jewish community in Park Forest was

[10]No one has ever studied why one community or subdivision gains Jewish residents while another area is avoided. Dr. Julian L. Greifer reported that in the Philadelphia area:

> Some of the new private housing developments have become almost exclusively populated by Jews, as friend followed friend, and relative moved near relative. . . . I know of several pioneering Jewish families that settled in new suburban communities but after a few years moved back, at great personal loss, to localities more heavily populated by Jews. Apparently the failure of additional Jewish families to settle in the new communities isolated the pioneers from Jewish contacts and communal institutions.

"Relationships in a Large City," *Jewish Social Studies,* July 1955, pp. 269–270. One factor in this decision is probably the ethnic identity of the developer. If he is Jewish he is likely to advertise in Anglo-Jewish papers, as well as invite friends to move into his project.

almost predestined.[11] Before the opening of the development, its officers had invited several friends to move out, and these were among the first tenants.

For those not personally known to the officers, the recognition process began in each court, as families stood beside their moving van and eyed the strangers who were to be their neighbors. Recognition was initiated even before contact was made, for with the first glance, Jewish people were attempting to figure out whether one or another person could be Jewish. This hypothesizing sometimes went on for days; or, if there was relative certainty, and one person was aggressive enough, it lasted a matter of minutes. Mrs. H. described it thusly:

> Mrs. F. came over and talked to me while we were outside with the moving van. It was not a question of religion, but of recognition, I knew she was Jewish by her name, and she looked Jewish, I don't know if the thing was ever discussed, I don't know if she knew I was Jewish that first day.

Mrs. F. said of that meeting:

> I didn't know Mrs. H. was Jewish, I kind of thought as much, by her looks.

In this case there were two signs of recognition, the Jewish "look" and a Jewish "name." Frequently people used a customary request for each other's names to test hypotheses of recognition based on the Jewish "look."

Anthropologists are agreed that there is no Jewish race. Nevertheless, many people, and especially Jews, tend to identify Mediterranean and Armenoid facial features as Jewish. This, plus the fact that certain names are almost monopolized by Jews, has created a stereotypical recognition formula which is realistic enough to be correct more often than it is not. This formula was used in a large number of cases for determining who were the other Jews in the court; its role in the formation of the Jewish community cannot be underestimated.

The look and the name were sometimes reinforced by what might be described as Jewish mannerisms, that is, a set of gestures or verbal expressions that are—again stereotypically—ascribed to Jews:

[11]In 1953 the president of A.C.B. became the international president of B'nai B'rith.

It was obvious he was Jewish, by name and appearance. I thought he was from New York, by his speech and action. I've run into a lot of Brooklyn people and can tell them apart. Then I went into his house, and saw the candlesticks.

As the above respondent indicated, there were other signs of recognition, for some people displayed Jewish ritual objects which quickly resolved all doubts.

Sometimes, however, people turned to systematic techniques of exploration. For example, initial conversations were skillfully directed toward attempts to discover the other's religion, or to offer clues as to one's own. When that failed, or seemed imprudent, the conversation turned to food habits:

. . . we have a taste for Jewish food . . . we told them what kind of food it was we liked: cornbeef, lox [smoked salmon]. . . .

The day I moved in I advertised that I was Jewish by asking for Jewish women who kept kosher. . . .

Sometimes there were no symbols or formulas which could be applied, and people found out by accident:

My next door neighbors, they didn't look Jewish, nothing Jewish about them, but then I asked before Passover if they wanted to try some macaroons, and we found out.

I knew them as neighbors, knew them for a month, then the name was given me on a mailing list. I was amazed, I didn't know they were Jewish.

The recognition process was somewhat facilitated by the presence of a minister who conducted a religious survey soon after each court was occupied, and informed curious Jews who the other Jews in the court were. In addition, there were a number of Jewish men who made a point of getting to know the entire Jewish community, and thus they were able to introduce individuals to each other.[12]

There was no automatic progression from recognition to *acquaintance* without a desire for further association. In many

[12]In most cases, however, the recognition as well as many other parts of the community formation process were handled by the women, for they were in the community all day long while the men commuted to Chicago. This sexual division of the social labors held also in the non-Jewish community.

cases, however, this desire for association with Jews was implied if not expressed already at the recognition stage, by the aggressiveness of one person or the other in creating conditions that allowed recognition when the Jewish-look-or-name formula alone was not conclusive.

Mutual recognition was followed by further exploration of each other's ethnic characteristics and affiliations. Neighbors asked each other where they were from, where they lived last, whom they knew there, what congregation or groups they belonged to, and later turned to discussing their attitudes toward Jewish traditions and observances. The question, "Did you know the So-and-So's in ———?" was perhaps most important. People who had mutual friends, or even mutual acquaintances in previous places of residence, very quickly passed to the acquaintance and friendship stages, thus accelerating the rate of community formation.

The abundance of these prior contacts is a function of the fact that the world of the middle-class Jew is comparatively small. Even in the larger cities, there are only a limited number of Jewish organizations, temples, and neighborhoods. Furthermore, Jewish families are still extensive, and maintain communication contacts even when kinship solidarity is much reduced. Consequently, people who are socially active tend to meet, or at least know about, a considerable proportion of their community's Jewish group. Many Park Forest Jews thus encountered neighbors with whom they could initiate relationships on the basis of some previous bond, even if it was nothing more than an introduction at some social function. In a new community of strangers, these prior contacts were invested with a greater significance than they would have elsewhere, and the relationships which grew from them achieved regularity and stability rather quickly. They became the foundations for the informal community, which was then completed by the slower development of social relationships among total strangers. The exchange of names also provided an opportunity for the parties involved to measure each other's social status and interests by those of the mutual acquaintance.

While it is difficult to determine at what point an acquaintance relationship became one of *friendship*, the overall timetable of the process of informal community development was fairly uniform. Usually ten days to two weeks passed before any but the exceptionally gregarious and mobile people made any serious attempts at getting out of the house to make contacts. However, after this moving-in period, contact, recognition, and acquaintance relationships developed quickly. In general it was a matter of only four to eight weeks before people said they had friends whom they saw regularly. Some residents suggested that regularity did not yet mean intimacy: "We see the So-and-So's regularly but you really can't call them friends, we haven't been here that long." Nor was it certain that these relationships would persist. Nevertheless, in November of 1949 almost all of the families who were living in the village by July of that year had established some regular and stable sociability relationships with their fellow Jews.[13]

B. *Development of Formal Organizations*. The development of the formal community began with the organization of a B'nai B'rith lodge and a chapter of the National Council of Jewish Women.

Among the first arrivals in Park Forest were a handful of "Jewish professionals," men who work for American-Jewish agencies. They were interested in setting up Jewish organizations, and while their activity was voluntary, like that of any other resident, their interest was still more than purely social or civic. In March of 1949, when fifty Jewish families were living in the village, one of these professionals (employed as an organizer in Chicago) considered the time to be ripe and invited a small group of men to discuss the formation of a lodge. Several of the men had met each other previously in the course of a local political campaign. Many of those present at the meeting, although vaguely in favor of a group, were not interested in any specific organization. One of them said:

> We were contemplating some kind of a social club, recreational, then we hit on . . . B'nai B'rith. The fact is that we were influenced, I guess, by fellows who are with B'nai B'rith.

Consequently, the group decided to form a lodge. Some thirty-five men were invited to the next meeting. There the lodge was organized, with the professionals and a handful of other actives taking over the decision-making positions.

[13]The kind of friendship relationship discussed here is not the intimate lifetime friendship as it is classically defined, but rather a companionship in transitory surroundings (like a college dormitory or army camp) which is intimate while the surroundings are shared but may end when they are not. On the other hand, it may lead to permanent relationships, especially if the parties involved are traveling toward the same social goals. It would be interesting to discover whether contemporary social trends encourage such companionship rather than the permanent type of friendship.

The organization of the women's group took place about a month later. It was initiated by two women who had just entered the village. While they knew the Jewish residents of their court, they wanted to make contact with others. Through a mailing list already compiled by the men's group,[14] the women were contacted and invited to an organizational meeting. At this gathering the process which took place at the men's meeting was repeated. Most of those present expressed the desire and need for a women's group. The initiators proposed affiliation with Council. Their choice was approved, and they were named to leadership positions.

Attendance and active participation in the Council of Jewish Women was immediately greater than in B'nai B'rith, reflecting the women's greater desire for Jewish companionships. Furthermore, the Council meetings provided an efficient and easily available method for newcomers to make contacts with the older settlers. It facilitated the recognition process, and initially this was perhaps the group's major—though latent—function.

The early leadership structure of both groups in its relationships with the informal community was quite similar. The top leaders in both organizations were "lone wolves"—they belonged to no set clique in the village. The rest of the officers in both groups were drawn largely from a clique of the older, well-to-do people who had been active in formal organizational life elsewhere. This clique had become fairly well stabilized by the time the two formal groups were organized; consequently clique members worked actively together in the structuring of the formal community.

After the organizational period, both groups evolved in the direction of their urban counterparts. Thus B'nai B'rith had speakers, played poker, and offered refreshments; the Council ran a number of study groups, heard other speakers, conducted charity programs, and gave the Jewish women of the community a chance to dress up and meet. In November 1949, each had enrolled about fifty members. . . .

[14]Some comment should be made about the cohesive and social pressure functions of the mailing list. This list was carefully compiled soon after the formation of the lodge, and kept up to date so as to include everyone known or suspected to be Jewish. The existence of the community was stressed by frequent mailings which went even to people who rejected all contact with the Jewish group. Later, Sunday school announcements were sent to everyone, as its caretaker reported:

> Just to show people what was being done in the Jewish community and to keep their interest up. No names should be taken off the list just because people hadn't shown interest.

The Informal Community—
The Ethnic Cohesion of Sociability

While [some] Jewish Park Foresters . . . avoided involvement with adult Jewish activities, they were nevertheless willing and desirous of associating with other Jews. Groups were formed consisting usually of another couple or a clique[15] of couples. Together they composed the informal Jewish community.

A. *Sociability Patterns.* On the whole, the informal community existed only at night. In the daytime, Park Forest was inhabited by housewives and the ever present children, and the Jewish women participated in the social life of the courts in which they lived. They interrupted their household duties to chat and "visit with" a neighbor over a morning cup of coffee, or while watching the children in the afternoon. They also belonged to the bridge and sewing clubs that were established in many courts. In these nonintimate, quasi-occupational relationships, which in many ways resembled their husbands' relationships at the office, ethnic distinctions were minimized.[16]

In the evening and weekend social relationships of couples, however, the Jewish husband and wife turned primarily to other Jews. One housewife summarized matters as follows:

My real close friends are Jewish, my after-dark friends in general are Jewish, but my daytime friends are Gentile.

Table 1 shows the sociability choices of thirty respondents who volunteered the names of their friends living in the village.

Although the figures are small, it is apparent that the actives chose their friends among other Jews to a greater extent than the inactives. *However, about half the people who named both Jews and non-Jews pointed out that their best friends were Jewish,* and

---

[15]For a useful definition of clique, see W. Lloyd Warner and Paul Lunt, *The Social Life of a Modern Community* (New Haven: 1941), pp. 110–111.

[16]Ethnic distinctions were almost nonexistent in the all-male activities. Bowling teams, baseball leagues, and poker clubs were organized on a court basis. In this connection one of the women observed:

The boys are real friendly, I imagine they don't think about it [ethnic distinctions] but the women have different feelings. Women have little to do; they talk about it in the afternoons.

The extent to which class factors rather than ethnic factors determined participation in these activities was not studied.

two of the inactives who "saw" mainly non-Jews explained that they were merely visiting with nearby neighbors and implied that the search for friends had not yet begun in earnest. Two of the respondents who named only non-Jews were attempting to avoid all relationships with Jews. Thus, for the purpose of "friendship" as distinguished from "neighboring," and especially for close relationships, the Jewish residents seemed to prefer other Jews. The informal Jewish community existed primarily for this function.

The cliques into which this community was subdivided varied in size from two to six couples. Sociometric factors as well as living-room size set this as an upper limit. A superficial sociometric analysis indicated that these cliques were connected into a network (which existed primarily for communication) by people who belonged to more than one clique, and by a few others who maintained loose memberships with a large number. These latter people, who made few close friends, chose to get to know as many people as possible and derived pride and satisfaction from the acquisition of such relationships. During the time of the study, the informal community came together only once. This was at a village dance. As both Jews and non-Jews later reported, the Jews at this affair congregated in one section of the hall.

The formation of cliques was accelerated by the people with previous acquaintances. However, loose as these contacts may have

TABLE 1

Sociability choices by activity status

"See regularly socially"	Actives		Inactives		All	
	No.	%	No.	%	No.	%
Jews only	4	57	6	26	10	33
Mainly Jews, some non-Jews	1	14	9	39	10	33
Mainly non-Jews, some Jews	1	14	5	22	6	20
Non-Jews only	1	14	3	13	4	14
TOTAL	7	99	23	100	30	100

been (a fleeting introduction at a meeting or party sufficed), such people established friendship relationships much more quickly than strangers who had first to explore each others' social attributes and interests. They generally became "charter members" of a clique which then attracted strangers into its circle. Of the approximately twenty-five cliques and combinations isolated in the sample, twenty had been formed, at least in part, on the basis of previous or mutual acquaintance. In this respect, the Jews differed sharply from other Park Foresters, most of whom knew no one when they arrived in the village.

Cliques were formed primarily on the basis of class, status, age, and ethnic background criteria. One of the largest and most powerful of the cliques was made up predominantly of relatively older, higher-income Park Foresters, many of them previously active in big-city Jewish congregations and groups. Most of the men held supervisory positions in business or industry, or were in the nonacademic professions. A second clique consisted largely of academicians, researchers, scientists, writers, and their wives (many of whom were active on the community newspaper). A third was made up of families who had come to Park Forest from areas of second and third settlement. They were torn between their lower-middle-class and still partially tradition-oriented ways of life, and the upper-middle-class ways of the first clique.

Despite the class-status homogeneity of the cliques, members often harbored the most diverse attitudes toward Jewishness. Respondents reported frequent clique discussions on Jewish topics, and commented:

> I don't start these discussions; it's a beautiful subject to steer away from; there are more fights about religion than anything else.

> There's a couple with whom we're very friendly; we like each other very much. They don't believe the way we do, and if we discuss it, it would just lead to arguments.

Whereas most non-Jewish Park Foresters chose their friends from within their courts, Jews tended to wander outside the court for their social relationships. Sometimes this was due to the absence of other Jews, but when this was not the case, clique membership and associated status- and age-criteria were more important than locational ones. One respondent described her relationship with the other Jewish women in the court:

We've never spent an evening together. Mrs. F. and I are good friends,
we walk together, but she is a bit older. . . . She travels in a different
circle of people . . . with an older, more settled crowd, better off; if
they have children, they're beyond the preschool age. . . .

B. Friendship and Ingroup Behavior. Many factors must be
considered in the explanation of this intraethnic friendship pattern.
A fundamental one is the age-old segregation between Jew and
non-Jew in Western society. Despite political emancipation, this
segregation has been maintained by cultural differences. While
many of these differences are being eliminated by acculturation, not
enough time has elapsed for this change to affect adult social, and
especially peer-group, relationships. As a consequence, current
Jewish–non-Jewish relationships are still based largely on the
historic segregation. Most Jews seem to assume its continued
existence. Also, some feel they would be rejected in non-Jewish
society, while others are not much interested in primary relationships with non-Jews.[17]

Perhaps most often, the long segregation has made association
solely with other Jews almost habitual. The interview material
indicated that most Park Forest Jews grew up in urban Jewish
neighborhoods. Their parental circle, and their own childhood,
adolescent, and adult peer groups, were predominantly Jewish. In
the absence of any strong incentives or socio-economic and
ideological pressures for greater social intimacy with non-Jews,
these patterns of association were rarely questioned.

An important functional basis for the choice of Jewish friends
was contained in the attitude shared by many Park Forest Jews that
"it's easier being with Jews." *Since sociability is primarily a leisure
activity, and in a suburban community one of the major forms of
relaxation and self-expression, the belief that there is likely to be less
tension in social relationships with other Jews becomes all-
important.* A respondent who had both Jewish and non-Jewish
friends pointed out:

> You can give vent to your feelings. If you talk to a Christian and say
> you don't believe in this, you are doing it as a Jew; with Jewish friends
> you can tell 'em point blank what you feel.

---

[17]For a discussion of Jewish–non-Jewish relationships, and of anti-Semitism in Park
Forest, see the writer's "Park Forest: Birth of a Jewish Community," *Commentary*,
April 1951, pp. 337–338.

However ambivalent their feelings toward Judaism, in a group of friends the Jews form a strong ingroup, with well-verbalized attitudes toward the non-Jewish outgroup.[18]

The group cohesion, the ingroup attitude, and the anti-outgroup feeling that often accompanies it, are expressed frequently at the informal parties and gatherings where the friendly atmosphere and the absence of non-Jews creates a suitable environment. These feelings are verbalized through the Jewish joke, which expresses aspects of the Jew's attitude toward himself as well as toward the outgroup, or through direct remarks about the outgroup. At parties which are predominantly Jewish, it is necessary to find out if everyone is Jewish before such attitudes can be expressed overtly. When someone in the gathering who is assumed to be Jewish turns out to be otherwise, the atmosphere becomes very tense and the non-Jewish person may be avoided thereafter.

The manifestation of this ingroup attitude was described by one respondent who was converted to Judaism in his twenties. He told of becoming disturbed over a discussion at an informal party, the subject being how to inculcate Judaism into the children "and keep them away from the *goyim* (non-Jews)." This resident was very active in the Jewish community and feared the consequences of revealing his origin. Nevertheless, he felt the time had come to announce that he had been born and raised a Christian. The declaration broke up the party, and shocked many people. He said afterward:

> From now on, they'll be on their guard with me in their presence. They've lost their liberty of expression, they don't express themselves without restriction now. At a party if anybody says something, everybody looks to see if I've been offended and people are taken into a corner and explained about me.

Despite the fact that this person had adopted the Jewish religion, was raising his children as Jews, and was active in Jewish life, he was no longer a member of the ingroup although he remained a member both of the community and of his clique.

[18]Some of the respondents had rejected Judaism as a culture and religion, had not joined any of the formal organizations of the Park Forest Jewish community, but yet remained in the informal community. However, since the cliques were not formed on ideological bases, those alienated from Jewishness and from participation in the formal community were not excluded.

In summary, ingroup feelings provided a solid base of emotional security for group members of the type which they felt they could not receive from strictly organizational and religious activities. It gave a cohesive function to the informal community.

C. Ethnic Cohesion Through Intellectual Positions and Leisure-Time Preferences. Some of the more highly educated members of the community rejected these ingroup feelings as "chauvinistic"; they pointedly responded that they did not distinguish between Jews and non-Jews in choosing friends. Nevertheless, they remained in the ingroup.[19] They made statements like the following:

> The funny thing is, most of our friends are Jewish even though we say we don't care.

Or they said, on a note of guilt:

> I think we should try to have friends that aren't Jewish. I don't like the fact that all my friends are Jewish.

Such Jews sensed that their failure to associate with non-Jews was not due to ethnic differences, but rather to their own special orientation toward American society and middle-class culture. Several reported such differences with honest misgivings and alarm:

> I think most Jews feel they are a little better than others . . . they won't admit it, they think they're smarter than the rest. I almost guess Jews live by brain more than anyone else.

> We're smarter, that's a prejudice . . . we have better intuition, but I know it's not true.

> The Jews are more conscientious, they get more involved as in the League of Women Voters. . . .

These feelings were summarized in extreme form by one respondent:

> I have a friend who is not Jewish who told me how fortunate I was in being born Jewish. Otherwise I might be one of the sixteen to eighteen

---

[19]Compare the letter, "Jews and the Community," by Deborah Dorfman, *Commentary*, January 1955, p. 85.

out of twenty Gentiles without a social conscience and liberal tendencies. . . . Being Jewish, most of the Jews, nine out of ten, are sympathetic with other problems; they sympathize, have more culture and a better education; strictly from the social and cultural standpoint a man is lucky to be born a Jew.

These attitudes had some basis in reality, for there seemed to be proportionately more Jews than non-Jews in Park Forest who expressed strong feelings of social consciousness, a personal concern in the political, social, and economic problems of the larger society, some interest in intellectual questions, and a tendency toward humanistic agnosticism.[20] Similarly, more Jews seemed to be interested in serious music and the fine arts, or at least the "highbrow" or "upper-middle brow" mass media fare,[21] in the so-called "higher quality" magazines, in the reading of books, and in membership in a Park Forest Cinema Club which showed foreign and art films.[22]

As a result, Jews who sought people sharing this subculture of intellectual interests and leisure preference tended to find them more easily among other Jews. In part this was due to the greater accessibility of other Jews. However, this was not a sufficient factor. Jews came together not only because they were Jews but because they shared the subculture, though it was actually devoid of Jewish

[20]No systematic comparative study was made of this phenomenon; the generalization is based on participant observation of Jewish and non-Jewish leisure activities of various "brow" levels, and the examination of close to 200 living-room bookshelves in the community. Note also the comments by Nathan Glazer, "Social Characteristics of American Jews 1654–1954," in the *American Jewish Year Book* Vol. 56 (New York: 1955), p. 33.

[21]See Russell Lynes' classic essay, "Highbrow, Middlebrow, Lowbrow," in *The Tastemakers* (New York: 1954), Ch. 13.

[22]Compare this with Berelson's description of the typical library user:

From related investigations, the most probable interpretation of the differences in interest and activity involves a general characteristic which might be called cultural alertness. Studies . . . have repeatedly identified a certain group of people who engage in all sorts of cultural activities, in the broad sense, more than does the rest of the community. They read more, and listen more and talk more; they have opinions and feel more strongly about them, they join more organizations and are more active in them, and they know more about what is going on and . . . they are generally more sensitive and responsive to the culture in which they live.

"The Public Library, Book Reading and Political Behavior," *Library Quarterly*, October 1945, pp. 297–298, quoted in his *The Library's Public* (New York: 1949), p. 49.

themes. Furthermore, when Jewish problems were discussed by this group (and they were discussed), these were seen from a generalized world view rather than from the ingroup perspectives described above.[23] Since the reasons for associating with other Jews were not primarily ethnic, ethnic distinctions were not made.[24] The Jewish scientists and academicians in the village formed a number of cliques organized on the basis of this shared culture. Membership, though predominantly Jewish, included non-Jews as well.[25]

The explanation for the fact that Jews seem to be more predominant in this culture than non-Jews is a complex one which can only be suggested here. In part, it stems from the fact that the second generation Jew is frequently a marginal person whose upbringing makes him sensitive to the world around him.[26] Furthermore, this culture is associated with upper- and upper-mid-

[23]These Jews shared many of the characteristics which Robert K. Merton has attributed to the cosmopolitan influentials. While Merton made no distinctions between Jews and non-Jews, the Jew's historic role on the fringe of the social structure has perhaps directed him into cosmopolitan (if not influential) roles. Some of the conflicts within the Park Forest Jewish community (and also in Park Forest generally) can be understood in terms of conflicts between locals and cosmopolitans. Park Forest differed from the community studied by Merton in that a large number of cosmopolitans who were among the first arrivals in Park Forest saw the then unformed community as a place in which they might attempt to implement some of their cosmopolitan ideals. They thus took on many of the characteristics of "locals." In time, these cosmopolitans relinquished their positions to more genuine locals, for their utopian aspirations were rejected by the more conservative residents. See Robert K. Merton, "Patterns of Influence, A Study of Interpersonal Influence and of Communication Behavior in a Local Community," in *Communications Research 1948-1949*, ed. by Paul F. Lazarsfeld and Frank N. Stanton (New York: 1949), pp. 180-219.

[24]Milton Gordon has described these as "passive ethnic intellectuals." See his "Social Class and American Intellectuals," *Bulletin of the American Association of University Professors*, Winter 1954-1955, p. 527.

[25]The role of the non-Jewish intellectual in the Jewish group is discussed in Chandler Brossard's "Plaint of a Gentile Intellectual," *Commentary*, August 1950, pp. 154-156.

[26]Robert Park originally applied the concept to the Jews in his essay "Human Migration and the Marginal Man," *American Journal of Sociology*, May 1928, pp. 881-893. This is reprinted in his *Race and Culture* (Glencoe: 1950), pp. 345-356. See also Everett Hughes, "Social Change and Status Protest; An Essay on the Marginal Man," *Phylon*, First Quarter 1949, pp. 58-65; Everett Stonequist, "The Marginal Character of the Jews," in Isaque Graeber and Steuart H. Britt, *Jews in a Gentile World* (New York: 1942), pp. 296-310; and Thorstein Veblen's perceptive essay, "The Intellectual Pre-Eminence of Jews in Modern Europe," in *Political Science Quarterly*, March 1919, pp. 33-42. David Riesman has elaborated on the theme in "Some Observations Concerning Marginality," reprinted in his *Individualism Reconsidered* (Glencoe: 1954), pp. 153-165.

dle class circles,[27] and in Park Forest was shared by Jews who were either already upper-middle class, or moving in that direction. However, people did not choose this culture for its status implications, for they did not choose it consciously. Rather, they were drawn to it as much by their marginality as their mobility. . . .

[27]See, for example, the analysis of reading and class in the Yankee City class structure in Warner and Lunt, op. cit., Ch. 19, and similar analyses in *Middletown, Middletown in Transition, Elmtown's Youth,* and other community studies.

THE FRIENDSHIP PATTERN
OF THE LAKEVILLE JEW
by MARSHALL SKLARE and
JOSEPH GREENBLUM

INTRODUCTION

*I*F THE INFORMAL COMMUNITY is fundamental to group
*cohesion and survival we need to know why it is that most Jews
make friends with other Jews rather than with Gentiles, at which
point in the life-cycle such friendships emerge, which segment of
the Jewish group is most likely to form such friendships, and what
the prognosis is for the maintenance of the present pattern of clique
interaction.*

*These questions are analyzed by Marshall Sklare and Joseph
Greenblum in their study of the Jews of Lakeville, The Lakeville
study focused on many aspects of Jewish identity but what Sklare
and Greenblum call the phenomenon of "associational Jewishness"
(the same phenomenon which Gans labels the "informal community") turned out to be a central feature of their analysis. Sklare and
Greenblum found that while many aspects of Jewishness had
declined, and that while Jews were reshaping their style of life and in
the process were increasingly coming to resemble non-Jews,
associational Jewishness continued to maintain itself.*

*One of the central shifts in Jewish life has been the sharp
decline in kinship interaction: Lakeville Jews are not involved with
extended kin with anything like the frequency and intensity of their*

parents. * Lakeville Jews are considerably less observant of religious ritual than were their parents, and the culture patterns they follow are much less Jewish than those of their parents. Furthermore, even if the area in which they happen to live has as high a proportion of Jews as was true of the neighborhoods in which they were reared in Lake City or in some other metropolis, Lakeville has no "Jewish" neighborhoods—that is, Jews have not affected a fundamental change in Lakeville's Gentile ambience.

All of these changes make the level of associational Jewishness crucial to the continuance of group cohesion. Sklare and Greenblum find that despite a weakening of kinship interaction, a decline in Jewish observance, and a sharp rise in the level of acculturation to Gentile norms and styles, Lakeville Jews maintain a strong pattern of associational Jewishness. Despite the fact that Lakeville Jews have Gentile acquaintances, on the whole they make their close friendships among Jews. Furthermore, Lakeville Jews do so with virtually the same frequency as was true of their parents. As Lakeville Jews move away from the pattern in which they were reared—that of intense involvement with kin—they appear to substitute in its place an intense involvement with Jewish friends. The pattern is all the more remarkable given the fact that in adolescence a significant percentage of Lakeville Jews had close friends who were Gentile. Furthermore, subsequent to their high-school days Lakeville Jews lived in environments such as college dormitories or Army barracks where Gentiles predominated. In sum, given the erosion of many significant aspects of Jewish identity among Lakeville Jews in comparison with their parents, it seems evident that a high level of associational Jewishness has been crucial for the development of a formal Jewish community in Lakeville and for its continued maintenance.

In a sense the high level of associational Jewishness prevailing in Lakeville is of greater significance than the same pattern in Park Forest. While Park Forest is a minor center of Jewish life whose residents could assimilate without vitally affecting the future of Jews in the metropolitan region, Lakeville is quite another matter. Located in the mainstream of Jewish suburbia, Lakeville is one of several communities on the Heights—a chain of elite suburbs located outside of Lake City, a large Midwestern metropolis. The

---

*To be sure Lakeville Jews are still highly involved if judged by the prevailing standards among their counterparts in the Gentile community.

price of its homes as well as the educational and professional status of its residents make Lakeville beyond the reach of the mass of middle-class Jews of Lake City, but it is also the object of their envy and aspiration.

Lakeville, unlike Park Forest, was a town long before it became a suburb. In the last quarter of the nineteenth century it began to lose its industrial and commercial importance but its favorable location and its combination of beaches and wooded hills ensured its future as an elite summer colony, and later, with the development of rail commuter service and the improvement of cars and roads, a year-round place of residence for upper- and upper-middle-class businessmen of Protestant extraction. Since Lakeville had once been a town, certain sections of the community were still inhabited by working-class people, whose numbers now increased as Lakeville came to function as a service center both for its own prosperous residents and for similarly-situated families in other Heights communities.

It was Lakeville's mixed character that made it the most hospitable of all the Heights communities to the settlement of Jews. Unlike neighboring suburbs which barred Jewish residents, Lakeville was comparatively open, and Lake City's German-Jewish elite proceeded to build or buy large summer homes and small estates in the community. In conformity with the pattern of the time they were excluded from country clubs and other facilities patronized by the Gentile elite, but they soon established a golf club of their own—the Wildacres Country Club—which became the first Jewish institution in the area.

In the course of time Jewish summer residents also became year-round commuters. After World War I the Jewish elite was joined by other prosperous Jewish families and a Reform synagogue—the Isaac Mayer Wise Temple—was established on the Heights. However, German-Jewish dominance could not long endure. While East European Jews were excluded from Wildacres and were given a lukewarm reception at the Wise Temple, in the 1940's East Europeans began to move out to Lakeville in significant numbers. Lakeville soon became a mixed Jewish community, with upper-class German and East European Jews, an upper-middle-class of both German and East European extraction, and a continual inflow of young families who were prosperous but not yet wealthy. These families were attracted by the community's physical surroundings as well as by the excellent reputation of its school system.

While Lakeville continued to be dominated numerically by Protestants the influx of Jews had the effect of making it unattractive to young Gentile upper-class couples who had been raised in Lakeville or in other suburbs on the Heights. Gentiles who did settle in Lakeville tended to be new to the Lake City area and to be less prosperous than many of Lakeville's Jewish residents. In contrast to the Jews some of the Gentile residents were organization men—they worked for giant corporations and in the normal course of events would be transferred to another community.

Despite its loss of social éclat Lakeville has retained its elite reputation among Jews. The blighting of several important Jewish residential districts in Lake City has meant a steady influx of upper- as well as of middle-class Jews. Some of the wealthiest Jews of the Lake City metropolitan area reside in Lakeville, together with a heavy representation of upper-middle-class Jews. There is even a section of Lakeville which—Jewishly speaking—is on the wrong side of the tracks although it also includes some Jews of considerable wealth and/or high education—individuals who consider themselves superior to the "strivers" who live in the more prestigious areas of Lakeville. Most Jewish oldtimers have remained in the area, although a small number of great wealth and high acculturation have left. There has also been something of an exodus of elderly Jews who find it burdensome to maintain an elaborate home; some have bought cooperative apartments in the most exclusive area of Lake City (luxury high-rise apartment buildings have also been put up on the Heights).

Lakeville is a community of well-educated Jews. As many as 34 percent of the men have attended graduate school—they are lawyers, judges, internists, surgeons, psychiatrists, and dentists. And even the 11 percent who have gone no further than high school are almost without exception members of the upper-class—German Jews who inherited considerable wealth but lacked the taste for higher education, or self-made East European millionaires whose families could barely manage to help them through high school. Lakeville Jews tend to be much more diverse in their Jewish identity than Park Forest Jews. Some are religiously observant (at least by Park Forest standards), while others are indifferent, if not hostile. Most of the leaders of Lake City's philanthropic, educational, and pro-Israel organizations who reside in the suburbs live in Lakeville. On the other hand there is also a definable group in Lakeville with no connection to the formal Jewish community. The twin facts of wide diversity in Jewish identity and elite status among Lake City Jews make the study of the friendship patterns of Lakeville residents of considerable significance in gaining an understanding of the foundations of communal sentiment among American Jewry as a whole.

M. S.

LIKE ANY SIMILAR collectivity, the specifically Jewish friend-ship group exists for the satisfaction of personal needs and interests, rather than for advancing any special group purpose. Nevertheless, the Jewish friendship group may constitute an important influence in developing and solidifying in-group sentiment: by providing a mode of Jewish association in a predominantly non-Jewish society, it is capable of confirming Jewish identity and consequently contributing to Jewish survival. The fact that the friendship group lacks many of the characteristics of an organization—a set time for meetings, an annual election of officers, a machinery which both advances the cause espoused by the agency and assures its perpetuation—is one of its greatest strengths; it can confirm and strengthen Jewish identity in a much more personal manner than an organization. Indeed, the overriding personalism of the friendship group is one of the most significant elements in its attractiveness. Thus the Jewish friendship group can work indirectly but nevertheless effectively to preserve group identity. It may constitute as great an influence, or an even greater influence, on the preservation of that identity than instrumentalities whose manifest purpose is the advancement of group survival.

The Character of Friendship Ties

. . . when our respondents were growing up, 42 percent of their parents spent more time socializing with friends than they did with relatives. On the other hand, as many as 88 percent of our respondents spend more time socializing with friends than with relatives. A shift of this magnitude occurring within the space of a single generation carries with it the potentiality of fragmenting patterns of in-group interaction, for a high level of interaction with a family group minimizes the possibility of meaningful involvement with members of the out-group. The shift to a group which is self-selected rather than inherited may portend the end of in-group solidarity.

This potentiality is particularly high given the fact that Jews constitute a rather small segment of the population in the Lake City area. Even if adjustments are made for factors which strongly delimit the choice of friends—race, class, educational level, and the like—Gentiles still outnumber Jews by a substantial ratio. Furthermore, most of our respondents have spent extended periods of time—particularly during the period of their late adolescence and early adulthood—detached from traditional familial and neighborhood relationships. Frequently, Jews constituted a minority in such settings. New patterns of shared experiences in such settings may give rise to cross-ethnic friendships that might endure long after these experiences have passed.

One example of such a setting is the Armed Forces, in which many of our male respondents have served. A better example—because it encompasses a more like-minded population and also includes the great majority of our female respondents—is the college or university.[1] While the schools which our respondents attended had a much higher proportion of Jews than was true for the Armed Forces, in most cases they were in a decided minority on their particular campus. The state universities which our respondents attended drew on the varied segments of the population of the area in which they were situated; the private institutions of higher learning generally chose their students on a variety of criteria which operated to select a so-called "balanced" student body. Furthermore, many respondents who attended colleges distant from their homes were almost completely dependent on the social life that they found in such campus situations. Taking into account, then, the shift from family to friends, as well as the exposure to environments where people of diverse backgrounds associate, what is the character of the friendship ties of the Lakeville Jew?

We find that such ties are predominantly—almost overwhelmingly—with other Jews. Some 42 percent of our respondents report that their circle of close friends[2] is composed exclusively of Jews.

---

[1] More than eight out of ten women and almost nine out of ten men had at least some college education.

[2] While such terms as "friendship circle," "friendship group," or "clique" generally refer to a distinguishable set of persons who are bound together by friendship ties, our data refer only to the aggregate of persons considered as "close friends" by the respondent. These data do not tell us, of course, the extent to which such friendship choices are reciprocated or whether the respondent's collection of close friends constitutes a functioning group.

We employed the following item for the purpose of distinguishing between close friends and others: "When you think of all the persons you are friendly with at this moment, about how many of them are people you consider really close friends?" Respondents were then probed as to the religious identity of their close friends. They

Another 49 percent say that their circle is composed of a majority of Jews. Only 7 percent report that Gentiles constitute a majority in their circle of close friends or that their circle is equally divided between Jews and Gentiles.[3] The Jewish character of the friendship circle of the Lakeville resident is clearly revealed when we look more closely at the 49 percent who say that their circle includes a minority of one or more Gentiles. We discover that approximately one-half of these respondents report that all or most of their Gentile friends are married to Jews.[4]

Perhaps the most remarkable aspect of this pattern of pervasive Jewish friendship ties is that in spite of being more acculturated than their parents and moving in a more mixed environment, our respondents make their close friendships with Jews virtually as often as did their parents. Thus, while 87 percent of the parents had most or all of their close friendships with Jews, the same holds true for 89 percent of our respondents (Table 1).[5] To realize the significance of this overlap between the generations, it is only necessary to recall the amount of disjunction in the area of religious behavior. And the continuity in friendship patterns between the generations is all the more remarkable, given such strong differences in the level of involvement with the family group.

Since friendship ties with Gentiles who are married to Jews are frequent enough to be of significance and will presumably bulk even larger in the future, a detailed analysis of them is required. The phenomenon suggests that a certain proportion of intermarried couples have found a place inside the Jewish group—that they have not assimilated into the non-Jewish world in a meaningful sense.

were also asked a series of questions regarding the type of relationship they had with the person whom they considered their closest Jewish friend as well as with the person whom they considered their closest Gentile friend.

[3] Some 2 percent did not know the religious identity of their close friends or did not report any close friends.

[4] Four in ten of these respondents say that all such Gentile friends are married to Jews. Another one in ten say that most such Gentile friends are married to Jews. If these cases, which constitute about one-fourth of all respondents, are added to those whose friendship circle is exclusively Jewish, we find that as many as two-thirds of Lakeville Jews make all their close friendships either with Jews or with Gentiles who are all or mostly married to Jews.

[5] The comparison with parents required that "most" friendships be defined as over 60 percent, rather than over 50 percent, and that "about half" be defined as 41 to 60 percent (Table 1). Therefore, the 89 percent figure is slightly less than the comparable total of the relevant percentages in the previous paragraph.

TABLE 1

Proportion of close friends Jewish among respondents and among their parents

Percent with following proportion of Jews among their close friends[b]	Parents[a]		Respondents	
All (100%)	30	⎫	42	⎫
Almost all (91-99%)	31	⎬ 87	10	⎬ 89
Most (61-90%)	26	⎭	37	⎭
About half (41-60%)	5		6	
Some (1-40%)	2		—	
None (0%)	2		—	
N.A., no close friend	1		2	

[a]During the period when respondent was growing up.
[b]The proportions stated in percentages apply to respondents. These have been calculated from data supplied by respondents in answer to separate questions on the total number of their close friends and the total number of their close Gentile friends. These percentages are grouped in intervals which most approximate the descriptive categories used in the question applicable to the parents.

Furthermore, we discover the startling fact that some of the spouses identified by our respondents as Gentile have actually been converted to Judaism. Of course, their categorization as Gentile indicates incomplete assimilation, this time into the Jewish group. Such categorization is also an aspect of the remarkable influence of ethnicity on our respondents—an influence which persists in spite of the prevalence of an extremely high level of acculturation.

While our respondents may not categorize all converts as Jewish, there is no question that they feel that such individuals, as well as non-Jews married to Jews, are quite different from the average Gentile. The distinction mentioned most frequently is that these intermarried Gentiles have adopted a Jewish identity and a Jewish way of life. In some instances, the attitudes and behavior of Gentile friends who are married to Jews are felt to be so typically Jewish that respondents are prompted to remark—as does a pharmacist's wife who is active in ORT—that their Gentile friend is "more Jewish than anyone else is." And according to a prosperous salesman whose only ethnic affiliation is with a local Jewish country club,

> This Gentile woman considers herself a Jew. We will kid her that: "We know you're not a Jew, so you don't have to bother acting like one." Yet in fact she does act like a Jew as much as the rest of us do.

A young and highly observant insurance broker, a member of the Schechter Synagogue who is quite active in B'nai B'rith, says of still another Gentile woman, "She has a warmth and attachment to things Jewish and follows its customs." And a lawyer's wife who is active only in non-sectarian groups and does not follow Jewish rituals in her own home details some of these customs and "things Jewish": "After her marriage this Italian girl started keeping a kosher house. She encourages her husband to go to temple and sends her kids to Jewish Sunday School."

Our respondents also emphasize that not only have such Gentiles become acculturated to Jewish ways, but they have become detached from Gentile clique groups. The insurance broker quoted above says of the Gentile woman whom he includes in his circle of close friends, "She primarily associates with Jews, and most of her friends are Jewish." An affluent salesman who does not feel entirely comfortable in the company of Gentiles nevertheless experiences no anxiety with his two close Gentile friends who are married to Jews: "[It is because] they move in a Jewish circle and are outside the pale of circle of their own kind." A further indication of the movement of such Gentile friends into Jewish clique relationships is the fact that when the most intimate of such friends is entertained, in seven out of ten cases most or all of the other persons present are Jewish.[6]

With respect to those whose friendship circle is predominantly Jewish but whose Gentile friend is not married to a fellow Jew, several types of relationships with such Gentiles are possible. For example, such a friend could be a detached Gentile who feels alienated from his peers and who as a consequence is willing, even eager, to join a Jewish clique group. Or the friend could be a Gentile

---

[6]When the most intimate Gentile friend who is not married to a Jew is entertained, in only a third of the cases are most or all of the other persons likely to be Jewish. Such information was gathered only in respect to the most intimate Gentile friend, the person who is referred to in the relevant questionnaire item as "the one with whom you are most friendly."

who is well integrated with his traditional group and as a consequence may be eager to have the Jewish friend join *his* Gentile clique group. In the first instance, the character of the Jew's friendship ties would not be shifted, while in the second instance they could be strongly affected. There is also a third possibility, however: that the Gentile to whom the Jew is close is neither well attached to nor strongly alienated from his traditional group and that in any case this aspect is not a significant element in the relationship. Rather, for both Jew and Gentile their friendship is a very special relationship—a relationship which does not disturb their respective friendship ties. Tending to see each other alone, neither Jew nor Gentile becomes incorporated in the other's homogeneous friendship group.

While further analysis is needed to discover the character and dynamics of such relationships, what is presently apparent is that most Lakeville Jews who have Gentile friends who are not married to Jews do not seem to be in the process of shifting their friendship circle. Instead of utilizing their contacts in the Gentile world to build a new pattern of friendship ties, they appear to pursue their interfaith relationship apart from their Jewish network. In summary, there tends to be no disruption of the predominantly Jewish friendship circle, even among those who have a Gentile friend who is not married to a Jew. . . .

The Shift to a Homogeneous Friendship Circle

While the pattern of friendship ties of our respondents is so strongly Jewish as to duplicate the one prevalent in the parental generation, it was not always so. During adolescence, our respondents had many more Gentile friends than they do today. To be sure, in the majority of cases teenage friendship ties were predominantly with Jews. However, almost four in ten of our respondents report that in adolescence only half, or less than half, of their circle of close friends consisted of Jews (Table 2). In actuality, the increased homogeneity of friendship ties is greater than these figures indicate, for, as we have noted, some of the present Gentile friends of our respondents have ties to Jewish life through marriage to a Jew.

While close friendships with Gentiles are much more exceptional today than they were in the past, adolescent patterns still retain their influence. Thus the greater the proportion of Jewish friends in adolescence, the greater the proportion today (Table 3). However, the trend is toward a homogeneously Jewish pattern for

TABLE 2

Proportion of close friends Jewish during adolescence and today

*Percent with following proportion of Jews among their close friends**	*Adolescence*		*Today*	
All (100%)	14		42	
Almost all (91-99%)	20	63	10	89
Most (61-90%)	29		37	
About half (41-60%)	18		6	
Some (1-40%)	15		3	
None (0%)	4		—	
N.A., no close friend	—		2	

*The proportions stated in percentages apply to respondents as adults and were calculated and grouped as described in Table 1. The matched descriptive categories were used in the question referring to their teen-age period.

all, even for those who had only some or no Jewish friends in adolescence, with those who had more Jewish friends to begin with having the highest proportion of all-Jewish friendships.

It appears that our respondents acquired and stabilized a relatively homogeneous pattern of close Jewish friendships while emerging from adolescence to adulthood, or at least before achieving parenthood. We find that throughout the parental phase of the life cycle, their sociability pattern remains stable: there is little difference between our younger and older respondents with respect to the ethnic composition of their friendship circles. Thus the friendship pattern acquired in the earliest phase of the parental life cycle remains constant through the mature years.

The trend to homogeneity in friendship behavior is comparable in some aspects to that which obtains in respect to religious behavior. Religious behavior is also at minimal levels during the adolescent and early adulthood years—transitional phases of the life cycle when the individual is in the process of loosening his bonds to

TABLE 3
Proportion of close friends Jewish today by proportion of
close friends Jewish during adolescence

Percent with following proportion of Jews among their close friends	Proportion of close teen-age freinds Jewish			
	All or almost all	*Most*	*About half*	*Some or none*
All	55	47	31	27
Most: Gentiles married to Jews	23	29	24	20
Most: Gentiles not married to Jews	21	23	37	31
Half or less	1	1	8	22
Number	(149)	(123)	(78)	(81)

his parental home, but has yet to establish his own household. Nevertheless, the trend to homogeneity of association occurs earlier than the maximization of the religious aspect of Jewishness. Thus the intensification of Jewish association may constitute a kind of preview of the reintegration of the young Jew into a variety of other aspects of his Jewish identity.

What accounts for the increase in homogeneous friendship ties before the onset of parenthood as well as for their maintenance through the ensuing years? This question is deserving of extended research; we are only able to supply preliminary answers along one or two of many relevant dimensions.

If we focus on those whose present circle is composed exclusively of Jews, we find that in many cases they once had Gentile friends. These Gentile friendships were often formed in a mixed setting into which they had been thrust for a relatively limited period. When the situation terminated, their relationships with Gentiles ended. We cannot be certain why these friendships never deepened; all that we can say is that the relationship was not firm enough to withstand separation. A young woman who is very active in non-sectarian organizations recalls that when she attended a small women's college in the East, she had friends who were "Christians and Negroes. I went to their parties . . . and I also dated Gentile boys." While she describes her college chums as "old friends" and retains membership in her alumnae association, she has not seen her college friends in some years; she considers none of them to be her close friends today. A professional man recalls the peculiar quality of the relationships with his Gentile friends in the Army and later in dental school. In each instance, the friendships were terminated after his connection with the respective institution came to an end: "At the time, it's like being on a desert island. . . . But when it's over, you just break up." A young matron who had a mixed group of close friends as a teenager reports that she also had mostly Gentile friends when she accompanied her husband during his military service. She sums up the situational nature of these relationships: "Of course, we broke up as we went from post to post. In making friends, I guess you take the path of least resistance, and these people were there."

Another relevant factor is that relationships with Gentiles did not receive the institutional, communal, or familial reinforcement that occurred with respect to relationships with Jews. Such reinforcement was apparently a factor which helped such relationships to endure long after the situation in which they developed had passed. Jewish friendships that have persisted since childhood and adolescence are especially instructive in this connection. We find cases where respondents trace their present homogeneous Jewish associations to the Jewish neighborhood of their childhood or even to their parents. For example, an executive in the entertainment industry who is somewhat active in Wise Temple soon lost contact with the close Gentile friends he made in adolescence. However, with respect to the Jewish friends he made during the same period, with some of whom he currently associates, he recalls, "Most of us came out of the same neighborhood; our communities were Jewish, and our families were heavily Jewish and traditional." Although as a teenager she had some Gentile boyfriends, a young fourth-generation wife of a buyer—a woman who is active only in non-sectarian groups—says much the same thing about her Jewish circle: "Most of us grew up together. Our parents knew each other, and we are all Jewish." A sales executive who also has little attachment to Jewish religious or organizational life points out how his Jewish friendships were formed in the close world of the neighborhood in which he was raised in Lake City:

> Most of this circle [of friends] is an old-time relationship dating back to public school and Hebrew school where our activities kept us close together. Why should we bring newcomers into the group? One of the important things about it is that it's such an old group.

The tendency to homogeneity becomes particularly discernible in late adolescence. Some of the all-Jewish cliques formed during this period have no institutional connections, while others have as their locus formal organizations such as high-school or college fraternities and sororities. The wife of a prosperous salesman, who is equally active in Jewish and non-sectarian groups, traces her Jewish friendship circle to her sociability pattern as a teenager: "It all goes back to the local high-school sorority that was all Jewish." A minimally observant woman with a similar pattern of organizational involvement had many close Gentile friends as a teenager, including those of the opposite sex, but she lost these contacts after joining a Jewish sorority in college. She says of her Jewish clique, "We are a closed group from college. Most of us are sorority sisters or fraternity brothers. We've been together for years." The young owner of an automobile parts business, a minimally observant second-generation man who is not affiliated with any Jewish organization, relates how his clique group became increasingly Jewish as he grew from adolescence to adulthood:

> I was active in a high-school fraternity—all Jewish. Until high school, I had more non-Jewish friends than Jewish ones. Though I held on to the non-Jewish friends, they decreased in proportion; we weren't in the same fraternity and we did little or no double dating. . . . This pattern increased as I got older, dated, and got married.

. . . while some of our respondents account for their homogeneous friendship pattern by highlighting factors that operated at an ·earlier period of their life, in the majority of cases it appears that present ties were formed during adulthood. Queried as to how they developed an all-Jewish circle, about half of our respondents feel that it results from the fact that Jews are more available and accessible to them. "There's more opportunity to make friends with Jews. We're with them a thousand times more: the Jews are around," explains a publisher who is somewhat active in Wise Temple and in a Jewish community-relations group. As a teenager, most of his close associations were with Gentiles, including a serious relationship with a Gentile girl. Such ties were dissolved, however, when he joined a Jewish fraternity at college. Another man who gives much the same type of response is a minimally observant advertising agency executive whose Jewish organizational affiliations are limited to a Jewish city club and to the Einhorn Temple. He grew up in a prestigious suburb on the Heights among predominantly Gentile friends, but he joined a Jewish fraternity at college. Today his close friends are all Jewish. He says, "I'm thrown into contact with [Jews] in many places and in many ways. It's easier. I don't feel the need to cultivate people. Proximity is the thing."

While many respondents allude to these Jewish associational opportunities in a general way, some specify the settings in which they occur: chiefly the neighborhood in which they live, the Jewish organization with which they are affiliated, and the synagogue in which they are active. "We all came into the neighborhood at around the same time about five years ago and have known each other as long," remarks a young second-generation mother of two children, who was reared in a small town on the West Coast where her close friendships were mainly with Gentiles. She has few ties to Jewish religious and organizational life. A physician's wife, a relative newcomer to the community, states that she "became friendly [with an all-Jewish friendship group] through organizations." She is a member of several Jewish women's groups, including the Sisterhood of Wise Temple. And a highly observant middle-aged owner of a men's clothing business states that he developed his friendships as a result of his activity in a Conservative synagogue in Lake City:

> I haven't had the occasion to mix with any [Gentiles] socially. I've never been in mixed community affairs. I developed a social life through the [X] Synagogue—the one place where I had causes plus friends and social activities.

While it is true that such associational opportunities are part of the situation in which individual Jews find themselves, in another fundamental sense they can be the outcome of individual preferences—the result of an attraction to fellow Jews and a desire for personal contact with them. It is apparent that because of this attraction many of our respondents place themselves in situations where it is Jews, rather than Gentiles, who are more available and accessible to them.

Jewish accessibility could, of course, be the result of nothing more than Gentile inaccessibility. This is not the picture which our respondents present, however. While one in ten of those who have a homogeneous Jewish friendship circle accounts for the pattern on the basis of exclusion by Gentiles, some four in ten say that it is a result of a preference for Jews. Some of these respondents consider such a preference to be self-evident, as does a moderately observant accountant who had some close Gentile friends as a teenager, but feels that "it's normal that Jewish people befriend other Jewish people." A college-educated and religiously unobservant wife of an executive in the construction industry, who also associated with Gentiles in adolescence, presents a more thoughtful formulation: "Today . . . Jews and Gentiles have much in common. But somehow a social barrier exists. Jews don't go seeking people different from themselves."

Other respondents emphasize that Jews are predisposed to social contact and intimate association with other Jews because of a common religio-ethnic heritage and a pervasive group identity. "It's because Jews go with Jews and Gentiles go with Gentiles. My background is so Jewish and my life is so Jewish that I'm happier surrounded by Jews," explains a young salesman's wife who is now active in Lilienthal Temple, although as an adolescent she had some close friends who were Gentile. "It's the identity, the background, the religion. It would be hard for a Gentile to be comfortable without these common bonds," elaborates an affluent lawyer and business executive who came to the United States from Russia when he was a youngster and is quite active in a variety of Jewish organizations. "There's a common notion of 'fate,' so we don't seek out non-Jews," is the concise reason given by a mother of three school-age children, who finds time for activity in several Jewish welfare groups despite her intense involvement in her local PTA group.

Some account for their preferences for Jewish social contacts by emphasizing life styles and manners which they believe are more commonly encountered among Jews. "There are cultural differences; we have common backgrounds, interests, and standards as Jews," is the general and somewhat cautious comment made by an affluent businessman, a member of Einhorn Temple, who did not receive a Jewish upbringing by his parents and claims to be entirely uninterested in religious matters. He considers none of the many Gentiles with whom he mixes socially to be a close friend. A more specific explanation is offered by a prosperous accountant highly active in a Jewish youth welfare group: "It's just our way of life—our parental background, our closer family and home ties, and our social tastes." He is no longer friendly with the Gentiles whom he met in college and in the Navy. And a young businessman who observes almost none of the traditional religious practices to which he was exposed in childhood mentions similar reasons to account for the fact that he lost contact with the non-Jewish friends he had before marriage:

> They went different paths because of differences in economics, education, and a different mode of living. The others bought homes earlier, but homeowning is only a recent thing for Jews.

Seeking out other Jews with whom one shares common attitudes and a way of life results in the strengthening of feelings of ethnic solidarity. Such solidarity, in turn, contributes to the formation of homogeneously Jewish cliques. "Jews seem to stick together. There's more security that way. It makes for a feeling of belonging," notes the wife of a prosperous businessman, whose intimate friends since childhood have been Jewish and is quite active in the PTA of the Wise Temple. A young salesman with a business degree who had some Gentile friends at college refers to "that family feeling" among Jews; his religious observance is minimal, but he is about to join the Schechter Synagogue. A fairly observant housewife who was close with several Gentile girls with whom she worked before marriage and is now active in the PTA and the Scouts summarizes the emotional basis of in-group solidarity in the following terms:

> My association with non-Jews has been good. But there's a warmth amongst Jews that couldn't be in a Gentile. A Gentile can't be as warm; he would have a different philosophy.

While this respondent and many others whose close friends are all Jewish account for their pattern by stressing the "positive" fact of attraction to Jews rather than such "negative" reasons as alienation, suspicion, or uncomfortableness with Gentiles, the possibility exists that their explanations contain an element of rationalization. In response to a direct query, we find that less than one in ten of those who have homogeneous Jewish friendship ties reports that either he or his friends would have an unfavorable reaction if a Gentile were to join the circle. On the other hand, we find respondents who, in trying to account for the fact that all their close friends are Jewish, are frank to admit that the presence of a Gentile would create strain. Thus a middle-aged housewife affiliated with a variety of Jewish groups, who recalls that half of her close friends during adolescence were Gentile, states:

> We have Gentile friends, but we'd never think of mixing them. It wouldn't work. We're very small drinkers. We like to have a nice dinner and play cards. We'd feel self-conscious, especially if they'd lose.

The presence of Gentiles would mean that conversation would have to be guarded. A woman who is highly active in the Schechter Synagogue as well as in ORT and is married to an attorney says of her Jewish clique, "They wouldn't be able to speak as freely about politics and religion if non-Jews were present." She is familiar with the ways of both groups, for as an adolescent she had close friends among Gentiles, and she still has Gentile acquaintances. . . .

We see, then, that the Lakeville Jew who has an all-Jewish circle explains his pattern of friendship ties in a variety of ways. What seems to charaterize these respondents, and others as well, is that they feel more comfortable with Jews than with Gentiles—a feeling which they experience in spite of their high level of acculturation and their affirmation of the value of Jewish–Gentile integration. The sense of feeling comfortable with another person is, of course, a precondition for intimacy; it is difficult to establish a close and abiding relationship without such rapport.[7]

The varied responses of these Lakeville Jews who have homogeneous Jewish friendship ties not only are characterized by

---

[7]See Vol. II of the Lakeville Studies for a discussion of the relationship between comfortableness, social anxiety, and integration-mindedness (Benjamin B. Ringer, *The Edge of Friendliness* [New York: Basic Books, 1967], pp. 138–154). It should be remembered that this material refers to any social contact with Gentiles, rather than to close friendships.

feelings of being at ease with Jews but also appear to involve a deep sense of kinship with other Jews. The composition of clique groups aside, if we take our respondents as a whole and compare their most friendly Gentile relationship with their most intimate Jewish one, we find that 76 percent say that they are closer to their best Jewish friend and only 9 percent say they are closer to their best Gentile friend. Some 14 percent claim that they are as close to their best Gentile friend as they are to their best Jewish friend. Indeed, while our respondents generally refer to their best Gentile friend as a "friend," they frequently speak of their best Jewish friend as being like a "sister" or "brother." An active alumna of a leading Eastern women's college, who is also involved in several Jewish and non-sectarian groups, characterizes her relationship with her most intimate Gentile friend as "friendly" and finds the Gentile friend as stimulating as her closest Jewish friend: "They're both intellectually stimulating. Both are very good for my ego; I feel like a whole person when I'm with them." But she states that she has a "deeper relationship" with the Jewish friend. Her insightful characterization of the relationship with the Jewish friend is as follows: "It's like being [in] a family without the tension."

The Alienated Jew and the Homogeneous Friendship Circle

It is clear from the personal information which has been supplied about the respondents whom we have been quoting that some are apathetic to traditional Jewish concerns and affirmations. Since they are nevertheless involved in homogeneous friendship groups, it is apparent that the kind of group solidarity demonstrated by their "associational Jewishness" is not necessarily related to what may be described as more "positive" expressions of Jewish identity. Such solidarity can and does exist apart from any commitment to Jewish religious or organizational life and even apart from any affirmation of the concept of Jewish peoplehood as manifested in pro-Israel sentiment. While "associational Jewishness" may go hand in hand with strong Jewish attachments . . . associationalism is highly prevalent even among alienated Jews.

Thus we find that those who are uninvolved in religion and synagogue life have almost as Jewish a friendship circle as those who possess religious commitments. As many as six in ten of the unobservant, compared with about seven in ten of the most observant, claim that all their close friends are Jewish or are

Gentiles married to Jews.[8] Barely more than one in ten of the unobservant claim that their circle of close friends is either ethnically balanced or predominantly Gentile. Furthermore, almost six in ten of those who lack an affiliation with a synagogue, although they have already reached that stage in the life cycle where the great majority join, report a homogeneously Jewish friendship circle.[9] This is not much different from the seven in ten among active synagogue members who have such a circle. Furthermore, only one in eight of the unaffiliated claim that Gentiles constitute half or more of their circle of close friends. . . .

It is only in respect to involvement in Jewish organizations that the situation is different. While 73 percent of those who are active in such organizations, whether they be less or more active, have homogeneous ties, only 56 percent of the unaffiliated possess such friendship ties.[10] Furthermore, a larger percentage of the un-affiliated—although no more than 14 percent—in contrast to the actives have a circle of close friends which is not predominantly Jewish or all-Jewish.[11] These findings highlight the function of the Jewish organization as a framework for social relationships; they suggest that the organization reinforces the tendency toward homogeneous friendship ties.

This pattern is accentuated among women. . . . Among men, there is only a slight difference between the unaffiliated and the actives with respect to homogeneous friendship ties: while the unaffiliated less often report exclusively Jewish friends, more often they have a minority of Gentile friends who are married to Jews. Among women, however, homogeneous Jewish cliques are found among as many as 75 percent of the actives, but only among 45

[8]The "most observant" group here are those who observe five or more home rituals. The finding remains the same even if we compare the unobservant with those who observe seven or more rituals. A strikingly similar finding emerges when those who never attend synagogue services are compared with those who attend quite regularly.

[9]In this section, a homogeneously Jewish circle of friends refers to a collection of close friends which is either all Jewish or includes a minority of Gentiles who are all or mostly married to Jews.

[10]The "unaffiliated" are persons who do not hold membership in either a general Jewish organization or a synagogue-related organization. Some, however, may belong to a synagogue.

[11]Only among a small segment who are consistently alienated from Jewish organizations is there a sizable proportion who participate in ethnically balanced or mostly Gentile cliques. Among those who are not affiliated with a Jewish organization or with a synagogue (despite the fact that their children have reached or passed the peak age for religious education), as many as 31 percent claim such friendship circles, while only 54 percent are part of homogeneously Jewish cliques.

percent of the unaffiliated. It should be noted that the divergence between the sexes occurs chiefly among the unaffiliated; men and women who are active or nominal members resemble each other fairly closely with respect to their pattern of friendship ties. Thus while most unaffiliated men retain a homogeneously Jewish circle of friends, most unaffiliated women have one or more Gentile intimates who are married to Gentiles. It should be remembered, however, that an overwhelming majority of those of both sexes who are alienated from Jewish organizational life have their friendship ties primarily or exclusively with their fellow Jews.

One of the remarkable aspects of the friendship pattern of the Lakeville Jew is that it remains so Jewish despite the pervasiveness of integrationist sentiment. Almost without exception, Lakeville Jews tend in the direction of integration, but an all-Jewish or predominantly Jewish friendship circle is even characteristic of more than nine in ten of those who score extremely high on our measure of integration-mindedness (Table 4).[12] Such respondents do differ from others, however, in respect to the ties which their minority of close Gentile friends have with Jewish life: as many as half of the integrationists, in contrast to only two or three in ten among others, have Gentile friends who are not married to Jews.

Why does the Jew who is highly alienated or strongly integrationist-minded tend to make so many of his close friendships within the Jewish group? Some would answer this question in a suprasocial framework, viewing associational Jewishness as a kind of Jewish affirmation and stressing that it is characteristic of the "wondering Jew." According to this perspective, associational Jewishness expresses a desire to preserve a link with Jewish tradition with its basis in inspiration in God; the individual hesitates to sever his one remaining link with the group lest he foreclose all possibility of encounter with God.

The conventional sociological approach shies away from such a perspective. Instead, it highlights the function which Jewish

[12]The measure of "integration-mindedness" is a composite index summarizing several dimensions of Jewish attitudes and behavior vis-à-vis the Gentile community. The index has five component items: 1) attitudes with respect to whether it is essential for a Jew to promote civic improvement in the community and to gain the respect of Christian neighbors; 2) feelings and behavior with respect to having a Christmas tree in one's home; 3) the ratio of Gentiles to Jews desired in the neighborhood; 4) involvement in non-sectarian organizations; and 5) participation in leisure-time activities that are characteristic of non-Jews in Lakeville.

TABLE 4

Proportion of close friends Jewish by level of integration-mindedness

Percent with following proportion of Jews among their close friends	Integration-mindedness score						
	High 8–9	7	6	5	4	3	Low 1–2
All	33	44	33	46	44	50	50
Most: Gentiles married to Jews	10	25	22	26	31	21	25
Most: Gentiles not married to Jews	50	23	33	23	21	24	20
Half or less	7	8	12	5	4	5	5
Number	(30)	(52)	(80)	(86)	(77)	(60)	(40)

friendship ties serve for the alienated. Accordingly, such ties may be seen as a buttress compensating for weak attachment to Jewish life. Thus the Jewish friendship circle might be viewed in the framework of the contribution it makes to Jewish survival.

The function of such ties aside, we are still left with the problem of explaining the persistence of a relatively homogeneous friendship pattern among strongly alienated and highly integrationist-minded Jews. Thoroughgoing research on this type of individual is necessary if we are to arrive at a definitive explanation for his puzzling behavior. However, our knowledge of the psychological orientation of the Lakeville Jew vis-à-vis the Gentile places us in a position to suggest an approach to such an explanation.

Earlier . . . we described one aspect of the orientation of those whose friendship circle is composed entirely of Jews: their feeling of greater comfort with Jews than with Gentiles. Comfortableness may arise from a variety of sources. One is the belief that the style of life and values of the Jewish group are closer to one's own. Another is the fear that Gentiles hold negative attitudes about Jews. However, almost half of our respondents—among them many alienated and highly integrationist-minded individuals—claim that they are as comfortable with Gentiles as with Jews. But while they are sufficiently comfortable in more casual social contacts with members of the out-group to maintain a relationship, we suggest that their level of comfort drops sharply in more intimate social relationships. Thus we reason that their lack of ease in truly intimate relationships with Gentiles explains their peculiar pattern. While we have no direct evidence to support this conclusion, the indirect evidence is strong indeed. We find that the majority of Lakeville Jews see themselves as ambassadors to the Gentile world.[13] We also find that our alienated and integration-minded respondents are even somewhat more committed to this role than other Jews.

To specify this idea further, if the Lakeville ambassador performs his duties well, his lot, and that of his children as well as of Jews generally, will improve. If not, the relationship between the Jewish "world" and the Gentile "world" will deteriorate. It is apparent that the assumption of an ambassadorial role places a strain on the individual, for in his contacts with Gentiles he must constantly manipulate himself so that he may succeed in manipulating them. Such manipulative conduct is acceptable in a variety of secondary relationships, but inappropriate in the context of intimacy. Even strongly alienated and highly integrationist-minded respondents, then, find it difficult to establish and maintain the type of close contact with Gentiles which their ideological proclivities suggest. Like all people, they are most at ease in a psychological climate characterized by candor and trust, and it is precisely such a climate which favors the growth of intimate association. Thus, given their orientation to intergroup relations, they find it easier to develop such a climate with fellow Jews than with Gentiles.

Because the Lakeville Jew sees himself as a representative of the Jewish group, he feels that he shares responsibility for its public image. As a consequence, he tends to become extremely self-conscious in the presence of Gentiles, which is another way of saying that he becomes highly aware of being Jewish. Such a fixed attitude of group consciousness and responsibility encompasses the range of manners by which the Lakeville Jew attempts to alter and

[13]Note, for example, our respondents' image of the "good Jew," particularly their feeling about gaining the respect of Christian neighbors.

redeem the Gentile stereotype. "I have to be careful with my manners, my dress, my expressions," says a middle-aged lawyer. He is active only in non-sectarian organizations, but he claims no close Gentile friends. "I'm always on my guard as to whether I laugh too loud or my voice is too shrill," says a minimally observant woman whose close friends are all Jewish. "I feel that I have to count my words," says a chemist's wife who observes hardly any religious practices, but has a predominantly Jewish friendship circle.

One aspect of inhibition and self-consciousness is the fear of the Jew that in the encounter with the Gentile he may be regarded stereotypically and not appreciated as an individual; in the eyes of the Gentile, he will be a Jew first and an individual a poor second. Thus an unobservant businessman who believes it "fitting and proper" to have a Christmas tree each year, but confines his organizational life to a Jewish city and country club and his clique participation to Jewish friends, observes about Gentiles, "You have to be on guard and careful about subjects you discuss. I don't have the freedom of personality I have with Jews." This crucial aspect of psychological climate is described even more insightfully by a thoughtful young housewife who is a newcomer to Lakeville. A college graduate and the wife of a prosperous businessman, she is completely alienated from Jewish organizational and religious life and highly integration-minded. One of those respondents constituting the 7 percent who do not have a predominantly or all-Jewish friendship circle, she has such a tenuous in-group connection that even the Jewish friend to whom she feels closest is intermarried. But with all that, this woman confesses, "I'm less comfortable with non-Jews because you feel that they think of you as a Jew. Jews don't really think of you as a Jew."

While the persistence of Jewish friendship ties among the alienated may contribute to Jewish survival, the pattern may not continue indefinitely. The ambassadorial function and the self-consciousness of the Jew in intergroup relationships is, among other things, related to the prevalence of prejudice and discrimination in the immediate past. Thus the involvement of the alienated in a Jewish clique structure not only grows out of the psychological situation which we have delineated but is also related to the fact that such cliques were reinforced by anti-Jewish sentiment and behavior on the campus, in public life, in business and professional affairs, and in club life.

Some of this prejudice and discrimination was experienced personally, more was experienced through significant others, and even more was experienced vicariously through exposure to various channels of communication.

Since it is an unresolved question whether the old pattern of prejudice and discrimination will occur in the future (it has already declined sharply), the Jewish clique may represent a residual form of Jewishness, a "holding operation" preliminary to the assimilation of the individual—or of his offspring—into the majority community.[14] It may be assumed that even with the trend to a more open society, those who are less integration-minded—and who are closely attached to religion, the synagogue, Israel, and the network of Jewish organizations—will retain friendship ties with their Jewish peers. But at the very minimum, the trend to openness suggests that the remarkable discrepancy between the real and the ideal betrayed by the alienated will become ever more apparent. Those who are most firmly committed to the ideal of a mixed society and whose ties to Jewish life are extremely attenuated will be confronted more directly with the choice of transforming their associational life in accordance with their value system or of continuing to journey along the Jewish "Indian path" which they presently tread.

Even if they demur to affect any substantial change in clique behavior, it is questionable whether their offspring will tolerate—or find it necessary to abide—the same disparity between the real and the ideal. Presumably, the children of most alienated Jews will be no more firmly involved in traditional aspects of Jewishness, and it may also be assumed that they will be at least as integrationist-minded as their parents. The open society having been achieved, members of the younger generation may feel free to shed the ambassadorial role and with it their Jewish self-consciousness. At that juncture, close friendships with Gentiles might burgeon, many more Jews finding it psychologically possible to take their place as members of otherwise all-Gentile or predominantly Gentile cliques. Significant numbers might enter such cliques as the spouses of Gentiles, thus reversing the situation of the present Lakeville Jew whose friendship circle, as we have noticed, sometimes includes the Gentile spouse of a Jew.

[14]Regarding the relevance of religious and ethnic identity in assimilating successful members of minority groups to elite social life, see E. Digby Baltzell, *The Protestant Establishment* (New York: Random House, 1964). See also Richard L. Rubenstein, "The Protestant Establishment and the Jews," *Judaism*, XIV (Spring 1965), 131–145.

DECISION-MAKING IN
THE AMERICAN JEWISH COMMUNITY
by DANIEL J. ELAZAR

INTRODUCTION

*E*UROPEAN OBSERVERS of the American scene have long
commented upon the unique role of the voluntary association in
American society—how citizens join together for the most diverse
purposes, and how they seek to meet needs which in other societies
are considered to be the responsibility of official bodies. Although it
has not received similar attention, a related development of equal
significance is the existence of "sub-communities" based on
common descent and on feelings of a common religious, ethnic, or
racial identity. While the legal system of the nation takes note of the
existence of sub-communities it does not grant them a corporate
status. Thus it comes about that the sub-community has no
coercive powers. Nevertheless, despite its unofficial character and
status, the sub-community has proved to be an enduring
phenomenon in American society.

The sub-community—especially its communal structure—has
not been the object of concentrated scholarly attention, perhaps
because of the pervasiveness of the melting-pot ideology. For many
decades it was assumed that the sub-communities were either
European holdovers or defensive structures erected as a response to
prejudice and discrimination. In either case it was thought that the
sub-community would wither away with the passing of the

immigrant generation and as barriers to fuller participation in American life were removed. As we know from the present concern with pluralism, these assumptions were grounded more in wishful thinking than in social reality.

Among American sub-communal structures the Jewish one is extremely elaborate, composed of a network of voluntary associations appealing to diverse constituencies. Part of the reason for the high development of Jewish communal structure is that it predates the American experience, though to be sure the Jewish organizations of the present are not duplicates of those of the past. The elaboration of a specifically Jewish network of social institutions is characteristic in Jewish history not only when Jews were excluded from the majority institutions but when they regarded such institutions as unacceptable on religious or cultural grounds. The fact that historically Jews had developed an institutional network of their own undoubtedly prepared them for the American experience of voluntarism and pluralism. Thus in addition to the factors of prejudice and discrimination, historical experience—and the feelings of Jews about their group identity—were elements which helped in the creation of an elaborate sub-communal structure in the United States.

The structure of the American Jewish sub-community is not a single entity; rather, it is a network of organizations. One becomes part of the formal community by affiliation with an organization— by joining a synagogue, contributing to a Jewish philanthropy, or participating in a Jewish voluntary association. However, those who do not participate in the formal community—or do so irregularly—are not outside of the community in the usual sense. Since the community rests on the kinship principle that Jews are Jews by virtue of birth and common descent, those who fail to participate in the formal community are not outcasts but rather "inactives" who can assume their place in the formal community at any time, at their own desire. Participation in the informal community is crucial, for it can easily be transformed into affiliation with the formal community.

Histories of local Jewish communities often include considerable detail about their voluntary associations, but there has been a dearth of knowledge concerning the basic structural features of the American Jewish community. Daniel Elazar, a political scientist interested in Jewish communal structure both in the United States and abroad, has analyzed the associations which make up the

Jewish community on the local and national levels. He has clarified the objectives of such associations, the roles played by various types of people, and the trends responsible for shifts in the status and direction of given voluntary associations.

It should be pointed out that while scholarly literature is sparse there has been considerable writing about the Jewish community by those active in it, as well as by those who would like to assume leadership. Much of this writing is critical in tone—for decades Jewish periodicals have published articles decrying the state of Jewish communal life and suggesting plans for its improvement. One chronic complaint centers on what is assumed to be the uncoordinated nature of Jewish communal structure, its tendency toward duplication. Another is that the Jewish community is undemocratic, that it is controlled by plutocrats who are said to rule by virtue of their fiscal potency.

Elazar's approach is different. He sees two large factors which have determined the shape of the community. The first is the growth of the federations, which he regards as a healthy development, accurately expressing the will, not of plutocrats, but of American Jewry as a whole. Federation leadership is made up, in his view, by a "trusteeship of doers" intensely committed to Jewishness. On the other hand, Elazar sees the main structural weakness of the Jewish community in the growth and development of the second large factor, the American synagogue. In his view the synagogue is localistic—it looks inward to its own constituency rather than outward toward the larger Jewish world. In an age of large and strong congregations, such localism becomes a significant factor in preventing the American Jewish community from effectively discharging the responsibilities thrust upon it by virtue of its numbers, wealth, and talent. Elazar's central proposals for the reform of American Jewish community structure center on the demand that congregational leaders come to consider their institutions as public rather than private institutions, and that the two key structures of the American Jewish community—the federations and the synagogues—be brought together in closer articulation.

M. S.

ಕೆಲ

ENVIRONMENTAL AND CULTURAL FACTORS

The Character of American Jewry

AMERICAN JEWRY forms the largest Jewish community in Jewish history and, indeed, is the largest aggregation of Jews ever located under a single government, with the possible exception of Czarist Russia on the eve of the mass migration. Its major local communities are larger than all but a handful of countrywide communities in the past.

The spread of Jews from East Coast to West and from far North to Deep South, despite the unevenness of the distribution, has given the Jewish community major concentrations of population at the farthest reaches of the country. Moreover, the density of Jewish population in the Northeast has been declining, at least since the end of World War II. California now has more Jews than any country in the world other than the United States itself, the Soviet Union, and Israel. Los Angeles, the second largest local Jewish community in the world, has as many Jews as all of France, which is ranked as the country with the fourth largest Jewish population. Simple geography serves to reinforce all other tendencies to disperse decision-making in the American Jewish community as in American society as a whole. It has proved difficult for any "central office" to control countrywide operations in the United States regardless of who or what is involved.

The five largest Jewish communities[1] in the United States contain close to 60 percent of the total Jewish population and the top sixteen communities[2] (all those containing 50,000 Jews or more) contain over 75 percent of the total. At the same time Jews are

[1] New York City, Los Angeles, Nassau County (N.Y.), Philadelphia, and Chicago.

[2] The aforementioned communities, plus Boston, Miami, Bergen County (N.J.), Essex County (N.J.), Westchester County (N.Y.), Baltimore, Washington, Cleveland, Detroit, San Francisco, and St. Louis.

distributed in over 800 communities ranging in size from just under two million in New York City down to a handful of families in the more remote towns and cities. Those 800 are organized into 225 local federations or their equivalent, of which only 27 have more than 20,000 Jews and only ten over 100,000. (Greater New York City, while really a region rather than a local community, is organized under a single limited-purpose federation, which includes the five boroughs plus Nassau, Suffolk, and Westchester counties.)

Local community size contributes directly to the organization of decision-making on the American Jewish scene. New York is not only in a size-class by itself but maintains its own—highly fragmented—organizational patterns while holding itself substantially aloof from all other communities. The federation system, which has become the norm throughout the rest of the country, is limited in New York City. There the major Jewish institutions and organizations, beginning with the United Jewish Appeal, conduct their own fund-raising campaigns and operate their own local programs outside of any overall planning or coordinating framework, often from their own national offices.

The major Jewish communities outside of New York are all structured so that the federations play a major, if not dominant, role in communal fund-raising and decision-making. All the significant ones among them are members of the Large City Budgeting Conference (LCBC) of the Council of Jewish Federations and Welfare Funds. While the LCBC itself is essentially an information-gathering body, its members together represent the single most powerful influence on communal fund-raising on the American Jewish scene and the leaders of its constituent federations are the major source of American Jewry's leadership across the spectrum of functional spheres. The communications network that is generated out of the interaction of those communal leaders may well be the heart of the countrywide Jewish communal decision-making system. Significantly, New York is not a member of the LCBC.

Communities too small or too weak to be members of the LCBC stand on the peripheries of the countrywide decision-making processes, no matter how well-organized and active they may be locally. Occasionally notable individuals from such communities do attain national prominence, but that is rare. Only in the last few years have the stronger of these communities begun to devise ways to enhance their national visibility in the manner of the LCBC.

Local decision-making has not been systematically studied in more than a handful of these organized communities. What we do know, however, is that there are variations among cities simply as a result of the differences in scale that change the magnitude of the communications problems. The ways in which patterns of communication are organized vary in communities of different sizes, not to speak of other cultural, historical, social, and economic factors. Size, for example, does much to determine who knows whom and how comprehensive or exclusive are friendship and acquaintanceship nets. These, in turn, determine who speaks to whom on communal matters.

There is also considerable evidence that the percentage of those affiliated with and active in communal life stands in inverse ratio to community size. Since there is always a certain minimum of positions to be filled, regardless of community size, smaller communities will, *ipso facto*, involve a greater proportion of their population than larger ones, not to speak of the greater social pressures for participation often manifested in smaller communities where people know who is and who is not participating.

The size factor works in other ways as well. To some extent, the number and spread of Jewish institutions is dependent upon the size of the community. A community of 10,000 Jews is not likely to have the range of institutions of a community of 100,000. Consequently it will not have the complexity and diversity of decision-making centers or channels nor the problems of separated leadership that are likely to prevail in a very large community where people can be decision-makers in major arenas without knowing or working with their counterparts in others.

The impact of size of place also has a dynamic quality. From the early eighteenth century, when Jews first arrived in the American colonies, until the mid-nineteenth century, Jews lived in a number of small communities of approximately the same size, none of which were able to support more than the most rudimentary congregational institutions. All this changed with the subsequent mass immigration of Jews from Eastern Europe, who settled overwhelmingly in the major urban centers. At the same time, the Jews in the hinterland communities continued to migrate to the metropolises because that is where the opportunities lay.

Since the end of World War II there has been another shift in the scale of Jewish settlement that is only now beginning to be fully reflected in the structure of local decision-making. Increasingly, Jews have been moving out of the big cities into suburbs which, while nominally parts of the same metropolitan area, in fact have fully separate governmental structures and substantially distinctive socio-economic characteristics, both of which they guard jealously. This migration is leading the Jews back once again to small communities where, unless they are involved with a great metropolitan federation, they are able to maintain only the minimum in the way of local Jewish institutions. Scattered widely among many small towns, they are tied together at most by a common fund-raising system for overseas needs. From the available data it would seem that 60 percent of American Jews today live in separate suburban communities or in metropolitan communities of less than 20,000 Jews.

New York, with its 31 percent of the total American Jewish population, is the *de facto* capital of the American Jewish community. Moreover, because New York is really a region rather than a single community, and is additionally surrounded by perhaps another 15 percent of American Jewry living within the orbit of Manhattan, the Jews of New York tend to believe that all Jewish life in the United States is concentrated in their city and environs. At the same time, what would be considered very large Jewish communities in their own right are well-nigh buried within the metropolitan area and maintain only those institutions that meet local needs.

The other very large Jewish communities are regional centers of Jewish life as well as major communities in their own right. Los Angeles is clearly the center of Jewish life west of the Rocky Mountains and the second city of American Jewry institutionally as well as in numbers, with branches of all the countrywide Jewish organizations and institutions located within its limits. Because of its distance from the East Coast it has a greater degree of independence from "New York" than any other regional center in the United States. Chicago is the capital of the Jewries of mid-America in much the same way, although in its case relative proximity to New York has prevented it from developing the same range of national institutions or local autonomy as Los Angeles. Once the great western anchor of American Jewish life, its overall position has been lost to Los Angeles along with so much of its Jewish population.

Philadelphia and Boston, although now almost within commuting distance of New York, remain equally important secondary national centers for American Jewry because of historical circumstance. Philadelphia's old, established Jewish community has long played a national role that at one time even rivaled that of the Empire City. It continues to maintain some institutions of national significance. Perhaps more important, as the first major Jewish community outside of the New York metropolitan area, its leaders have easy access to the national offices of Jewish organizations where they frequently represent the point of view of the rest of American Jewry (insofar as there is any common one) vis-à-vis that of "New York."

Boston Jewry, though a far younger Jewish community, has capitalized on its city's position as the Athens of America to create major Jewish academic institutions of national scope and to become the home of whatever Jewish academic brain trust exists in the United States.

Only in the South is the largest city not the regional center. Greater Miami, still a very new community, the product of the post-World War II migration southward and heavily weighted with retirees, has had no significant national impact as a community (as distinct from a location for the conduct of the winter business of American Jewry as a whole). The capital of Jewish life in the South is Atlanta, the region's general capital. Despite its small Jewish population of 16,500, it possesses the panoply of regional offices associated with much larger Jewish communities in other parts of the country. The pattern of Jewish activity in Atlanta is markedly different from that of any of the other regional centers because of the intimacy and proximity within which the regional offices and local institutions must live.

Jewish communities of medium size (here defined as 20,000 to 100,000 population) all play tertiary roles (as communities) in the hierarchy of American Jewish communities. They are generally able to provide the full range of local institutions and organizations found in any American community, although often in rudimentary form, but serve no particular national functions except as a result of historical accident. Among them, national importance is determined by factors other than size. The subsidiary regional centers, all located between the Mississippi and the Pacific, represent nodes of Jewish population. These centers serve wide areas, sparsely settled by Jews, and thus occupy a more important role in the overall scheme than either their size or, in most cases, the quality of Jewish life within them would otherwise warrant. . . .

Associational Framework

Still another environmental factor that is vital in shaping decision-making in the American Jewish community is the extraordinary variety of forms of Jewish association possible. Any organized interconnections within the maze of institutions and organizations of American Jewry have had to be forged in the face of many obstacles, including the lack of any inherent legitimacy attaching to any coordinating institutions, the penchant for individualism inherent in the American Jewish community derived from both American and Jewish sources, and the difficulties of enforcing any kind of coordinating effort within the context of American society which treats all Jewish activities as private, voluntary ones.

Thus the pattern of relationships within the matrix of American Jewish life must be a dynamic one. There is rarely a fixed division of authority and influence within American Jewry but, rather, one that varies from time to time and usually from issue to issue with different elements of the matrix taking on different "loads" at different times and in relation to different issues. Moreover, since the community is a voluntary one, persuasion rather than compulsion, influence rather than power, are the tools available for making decisions and implementing policies. All this works to strengthen the character of the community as a communications network since the character, quality, and relevance of what is communicated and the way in which it is communicated frequently determine the extent of the authority and influence of the parties to the communication.

The World Jewish Environment

Decision-making in the American Jewish community is further shaped by the impact of the world Jewish environment. This is most immediately evident in the role which Israel plays in American Jewish life. Israel has become the major unifying symbol in the community, in effect replacing traditional religious values as the binding ties linking Jews of varying persuasions and interests. Fund-raising for Israel has not only come to dominate all communal activity, but has been the stimulus for the general increase in funds raised for across-the-board Jewish purposes in the United States since the end of World War II. . . .

Indeed, Israel has become, *de facto*, the authority-giving element in Jewish life today in the way that the Torah was in the pre-modern world. The ascendancy of Israel appears to have ended a period of well over a century in which there was no clear-cut source of authority in Jewish life at all. The fact that Israel has become the new source of authority is not without problems of its own, but nevertheless this new situation provides a means for uniting a people with very diverse beliefs.

The authoritative role of Israel functions in two ways. First, Israel is itself authoritative. Those who wish to dissent from any particular Israeli policy or demand must be very circumspect when they do so. Those Jews who reject Israel's claims upon them are more or less written off by the Jewish community. They are certainly excluded from any significant decision-making role in the community. Second, leaders who can claim to speak in the name of Israel or on behalf of Israel gain a degree of authority that places them in very advantageous positions when it comes to other areas of communal decision-making. Even the synagogues, which are expected to be bastions of support for the Torah as the primary source of authority in the community, have come increasingly to rely upon Israel and Israel-centered activities to legitimize their own positions.

INSTITUTIONS AND ORGANIZATIONS

Institutional Roles

The organizations and institutions within which the decisions of the American Jewish community are made group themselves into four categories based on the kinds of roles they play within the community as a whole. They are: *1) government-like institutions; 2) localistic institutions and organizations; 3) general-purpose, mass-based organizations;* and *4) special-interest institutions and organizations.*

Government-like institutions are those that play roles and provide services on a countrywide, local, or (where they exist) regional basis which, under other conditions, would be played, provided, or controlled, predominantly or exclusively, by governmental authorities. The Jewish federations and their constituent agencies are the most clear-cut examples of government-like institutions in the American Jewish community. Locally, the federations themselves have become something like roof organizations. They are constantly expanding their role in community planning, coordination, and financing. While they are not always comprehensive in the sense of embracing all organizations in the community directly, in most cases, they do maintain some formal connections with all significant ones performing government-like services which are either their constituent agencies, beneficiaries, or affiliates. Thus the bureaus of Jewish education, the Jewish community centers, Jewish community-relations councils, the community-wide welfare institutions, and the like, all of which perform functions which would otherwise be performed by government, are generally linked to the federation.

On the countrywide plane the analogous organizations are not as easily identifiable. The Council of Jewish Federations and Welfare Funds, the Synagogue Council of America, the National Jewish Welfare Board, the National Community Relations Advisory Council, and the American Association for Jewish Education at least make claims in that direction. In fact, however, the Jewish communities of the United States are no more than leagued together; they are not really federated on a countrywide basis in a sufficiently comprehensive manner to have generated comprehensive institutions that are comparable to those on the local scene.

Localistic institutions and organizations, primarily synagogues now that the *landsmanshaften* have virtually disappeared, are those whose first and foremost task is to meet the primary personal and interpersonal needs of individual Jews and Jewish families. By their very nature, synagogues are geared to be relatively intimate associations of compatible people. While the growth of the large American synagogue has led to a confusion of functions (which has contributed to the present difficulties of the synagogue as an institution), it still retains primary responsibility for meeting those needs.

General-purpose, mass-based organizations are those that function to a) articulate community values, attitudes and policies;

b) provide the energy and motive force for crystallizing the communal censensus that grows out of those values, attitudes, and policies; and c) maintain institutionalized channels of communication between the community leaders and "actives" ("cosmopolitans") and the broad base of the affiliated Jewish population ("locals") to deal with the problems and tasks facing the community in light of the consensus. These mass-based organizations provide the political structural parallel to the government-like ("cosmopolitan") and localistic institutions, bridging the gaps between them, providing a motivating force to keep them running, and also functioning to determine their respective roles in the community as a whole. In a sense these organizations function as the equivalent of political parties in a full-fledged political system (in some Jewish communities in other countries they are indeed political parties) to aggregate and mobilize interests in the community.

In the American Jewish community, these organizations are to be found in three varieties. First, there are the quasi-elite organizations which have begun to reach out to develop a larger membership base but in such a way that only people with special interests or backgrounds are likely to find their place within them. The American Jewish Committee is perhaps the best example of such an organization and in many respects is the most important of these organizations. Beginning as a small select group, the Committee has developed a larger membership base as it has become more democratized, but its base still includes a relatively select group of people (even if they are more self-selected than they used to be). At the same time, it is a very powerful group since its major principle of inclusion seems to be influential or potentially influential leaders. It, more than any other organization, has a membership strategically placed in the ranks of the leadership of the government-like institutions and the major synagogues.

The American Jewish Congress is another organization of this type. Its history has followed exactly the reverse pattern of that of the Committee. It was founded with the intention of becoming a mass-based organization but has instead become the preserve of a self-selected group interested in a particular kind of civil-libertarian approach to Jewish communal affairs.

The second variety consists of mass-based organizations that remain widely open to all types of Jews but have not been able to develop the mass base they desire. The Zionist organizations in the United States (with the exception of Hadassah) are the principal examples of this group. They have not only fallen short of their basic aim but have also failed to develop an elite cadre that would place them in the first group.

Finally, there are the truly mass-based organizations of which two stand out: B'nai B'rith and Hadassah. These organizations, whose members number in the hundreds of thousands each, reach out to the lowest common denominator in the American Jewish community on one hand, while at the same time speaking for the most sophisticated and complex communal needs.

Special-interest institutions and organizations are what their name indicates. They reflect the multitude of special interests in the community, either by maintaining programs of their own or functioning to mobilize concern and support for the various programs conducted by the government-like institutions in the community by exerting pressure for their expansion, modification, or improvement. The number of special-interest organizations is well-nigh myriad and they cover the gamut of interests which any Jewish community could possibly possess. They perform the important functions of concentrating on specific issues and trying to raise those issues before the larger Jewish public on the one hand, and before the leaders and decision-makers of the Jewish community on the other. No one of these special-interest groups is likely to have a great deal of influence in the community as a whole, though some will be of decisive importance in those specific areas of interest in which they are involved. A whole host can wield some influence on communal decision-making, depending on the character of the interest they represent, the degree of sympathy it invokes as an interest among the decision-makers in the community, and the caliber of leadership attached to the special-interest group.

It should be noted that the description presented here is idealized to the extent that particular organizations and institutions have functions that overlap the categories. For historical reasons that relate to the evolution of the American Jewish community from discrete institutions, functions were assumed in unsystematic ways. Thus B'nai B'rith is responsible for welfare institutions and the Hillel Foundations because, at the time they were founded, no more appropriate organization was available to initiate, finance, or operate them. Today they are slowly being transferred to more appropriate communal bodies.

The patterns of decision-making in the American Jewish community must be traced in light of the foregoing four-fold division which contributes so much to the shaping of the community's structural matrix. However it does not do so alone but only in combination with the territorial and non-territorial patterns of organization that inform the community.

Territorial and Non-Territorial Organization

The American Jewish community, like every Jewish community before it, is organized on a mixture of territorial and non-territorial bases. The territorial organizations are invariably the most comprehensive ones, charged with providing overall direction for the community as a whole or some otherwise fragmented segment of it, while the ideological, functional, and interest organizations generally touch the more personal aspects of Jewish life. One consequence of this has been that Jewish reformers in the United States seeking to improve the organization of the American Jewish community have constantly emphasized the need to strengthen territorial organization as against other kinds, while partisans of particular interests in the Jewish community have emphasized non-territorial forms of organization as the most appropriate forms in a voluntary community.

At the same time, because of the nature of the Jewish community, the territorial organizations rarely have fixed boundaries except by convention. Furthermore because ideological commitment in American Jewish life tends to be very weak, the ideological groupings have little internal strength of their own except insofar as they serve the interests of their members by taking on specific functional roles.

Ideologically based organizations have had more success on a countrywide basis where the absence of comprehensive territorial institutions has been marked until recently. Such countrywide organizations as developed prior to the 1930's became committed to specific ideological trends whether they were founded that way or not. However the impact of American life constantly serves to emphasize the territorial over the non-territorial elements wherever given half a chance and to reduce ideologically based organizations to functional specialists responsible for specific tasks. A major result of this has been to limit the powers of the countrywide organizations and to make the primary locus of decision-making for the American Jewish community local.

With the exception of a few institutions of higher education (and, once upon a time, a few specialized hospitals which are now non-sectarian), all Jewish religious, social, welfare, and educational institutions are local both in name and in fact. Some are casually confederated on a supra-local basis but most are not, and those claiming national status with no local base soon find themselves without a constituency. Indeed, the major institutions of the American Jewish community—the federations and the synagogues —developed their countrywide bodies after their local institutions had become well-established. Among the organizations which have been built out of a national headquarters, the only ones that have succeeded are those which have been able to develop meaningful local operations under local leadership.

The three great synagogue movements which are conventionally viewed as the primary custodians of Jewish affiliation in the United States since the end of World War II are excellent cases in point. All are essentially confederations of highly independent local congregations linked by relatively vague persuasional ties and a need for certain technical services such as professional placement, the organization of intercongregational youth programs, and the development of educational material. The confederations function to provide the requisite emotional reinforcement of those ties and the desired services for their member units. They have almost no direct influence on crucial congregational policies and behavior except insofar as the congregations themselves choose to look to them as guides. Short of expulsion from the movement, they have no devices which they can use to exercise any authority they might claim even in those cases where the congregation was originally established by the parent movement (which is not the usual pattern but does occur). Once a congregation is established it becomes as independent as all the rest.

The other great countrywide institutions of American Jewry are similarly organized. The Council of Jewish Federations and Welfare Funds is an equally loose confederation of hundreds of local Jewish federations which have emerged in the past four decades as the most powerful institutional forces in Jewish life. The role of the CJFWF is definitely tributary to that of its constituents who do not hesitate to give it direction. As in the case of the synagogue movements, the power of the national organization flows from its ability to provide services to the local affiliates, generate ideas for them, and manage the flow of professionals.

So, too, the National Jewish Welfare Board is the countrywide service agency of the clearly autonomous local community centers, the American Association for Jewish Education is the service agency of the local bureaus of Jewish education plus the countrywide organizations that claim to have a major interest in Jewish education, and the National Jewish Community Relations Advisory Council is the service agency of the local Jewish community-relations councils and the umbrella agency for the countrywide community-relations agencies and organizations. Exercise of these service functions brings with it a certain power which the professionals who staff the national agencies have developed in various ways, but it is a limited power, usually more visible at conferences than in the daily affairs of the local bodies. In recent years, the countrywide federations have been supplemented by even more loosely knit confederations of national bodies such as the Synagogue Council of America, a confederation of the major synagogue movements and, most recently, the Presidents' Conference, a loose league of the presidents of major Jewish organizations organized for "foreign-relations" purposes.

Whether the federative arrangements involved are of near-universal scope and have broad-based, multipurpose goals or are limited to single functions with rarely more than consultative or accreditation power, it is the consistent use of such arrangements that enables American Jewry to achieve any kind of structured communal unity at all. What emerges is not a single pyramidal structure, nor even one in which the "bottom" rules the "top" as in the case of Jewish communities with representative boards in other parts of the world. There is no "bottom" and no "top" except on a functional basis for specific purposes (if then). Thus it is the absence of hierarchy which is the first element to recognize in examining the decision-making process.

The Role of Functional Groupings

The institutions of the American Jewish community can properly be grouped into five spheres based primarily on function: 1) religious-congregational; 2) educational-cultural; 3) community relations; 4) communal-welfare; and 5) Israel–overseas. Decision-making in the community is organized accordingly.

Religious-Congregational Sphere: Even the synagogues can be seen as a functional grouping since American Jews' ideological commitment to a particular synagogue movement is very weak except at the extremes of Orthodoxy and Reform. In essence, they provide the immediately personal and interpersonal ritual- *cum*-social functions demanded by the community and do so primarily through individual congregations. They have an essential monopoly on those functions locally while the synagogue confederations, rabbinical associations, seminaries, and *yeshivot* maintain a parallel monopoly over the community's theological and ritual concerns countrywide.

Nationally, the three great synagogue confederations dominate the religious-congregational sphere. Over the years, each has expanded its scope and intensified its efforts on the American Jewish scene. In their common quest for an expanded role in American Jewish life, they leagued themselves into the Synagogue Council of America which, for a few years during the height of the "religious revival" of the 1950's, tried to capture the leading role as spokesman for American Jewry and which remains the Jewish religious counterpart to the national church bodies.

Each of the synagogue confederations has a seminary of its own which, because of its academic character, projects itself on the American Jewish scene in a quasi-independent way. Even with the growth of Judaic studies programs in academic institutions, these seminaries remain the backbone of organized Jewish scholarship in the United States. Their alumni lead the congregations of American Jewry and, through their rabbinical associations, link seminaries and the confederations. In addition, there are a growing number of yeshivot in New York and many of the other major Jewish communities that reflect the great growth and proliferation of the new ultra-Orthodox elements in the community. They preserve and extend traditional Jewish scholarship on a scale never before experienced in American Jewish history.

Since World War II, there has been an increasing involvement of power centers outside of the United States in the religious-congregational spheres. The Israeli rabbinate is a growing force on the American scene by virtue of its role in deciding the personal status of individual Jews. In an age of jet travel between Israel and the Diaspora, such decisions have ramifications which reverberate throughout the Jewish world. In this connection, the Knesset is also acquiring influence in the religious-congregational sphere and, indeed, is the first "secular" body anywhere to do so, simply because of its central role in defining the question of "Who is a Jew"? in a setting where separation of "church" and state does not prevail.

The controlling power of the synagogue in the religious-congregational sphere means that a very large share of Jewish activity—involving perhaps half of the total revenue and expenditure of American Jewry—is managed outside of any communal decision-making system. American synagogues have traditionally considered themselves (and have been considered) to be private institutions, like clubs or fraternal lodges, accountable to no one but their own members for the decisions they make. This reflects their status in American law and has simply been carried over unquestioningly into Jewish communal affairs.

Educational-Cultural Sphere: The synagogues also play a major role in educational matters, having acquired that role after a contest of some forty years' duration during which the non-synagogue schools were defeated in the struggle over who was to assume responsibility for elementary and secondary Jewish education. Today the great majority of Jewish Sunday and afternoon schools at the elementary level and a large number of those at the secondary level are housed in and controlled by synagogues. Synagogue control is so complete where it exists that we do not even have decent estimates of how much is spent on Jewish education since they do not make their budgets public.

Management of elementary and secondary Jewish education carried on outside of the synagogues is vested in three categories of institutions. There are a few surviving "secular" schools, usually Yiddishist in orientation, managed by what are secularistic equivalents of congregations, that is to say, groups of families that carry out the same functions together that conventional congregations do, eliminating their overtly "religious" character. There are also some remnants of older non-congregational school systems, generally confined to serving the older neighborhoods. Finally, there are a handful of communal school systems, the largest of which are in Detroit, Minneapolis, and St. Paul, that function as the comprehensive educational arms of the Jewish community and dominate Jewish educational activity locally.

Aside from the latter, the only movement in Jewish elementary and secondary education outside of the synagogue that is growing is the day-school movement. Day schools, whether formally attached to some national "ideology" or not, tend to develop with communal support by default, though, because few communities have any well-defined way to deal with them, they are rarely tied to the central institutions of communal governance but remain nominally "private" schools that receive subsidization to some degree.

Central agencies of Jewish education in the larger Jewish communities do have some formal responsibility for developing curricula, setting professional standards and the like for the synagogue schools, and in some cases have acquired responsibility for directly managing secondary afternoon schools and colleges of Jewish studies. Occasionally, they even maintain "experimental schools" which usually provide such intensive supplementary Jewish education as exists in a given community. While their operational role is limited, they usually represent the only links between the synagogue educational programs and the central institutions of the local Jewish community.

Higher Jewish education is also divided into three segments, the colleges of Jewish studies, the seminaries and yeshivot, and the emerging Jewish-studies programs in general colleges and universities. The latter, whatever their name and format, are beginning to acquire a certain amount of importance within the overall scheme of Jewish education locally and are even beginning to affect the character and content of the traditional institutions of Jewish education. It would be wrong, however, to overestimate the importance of such programs—as against the seminaries and yeshivot—as sources of Jewish scholars or to view the colleges of Jewish studies as influences on local communal life.

If anything, Jewish educational activities are even more localized than the religious-congregational activities. The American Associaton for Jewish Education, the umbrella body for the central agencies and itself a confederation of local and national groups, is limited in the technical services it renders to studies of local needs and problems. The Orthodox day schools are somewhat more clearly linked to their countrywide bodies, particularly in the case of the *Torah Umesorah* schools. The Conservative day schools are linked formally to umbrella bodies which exist in name only and many such schools have no extra-community ties at all. The most important ties linking any Jewish schools are the professional associations linking Jewish educators. Increasingly, the Council of Jewish Federations and Welfare Funds is becoming involved in the educational and cultural sphere in an attempt to develop some countrywide input, but its role must still be considered peripheral at this point.

Worldwide bodies involved in the educational-cultural arena

include the Jewish Agency, which represents the Zionist point of view and Israel's interests and which works most extensively in the realm of adult education and in linking Jewish students with Israel. The Memorial Foundation for Jewish Culture, an international body with headquarters in New York, has become the most potent source of support for Jewish scholarly and cultural activities since its resources exceed those of any other institution on the scene.

Among the scholarly associations and research institutes, the YIVO Institute for Jewish Research and the American Jewish Historical Society are probably the most potent independent bodies actually engaged in projects and their activities are distinctly limited, if only because of monetary limitations. In general, these bodies are small, independent, and outside the mainstream of American Jewish life.

Except for the Jewish Publication Society and the small seminary and movement publication programs, publication is a private enterprise in American Jewish life. The JPS is the most significant publishing force on the American Jewish scene and the only one seriously linked with other institutions in the Jewish community. Only recently has the publication of Jewish books for profit expanded much beyond the textbook business.

What is important about the cultural activities of American Jewry is how peripheral they and those engaged in them are in the context of American Jewish public affairs. Since the cultural institutions do not even have the advantage of feeling needed by the decision-makers, as is true of Jewish education, and rarely have the prestige of Jewish academics in general universities, they are at a great disadvantage in a community that is not much oriented to scholarly or cultural concerns.

Community-Relations Sphere: Most major Jewish communities have a Jewish Community Relations Council which considers itself the central agency for handling community-relations problems. In addition, communities often have local offices or chapters of the American Jewish Committee, the Anti-Defamation League of B'nai B'rith, the American Jewish Congress, the Jewish War Veterans, and the Jewish Labor Committee that also engage in community-relations work, whether in cooperation with the Jewish Community Relations Council or independently. Indeed, the classic pictures of fragmentation in American Jewish life are usually drawn in regard to the community-relations field, and it was in that field that the most publicized countrywide efforts have been made to bring order out of chaos, beginning with the development of the National Community Relations Advisory Council in the 1940's. The latter is a confederation of independent agencies combining both local agencies and countrywide bodies in one common league. Of course it is limited in its role precisely because it is a confederation of what are powerful and independent bodies, each in its own right.

In the educational-cultural and religious-congregational spheres the situation is so structured that the many separate organizations engage in relatively little direct competition. In the community-relations sphere, on the other hand, the smaller number of separate organizations overlap one another because they deal with the same problem—often the same explicit issues. The effects of that competition are potentially great because they are directed toward "foreign affairs" matters, that is to say, matters that reach outside of the Jewish community and directly affect its relations with the larger world. Consequently, a considerable amount of self-policing and specialization has developed within the sphere in the past two decades.

The American Jewish Committee, the Anti-Defamation League, and the American Jewish Congress, conventionally recognized as the "big three" in community-relations work, are the most centralized of all countrywide Jewish organizations. Their role in American Jewish life was once enhanced by their centralized structures at a time when the local Jewish communities were barely organized and the individual institutions within them were far too parochial to reach out to the general community. Today, their situation is reversed. Only those that have managed to decentralize are thriving. The American Jewish Congress, perhaps the most centralized among them, has not properly taken root on the local plane and as a result is suffering tremendously as a countrywide organization. The Anti-Defamation League and the American Jewish Committee began earlier to achieve substantial decentralization with greater success, though in both cases the national office still plays a very great role even in local activities.

More recently, the synagogue movements have attempted to enter the community-relations field as part of their drive toward dominance in American Jewish life. Bodies such as the Synagogue Council, the Commission on Social Action of Reform Judaism, and the National Commission on Law and Public Affairs of the Orthodox movement reflect this. However, they still play a relatively limited role on the overall scene.

Increased American Jewish involvement in the concerns of the

Jewish people as a whole has sharpened the need for a communal voice that speaks as one, at least in the foreign-relations field. This, in turn, has led to the establishment of the Presidents' Conference, consisting of presidents of the major countrywide Jewish organizations who meet together to make policy decisions that the more institutionalized consultative bodies cannot. Since the Presidents' Conference must make all decisions unanimously, it is limited in the degree in which it can play an active role in its prescribed area, but it has brought some order at least in matters strictly pertaining to foreign relations.

Since support and assistance for Israel have become key items on the community-relations agenda, the Israel government has become a prime mover in this sphere. Despite occasional protests to the contrary, official American Jewish action on behalf of Israel in the public-relations field is conducted in close consultation with and in response to the initiatives of the Israel authorities. In certain respects, Israel's role in the community-relations sphere may well be greater than its role in any other sphere of decision-making in the American Jewish community.

Communal-Welfare Sphere: The communal-welfare sphere has undergone the greatest change in the past generation. As late as the 1950's it was simply another functional grouping among several, considerably better organized internally; the various Jewish social service and welfare agencies plus the Jewish community centers had federated with one another a generation or more earlier. While the local federations had already expanded to include fund-raising for overseas needs, their pretensions to centrality in the community were limited by the fact, that on the domestic scene, they remained primarily concerned with the traditional social service functions.

By the end of the 1950's, the federations had been transformed into the major fund-raising bodies in the community and stood on the threshold of a whole new world of responsibilities. The latter transformation came as federations realized that proper execution of their role as allocating agencies necessitated greater involvement in community planning of a scope that at least touched all the activities defined as being communitywide in character in any given locality. At the same time, the old "German" leadership in the communal-welfare field was being broadened to include "Eastern European" elements as well, selected from the same income, occupational, and observance levels.

The decade of the 1960's saw the federations undertake

community planning on a large scale, beyond that required for the simple allocation of funds. They also acquired greater responsibility for and interest in Jewish education as well as continuing and even deepening their relationships with their constituent social-service and welfare agencies. In the process, most made strong efforts to broaden their leadership base to include new segments of the community.

All this has served to enhance the central role of the federations locally and to give them the best—if not the unrivaled—claim to being the umbrella organizations. There is no question that the key to the growth of the power of the local federations is that they have become the major fund-raising bodies on the American scene. Even though money and influence are not necessarily correlated on a one-to-one basis, there is unquestionably a relationship between the two. Locally, as agencies become more dependent upon the federation for funds, they are more likely to be included in the ambit of federation planning and policy-making.

The same pattern has repeated itself on the countrywide plane though in a less clear-cut way. The difference is that the Council of Jewish Federations and Welfare Funds does not have the fund-raising power which the local federations have and consequently has no such monetary power to exercise over the parallel national associations. The Jewish Welfare Board, for example, is funded the way the CJFWF is—by grants from its local constituents and the local federations directly, thus limiting the possibilities of CJFWF influence on indirect grants. The national community-relations and religious organizations are even more independent.

A new addition to the communal-welfare scene is the Israeli element, the result of the large role played by the federations in raising funds for Israel's needs. The government of Israel has its special concerns in American Jewish life which it pursues in many ways, but is finding it increasingly advantageous to pursue within the context of the communal-welfare sphere. The Jewish Agency, particularly since its recent reconstitution, has virtually coopted the federation leadership as its "non-Zionist" representatives, creating an even tighter bond between the institutionalized representatives of the World Zionist movement and the American Jewish community than ever before. In both cases, the institutionalization of relationships is still in its incipient stages.

Israel-Overseas Sphere: This area is both the best organized and the best integrated of all the spheres. Integration here dates back to

World War I and the founding of the American Jewish Joint Distribution Committee (JDC). In general, the sphere has two interlocking wings, one concerned with fund-raising and the other with political-*cum*-educational activity. Responsibilities for fund-raising are divided between the federations which handle the United Jewish Appeal (UJA) the Israel Bonds Organization, the Jewish National Fund, and the various "friends" of Israeli or overseas institutions. Political-*cum*-educational activities are conducted primarily through the Zionist organizations that are now at least nominally united (except for the Zionist Organization of America [ZOA]) into an American Zionist Federation, locally and country-wide.

Since the potentiality for competition among these organizations is great and the need to cooperate for the common good of Israel felt universally among them, a system of negotiated sharing has been developed through a network of agreements dividing the funds and/or the campaign arenas. The basic agreements are those reached nationally between the representatives of the federations working through the CJFWF and the UJA on an annual basis, dividing the funds raised in the local campaigns. A second agreement, between the UJA, the Israel Bond Organization, and the various "friends" groups more or less spells out their respective jurisdictions and claims to various methods of fund-raising. Thus Israel Bonds has a right to make synagogue appeals, while direct solicitation is a province of the UJA through the federations. The problem of cooperation among the Zionist organizations has consistently been more difficult. Since, with the exception of Hadassah and the ZOA, they are tied to the great "national" (read "worldwide" Jewish) Zionist parties that participate in the political life of Israel, they have been less than willing to cooperate on the local scene until very recently.

Naturally, the Israel-overseas sphere is substantially influenced by sources outside of the United States. The Israel government and the Jewish Agency take a very active role in the fund-raising process. Similarly, the Jewish National Fund and the *Keren Hayesod* become active participants both through the Jewish Agency and to some extent directly on the American scene as well. Aside from these Israel-based bodies, the JDC, the Organization for Rehabilitation and Training (ORT), and the Claims Conference are also involved in the worldwide activities of the Jewish people, both as beneficiaries and constituents of the American Jewish bodies functioning in the field. Their role has been of great significance in the postwar period. The JDC in particular has become the bearer of American Jewish "know-how" as well as money wherever there are Jewish communities in need of redevelopment.

BASIC DIVISIONS IN THE DECISION-MAKING ARENAS

Religious and Secular

The division between the "religious" and the "secular" developed out of the American milieu and was enhanced in the early days of the twentieth century by the relatively sharp division between those Jews who concerned themselves with their *shuls* and those who, while members of synagogues and temples, were really far more interested in welfare and community-relations activities which they saw as divorced from "religion" *per se*. This led to the rise of two separate groups of decision-makers. By their very nature, synagogues were localistic institutions, while the secular services became the province of the cosmopolitans.

Despite all the forces making for separation, the division could not and did not remain a hard and fast one. Indeed, it has been breaking down since the end of World War II. In the first place, there was the great expansion of those educational and cultural functions which could not be neatly divided between the two. Moreover, as the synagogues grew in power in the 1950's and began to see themselves as the true custodians of American Jewish life, they began to claim authoritative roles in areas previously reserved to the "secular" side. Finally, the whole thrust of Jewish tradition militated against such a separation as artificially enforced. As those concerned with the "secular" side became more involved in Jewish life and began to see their services as functions that had a specifically Jewish content, they began to think of them as no less religious in the traditional Jewish sense than the functions of the synagogues. Nevertheless, while ideologically and functionally the lines between the two are weakening, structurally the separation between "religious" and "secular" institutions remains as strong as ever.

Public and Private

While there is little conscious perception of the distinction between "public" and "private" (partly because there is some notion that vis-à-vis governmental activities all Jewish communal activities are private), nevertheless the activities sponsored or funded by the federations and their constituent agencies are implicitly understood to be the public activities of the American Jewish community. The argument for "communal responsibility" essentially has been an argument designed to define them in that manner.

Synagogues, on the other hand, have continued to be regarded as "private." Only in the last few years has the notion of the synagogues as private enterprises been questioned within Jewish communal circles, and then only privately, in a belated recognition of the fact that a congregation of 1,000–2,000 families, providing a range of services far beyond simple maintenance of the weekly and yearly prayer schedule, is not the same as a collection of twenty or forty men gathered together primarily for a *minyan*. In part, this recognition is a response to the synagogues' encroachment upon the traditionally communal sector. In part, it is also a reflection of the suburbanization of American Jewry whereby synagogues have become major centers of community activities in their respective suburbs—if not the *only* centers—and where movement of a major synagogue from one neighborhood to another affects the whole course of Jewish life within a particular locale.

"Cosmopolitans" and "Locals"

The "public-private" distinction as it is implicitly recognized in Jewish life today follows very much along the lines of the dichotomy between "cosmopolitans" and "locals" described by social scientists. Briefly, cosmopolitans are those who see the whole community as a single entity and maintain connections and involvements across all of it. While their cosmopolitanism is first defined in relation to a particular local community, once they develop a cosmopolitan outlook toward the local community, they almost invariably take a cosmopolitan view of the larger world of which that community is a part, as well. Locals, on the other hand, are those whose involvement and connections are confined to a small segment of the total community—a neighborhood, a particular social group or, in Jewish life, a particular synagogue, organization, or club. Their involvement rests overwhelmingly on their commitment to that point of attachment and does not extend to the community as a whole except indirectly. Moreover, their perceptions of the larger world are also quite limited, based as they are on their localistic involvements.

To a very real extent, this is a natural division in society. At the same time, all cosmopolitans have clearly localistic needs—to be tied to something more intimate than the community in the abstract, or even to a set of institutions which must inevitably be depersonalized to some degree. Similarly, locals can be mobilized for essentially cosmopolitan purposes when those purposes are made to strike home at the source of their involvement. Thus every community needs institutions devoted to serving both cosmopolitan and local needs as well as the local needs of cosmopolitans and the cosmopolitan needs of locals.

In the Jewish community, the organizations and agencies that fall within the federation family generally represent the cosmopolitan interest and consequently attract cosmopolitans to leadership positions within them. The synagogues, on the other hand, represent localistic needs and interests first and foremost. Indeed, that is their primary role (if one that is often neglected in the large contemporary American congregation). Consequently, the leadership they attract consists of a very high percentage of locals.

Professionals and Volunteers

The other major division among decision-makers in the American Jewish community is that between professional and voluntary leaders, with the professionals further subdivided into those whose training is obtained through religious institutions and those whose training is through secular ones. The American Jewish community has the most professionalized leadership of any in the world, probably the most of any in Jewish history. The roots of this undoubtedly lie in the commitment to professionalization which envelops the larger American society.

Today, the day-to-day business of the Jewish community is almost exclusively in the hands of professionals or, at the very least, people who are paid for their services even if they do not meet professional standards or consider themselves as forever committed to Jewish careers. Because these professionals are involved on a daily basis with the problems of the community, they exercise great influence in the decision-making of the community. On the other hand, there has been no diminution in the number of voluntary leaders. Parallel roles for professionals and volunteers have developed in virtually every Jewish organization and institution, allowing for extensive participation by both. What is not fixed is the way in which they relate to each other.

In some cases, the relationship between professionals and volunteers is resolved by separation of functions and in some by a mixing of functions. As a general rule, wherever the requirements of the profession are most exclusive and demanding, and the need for professional expertise established, separation of functions tends to be the norm. Wherever the line between professional competence and volunteer talent is least distinct, sharing tends to be the norm. Thus, in the rabbinate, Jewish education, and certain of the Jewish social services, not only operations, but many policy-making powers are placed in the hands of professionals who are viewed as specially trained experts, bringing to their tasks an expertise that endows them with a special role. In such cases, the voluntary leadership often confines itself to endorsing or ratifying policies suggested by professionals, developing and approving very general organizational goals and principles, and finding the necessary monetary and community support for their enterprise, only intervening more actively when the professionals fail to provide the requisite leadership.

On the other hand, in community relations and fund-raising, the lines that divide professionals and volunteers tend to be relatively weak. Professionals are often treated as if they cannot claim very much in the way of special expertise (other than the expertise of experience) for handling what are essentially political tasks. In fact, they gain their substantial influence because they, too, are specially trained and, most important, spend all of their working time at what they do, enabling them to know the situation better than the voluntary leadership. Like all professionals, their special power is based on the extent to which they control (willy-nilly, deliberately, or for traditional reasons) the amount and kind of information that reaches their volunteer counterparts. In addition, their control of in-house planning, their ability to strongly influence the appointment of voluntary leaders to particular committees, and the fact that they provide continuity in the life of the organization adds to their power. At the same time, some of the volunteers may indeed have special talents, capabilities, or positions, particularly political ones, which place them in very strategic positions within the organizations and give them major roles in the decision-making process hardly different from those of the professionals in those arenas where their talents, capabilities, or positions are useful. In fact, the process usually finds volunteers and professionals working in tandem on common problems with minimum conflict.

The sources of professional and volunteer leadership in the community themselves help to mark the division. By and large, the volunteers are recruited from among the wealthier elements associated with any particular function or institution. This is partly because the hierarchy of influence among the voluntary leadership is often set in terms of the size of their contributions and partly because the costs of playing a leadership role are such that only the well-to-do can afford the time and the money to do so. Aside from successful businessmen and professionals and perhaps young lawyers associated with law firms where there is a tradition of participation in Jewish communal life, the only people who can contribute the requisite time are academicians and they are limited by their inability to spend the money required to maintain an active role. Thus, willy-nilly, wealth becomes an important factor in determining the voluntary leadership.

This situation is not quite as stark as it seems. Obviously it is far less true in the case of small synagogues and clubs (the most localistic institutions of all) and most true in the case of the UJA. Even where wealth is of great importance, it does not function as the only measure of leadership. The wealthiest men are not necessarily the most important leaders. There is apparently some threshold of prosperity past which most men are relatively equal in the pursuit of leadership roles. A man of still modest means from the perspective of the very wealthy may choose to allocate a high proportion of his resources to the Jewish community and get recognized accordingly, while a man of very great means may not be willing to make such a major allocation and remains unrecognized accordingly. Moreover, beyond the willingness to give there must be a willingness to serve.

THE DECISION-MAKERS: THEIR ROLES AND FUNCTIONS

There are at least five categories of decision-makers functioning in the Jewish community today. Three of these are dominated by professionals: rabbis, communal workers, and Jewish educators. Two are dominated by lay personnel: congregational boards and volunteers. These categories, in turn, fall into two divisions: congregational decision-makers (rabbis, congregational boards) and communal decision-makers (communal workers, volunteers). (The educators, as we shall see, form a kind of class of their own.)

Congregational Decision-Makers

Rabbis: At the very least, rabbis function as decision-makers within their congregations, while the more talented, important, well-known or cosmopolitan among them are able to build upon their rabbinical roles to become decision-makers in the larger Jewish communal life as well. In general, rabbis tend to be restricted to their congregations or to their synagogue movements by the secular sector and by their own reluctance to venture outside of the arena in which their authority is rarely questioned.

It is very difficult for rabbis to shift roles when they leave the congregational setting, as they would have to do if they were to participate, say, in communal-welfare activities. There they would have to participate as if among equals, but with neither the special competence of professionals in the particular field nor with any claim to special recognition by virtue of their rabbinical positions. A relationship of equality in such a situation is uncomfortable for both sides, since neither knows how properly to respond to the other. Thus it is more convenient for a rabbi simply not to participate.

The field of education and culture however, is one area in which rabbis can participate fully. At the same time, rabbis are not especially eager to become professional leaders in this area for at least two reasons. First, Jewish education tends to enjoy a relatively low status in the eyes of the voluntary leaders who control their destinies as rabbis; second, American rabbis rarely have the training or the time to develop excellence in Jewish scholarship to a degree that would give them the kind of status they demand—and get—in the pulpit.

When the Jewish community was smaller, its leadership concentrated in fewer hands, and its functions (and finances) more limited, a few dynamic rabbis could rise to positions of communal eminence by dint of their virtuosity. None of those conditions prevails today and the virtuoso rabbi has gone the way of his secular counterpart. Another reason why rabbis are not found in the forefront of American Jewish leadership is that synagogues are essentially localistic institutions and rabbis, no matter how cosmopolitan in outlook, in order properly to maintain their congregational bases must adapt themselves to localistic needs and interests.

Congregational Boards: Since synagogues account for so much of Jewish activity in the United States today, the men and (in some instances) women who comprise the congregational boards of trustees must be considered important decision-makers, though they are rarely recognized as such. The lack of recognition stems from the fact that there are so many congregations in the United States, each a little empire in itself, controlling its own budget, hiring its own personnel, establishing its own program, and building its own facilities with barely any reference to any outside body.

The congregations spend no less than $100 million a year and perhaps as much as $500 million. Nobody knows the exact figure, or even knows how to make a proper estimate. This is an amount of money equal to that contributed to the federations and the UJA in the very best years of their drives.

There are over 4,500 Jewish congregations in the United States according to the fragmentary figures available. Should the average size of the congregational board be ten members (probably an underestimate), this would mean that there are at least 45,000 congregational board members. In fact, the number is probably larger than that. When we add to the congregational boards the number of men who serve on congregational committees, the number of potential decision-makers increases even further and our knowledge of what they do and how they do it diminishes even more.

Every form of decision-making is to be found in the government of Jewish congregations in America, ranging from the most autocratic, where one man decides all congregational policy, holds the rabbi in the palm of his hand, so to speak, hires, fires, and decides as he pleases on all issues, to situations where the most open forms of town-meeting democracy prevail and the congregation governs itself without the mediation of any board.

In the larger congregations, with boards of thirty or more, actual policy-making may be confined to an even smaller group. Assume that decision-making is shared among five people in each congregation—again, probably an underestimate. That means that there are still 20,000 significant decision-makers governing the synagogues of the United States, all of whom function within their respective congregations with minimal, if any, ties among congregations.

At this stage of our knowledge, it would be difficult to describe the "typical" congregational board member or even the typical congregational board. What unites them all is their essentially localistic commitment to the primary needs of their own particular congregations. It is rare to find a congregational board that, in its official capacity, will concern itself with the needs of the larger community, even when its members may, in other capacities, be the major communal leaders.

This fragmentation of outlook has great consequences for the community as a whole, particularly in the case of the largest congregations, those with membership of a thousand families or more. The consequences are obviously far less important in connection with congregations of fifty families. What is most important is that even congregations of medium size, whose actions are not likely to jolt the Jewish community as a whole in the manner of the largest ones, have a tremendous impact on the character of the community by virtue of their control over the education of their children.

Relations between rabbis and congregational boards obviously stand at the heart of the congregational decision-making process. While, again, the variety is great, three general models can be found. On one hand, the congregational board, or the dominant authority figure in the congregation, may simply dominate the rabbi, confining him to a role that involves conducting services and carrying out similar ritual chores. In some cases, rabbis are not even allowed to attend congregational board meetings. In other situations, the diametrically opposite condition prevails: the rabbi is so strong that he dominates the congregational board, which exists primarily to mediate between him and the congregation as a whole or to carry out his wishes in areas where he does not want to be directly or extensively involved. Finally, there is the situation which prevails more normally, where some kind of division of functions is worked out between the congregational leadership and the rabbi, with decision-making shared in certain relatively clear-cut areas.

Communal Decision-Makers

Communal Workers: Communal workers gain their power on the basis of either expertise or their day-to-day involvement with the problems of the community. Their technical knowledge and perennial availability give them important decision-making roles unless they are directly challenged by the voluntary leadership. This rarely happens because, in most cases, the voluntary leadership does not feel interested or competent enough to challenge them.

At the present time it is likely that the majority of Jewish communal workers are drawn from the social-work professions and have been trained as social workers, with legal training in second place. In relatively few cases were the senior civil servants of the Jewish community trained specifically for Jewish positions. In most cases they simply fell into such positions as a result of happenstance or circumstance. This is less true among the younger members where Jewish agencies, in an effort to overcome the personnel problem, have made some effort to recruit people and provide them with the resources needed to attend secular schools to get social-work training on condition that they then serve the agencies for a specified period of time.

For the most part, the communal workers are not well-grounded in traditional Jewish learning or even in rudimentary knowledge of Jewish history, law, society, or customs. Consequently, their deficiencies are most glaring when it comes to making decisions involving the Jewishness of their programs. Since their expertise in other respects tends to be among the very best available in the country, the contrast is rendered even sharper than it might otherwise be. This is not to say that many—or most—of them have not become seriously and sincerely interested in fostering the Jewish aspects of their work, but they are in a difficult position when it comes to translating attitudes into concrete programs.

Volunteers: We have almost no data on the voluntary leaders of the American Jewish community, but one thing that does mark them is their relative wealth, although this is not the only criterion. They are very heavily confined to community-relations, communal-welfare, and Israel-overseas activity. Volunteers are a group for whom Jewish activity is a means of expressing Jewishness, no more and no less than synagogue worship or observance of Jewish tradition is for others. In effect, their activity becomes their religion, and their observance is conditioned by the demands of communal life. Some of them are involved in communal leadership primarily for the honor, but many others work as persistently as their professional counterparts for little recognition. Moreover, they expend large sums of money for the pleasure of participating.

Money and energy are thus key sources of such influence over decision-making as the volunteers have, although neither replaces talent when it comes to the actual decision-making process itself. Money may buy a man the presidency of an organization or agency. Energy may put a man in a leadership position, but some kind of talent is necessary if a person is actually to have a share in making decisions. This is true if only because of the role of the professionals in screening the advancement of the voluntary leadership.

In at least one area—that of fund-raising—volunteers are the dominant decision-makers. No matter how much professional help is provided, it is only the voluntary leadership—the men who give the money themselves—who are able to influence others to give money. Moreover, with respect to fund-raising they usually feel that they have as much expertise as any one else and therefore are less likely to defer to the ideas or demands of the professionals.

By and large, the volunteers are probably representative of the more Jewishly committed elements in the mainstream of the American Jewish community, this despite the fact that they are rarely elected to the offices they occupy in any meaningful sense of the term. (The elections, though not always formalities, are usually simply means of formally ratifying the choices of nominating committees and, even when contested, are rarely contested by candidates representing seriously different characteristics or points of view.) They are representatives because there is a certain sameness in American Jewry; their desires, tastes, attitudes, interests, and educational backgrounds probably depart very little from the norm among the majority of American Jews.

Jewish Educators: Jewish educators are here considered apart from rabbis and communal workers because they generally pass through different forms of training and pursue different career lines. While some men trained as rabbis become Jewish educators, most of the educators are men who had decided upon Jewish education as a career before entering rabbinical school. It can fairly be said that the educators' decision-making role is confined to the sphere of Jewish education, that is to say, to schools or camps where they exercise authority as professionals. However, their authority is limited by various external factors. Chief among these are the problems inherent in Jewish education in the United States—namely, the ambivalence of parents regarding the amount of Jewish education they wish their children to acquire, the problems of obtaining qualified teachers and adequate financial support, and the fact that education is lodged in the synagogue whose leadership has other priorities.

Still, within this framework there is usually little interest in what the Jewish educators teach except on the part of the rabbi who may intervene to assure that "loyalty to the institution" is given the first priority. Beyond that, even the rabbis tend to pay little attention to the day-to-day operations of "their" schools. A Jewish educator who wishes may do more or less what he pleases in his school with little outside interference, provided he does not do anything that violates the Jewish communal consensus.

DECISION-MAKING TASKS AND MODES

The tasks to which the various categories of decision-makers address themselves are all ultimately geared to the question of Jewish survival. Given this overriding interest, the Jewish community's two most important concerns are defense and education.

Defense: The major defense concerns have changed radically within recent years. From the 1870's through the 1930's domestic anti-Semitism was the dominant defense concern of the community. Beginning with the 1930's, however, this was gradually replaced by efforts to defend Jews in other parts of the world. However, after 1948, Israel became the major focus of Jewish attention; and since 1967 particularly, insuring the survival of Israel has become the heart of the defense function of the American Jewish community.

Even the community-relations agencies are now spending a high proportion of their time and resources trying to increase support for Israel in the United States. As a result, the most important decision-makers in the community are those who are related to the defense of Israel, namely the federation and UJA leadership, voluntary and professional.

Education: Education is now being recognized as an equally essential concern. Meeting Jewish educational needs is a somewhat problematic matter for the community since it exposes all the ambivalences of contemporary Jewish life, creating a clash between the desire for survival as a people with the desire for full integration into the general society. Jewish education therefore requires a great measure of commitment to the notion that Jews are different and must educate their children to be different. All agree that Jewish education is important, but the character of the commitment is something else again. American Jewish education reflects all the ambiguities, and that is one reason why major decision-makers rarely play any real role in the educational field and why those who are professionally involved in Jewish education are not major decision-makers in the community.

Since these ambivalences are not easily overcome there is not likely to be any dramatic change in the foreseeable future although there has been a consistent and gradual increase in support for Jewish schools over the last twenty years. It is now clear that the major decision-makers are willing to provide some kind of "minimum base" support for Jewish education locally through the federations and their appropriate constituent agencies. This minimum base is progressively being defined upward but it remains a base line, not an aggressively advancing one. Moreover, the federations are discouraged from moving beyond the minimum by the unresolved division over control of Jewish education between the community as a whole and the individual synagogue.

Social Services and Welfare: The decision-makers who are most involved in this area have been losing importance on the communal scene. This is partly because the social services themselves have become progressively less Jewish in appearance, if not in fact, and partly because the rise of the welfare state has reduced their significance in American Jewish life. Jewish hospitals, for example, are now simply institutions sponsored by the Jewish community as one of its contributions to the welfare of American society as a whole. The Jewish community maintains its stake in such institutions partly because it is a customary way of making a contribution to the life of the general community, partly because it provides a bridge to other minority groups with whom the Jewish community wants to maintain good relations, and partly because there is some strong, if unspoken, sentiment in the Jewish community that it is well for Jews to have such institutions under their supervision "just in case."

Pressures are also mounting for the social welfare agencies to give representation on their governing bodies to their non-Jewish clients. While most Jewish communities have resisted those pressures, the fact that the institutions are supported only partially from Jewish funds and heavily by United Fund and government contributions or grants makes it more difficult to hold the line.

Certain of the institutions which are presently considered to be within the social-service sphere are now seeking to broaden their interests, usually by moving into the area of education and culture as well. This is particularly true of the Jewish community centers whose social-service functions have been reduced as their educational and cultural functions have increased. Today some Jewish community centers often appear to be secular rivals of the synagogues.

Finance: Community finance is obviously a central task of the American Jewish community and the raising of money is a continuing and unrelenting activity. Indeed, such is its importance in determining the organization of Jewish communal life that from a strictly organizational point of view it may be considered the most important task of all.

Two major struggles have developed and have been essentially resolved in the area of fund-raising, both of which have had significant consequences for the organizational structure and the patterns of decision-making in the community. The first was the struggle within each locality as to whether or not to centralize the raising of funds for Jewish communal purposes. By and large, the decision has been to centralize fund-raising for all purposes other than those that fall within the religious-congregational sphere. This struggle led to the creation of the Jewish federations which by standing astride of general fund-raising have acquired the central decision-making role in the community.

The second struggle that took place was between local and

national organizations over who should be responsible for the raising of funds. The local organizations won the lion's share of the victory, gaining control over fund-raising for even the most national and international purposes. This victory has substantially strengthened the power of the local communities in the overall framework of American Jewish life.

Decision-Making Modes

In the final analysis, what can we say about the decision-making modes of the American Jewish community? A number of modes may be identified. We will consider six of these: 1) the penchant for government by committee; 2) the urge to avoid conflict; 3) the legitimacy of tension between the "national office" and the "local affiliates"; 4) the patterns of "duplication" and inter-organizational competition; 5) the sources of innovation and the initiation of programs; and 6) the role of personalities in the decision-making process.

Government by Committee: The immediate organizational tool of decision-making in the American Jewish community is the committee. Committees—in all shapes, sizes, and forms—carry out all the variegated business of the community. The multiplicity of committees within organizations and institutions provides for a certain degree of diffusion of power among many decision-makers and something akin to an intra-institutional "checks and balances" system.

Power and influence accrue to those who can control the committees and their work. Personality conflicts may well be focused more sharply in committees but, then, the business of the community is conducted through committees, from the smallest synagogue to the President's Conference (itself simply a high-level committee). Consequently, the dynamics of committee behavior are at least a partial factor in any decision taken by the leadership of the American Jewish community.

Conflict Avoidance: Despite the existence of conflict as part of life's reality, conflict avoidance is a major principle in American Jewish decision-making. By and large, especially where voluntary leaders are involved, every effort is made to avoid open conflict. Where issues are such that they are likely to provoke conflict there is every tendency to avoid raising them in the first place. Where an issue is likely to provoke conflict and must be raised, every effort is made to develop a decision in such a way that there is no chance for the conflict to be expressed.

In part, this avoidance of conflict reflects the traditional desire of a minority to avoid risking any weakening of the ties that bind its members together. But, in part, it also reflects the fact that the voluntary leaders in the American Jewish community are over-whelmingly recruited from the world of business and commerce where open conflict is considered "bad form" and decisions are reached in such a way as to minimize the appearance of conflict if not its reality.

The desire to avoid open conflict clearly rules out some issues from consideration no matter how important they might be. It also enhances the role of the professional leadership since it enables them to administer the community rather than requiring the voluntary leaders to *govern* it. In such situations, the tendency is to rely upon the men trusted with the administration to make what still are, in the end, political decisions. Thus the professionals continue to gain power simply because they can organize decision-making in such a way as to minimize the emergence of conflict, thereby earning the appreciation of the voluntary leadership.

Local Affiliates vs. the "National Office": One perennial conflict which is considered legitimate, provided that it is not allowed to spread beyond limited tactical skirmishes, is the tension between the "national office" and the local "affiliates". In part, it reflects the simple difference in constituency and interest of the national office and the local affiliates or branches. In part, it reflects a difference in the situation between Jews in the New York metropolitan area with its particular set of problems and Jews in other smaller communities which have a different scale of operations.

This tension is a perennial one which, by its very nature, can never finally be resolved. But shifts do take place in the structure of the tension, and these bring about immediate changes in the community's decision-making patterns. What can be said about the present situation, in general terms, is that those organizations which have traditionally been New York-centered are losing power in the community as a whole, while those whose locus of power is in the localities are gaining.

"Duplication" and Inter-Organizational Competition: Inter-organizational competition within the same sphere (duplication) is

another perennial feature of the American Jewish scene, stemming from the voluntary and associational character of the community. The attack on duplication is part of the standard rhetoric of American Jewish community life. At the same time, competition itself is not always a negative phenomenon. Moreover, on the local plane, organizations functioning within the same sphere often develop patterns of sharing that effectively divide tasks so as to minimize overlapping. Duplication is not likely to disappear on the American Jewish scene nor even to be substantially reduced in the ways in which reformers usually suggest because there is no realistic way to curb the proliferation of organizations. When organizational consolidation does take place, it usually reflects a tightening of the organizational belt to cope with decline, a retreat rather than a step forward, such as in the case of the recent formation of the American Zionist Federation.

This is not to say that all efforts to control duplication reflect weakness. Within the sphere of community relations, for example, coordination came about at a time when the individual organizations were all fluorishing. Furthermore, even though some of the same organizations are now doing poorly, they are not interested in consolidation. Rather they are redoubling their efforts to survive.

Recognition of the realities of interorganizational competition is not the same as condoning the semi-anarchy which prevails in some sectors of American Jewish life and which is justified in the name of a specious "pluralism" that is no more than a reflection of organizational self-interest. What is needed are better means of enhancing coordination and limiting harmful duplication in ways that are consonant with the American situation.

Innovation and Program Initiation: While decision-making in connection with established programs is more or less shared by the professional and voluntary leadership, innovation and program initiation are more often than not dominated by the professionals, if only because they are involved in organizational and institutional affairs on a day-to-day basis and are recognized as the custodians of programmatic expertise. Their positions, then, make them the initiators of a very high proportion of new activities and programs and the prime generators of new ideas. This is not to say that they are the only innovators and initiators; but there is no question that they bear a disproportionate share of the responsibility in these areas.

Personalities: The role of personalities in decision-making is not to be underestimated even though there have been substantial changes in this regard in recent years. Ironically, personality conflicts are particularly significant at the highest levels in the national organizations. Perhaps because they are so detached from operational responsibilities, the top leaders can indulge in the luxury of personality conflicts. In the local communities, operational necessities lead to greater efforts to control such conflicts.

Problems and Prospects

Despite the limitations of the data, it is not unfair to conclude that the American Jewish community is governed by what may be termed a "trusteeship of doers" in which decision-makers who are generally self-selected on the basis of their willingness to participate hold the reins of communal life in all of its facets. They perceive of their function as managing the community's affairs in trust for its members, the Jewish people as a whole, just as earlier generations of leaders saw themselves as managing the community's affairs as trustees of God. It is this sense of trusteeship which keeps the communal leadership from being an oligarchy, or a small body that manages the community for its own profit. Every significant Jewish interest has the right to claim a place in the trusteeship of doers and is accorded that place once it brings its claim to the attention of the appropriate leadership by "doing."

Although it is not elected in any systemically competitive manner, the trusteeship is representative of American Jewry in that it reflects the attitudes, values, and interests of the community—except perhaps in one respect: the leaders are probably more positively Jewish then the community's rank and file.

A trusteeship of doers seems to be the system that is fated for American Jewry and probably for any Jewish community living in a voluntaristic environment like the United States. Those modern Jewish communities which have experimented with communal elections have not found them any better a solution to the problem of representation, because the turnout in these elections tends to be extremely low. Moreover, a voting procedure does not guarantee the election of statesmen to communal leadership either. Elections do have one important consequence, however. They raise to the inner circles of leadership men whose qualifications are not simply financial. In most cases these are men who have gained leadership of some important organizational bloc within the community which is able to turn out its members to vote. As such they are more likely to be attuned to straightforward political considerations than big donors who do not have to conciliate constituencies in any way. . . .

The fact that elections are not likely to accomplish the purposes for which they are instituted does not mean that ways cannot be developed better to involve a wider segment of the American Jewish community in its crucial decision-making bodies. In any case, efforts in that direction must be founded on the recognition that oligarchy is likely to be the persistent form in American Jewish life. What is called for, then, is an attempt to make the oligarchies properly representative.

This might involve the encouragement of a whole host of tendencies already present on the American scene and the addition of others. The strengthening of the federation movement, for example, might offer the best opportunity for creating a systematic decision-making structure on the American Jewish scene. In this connection, it is absolutely vital that the synagogues cease to be considered the private property of their members and be recognized for what they are—public institutions bearing significant communal responsibilities. This is not an argument against congregationalism; indeed, there is every reason to want to foster true congregational spirit in synagogues of proper scale, provided that it is not a euphemism for communal anarchy.

If this could be accomplished, it might then be possible to devise ways in which elections conducted through the congregations would form a major part of the basis of representation in the federations, so that the leadership recruitment process would reach down into every segment of the community. Under such circumstances federations would become more completely and thoroughly communal agencies. Moreover, under such circumstances it will be possible to make better determinations as to who should conduct and finance the different activities of the Jewish community. The advances suggested here should be made on a proper federal basis . . . not through a centralization of power either locally or nationally, as is often suggested. . . .

JEWISH RELIGION AND THE AMERICAN JEW

THE RELIGION OF AMERICAN JEWS
by CHARLES S. LIEBMAN

INTRODUCTION

*C*HARLES S. LIEBMAN *takes us backstage, as it were, in order to detail the inner workings of American Jewish religion. His analysis consequently differs from the usual portraits of Jewish religious life, whether of Reform, of Conservatism, or of Orthodoxy. Furthermore, Liebman's perspective makes him particularly critical of the portrayals of Jewish religiosity which have appeared in the mass media. He suggests, however, that false portrayals may create their own truth: they may motivate individuals to conform with stereotypes projected about them.*

Liebman's analysis of the kind of immigrants who came to the United States and the social situation with which they were confronted is crucial to his argument, as is the distinction which he draws between elite religion and folk religion. He stresses that both the German Jewish immigration of the mid-nineteenth century and the East European immigration of the late nineteenth and early twentieth century were dominated by followers of folk religion.

Because America was different and emancipation was not a problem, the kind of Reform Judaism that evolved in the United States differed from its European prototype. As Liebman puts it: "American Reform at its outset was the folk religion of the German-American Jew." The European-trained Reform rabbis who came to the United States later succeeded in formulating an elite version of Reform Judaism, but in any case the folk content of Reform Judaism was destined to be reshaped by the East European Jew, whose gradual infiltration of the movement caused Reform to take on the folk patterns of East European rather than of Western Jewry. To be sure, such patterns had themselves been extensively reshaped by the confrontation with American culture.

Liebman is particularly acute in his analysis of American Orthodoxy. He stresses that the leaders of the elite religion of Orthodoxy remained in Eastern Europe until after World War I, and in fact did not arrive in substantial numbers until World War II. America gave Jews the freedom to construct their own Judaism and ". . . to a greater extent than ever before the folk now set their standards independently of the elite." Thus it came about that American Orthodoxy was an Orthodoxy pervaded with folk religion. Furthermore, the acculturation which Jews underwent meant that the Orthodox norms of Eastern Europe were widely disregarded. Yet, given its structure, Orthodox Judaism never lost its elite tradition, which maintained a foothold even during the chaotic days of mass immigration. In recent decades the elite version of Orthodoxy has reasserted itself with the arrival of new immigrants fully committed to Orthodoxy and more particularly with the settlement in the United States of a group of religious leaders of East European Jewry. In Liebman's view the rise of Conservatism, and to a lesser extent of Reform, provided a haven for those dissatisfied with Orthodoxy and helped make possible the rise of a new elitist leadership within Orthodoxy.

It is Liebman's contention that Conservatism represents the purest expression of the folk religion of the American Jew (though there is an elite version of Conservative Judaism as well). He emphasizes that Conservatism appealed to traditionally minded East European Jews who were seeking a way to combine their traditionalism with the American cultural patterns which they had adopted. The folk religion which they created had a particularly strong emphasis on the ethnic aspect of Jewishness. Liebman believes that the stress on ethnicity under the umbrella of religion, and as institutionalized in the American synagogue, was responsible for the rapid growth of Conservatism. He describes the individuals who proceeded to establish hundreds of Conservative synagogues across the nation as ". . . quite concerned with group survival, not very interested in religion, and in search of institutions which expressed values of both communal survival and integration or acculturation to middle-class American standards."

If the folk religion of American Jewry has had a strong ethnic-communal thrust in contrast to a universalist-pietistic thrust, then the Reconstructionist movement initiated by Mordecai M. Kaplan should not only have constituted a fourth religious group but should have achieved primacy over its competitors. No one has been more of an admirer of folk religion than Kaplan. He has been unique in his ability to reconceptualize the essence of American Jewish folk religion, giving it ideological justification and thus conferring intellectual respectability. But Reconstructionism never became a fourth wing of American Judaism. Liebman is obliged to account for its failure as an institutionalized movement, for his theoretical perspective would lead us to believe that a Reconstructionist triumph was inevitable. His explanation of Reconstructionism's failure constitutes a significant extension of his theory of folk religion versus elite religion and should provoke an interesting debate among students of the religion of American Jews.

M. S.

. . . IN ORDER to understand fully the religion of American Jews we must . . . define two concepts: "folk religion" and "elite religion." Folk religion is the religion of a community which delineates the peculiarity of the particular group and which is generated by the community itself. . . . The popular religious culture of folk religion can be better understood if we first understand elite religion. The term religion refers here to a formal organized institution with acknowledged leaders. Within the institution, symbols and rituals are acknowledged as legitimate expressions or reenactments of religious experience, and a set of beliefs is articulated as ultimate truths.[1] Elite religion is the symbols and rituals (the cult) and beliefs which the leaders acknowledge as legitimate. But most importantly, elite religion is also the religious organization itself, its hierarchical arrangements, the authority of the leaders and their source of authority, and the rights and obligations of the followers to the organization and its leaders.

For various reasons—the evolution of religion, the conflict of different cultures, differentiated levels of religious and even nonreligious education, and psychological propensities—large numbers of people may affiliate with a particular religious institution, and even identify themselves as part of that religion, without really accepting all aspects of its elitist formulation. What is more, a kind of subculture may exist within a religion which the acknowledged leaders ignore or even condemn, but in which a majority of the members participate. This is called folk religion. Why consider folk and elite religion to be two aspects of the same religion? Why not call them two separate religions? The answer is that both share the same organization and at least nominally recognize the authoritative nature of the cult and beliefs articulated by the elite religion. Folk religion is not self-conscious; it does not articulate its own rituals and beliefs or demand recognition for its informal leaders. As far as elite religion is concerned, folk religion is

[1]This discussion follows O'Dea's treatment of institutional religion, in which he distinguishes three levels: cult, belief, and organization; Thomas O'Dea, *The Sociology of Religion* (Englewood Cliffs, N.J.: Prentice-Hall, Inc., 1966), pp. 36–51.

not a movement but an error, or a set of errors, shared by many people.

Folk religion is expressed primarily though rituals and symbols. These rituals may be rooted in superstition; they may originate from an older localized religion which has been replaced by the elite religion; or they may arise from a need on the part of people for the sanctification of certain social, economic, or even sexual activity which elite religion refuses to legitimize. Folk religion tends to accept the organizational structure of the elite religion but to be indifferent to the elite belief structure. Of course, its rituals and symbols imply a belief system, but this tends to be mythic rather than rational and hence not in opposition to the more complex theological elaboration of the elite religion. Where the beliefs of the folk religion are self-conscious and articulated, they tend to be beliefs about which the elite religion is neutral. . . .

The potential for folk religion to become institutionalized always exists; if it does, it will become a separate religion or an official heresy. The history of Catholicism is filled with such examples. Yet folk religion permits a more intimate religious expression and experience for many people, and may, in fact, integrate them into organizational channels of the elite religion. It is a mistake to think of folk religion as necessarily more primitive than elite religion. While its ceremonies and sanctums evoke emotions and inchoate ideas associated with basic instincts and primitive emotions, it is also more flexible than elite religion. Hence it is also capable of developing ceremonial reponses to contemporary needs which may be incorporated into the elite religion. Much religious liturgy arises from the folk religion and is incorporated into the elite religion.

The absence of an elaborate theology within folk religion and the appeal of folk religion to primal instincts and emotions does not mean that folk religion is less attractive to intellectuals than is elite religion. Quite the opposite may be true under certain circumstances. In secular America, elite religion has been forced to retreat before the challenge of science, biblical scholarship, notions of relativism implicit in contemporary social science, and the whole mood of current intellectual life. . . .

The problem for the religious elite has been that most intellectuals cannot accept dogmatic formulations which purport to be true or to have arisen independent of time and place. Hence intellectuals have special difficulty with elite religion. But the same intellectual currents which challenge religious doctrine can also serve to defend behavioral and even organizational forms against the onslaught of such secular doctrines as twentieth-century positivism or eighteenth- and nineteenth-century deism. Thus folk religion, with its stress on customary behavior and traditional practices, may be legitimized functionally without an elitist prop. An intellectual today may well be attracted to folk religion because it provides him with comfort and solace, a sense of tradition, a feeling of rootedness, a source of family unity. His worldview may remain secular, and from the point of view of elite religion his beliefs will therefore be quite unsatisfactory. But it is, at least in the first instance, elite religion, not folk, which is challenged by his worldview.

In traditional Judaism, folk religion has always existed side by side with elite religion. Many of its ceremonies and rituals were incorporated into the elite religion; others were rejected; still others achieved a kind of quasi-incorporation. They were and are widely practiced and even have a certain liturgical legitimacy; but they are still outside the boundaries of elite religion. Such ceremonies, for example, are associated with Jewish holidays. Best known, perhaps, are Jewish New Year rituals of eating apple and honey and the ceremony of *tashlich,* at which Jews throw crumbs representing their sins into a body of water. The essentially healthy relationship between the folk and elite religion in traditional Judaism is exemplified by the fact that Jews who participate in *tashlich* feel the need to accompany the act with the recitation of a traditional psalm. That is, the sanctums of the elite religion must accompany a purely folk religious act.

Every religious group has both its folk and elitist aspect. They may differ from one another, and, as we shall see, branches or denominations within Judaism do differ from one another as to the extent to which the folk and elite formulations are in tension with each other. But first some historical background is necessary.

ʚϤɞ

AMERICAN JUDAISM BEFORE
THE TURN OF THE CENTURY

In 1880 there were approximately 250,000 Jews in the United States. During the next forty years over 2,000,000 Jews immigrated, the great majority from Eastern Europe. The intensity of the immigrants' Jewish identification and Jewish concerns, and even more, their large numbers and the problems created by such a vast lower-class segment of people, overwhelmed the existing Jewish institutions and transformed the very nature of American Judaism. Consequently, the turn of the century is a convenient starting place for anyone who wishes to understand the roots of the contemporary Jewish community.

Early Reform

Before the arrival of the East Europeans, most American Jews were German in origin and Reform in religious orientation. But there was a great difference between American Reform and German Reform. . . . German Reform represented a conscious break with the Jewish tradition. Under the influence of the European Enlightenment and concerned with the requirements for Jewish emancipation, it defined itself in opposition to the traditional patterns of Jewish belief and practice. It was a new elitist formulation of Judaism. In contrast, American Reform was the religious organization of the German-American Jew who came searching for personal liberty and economic advancement. That Jew was neither ideologically oriented nor purposefully assimilationist. He had no need to rebel consciously against the tradition, because there were no traditional institutions in the United States which were of any concern to him. American Reform at its outset was the folk religion of the German-American Jew.

Jews had lived here prior to the large German immigration, which began in the 1840's. They included Sephardic Jews . . . and Germanic Jews, who came in numbers small enough to be assimilated into Sephardic institutions. But these institutions, centered around the synagogue, were confined mostly to the East

Coast, were wealthy, followed traditional Sephardic practices quite different from those of the Germans, and were indifferent, if not hostile, to the new German immigrants.

The new immigrants, many of whom settled away from the older Sephardic communities, naturally established their own synagogues. At least, those who bothered about Judaism did so. But they did not think of these institutions as particularly denominational. The new German synagogues were not established in deliberate opposition to any other synagogue or ideology. With the arrival of German rabbis, preeminently Isaac Mayer Wise, who was already identified with German Reform, some deliberate and successful efforts were made toward organizing these synagogues into a central body with a uniform liturgy and a single ideology.

In 1857 Wise published a prayerbook which he hoped would meet the needs of these congregations. He called it *Minhag America*, The Custom of America. To Wise, Jewish denominationalism was not the division between Reform and Orthodoxy. At this period in his life Wise believed that the only type of synagogue which would survive was the indigenous American congregation, which he saw as Reform in orientation. Wise did not fear the opposition of Orthodox or traditionalist Jews. The great Jewish problem in America was not to fight the tradition but to retain the Jewish allegiance of the immigrants and their children. Consequently, Wise thought of his prayerbook and liturgy as reflecting, not so much Reform, but rather the needs of American Jews.

In 1873 Wise founded the Union of American Hebrew Congregations and in 1875, Hebrew Union College (HUC) for the training of American rabbis. The word Union in the name is significant because it suggests the absence of schism. As Samuel Cohon has noted, the term Union expressed the founder's hope "to have one theological school for all Jews of the country,"[2] at least for all but the "ultra-Orthodox," to use Cohon's formulation. Certain segments of American Judaism found the practices of HUC "too Reform," however, and in 1886 they founded the Jewish Theological Seminary Association to organize a more traditional institution to train rabbis. Even then an Orthodox leader, Judah David Eisenstein, objected to the new seminary, and argued that if HUC

[2]Samuel S. Cohon, "The History of Hebrew Union College," *Publications of the American Jewish Historical Society* 40 (September 1950), p. 24.

was indeed too Reform, one solution was for the non-Reform to identify themselves with it and change its character.[3]

American Reform, however, had already begun to take shape as a distinctive movement with its own ideological position. In 1885 a group of Reform rabbis met in Pittsburgh and adopted the famous statement of principle known as the Pittsburgh Platform. These rabbis represented the more radical and ideological wing of Reform. Wise himself was not present at the meeting. But after 1885 and until the repudiation of the Pittsburgh Platform in 1937 by the Central Conference of American Rabbis (the Reform rabbinical organization), this statement represented, one might say, the elitist formulation of American Reform.[4] It repudiated the binding character of "Mosaic legislation," that is, Jewish law and its divine revelation. It is doubtful, however, if this rejection of traditional Jewish law and dogma was more shocking to the sensibilities of the East European immigrant than the assertions that Judaism was *only* a religion; that "we consider ourselves no longer a nation but a religious community"; and that "we recognize in Judaism a progressive religion, ever striving to be in accord with the postulates of reason." This was the spirit of American Reform which the East European Jew found upon his arrival in the United States.

The New Immigrants

Who were the new immigrants? The important fact to be noted is that a disproportionately large number of them, relative to a cross-section of East European Jewry, were nontraditionalists, secularist Jews, Socialists, and Zionists. A few of them, particularly the Socialists, were militantly antireligious. Most, however, were not ideologically oriented. They were traditionalist in orientation but without the political, economic, or ideological stake that many East European Jewish leaders had in traditionalism. They were adherents of the folk, rather than the elite, religion of traditionalism.

Within traditional Judaism, folk religion and elite religion may be distinguished from each other by their orientation to change.

---

[3]Judah David Eisenstein, *Ozar Zikhronothai* (New York: Published by the author, 1929), pp. 206–211. The pages are reprinted from an article by Eisenstein in the *New York Yiddish Zeitung*, 1886.

[4]The text of the Pittsburgh Platform is reprinted in Nathan Glazer, *American Judaism* (Chicago: University of Chicago Press, 1957), pp. 151–152.

Traditional society differs from modern society, not in the occurrence of change (all societies change), but in its orientation to the concept of change.[5] Traditionalists accept only change which can be legitimized by past values and practices. The hallmark of the elite religion of traditional Judaism is the fact that the touchstone of legitimacy is the sacred textual tradition and the codes of Jewish law. The traditional elite are represented by the Talmudic scholars and sages. The traditionalist folk, on the other hand, find the touchstone of legitimacy in the practices of the community. In this sense the traditionalist folk are more innately conservative than the elite but are more susceptible to a radical break with the past, once the consensus within the community is broken.

The first traditionalist immigrants found themselves surrounded by a disproportionate number of nontraditionalists. Not only were the vast majority of new immigrants adherents of folk, rather than elite, traditionalism, but there was also a decided absence of distinguished scholars and rabbis. Israel Rosenberg, one of the leading Orthodox East European rabbis in America, noted the miserable state of Jewish education and commented at the 1924 convention of the Union of Orthodox Rabbis (Agudat Horabbonim): "To a certain extent the Jews of Europe are also responsible for this situation. When they saw that the stream of emigration to America was increasing, it was incumbent among them to send us the spiritual giants, those who had it in their powers to influence and to work."[6]

Although most of the estimated fifty thousand Jews who immigrated to the United States from 1881 to 1885 settled in New York, the leading East European congregation of the city had only a part-time rabbi of meager scholarship. When twenty-six Orthodox congregations met to choose a joint leader for New York Jewry, no American rabbi was even considered. In 1887 the secretary to Rabbi Isaac Elhanan Spektor, the outstanding rabbinic authority from Russia, referred to American rabbinical leaders as "improper men."[7] The few Talmudic scholars who did come "were without honor or

[5]The distinction and some application to contemporary Judaism is made by Jacob Katz, "Traditional Society and Modern Society," *M'Gamot* 10 (March 1960), pp. 304–311 (Hebrew).

[6]Agudat Horabbonim, *Jubilee Volume* (New York: Arius Press, 1928), p. 110.

[7]Cited in Abraham J. Karp, "New York Chooses a Chief Rabbi," *Publications of the American Jewish Historical Society* 45 (March 1955), pp. 129–198.

support even in their own poor communities."[8] One contemporary, commenting on the Talmudic saying that "the sages are kings," noted that in America this should read "the shoemakers, tailors, and usurers are the sages."[9]

The absence of a religious elite meant that the traditionalist immigrants were especially susceptible to a breakdown in religious consensus. To a greater extent than ever, the folk now set their own standards independently of the elite. The traditionalist immigrants were certainly not irreligious, nor did they wish to conceal their Jewish identity. But they did desire to be accepted and integrated into American society. . . . And while they were not irreligious, neither were they religious in the elitist sense in which one's life is bounded and guided by a legal textual tradition. Their piety was what Leo Baeck called *Milieu-Fromigkeit,* and what we have called a manifestation of folk religion. Willing as they were to take extended leave of family and home, they were less committed to tradition and more accepting of new values than their relatives and neighbors who came much later.

When the rabbi of Slutsk visited America and appeared at a public meeting of the Union of Orthodox Jewish Congregations during the first wave of immigration, "he chastised the assemblage for having emigrated to this *trefa* [impure] land."[10] Similarly, would-be emigrants were warned by such renowned rabbinic authorities as the Hafetz Hayim, Rabbi Israel Meir Hacohen, to stay home and not endanger their Judaism.[11] Those who did emigrate

[8]Ezekial Lifschutz, "Jewish Immigrant Life in American Memoir Literature," *YIVO Annual of Jewish Social Science* 5 (1950), p. 232.

[9]Shlomo Noble, "The Image of the American Jew in Hebrew and Yiddish Literature in America, 1870–1900," *ibid.*, 9 (1954), p. 87. A Yiddish story relates how Jews in a small East European town raised money to send a young man to America to prevent him from marrying a Gentile: Isaac Metzker, "To the New World," *A Treasury of Yiddish Stories,* ed. Irving Howe and Eliezer Greenberg (New York: Meridian Books, 1958), pp. 504–515. Milton Himmelfarb has noted: "After all, who went to America? Overwhelmingly, it was not the elite of learning, piety, or money but the *shnayders,* the *shusters* and the *ferdgenevim*"; Milton Himmelfarb, "The Intellectual and the Rabbi," *Proceedings of the Rabbinical Assembly of America,* 1963, p. 124. See also Mark Zborowski and Elizabeth Herzog, *Life Is With People* (New York: Schocken Books, 1952), pp. 260–261, and Arthur Hertzberg, "Seventy Years of Jewish Education," *Judaism* 1 (October 1952), p. 361.

[10]Moshe Davis, "Jewish Religious Life and Institutions in America," *The Jews: Their History, Culture, and Religion,* 2d ed., ed. Louis Finkelstein (Philadelphia: Jewish Publication Society, 1955), I, p. 539.

[11]Lloyd P. Gartner, *The Jewish Immigrant in England, 1870–1914* (Detroit: Wayne State University Press, 1960), p. 30.

were unable to separate the distinctively religious or legally essential elements from the nonessential elements of Judaism. We find that the "religious" practices which persisted among the immigrants were those most closely associated with the cultural life-style of Eastern Europe and were irrelevant to the process of American acculturation. In contrast, practices which were more deeply rooted in the textual religious tradition were readily abandoned.

Among the most important set of rituals in Jewish law are those surrounding Sabbath observance. The Torah commands the Jew, under penalty of death, to refrain from work on the Sabbath. The Sabbath rest is connected to creation itself. By resting on the Sabbath, the Jew refreshes and renews his spirit through prayer, study, good food, and even sexual intercourse, to which he is commanded. In the elitist formulation the Jew also affirms, by abstinence from forbidden work, his belief in God the Creator, who also rested on the Sabbath. But Sabbath observance entailed economic hardship for the immigrants and often did not survive the voyage across the Atlantic. A survey of Jewish workmen on the Lower East Side revealed that only 25 percent rested on the Sabbath; 60 percent of the stores owned by Jews were open. . . .[12]

Kashrut, the laws pertaining to permissible and forbidden foods, survived longer than Sabbath observance, though in an attenuated form. The parts which survived were rooted in the folk, rather than in the elitist, aspects of Judaism. The laws of kashrut govern which animals may be consumed, as well as which cuts of meat may be eaten, and prohibit mixing dairy and meat dishes. Kashrut resulted, therefore, in certain styles of food. Long after most Jews ceased to observe kashrut they continued to eat "kosher style." Among the animals which are forbidden to the Jew is the pig. In the elitist formulation eating pork products is sinful, but no more sinful than eating shrimp. Further, the laws make no distinction between consuming forbidden foods in one's home and consuming them in a restaurant. But the folk religion made both these distinctions. Pig was anathema, and it is not uncommon today to find Jews who will eat all nonkosher food except pork. Similarly, a newly emerging folk religion of American Judaism gave special sanctity to the home and forbade eating certain foods in the intimacy of the family but not outside. Many new immigrants in

---

[12]Cited in Moses Rischin, *The Promised City* (Cambridge, Mass.: Harvard University Press, 1962), pp. 146–147.

particular would have been shocked at the thought of eating nonkosher meat at home or outside long after they ceased observing the Sabbath. Behind all this is the special association between eating and cultural or life-style patterns which the Jew retained.

An elitist Jew might be expected to provide extensive Jewish education for his child, but as late as 1916 there were only two religious elementary schools (yeshivot) in the United States. According to an educator of that period, Jews opposed parochial schools, which they felt were harmful to democracy.[13] Less than 24 percent of the estimated number of Jewish children of elementary school age in New York received any form of Jewish education in 1917, and less than 1 percent received any training at the high school level.[14] It was primarily the elderly or the very poor who studied the Talmud, and then only at a very low level.

Jewish law extends to the most initimate details of family life—laws of family purity—and requires a married woman to immerse herself in a lustral bath (mikvah) at a specified time following each menstrual period. Writing in 1928 about the immigrant era, an observer commented that lustral baths were simply unavaliable and that "the daughters of Israel had ceased to guard their purity."[15] The Union of Orthodox Rabbis, in the first issue of their publication in 1918, noted that family purity had been "erased from our lives." Requirements of family purity did not involve economic hardship, but they were an anachronism in the values of middle-class American culture toward which the immigrants aspired.

Many Jews did retain an attachment to the synagogue, but this was a broadly cultural, rather than a specifically religious, commitment. As early as 1887 one commentator noted that when the immigrants had built beautiful synagogues they felt they had fulfilled their obligation to Judaism.[16] The large majority of Jews attended a synagogue only on Yom Kippur, the most sacred day in the Jewish calendar.

The new immigrants did found countless small synagogues almost immediately upon arrival, but that in itself was no evidence

[13]Alexander M. Dushkin, Jewish Education in New York City (New York: Bureau of Jewish Education, 1918), p. 21.

[14]Ibid., p. 156.

[15]Agudat Horabbonim, Jubilee Volume, p. 16.

[16]Moses Weinberger, Ha-Yehudim Vehayahadut B'New York (New York: 1887), p. 2.

of religiosity. If the function of the synagogue was primarily for worship there was no need for such proliferation. But if its primary purpose was to meet the social and cultural needs of small groups originating in different European communities this proliferation is more understandable. The synagogues were social forums and benevolent societies adapted to the requirements of poor, unacculturated people. The evidence suggests an absence of religious, as distinct from ethnic, commitment on the part of the East European immigrants to the United States. But the older Jewish community made no such distinctions. To them the bulk of the immigrants were very religious unacculturated Jews. . . .

THE RISE OF CONSERVATIVE JUDAISM

We are now in a position to understand the emergence of a distinctly American brand of Judaism. American Judaism in its religious aspects is not quite synonymous with Conservative Judaism, but it is intimately connected with its growth.

In 1902 the Jewish Theological Seminary was reorganized, and Solomon Schechter was brought from England to head it. Its new financial benefactors were primarily nontraditionalists (Reform Jews) who hoped that the institution and its future rabbinical graduates would Americanize and acculturate the East European immigrants. It is most interesting that the Reform Jews sought to use a nominally traditionalist institution to reach the new immigrant. However, their own status in American society was threatened by the masses of Jewish immigrants.[17] Indeed, the rising anti-Semitism in this period was attributed to the nonacculturated character of the immigrants which reflected unfavorably on the native American Jews.[18] They apparently believed that the seminary could reach the new immigrants since it shared their commitment to religious tradition. . . .

In its infancy, the Conservative movement (with some

[17]Marshall Sklare, *Conservative Judaism* (New York: Free Press, 1955), pp. 161–165, 191–193.

[18]*Ibid.*

exceptions) represented an upper-class formulation of elitist traditional Judaism. But its synagogues were more adaptable to the changing needs of American Jews than were those of Orthodoxy. Some Conservative rabbis were themselves in the forefront of those clamoring for change. But the changes which the rabbis sought were rooted in ideological convictions about the nature of Judaism. The masses sought change for very different reasons.

The alliance between the masses of East European immigrants or their descendants and the Conservative movement finally took place as the East Europeans abandoned the traditional folk religion of Orthodoxy and sought new forms of Jewish expression. Conservatism became predominant in areas of "third settlement." This was the most fashionable ethnic settlement and typically was located near the city limits, where residence "symbolized the attainment of solid middle-class position or better and is indicative of a relatively high level of acculturation."[19] Here Jews constituted a distinct minority of the population and were surrounded, not by other ethnic groups over whom they might feel a sense of status superiority, but rather by Protestants and "old Americans" to whom they were subordinate in status. "The importation of the Orthodox synagogue to areas of third settlement would not have helped to reduce this status hiatus; it would in fact only have served to underline it."[20]

It is not surprising, then, that Jews sought to develop a new form of worship. The surprise is that Conservative synagogues still conformed so closely to traditional Orthodoxy. The content was not changed because the new Conservative Jews had no interest in content. They were folk traditionalists or "reformed" secularists with a communal or ethnic definition of Judaism. They were quite concerned with group survival, not very interested in religion, and in search of institutions which expressed values of both communal survival and integration or acculturation to middle-class American standards.

To the upwardly mobile, status-conscious, economically successful East European Jews of the second or even first generation, there was a tremendous socio-economic cost in being Orthodox. The economic cost came from not working on the Sabbath and the holidays. A social-status cost resulted from

[19]Sklare, *Conservative Judaism*, p. 217.
[20]*Ibid.*, p. 67.

affiliation with an institution lacking in decorum, unconcerned with physical amenities, and chaotic in worship. There was an intellectual cost in paying lip service to a faith burdened with real and imagined superstition which was out of keeping with the prevailing spirit of rationalism and secularism. Hence the immigrant sought new institutional outlets for his Judaism. These outlets had to be outwardly religious, since this was the most legitimate expression of Judaism in America; but they also had to provide a focus for expressing his essentially communal concerns.

The growth of Conservatism in turn took the pressure off Orthodoxy to accommodate itself rapidly to the American environment. Conservative Judaism provided a safety valve for discontented Orthodox Jews and reduced the demand for radical innovation within Orthodoxy, leaving it relatively unconcerned with integration. However, this also changed with the growth of an American-born rabbinate and laity.

Conservative Judaism is the primary Jewish expression of the East European immigrant and his descendants. It is fair to say that the folk religion of the contemporary American Jew is more adequately expressed through Conservatism than through any other movement. But it was not just shaped by the Jewish folk religion; it developed its own elite religion, its own ideology and practices which were shared by its leadership but not by the masses of Conservative Jews. In Conservatism, far more than in Orthodoxy or Reform, there is a sharp division between folk religion and elite religion. The original adherents of Orthodox folk religion have died out or become Conservative. Reform is experiencing a crisis in its own formulation. In fact, considerable numbers of Reform Jews, especially in the East, and many of its leaders share the folk religion of Conservative Judaism. Some nominally Orthodox Jews (though none of its leaders) also participate in the folk religion characteristic of Conservatism. Consider first, however, the elite religion of Conservative Judaism.

The Elite Religion of Conservative Judaism

Conservative Judaism traces its intellectual origin to the Historical School of Judaism in nineteenth-century Europe.[21] It represents a commitment to the historical traditions of Judaism, which it

[21]Moshe Davis, *The Emergence of Conservative Judaism* (Philadelphia: Jewish Publication Society, 1963).

acknowledges as primarily legalistic and textual. Unlike Orthodoxy, however, Conservative Judaism sees the Jewish people and their history—through which God acts—as the source of authority, rather than the sacred texts—through which, according to the Orthodox, God speaks. Thus Conservative Judaism opens the theoretical possibility for reform and even radical change in Jewish law, depending upon how one interprets Jewish history and law, the needs of the time, and the mix between past and present authority. The elitist ideology of Conservatism is shared by most of the nine hundred or so members of the Rabbinical Assembly (the rabbinical arm of Conservatism) and by a few hundred, perhaps as many as a few thousand, Conservative educators and Jewishly literate laymen.

The center of Conservative Judaism for this small community of elite is the Jewish Theological Seminary (JTS). JTS is more traditional in orientation than even its elitist constituents, and its leaders have opposed the introduction of changes in Jewish law. This opposition has been generally successful (somewhat less so in the last few years), because the Talmudic scholars who might introduce the changes or reforms with textual or legal justifications are on the JTS faculty and are generally the more traditional element within the Conservative movement.

But more significantly (for many Conservative rabbis would accept change even if it could not be legitimized by textual exegesis of some kind), JTS as an institution maintains a strong hold over its graduates and friends. This is due in part to the interpersonal relationships developed during student days between future rabbis and the JTS leadership, and in part to the enormous prestige of JTS as a center for scholarly research. In addition, many Conservative rabbis harbor feelings of guilt toward JTS. While this last point is highly speculative, it is based on the observation that many JTS graduates are disturbed by the kinds of compromises they have made with lay leaders of their congregations and feel that they have thereby betrayed the seminary. Many Conservative rabbis have very ambivalent feelings toward JTS, to whom they relate as sons to a father. The same individuals who are willing to follow its leadership on matters of religious reform often express a sense of bitterness and even hostility toward the institution.

In recent years the faculty, curriculum, and standards of conduct within JTS have become even more traditional. This has produced some serious strains among the elite themselves, particularly between the rabbinical students and the JTS leadership.

The problem is that JTS, whose students at one time came primarily from Orthodox homes, now recruits its students from homes where the prevailing atmosphere is Conservative folk religion. Before they come to JTS these students are socialized somewhat to the elite religion by the youth and camping movements of Conservatism. However, these institutions are staffed by individuals whose ideology is less traditional than that of the JTS leadership.

There is one central value, however, which is shared by both the elite religion and the folk religion of Conservatism: the value of integration into American life and a rejection of the notion that integration can only be sought at the expense of survival.

THE FOLK RELIGION OF AMERICAN JUDAISM

First- and second-generation American Jews of East European origin created the folk religion of American Judaism. Its adherents, as noted earlier, included virtually all the nominally Conservative Jews, many Reform, and some Orthodox.

Ritual of the Folk Religion

It is clear that the immigrant was willing to sacrifice a great deal that was basic and fundamental to the Jewish religion. He quickly denuded Judaism of much basic ritual. The laws of the Sabbath, kashrut, and family purity—the basic elements of Jewish ritual life—were abandoned by most of the first- and second-generation Jews. (Kosher-style, however, replaced kosher, a substitution which, as we noted, suggests that we are dealing with a choice for the sake of convenience, not a deliberate variation of life-style in an effort to conceal or lose one's identity.)

Despite the abandonment of the basic Jewish ritual, objections to intermarriage were retained. Why? Many of the early Reform rabbis raised no objections to intermarriage; indeed, they welcomed it. It is certainly consistent with Reform's definition of Judaism as a religion stressing morality and ethics which the Jew is obligated to diffuse among non-Jews. Why is intermarriage any more horrendous than violation of the Sabbath? In the catalog of ritual Jewish sins, there is hardly anything worse than desecration of the Sabbath. But obviously in the catalog of Jewish communal sins there is nothing worse than intermarriage. Countless Jewish mothers and fathers have cautioned their children before they left for college: "Forget Sabbath observance or kashrut if you must, but just make sure you don't fall in love with or marry a non-Jewish student." The proper ritual advice should be: "Marry a non-Jewish person if you must, but remember to observe the Sabbath." Of course, such advice sounds ludicrous. And the fact that it is ludicrous says something about the ritual, as opposed to communal, priorities of Jews.

The pattern of ritual which Jews have maintained is supportive of Jewish communalism and ethnicity, of the Jewish home and peoplehood. The seder, now celebrated as an annual festive family meal, is the most widely observed Jewish practice. The rites of passage—circumcision, bar mitzvah, a Jewish marriage, and a Jewish funeral—all serve to integrate the Jew into the community of fellow Jews. Chanukah was elaborated by American Jews to protect the child and to defend Judaism against the glamour and seductive power of Christmas. These holidays are the major points of contact between the Jew and his ritual traditions. Obviously, even these celebrations have undergone considerable distortion as they developed. The joyful and child-centered aspects were stressed and the more historically symbolic and existential theological aspects de-emphasized. Of somewhat lesser, though still considerable, importance is the celebration of the High Holy Days inaugurating the Jewish New Year. These days, Rosh Hashana and Yom Kippur, have acquired particular religious significance as memorials for departed parents and as the holidays of Jewish affirmation.

Some East European immigrants, forced by economic circumstances to work on the Sabbath, attended religious services in the early morning and then went to work. Second- and third-generation American Jews have reversed the process for the High Holy Days (the Sabbath is totally ignored). The folk religion enjoins the Jew from working on these days, regardless of whether he attends the synagogue or not and regardless of whether he prays or not. At least a token appearance at the synagogue is a desideratum, particularly at the time when memorial prayers for the dead are said. But the stress is not so much on prayer, and certainly not on hearing the shofar (the ram's horn blown on Rosh Hashana), which is central to the religious service. Rather, the stress is on staying away from work and thereby publicly acknowledging one's Jewish identity.

One does not have to believe with Emile Durkheim, the seminal French Jewish sociologist, that all religion is the celebration and ritualization of communal ties to observe that this is the major function of Jewish folk religion in America. It is not without significance that Mordecai Kaplan, whose philosophy of Reconstructionism was an effort to provide an ideological and elitist framework for Jewish folk religion, was influenced by Durkheim's theory of religion.

In a number of community studies, Jews were asked what they considered essential for a person to do in order to be a good Jew. The answer most frequently given was "Lead an ethical and moral life." Close behind and affirmed by over three-quarters of the respondents was "Accept his being a good Jew and not try to hide it."[22] Less than half, however, thought it was essential for one to belong to a synagogue or temple, and less than one-quarter thought that it was necessary to observe the dietary laws or attend weekly services in order to be considered a good Jew.

Associationalism

The Jewish folk religion includes a commitment to Israel . . . and to group survival, but its essence is one's social ties to other Jews. The distinguishing mark of American Jews is less and less how they behave and is certainly not what they believe; it is that they associate primarily with other Jews. Gerhard Lenski, in his Detroit area study, found that ties binding Jews to their religion are weaker than those of Protestants or Catholics, but ties binding them to one another are much stronger. More than other religious groups, "the great majority of Detroit Jews find most of their primary relationships within the Jewish subcommunity."[23] Even the highly acculturated and assimilated, wealthy, predominantly third-generation suburban

---

[22]Marshall Sklare and Joseph Greenblum, *Jewish Identity on the Suburban Frontier* (New York: Basic Books, 1967), and studies of Jews in Miami, Baltimore, Kansas City, and White Plains, conducted by Manheim Shapiro for the American Jewish Committee.

[23]Gerhard Lenski, *The Religious Factor*, rev. ed. (New York: Doubleday, Anchor Books, 1963), p. 37.

American Jews studied by Sklare and Greenblum continue to make their friends almost exclusively among other Jews.[24] They noted that "87 percent of the parents had most or all of their close friendships with Jews; the same holds true for 89 percent of our respondents."

Schools

Most Jewish parents who send their children to Jewish schools do so because they expect the school to serve those functions which the acculturated, Jewishly ignorant parent can no longer fulfill, "to reinforce Jewish identification through learning about Jewish history and traditions."[25] In his study of the growth of a new Jewish community, Herbert Gans notes that the community organized a school before a synagogue because the school was necessary as "an institution which transmits norms of ethnic culture and symbols of identification, whereas the home and the family are run by secular, middle-class behavior patterns."[26]

A synagogue bulletin carried the following argument by the principal of the congregation's supplementary Hebrew high school, urging parents to enroll their children:

> Our adolescent youngster, for instance, begins to evaluate the Synagogue he once accepted unthinkingly. Does he really need worship or home observances? Does Jewish living do him or the world any good? Do Bible stories about tribes and miracles deserve all this fuss? These are really adolescent problems, not Jewish ones. If a child did not continue on to public high school, he would be assailed by the same doubts concerning the value of his secular elementary education. Such problems do not usually trouble a child who carries on his Jewish education through the high school level.

The writer's rationale for the child's continuing his Jewish education is worth noting. Jews traditionally educated their children in order to teach them how to live as good Jews. Now parents are urged to enroll their children so that the school may transmit to them the *value* of being Jewish. . . .

[24]Sklare and Greenblum, *Jewish Identity*, pp. 269–290.

[25]Herbert Gans, "The Origin and Growth of a Jewish Community in the Suburbs: A Study of the Jews of Park Forest," *The Jews: Social Patterns of an American Group,* ed. Marshall Sklare (New York: Free Press, 1958), pp. 217–218.

[26]*Ibid.*, p. 217.

The Synagogue

The synagogue plays a crucial role in the folk religion of the Jews. Statistics are difficult to ascertain, but the combined estimates of members of all Orthodox, Conservative, and Reform congregations suggest that about 60 percent of American Jews are affiliated with a synagogue. According to the most recent community surveys, less than 20 percent of the Jews reported attending synagogue services oftener than once a month.

But the synagogue is far more than a religious center. It tends to be the center for all Jewish activity. . . . It provides recreational and educational facilities, lectures, art classes, social outlets, golden age clubs, and a meeting place for other nonsynagogal Jewish organizations in the area. It raises funds not only for its own needs but for Jewish philanthropic purposes as well. The synagogue-based campaign provides a major source of funds for federations of Jewish philanthropies and for assistance to Jews abroad, particularly in Israel. Furthermore, secular Jewish organizations such as B'nai B'rith and the American Jewish Congress are not alternatives to the synagogue. Most members of the major Jewish communal organizations are synagogue members. Indeed, Jewish organizational membership tends to be a supplement rather than an alternative. Those who are affiliated with Jewish organizations are most likely to identify themselves with the religious community. According to Bernard Lazerwitz, "the two dominating factors of Jewish identification which are also strongly associated with one another are the religio-pietistic and Jewish organizational factors."[27]

The synagogue is the institutional center of Jewish life. Its public image is religious, its ostensible director is a clergyman, and its activity is therefore legitimate. The official ideology of the synagogue and the rabbi is that of an elite religion, but its content is that of the Jewish folk religion.

Reconstructionism

There was one effort, characteristically arising out of the Conservative movement, to reformulate the essence of American Jewish folk religion in ideological terms, and hence to institutionalize it and provide it with a formal leadership. This was the

[27]Bernard Lazerwitz, *A First Report on the General Components and Consequences of Jewish Identification*, mimeographed (Waltham, Mass.: National Jewish Welfare Board, 1968), p. 19. . . .

Reconstructionist philosophy and movement founded by Mordecai Kaplan in the 1920's. Kaplan's major work is *Judaism as a Civilization: Toward a Reconstruction of American-Jewish Life,* a title which suggests both a traditional view of Judaism and at the same time its reformulation in contemporary terminology.[28] The Reconstructionists challenged the notion of God as a Being. They redefined Him as a power and force in man and nature which makes for salvation, by which they mean freedom, justice, love, truth, and creativity. Under the influence of Durkheim and Dewey, Kaplan sought to explicate or make manifest in religion what others had seen as its latent function: social solidarity and the strengthening of peoplehood. Kaplan sought to retain the form of many traditional observances by reinvesting them with contemporary humanist meaning or national-historical significance.

The most remarkable feature of Reconstructionism is its failure as an institutionalized movment. Kaplan taught at the Jewish Theological Seminary from 1909 to 1963, serving also as dean of its Teachers Institute. He was a very popular teacher and for many years the most influential instructor there. Two generations of Conservative rabbis and educators came under Kaplan's influence. Since 1934 the Jewish Reconstructionist Foundation has published a lively biweekly periodical, *The Reconstructionist,* which has attracted many outstanding Jewish intellectuals as contributors and subscribers. And yet Reconstructionism has made few inroads into organized Jewish life. Only a handful of synagogues are associated with it, it has little money, and since the 1950's it has failed to gain the affection of young intellectuals, particularly within the Conservative movement.

Kaplan was not saying anything very new. He articulated in a provocative and intellectual manner the folk religion of American Jews. Why did his movement strike such a small chord if most Jews consciously or unconsciously are really Reconstructionists? The answer rests in the fact that to label one's religion explicitly as Reconstructionism is to identify it as a sham. Jews have preferred to deceive themselves and others about the nature of their faith and commitment. For the intellectuals of the 1930's, Reconstructionism had a more positive image. The Jewish Theological Seminary student, for example, knew he had lost the traditional Jewish faith in

[28]First published in 1934 by Macmillan, the volume has been reprinted by the Reconstructionist Press and most recently (1967) by Schocken Books in a paper edition.

God and belief in the divine authority of religious law. Coming as he generally did from an Orthodox home and attending an institution of Conservative Judaism, he was quite self-conscious about his divergence from tradition. But he did not want to break with Judaism. He not only wanted to remain Jewish but to believe that he could function as a rabbi within the traditional Jewish fold. Kaplan offered him a rationale and a justification. Reconstructionism had an appeal to Jewish intellectuals, particularly rabbis, as long as there were young men who wanted to be rabbis and did not want to be—or found they could not be—"religious." But the number of such young men, particularly in the Conservative rabbinate, is declining.

The institutional weakness of Reconstructionism lies partly in the fact that if one wants to be Jewish and not religious, there are secular Jewish organizations which can occupy one's energy and attention. Jewish philanthropic organizations, Zionist organizations, B'nai B'rith, the American Jewish Congress, the American Jewish Committee, and other groups provide outlets for one's Jewish identification outside a religious context. These secular Jewish organizations tend to specialize in one aspect of Jewish life or to concentrate on one type of Jewish problem. But they maintain secondary activities in the hope of appealing to all Jews, regardless of their particular interest.

Pure Jewish secularism has no legitimacy in America (witness the demise of Jewish secularist labor and Yiddishist schools, and the inability of Zionists to establish a network of schools, as they have done in a number of other countries). Consequently, the secular organizations themselves have increasingly incorporated religion into the structure of their activity. They generally have one or more rabbis on their staffs, they often introduce some minor religious service into their meetings or conferences, and they articulate their special interests—whether they be Jewish-Christian relations, defense against real or imagined anti-Semitism, support for Israel, or even battling for strict separation of church and state—in quasi-religious terminology. Thus even Jewish secular organizations are "religious." Many spokesmen for these organizations deny that they are secular. To many Jews they differ from Orthodox, Conservative, and Reform synagogues only in their nondenominationalism.

A second factor which has handicapped Reconstructionism is the increased "religiousness" of the American Jew. We have suggested all along that religion is the public façade for the essentially communal content of Jewish identification. But as Jews become increasingly acculturated they take the façade of their public image more seriously. This is the paradoxical result of the fact that more and more Jews learn about themselves from the outside world, particularly the mass media. Newspapers, magazines, and television are probably the primary sources of information for Jews about Judaism. But the mass media obtain their information from the façade of Jewish life, not from the inner content. . . .

The process of acculturation has led an increasing number of Jews to believe that Judaism is a religion. Consequently, if Jews are nonreligious, they more readily lose a sense of Jewish identification. But if they desire a continuing identification, they must be religious. For such Jews, God must be more than the impersonal force or power that Reconstructionism asserts.

Reconstructionism, then, has lost much of its appeal for Conservative Jews, particularly rabbinical students. These young men now come from Conservative backgrounds. They never broke with Orthodoxy; they have no nostalgia for replicas of East European life-styles, no guilt feelings about their religious beliefs or behavior. Furthermore, they are not attracted to the rabbinate by a depression economy which offers no occupational alternatives. They want to become rabbis because they believe Judaism has something to say of religious and social significance.

Reconstructionism has enjoyed some increase in popularity, however, among Reform Jews, though not among its theological spokesmen. Reform theologians either are far more committed to religious existentialism and belief in a personal God or, at the other extreme, are far more radical than Kaplan. The radical Reform Jews deny the utility of the God concept or the existence of meaningful Jewish tradition. Nevertheless, Reform, like every other American Jewish institution, was engulfed by the East European immigrant. This was not only true among the laity but also among the Reform rabbinate, and resulted in the introduction of more traditional symbols among the Reform, a greater emphasis on traditional observance, and greater sympathy toward Zionism. David Philipson, a member of the first graduating class of Hebrew Union College in 1883, viewed these developments at the 1931 meetings of the Reform rabbis with chagrin, and attributed them to "the large number of young rabbis who came from Zionistic and Orthodox environments."[29]

As Reform found an East European Jewish identity, Kaplan's notion of peoplehood and his justification of many ritual practices as folkways had special resonance for some. In a recent survey of first- and last-year students at rabbinical seminaries, respondents were asked to check the name of an individual who best reflected their religious, philosophical, or theological position. Between the first and the last year, the number of Jewish Theological Seminary students choosing Kaplan decreased, but at the Reform schools the number increased. To many Reform Jews of East European background, classical Reform Judaism appears schismatic. For them, Kaplan represents the route back to the unity of the Jewish people.

Religious Elitism and the Growth of Jewish Denominationalism

The religious definition of Judaism strengthens elitist religion within Conservativism and Reform as well as within Orthodoxy. Within Orthodoxy, the religious right wing and the Talmudic scholars—those most at home in the sacred textual tradition and those, therefore, with the greatest stake in the present system of religious authority—have assumed the leadership. In Conservatism and Reform, the influence of the rabbi, the bearer of their elitist religion, has been enhanced because only the rabbi has the requisite knowledge and "authority" to manipulate the symbols of the religion and organize its cult. Of course, this notion of rabbinic authority was borrowed from Christianity by the modern Jew, who, religious though he may be, tends increasingly to be religious in a Christian rather than in a traditional Jewish sense.

One result of the growth of elitism has been the development of Jewish denominationalism. Religious denominationalism among Protestants has often been associated with differences in social class. It might be well to explore the question of social change and question whether certain Jewish religious developments might not be ascribed more properly to change in social conditions.

The identification of individual Jews with Orthodoxy, Conser-

---

[29]David Philipson, *My Life as an American Jew* (Cincinnati: John G. Kidd & Son, 1941), p. 128.

vatism, and Reform in America is indeed associated with differential social characteristics. In view of the fact that a substantial segment of all three denominations shares in the Jewish folk religion, one might even argue that social and life-style differences have been the major source of differentiation among the denominations. Reform Jews were the wealthiest and best educated, Orthodox the poorest and least educated; indeed, many of the ritual and behavioral differences between Orthodoxy and Reform do reflect differences in social class. (Since Orthodox Jews tend to be older than other Jews and of more recent immigration, they are naturally the poorest and least educated. Whether differences in the social characteristics of the denominations will remain the same in the future is problematical.)

But if the major distinguishing features of the three Jewish branches are their social characteristics, then one might anticipate a lessening of Jewish denominationalism and perhaps even a merging of the three groups should their members become socially homogeneous. This is, after all, the process that has taken place among Protestants. Jews who rise in social class might simply leave one denomination, Orthodoxy, and switch their affiliation to Conservative or Reform. This unquestionably has happened. But the experience of Protestantism has been that not all members of a lower-status denomination change to a higher-status one as they rise in social class. Instead, whole groups or denominations tend to respond to changes in their members' social status by changes in their prescribed religious practices and beliefs. These changes help account for the growing ecumenism among Protestants.[30]

In order to examine changes in the social characteristics of Orthodox, Conservative, and Reform Jews, synagogues in the Greater New York area were examined during two periods: 1948–1952 and 1958–1962.[31] Synagogues were located by census tract, and the median income of the residents of each tract was examined. The assumption was that a new synagogue reflected the social characteristics of the area in which it was located, and that the relative class composition of Jews was proportional to that of the other residents within a given census tract. The study found that, on the average, Reform Jews have been and continue to be in the

[30]Robert Lee, The Social Sources of Church Unity (Nashville: Abingdon Press, 1960).

[31]For details of the study, see Charles S. Liebman, "Changing Social Characteristics of Orthodox, Conservative and Reform Jews," Sociological Analysis 27 (Winter 1966), pp. 210–212.

highest income bracket, Orthodox Jews in the lowest, and Conservative Jews between the two but closer to Reform. However, since World War II the overlap between the three groups is considerable. Reform Judaism is no longer confined to Jews of the highest income and Orthodoxy to those of the lowest. Instead, the social distance among Orthodox Jews themselves, or Conservatives, or Reform Jews, is growing. . . .

This overlapping may in the long run lead to increased cooperation between the three groups. But it is dangerous to make such a prediction without taking into account the growth of elite religion. Jews who share a folk religion may readily move from one denomination to another if the distinctions are based only on acculturation, style, and taste. But should elite religion continue to develop more rapidly than changes in the class composition of the three groups, there is no reason to believe that social homogeneity would inevitably lead to religious unity. In fact, Orthodoxy, which has the most highly developed elitist leadership and which has been most successful in repressing its folk elements (partly because its adherents of the folk element abandoned Orthodoxy for Conservatism), has become more sectarian with its rise in social status. The elite religion of Orthodoxy must be more sectarian than the folk religion because communal consensus carries much less weight in its scale of values. The increase in income among Orthodox Jews has simply meant that its elite leadership now has greater resources and is better able to strike out on an independent path from Conservatism and Reform.

Conservative and Reform leaders in turn have sought to delineate the particular boundaries differentiating their own groups from Orthodoxy. In part this has been a response to Orthodoxy's denial of their religious legitimacy in a period when religious legitimacy is increasingly important. In part it has been a response to the threat posed by the synagogues' peripheral nonworship activity which engulfs the religious center and reduces the rabbis' authoritative platform. This threat has always existed and has been an inherently unsatisfactory condition for the rabbi, who is now in a position to fight back. But most of all, the Conservative and Reform leaders have had to define their particular boundaries in response to the increasing sense of religious (as distinct from communal) Jewish identity among many young people. This identity requires that the rabbi assert a religious definition of his own denomination if his synagogue is to have any meaning.

But once boundaries are asserted in elitist terms, differences between the groups become significant. The folk religion also distinguished between Orthodoxy, Conservatism, and Reform— Reform being modern, Orthodoxy old-worldly, and Conservatism between the two. To the third- or fourth-generation American Jews, to whom the conflict over acculturation is a fight long past and for whom Judaism is a religion, these distinctions are trivial and hardly enough to sustain or justify independent religious establishments. The elitist distinctions in theology and practice appear to be of greater substance. In their efforts to impose elitist definitions on the masses of synagogue members, each group has paid increased attention to the development of synagogue-based youth groups and summer camps. Part of the impetus was to recruit young men for the elite ranks, particularly the rabbinate, but the enterprise can also be seen as an effort on the part of each movement to socialize the future synagogue members to the values and definitions of the elite.

PROSPECTS FOR THE FUTURE

The self-definition of Judaism in religious rather than communal-ethnic terms has been a major tendency in American Jewish life. But there are forces operating against this trend which might well become dominant in the future. These include the decline of Christian churches and the deterioration of organized religion's reputation, which may result in Jews being more comfortable with a different structural façade. In addition, there is the increasing significance of the role of Israel in the life of the American Jew, and the Jewish identity which is aroused by threats to Israel's safety. Support for and interest in Israel by some Jews represents a secular and ethnic outlet for Jewish expression which is not necessarily religious in nature. Should there be increasing manifestations of anti-Semitism in the United States, Jews will be drawn together across denominational lines. Anti-Semitism, like perils to Israel, will activate religiously uninterested Jews who might otherwise have left the community.

REFORM IS A VERB
by LEONARD J. FEIN, ROBERT CHIN, JACK DAUBER,
BERNARD REISMAN, and HERZL SPIRO

INTRODUCTION

*H*ISTORIANS *have done considerable research into American
Reform Judaism. The accessibility of Reform records and archives,
the interest in Reform Judaism by students of American Jewish
history, and the intellectual curiosity of members of the Reform
elite have resulted in the accumulation of considerable knowledge
about the origin and development of this movement.*

*Social scientists have come to the study of Reform Judaism
independently of historians. Furthermore, their findings have
centered on present-day Reform rather than on its historical
development. Their work has also taken on a different emphasis
from that of the historians, tending to highlight not the
accomplishments of Reform but the relative poverty of "Jewishness"
among present-day Reform Jews. Thus in the various community
surveys conducted from the 1930's to the present, Reform Jews
appear as highly secular. They practice very few Jewish rituals in the
home and, except for a small group, their attendance at religious
services is minimal. Furthermore, the more pious element in the
movement does not appear to have been motivated by its Reform
affiliation but by the fact of having been reared by parents who were
uncommitted or residual Orthodox Jews.*

Ritual deviance has been accompanied by attitudinal deviance: most social science research indicates that Reform Jews have a weaker Jewish identity than Orthodox or Conservative Jews. Part of this difference can be accounted for by the fact that Reform Jews generally exceed Conservative and Orthodox Jews in class level, secular education, and in the number of generations their families have been in the United States. There is also the fact that the designation "Reform" has functioned as a kind of catchall category. Thus in most studies "Reform" includes unaffiliated Jews who so designate themselves in response to a question such as: "Would you describe yourself as Orthodox, Conservative, Reform, or none of these?" Apparently a fair percentage of unaffiliated Jews of weak Jewish identity choose the rubric "Reform" because it corresponds more closely to their image of themselves than does "Conservative" or "Orthodox," or because they prefer to associate themselves with something positive—"none of these" suggests a lack of commitment.

In evaluating the findings of social scientists it is well to remember that there are two divergent interpretations of Reform. Both have been made in respect to Reform in Germany, where the movement originated, as well as in respect to Reform in America, where the movement grew much more rapidly than it did in European countries. The first interpretation is that Reform constitutes an effort to break with one's Jewish identity; since a sharp separation would threaten personality integration the individual looks for a way of remaining Jewish until such time as he (or his children) is ready to assimilate. According to this interpretation, Reform is a way of remaining Jewish for people who prefer to assimilate; its latent function is that of preparing the individual to separate himself from the Jewish community.

The second interpretation of Reform is that it serves precisely the opposite function—it constitutes a movement serving the individual who wants to remain Jewish but who feels that his Jewish identity is threatened. No longer able to conform to traditional patterns, such an individual becomes attracted to Reform because it offers him the possibility of remaining Jewish on terms which take into account his life situation, his extensive acculturation, and the pressures which he experiences living in a Gentile world.

It is apparent that the motivation of most present-day Reform Jews conforms more closely to the second interpretation than to the first. Most Jews who adhere to Reform do so because they wish to remain within the Jewish community—their Reform affiliation represents a desire to affiliate with the Jewish community rather than a desire to depart from it. Nevertheless, the identity pattern common to many Reform Jews suggests the possibility that, while they may wish to avoid assimilation, they may not prevail in their desire to remain Jewish. The social scientist must entertain the possibility that the Jewish identity of the Reform Jew, and particularly the identity of his children, is not sufficiently strong to resist further secularization or acculturation—for any additional secularization and acculturation would inevitably end in assimilation.

The communal studies sponsored by Jewish federations contain extensive data on Reform Jews. However, these studies are demographic in orientation. The problem of the Jewish identity of the Reform Jew was an important aspect of the Lakeville Study and is analyzed in Marshall Sklare and Joseph Greenblum: Jewish Identity on the Suburban Frontier: A Study of Group Survival in the Open Society. Since Lakeville was heavily Reform—the first synagogue established in the community was Reform, and of the four synagogues subsequently founded, three were Reform and the fourth was Conservative—the identity of the Reform group necessarily constituted an important focus of the research.

The Lakeville findings indicated a sharp contrast between the strong attachment to Jewish clique groups and the much weaker attachment to Jewish religious observance and to synagogue attendance. While most Lakeville Jews disapproved of intermarriage and were fearful that intermarriage might occur in their own families, they were prepared to adjust (as they put it) to "reality" should they be confronted with a son or daughter who insisted upon intermarrying. Furthermore, it became clear that for most Lakeville Jews the essential qualifications for being a "good Jew" were Jewish self-acceptance, moral excellence, good citizenship, and a kind of general acquaintance with the essentials of Judaism. Only a minority of Lakeville Jews viewed marrying within the Jewish group, contributing to Jewish philanthropies, or attending services on the High Holidays as essential to being a good Jew.

The concern of both Reform officials and lay leadership about the long-range viability of Reform resulted in the initiation of a research program under the auspices of the movement. One study, directed by Theodore I. Lenn, was published under the title Rabbi and Synagogue in Reform Judaism (New York: Central Conference of American Rabbis, 1972). A second study, named "The Pilot Project for Synagogue Change," was directed by Leonard J. Fein. It represented a collaboration among a political scientist, a psychologist specializing in group dynamics who was connected with a human relations center, an academician trained as a social worker, a group worker in the Jewish community-center field, and a psychiatrist specializing in the field of community mental health, and it resulted in Reform is a Verb: Notes on Reform and Reforming Jews (New York: Union of American Hebrew Congregations, 1972).

Both studies utilized self-administered questionnaires, as well as other techniques. Samples were drawn from a selected group of Reform temples. Respondents did not represent a cross-section of affiliated Reform Jews, however; they tended to be more highly committed to the Reform movement than other temple members and presumably their Jewish identity was stronger than is the norm among Reform Jews.

While the two studies proceeded independently their findings are similar in many respects. Observance of basic home rituals is far from universal, attendance at services is infrequent, a significant minority is not upset at the prospect of intermarriage, and the only two actions which a majority of adults endorse as being essential to being a good Jew are "Accept being a Jew and not try to hide it," and "Lead an ethical and moral life." Further, both studies came to the conclusion that the Jewish commitment of Reform youth is far less than that of Reform adults. Finally, it was found that even the committed Reform Jew lacks deep attachment to his temple. Instead of seeing his temple as an extension of himself he sees it as outside of himself—as a purveyor of services to be utilized when required. The committed Reform Jew leads his social life quite independently of his temple.

Since the Lenn study was commissioned by the Central Conference of American Rabbis, it not only includes material on the practices and attitudes of the Reform laity but devotes considerable attention to the state of the Reform rabbinate. The study discovered a relatively high level of rabbinical discontent —most rabbis dislike their seminary training, only 53 percent would choose the rabbinate if they had it to do over again, and 64 percent feel that their congregation is "undergoing a crisis of existence and commitment." The study concluded that if present trends continue an increasing number of rabbis will question the basic religious tenets of Reform Judaism.

A summary of the second project—"The Pilot Project for Synagogue Change"—is reprinted below. In addition to reporting on questionnaire findings the summary includes the results of a series of workshops utilizing an experiential and group-dynamics approach. The summary also includes an extensive section devoted to recommendations made to the sponsoring agency.

While the Synagogue Change team does not present the assumptions on which their recommendations are based, it is clear that they believe that Reform Judaism, as a belief-system, has come to a dead end. They proceed on the assumption that Reform's religious message not only lacks the power to attract the unaffiliated but that it is incapable of transforming the lives of its leaders and devoted followers. Thus they recommend that the movement look elsewhere for its salvation. Rather than calling for the adoption of a new belief-system, they suggest that the movement seek to serve the need for community among its adherents.

One irony of this recommendation is that Reform has been strongly influenced by the cathedral model—that is, by the concept of the large impersonal religious institution of imposing architecture, a structure in which diverse individuals assemble at periodic intervals to discharge their religious obligations. It might be assumed that given their diagnosis the Synagogue Change team would call for the destruction of Reform temples and the return to the old-style synagogue housing a small group of worshipers who know each other intimately and who are drawn together by a common ideological commitment if not by common occupation or place of origin. However, the Synagogue Change team calls neither for the elimination of the imposing "cathedral synagogues" erected decades ago or for the destruction of the more recently erected sprawling suburban-synagogues surrounded by acres of parking space.

The Synagogue Change team maintains that a feeling of community can be created in giant institutions and suggests, furthermore, that large size can be an advantage—since the congregants are so varied, only a large synagogue can offer the opportunity to meet others like oneself. The temple can facilitate the identification of peers and the formation of friendship groups—or what the sociologist would call cliques—through an experiential-workshop approach, the team maintains. This process would be guided by professionals skilled in the techniques of group-dynamics and capable of leading the group in exploring the resources of the Jewish tradition, especially as these relate to the problem of overcoming alienation and leading a more satisfying life.

Looked at from the perspectives developed in earlier readings in this volume, the approach of the Synagogue Change team is based upon the following premises: 1) the informal Jewish community is composed of a clique network which constitutes the basic foundation on which the institutional structure in the Jewish community rests; 2) the synagogue lacks vitality because it is insufficiently coordinated with this network; and 3) the synagogue can be revitalized if it can move its members away from their present cliques and integrate them into new cliques which are synagogue-based and directed.

The report of the Synagogue Change team is a significant example of a new type of policy research in the Jewish community, and the reception accorded to it is itself of interest. The report was received with enthusiasm by the sponsoring body—the Long Range Planning Committee of the Union of American Hebrew Congregations—which immediately sought approval to begin implementation of the report's recommendations. Even those critical of the report did not charge the research team with a lack of faith in the message of Reform Judaism but merely stressed the subjective nature of the team's recommendations and questioned the efficacy of the workshop strategy.

When Isaac Mayer Wise (1819–1900), the organizer of Reform in the United States, established the Union of American Hebrew Congregations in 1873, he was confident that Reform would become the Judaism of all American Jews. The truths which Reform taught, he believed, were irrefutable. A century later Wise's successors are unsure of the viability of their movement and even of its mission. Lacking his complete faith in the superiority of Reform they seem prepared to recommend a course of action which the founder would have considered at best indicative of a disbelief in Divine mercy and justice, at worst as heretical. In Wise's view man's greatest need was not for community but to be brought closer to Divine truth. Truth could only be discovered in encounter with God and in his holy Torah; it would never be discovered in encounter with people.

M. S.

PART I of this report ("The Actual Jew: A Research Report on Reform Jews and Their Temples") is based on the findings of a sample survey. Questionnaires were mailed to a randomly selected sample of the membership of twelve temples across the country as well as to college student "alumni" of those temples and to students in their confirmation classes. The overall response rate was a bit over 50 percent, providing a total of 1,643 completed question- naires. . . . The adult respondents represent accurately the views of the more involved and identified half of the membership of Reform temples in metropolitan areas outside the South; the confirmation class sample is accurately representative of the total population of confirmation class students who are enrolled and actually attend class; the college sample, in all probability, is somewhat more positively biased than the other two groups. . . .

. . . in respect to the statistical profile of the respondents the single most striking finding is the extraordinary level of educational attainment among the adult respondents, 60 percent of whom have at least four years of college (compared to 11 percent of the total American adult population). On the basis of comparisons with other studies, the report argues that this high level of educational attainment is not unique to the sample but likely reflects the high educational level of Reform Jews in general.

The study also finds that only 34 percent of the adult respondents were raised in Reform households, that a majority have only a minimal Jewish education (44 percent report Sunday school only and 17 percent report no formal Jewish education at all), and, that while a majority are at least third-generation Americans, those who are second generation are overwhelmingly of East European (rather than Central European) origin.

[In respect to] the beliefs and practices of Reform Jews . . . the major finding is that there is enormous variety in both behavior and in belief, both among temples and within temples. While the large majority report that they take part in a Passover seder and light candles on Chanukah, 62 percent report having a mezuzah on their door (the high is 80 percent in one temple, the low 40 percent in another); 50 percent light Sabbath candles (the range among the temples is from a high of 68 percent to a low of 38 percent); 50 percent read some Jewish publication other than their temple bulletin (the range is from 71 percent to 31 percent); over a third belong to no Jewish organization other than their temple; 10 percent have Christmas trees in their homes (the range here is from 29 percent to 1 percent); 31 percent attend religious services only on the High Holy Days, while, at the other extreme, only 7 percent report weekly attendance and another 17 percent report attending "a few times a month."

Diversity of response increases as we move from the area of behavior to the area of belief. A large number of questions deal with the area of belief. . . . The most intriguing responses are to a set of questions dealing with the qualities of a "good Jew." These answers permit us to compare our respondents to respondents in earlier studies . . . and especially to the sample reported by Sklare and Greenblum in *Jewish Identity on the Suburban Frontier.* Compared to the earlier sample, we find a significant attrition in support of general humanistic, or liberal, positions, and, save for one major exception, no concomitant increase in support for specifically Jewish positions. The major exception is the dramatic increase in the centrality of the State of Israel. . . . The evidence does not support the notion that Jews are involved in a significant backlash on social issues; rather, it suggests an increase in confusion, a disillusionment with traditional liberal precepts.

Further, there is a substantial gap between old and young on every item of specifically Jewish interest. Thus, for example, while 32 percent of the adult respondents hold that it is essential, in order to be a good Jew, that one contribute to Jewish philanthropies, only 4 percent of the young respondents agree; while 75 percent of the adults hold it essential or, at least, desirable that one marry within the Jewish faith, only 43 percent of the youth agree.

The overall conclusion of the report concerning the data on these questions is that there is "a general uncertainty regarding the 'requirements,' or even the desiderata, of Judaism, an uncertainty that is quite evident among adults and still more striking—substantially more striking—among youth. . . ."

We find also that there is no apparent segregation of Jewish belief into "religious" and "cultural" components. Those respondents who displayed a relatively high interest in, and commitment to, Judaism tended to do so across the board rather than selecting out one or another of the major "approaches" to Judaism for endorsement. In this, as in other ways, the evidence supports the conclusion that erstwhile points of significant difference between Reform Jews and other American Jews are not now significant. . . .

The chapter on beliefs and practices also includes a report of the answers to two hypothetical questions—one dealing with the distribution of the respondent's charitable dollar, the other with his preferences among several summer camps to which he might send his child. The first shows a distinct preference among adults for Jewish charities and especially the UJA and the respondent's temple. Among young people, there is a dramatic increase in support for political, as distinguished from welfare, causes, although they, too, accord a major allocation to the UJA. . . . As to summer camps, all respondents indicate a clear preference for a cosmopolitan, intercultural camp setting or, as a second choice, a recreational camp, as distinguished from camps with a distinctive substantive Jewish orientation.

The chapter closes with the observation that the one area of overwhelming consensus among all respondents concerns the possibility of anti-Semitism in America. Respondents were asked whether they agreed that "anti-Semitism will never be a major problem for American Jews." Only 7 percent of the respondents (in both the youth and adult populations) agreed with the statement. Given the wording of the statement, disagreement does not necessarily reflect a lively anxiety concerning the possible imminence of serious anti-Semitism in this country. It does, however, suggest that awareness of the possibility of anti-Semitism remains a factor, perhaps an important factor, in shaping the Jewish understanding. . . .

With respect to intermarriage, the study reports a major gap between the generations. While a substantial minority of adults do not appear particularly concerned with intermarriage as a "problem," most express both ideological and personal concern. Young people are much less concerned ideologically. But, although the young appear, in the main, to hold that intermarriage is not an ideological problem (e.g., 61 percent do not agree that "intermarriage is bad for the Jewish people"), the large majority report that the religion of a prospective mate would be a matter of important personal concern. One-third of the young would not marry a non-Jew under any circumstances, or unless the non-Jew were to convert, and another 54 percent would consider such a marriage only if they were certain they themselves could remain Jewish. The report suggests that the apparent discrepancy between ideology and (prospective) behavior is an important area for concern and for educational investment.

With respect to Israel, the report finds that more adult respondents attach importance to the relationships between American Jews and Israel than to a number of other "problem" areas, such as Jewish education, intermarriage, or "theological confusion." Indeed, only the "alienation of Jewish youth," among the items in the survey, was regarded as more important by adult respondents. And among young people, relationships with Israel were deemed more important than any other single item.

Over four-fifths of adults and two-thirds of young people believe that in order to be a "good" Jew it is either essential or desirable that one support Israel. This is the single most heavily endorsed item of specifically Jewish content in the entire survey (except for the importance of "accepting one's Jewishness"). At the same time, endorsement of Zionism is much less common. The indication is that non-ideological support for Israel is at the very center of the Jewish understanding of contemporary Reform Jews, and that this represents a major shift over time, a point confirmed by comparison of the data to those reported in earlier studies.

Several series of questions were devoted to the views of respondents concerning their temples. The general finding is that the temple is not, for most of its members, an object of important emotional investment. The three major reasons people say they joined a particular temple are the quality of its rabbi, their belief in Reform ideology, and the quality of the religious school. A very striking finding here is that friendship patterns do not appear to play a leading part in the determination of temple membership. Indeed, 60 percent of all adult respondents report that they have few, if any, close friends among the members of their temple. It appears that the temple is perceived chiefly as the site of certain desired services, rather than as the site for significant communal experience.

Worship services are not viewed critically. Forty percent of the respondents "like them very much," and most of the rest are neutral rather than dissatisfied. A major difference between young people and adults, in this connection, is that almost half of the young felt the opportunity for participation in the worship service was inadequate while 80 percent of adults were satisfied with the level of congregational participation.

In examining the rabbinic role, the report reveals that the single most important qualification people seek in a rabbi is his capacity to relate to young people. This is followed by his abilities as an educator, as a family counselor, and as a giver of sermons. Other aspects of the rabbinic role, such as interfaith activities, scholarship, involvement in social action, administrative ability, and interest in socializing with temple members, are viewed as much less significant, at least by adult respondents. Young people are rather more interested in "where a rabbi stands" than in "what a rabbi can offer."

Part II of the report ("The Potential Jew: Innovations in Experiential Techniques") contains a description of eighteen weekend workshops—three in each of six temples—designed to encourage people to examine themselves as Jews, both actual and potential, and to develop support systems for an intensified commitment to Jewish experience. The workshop design rested on two assumptions: first, the necessary prior step to any proposed program of institutional renewal is a program of personal renewal. Before people can plausibly ask whether their institutions are functioning adequately, they must have a reasonably clear sense of what it is they want their institutions to do, and the development of such a sense depends upon knowing what it is the person wants, or needs, the institution to do for *him*. Second, a simple reminder of the discrepancy between where most people are as Jews, and where most would ideally like to be, would in itself have little impact on behavior. Such reminders are, after all, part of the regular fare of many Jews. What might, however, prove useful is the conscious pursuit of a system of interpersonal supports, which would encourage people to join together to achieve fairly specific Judaic goals. . . .

Following from these assumptions, a series of workshops was designed. In the first workshop, a dozen members of the participating temple, each with some experience in human relations-oriented activities, were trained to act as "facilitators," para-professionals who would, together with the workshop leader, guide the subsequent workshop process. The subsequent weekends involved an additional fifty members of the temple who, together with the facilitators, engaged in a set of specifically designed experiential techniques intended to raise the following questions: What am I as a Jew? What would I like to be as a Jew? How do I move from what I am to what I would like to be? Does the temple, as it now exists, help or hinder me in that movement? How might it be more helpful?

In connection with Part II a detailed description of the 22 specific exercises that were developed for use in the workshops has been prepared. (This description, intended as a guide for future workshops, is available only to professionals engaged in such work. Experience shows that its use by non-professionals, though well intended, is often counterproductive.)

The report also includes data on the post-workshop evaluation by participants in the workshops. Of the 294 participants, 94 percent had a generally positive evaluation of the experience and over one-third found it an "extremely important personal experience." A number of spin-off groups resulted from the workshops and are still functioning today supporting the hope that the workshop impact is enduring rather than ephemeral.

IMPRESSIONS AND JUDGMENTS

Against the background of the findings which emerged from both the survey and workshops, those of us involved with the project have, inevitably, formed certain impressions regarding the present state and impending directions of Reform Judaism. In this last section of our report, we turn from specific findings and observations to personal impressions and judgments.

The Reform Jew. Through all of our work, no single conclusion registers so strongly as our sense that there is, among the people we have come to know, a powerful, perhaps even desperate, longing for community, a longing that is, apparently, not adequately addressed by any of the relevant institutions in most people's lives. It is possible, of course, that this need is unique to those who volunteered as participants in our workshops, that, indeed, this need is the reason they volunteered. Yet that is not our impression. So much other evidence is available to support the perception that

Americans in general, and middle- and upper-middle-class Americans in particular, have lost the sense of community, that we cannot believe that the problem is limited to those few whom we had the good fortune to meet and to work with. And so much of what we heard from them, about their neighbors, and their colleagues, and their fellow congregants, supports their own description of aloneness, that we feel safe in our generalization.

The need for community is not something people speak of easily. Most of us cope with our circumstances, take pleasure from the diverse symbols of our success, and recognize only a vague, though often pervasive, malaise, which we are reluctant either to analyze or to articulate. (Thus, at least, for adults; less for today's youth—here the generation gap is real.) In our own experience, people did not pour out poignant stories of loneliness. Such stories as were told came out in fragments, in bits and pieces of evidence that became a story only in retrospect. Our sense of the matter is that the need for community is so strong, and the prospect of community so weak, that people are reluctant to acknowledge the need, knowing, or believing, that it is not likely to be satisfied. Moreover, it is a sign of weakness, and hence of lack of success, to speak aloud of need. In the workshops that were developed for this project—that is, in a carefully designed and professionally directed process, in which hope emerges slowly, in which support and encouragement are offered freely—people do begin to talk about their own sense of human deprivation. And even then, not all do. Some, to be sure, are silent because they do not share the experience; others say nothing because they have so long been accustomed to segmented and superficial relationships that they can scarcely imagine the possibility of something different.

But the need is not less great for its being largely inarticulate. In the desperate search for warmth, many people are attracted to cultish, often bizarre groups that appear to offer some hope of intimacy. Still more, especially within the adult generation, simply accept the desperation, viewing it either as a necessary cost of modern times, or as a reflection of personal, rather than societal, incapacity. Whether the "solution" is frenetic cultism or quiet loneliness, large numbers of people never experience the warmth, the shared emotion, the sense of support, which community provides.

The need of which we speak here is obviously not specific to Jews, although it may be more keenly felt by those whose own memories go back to the life style of the organic folk-society which characterized the immigrant generation. It is not, in any case, a "Jewish" need, one whose satisfaction depends upon some agency or institution within the Jewish community. People who are prompted to seek more intimate, more open, more organic relationships may look to Jewish institutions for a response, or they may look elsewhere. Where they choose to look, if, indeed, they choose to look at all, depends in part on their tastes and predilections, but depends even more on where they sense the greatest likelihood of response.

In the next section, we shall have something to say about Reform Judaism's capacity to respond. Here, our focus is with the individual, and the point that wants making is that from the perspective of the individual Reform Jew, the Reform temple appears an unlikely site for the effort to create community. Our survey data show that most people are not disappointed in their temple; the demands and expectations they have of the temple are too minimal for them to experience disappointment, even when they experience alienation. The temple is assigned certain limited functions, notably with respect to the young, and it is judged in terms of its performance of these functions. The large majority of our respondents report very few close friends among their fellow temple members; over a third hold that the temple is a relatively unimportant institution in their lives; most attend the temple quite infrequently. The most important reasons our respondents give for joining a particular temple are its religious school and rabbi; among the least important is that their freinds or neighbors are members. And in our workshops, over and over, people spoke of joining, without belonging; they spoke of the "new member" problem, of the common lack of interest in making new members feel welcome; they spoke of the fact that the temple seems the "property" of a small handful of its most active members; they spoke of their own sense of nonpartnership in the temple.

To complaints such as these, there was usually a response that active membership was always welcome, that those who were infrequent visitors to the temple could hardly expect to find it a home, rather than merely a place to visit. More often than not, however, even the most active temple members among our participants were not prepared to argue that the temple was a warm and welcoming place; there was much to do, but even for those who did much, not much to feel. In fact, the word "cold" was not an uncommon description of the feel of the temple. Like Charles Silberman's classroom, the temple is a joyless place; the house of worship is not a home, except to a tiny few.

At a time, and with people for whom the experience of affective community is not natural, how does one set about creating it? Except as a temporary phenomenon, community happens when people share important experiences with one another, of which the most important is the experience of personal growth. But if the temple is not seen as a place where experiences are shared, is seen instead as a place where a limited number of services are consumed, then it appears an unlikely place for community to be pursued. And our data show that the primary expectation people have of their temple is that it will provide certain services, such as education, and a place to be on the High Holy Days, and a rabbi in time of personal need. Beyond these, people expect little; expecting little, that is what they get.

As we have noted, the need for shared community is not unique to Reform Jews. There is yet another respect in which Reform Jews are not unique. Like many, perhaps most Jews in America today, they are highly uncertain as to what it is that being Jewish implies, involves, demands. There was a time, not so very long ago, when Judaism was chaotic, a dozen ideologies and a hundred varieties of ideologies all clamoring for attention and competing for adherents. We have moved, it seems, from a chaotic Judaism to an inchoate Judaism, to a generation of Jews whose ties to Judaism, whether as faith or as peoplehood or as both, may be no weaker than the ties of their parents and grandparents, but whose "competence" as Jews is very shaky indeed.

In coming to this judgment, we are not adopting a specific normative stance. It is not that the views and beliefs of the Jews we encountered in the course of our work, whether through the survey data or through the workshop experiences, were different from our own. The problem, instead, is the prevalence of opinion as a substitute for belief, for any belief; the existence of belief, but the absence of belief systems. We are not at all convinced that there is a serious crisis in Jewish identity, at least among the people we encountered; there is a very clear crisis in Jewish ideology.

This ideological crisis is not, in the first instance, a question for theologians or philosophers. What we find is that people with very potent Jewish instincts feel that they have no way of supporting those instincts intellectually. Indeed, to the degree to which people have relatively coherent ideological tendencies, those tendencies often appear to contradict their Jewish instincts. This is a source of substantial personal distress, all the more so as it is extremely difficult to transmit instincts to the young when the justification for those instincts has been lost, or is uncertain. Nor is the question one of Jewish literacy alone. Jews may be more or less familiar with their history and their texts; it is the operational conclusions that may be derived from that history and from those texts that are inadequately perceived.

In former times, the question "Why be Jewish?" could not have arisen. There was no plausible alternative, even should one have been disposed to search for rationale. In modern times, the question not only arises, it is thrust upon us all, for we have become accustomed to demanding rational foundations for our commitments. For adults of this generation, the question, even if unanswered, is buried beneath enough Jewish memory and enough Jewish scar tissue so that it can, most often, be ignored. But when rich and private memory is replaced by a smattering of impersonal history, there is no defense against the question—which might be no matter, were the answers, whatever they be, more readily apparent.

We do not know whether the answers exist, or what they are; that is hardly our task. But we can attest that if they exist, and whatever they are, they are not widely known. Nor, for that matter, are the questions themselves widely discussed. Time and again in the course of the eighteen workshops (three in each of six temples) we conducted, the reaction to our initiation of serious discussions of Jewish values and beliefs was one of adventure and novelty; time and again we were told by participants how interesting it was to talk about such issues, and how rare.

So much entirely aside from normative commitment. We would be remiss were we not to add, from a more normative perspective, our very strong impression that in dealing with the matters raised above, the Reform movement has, in one important way, made them worse rather than better. Specifically: it is our view that there are inevitable tensions involved in being Jewish in the modern world. To be part of a religious brotherhood is necessarily to be a partner in mystery, in commitments that lie beyond rationality. And to be a Jew is not only to be a partner in a religious brotherhood, but also to be subject to the specific tension that arises from the Jewish situation, a situation in which the competing claims of particularism and universalism must continually be confronted. For Jews, that competition seems to us inevitable, difficult, and, potentially, productive.

A relatively common criticism of Reform Judaism is that it emphasizes Jewish universalism at the expense of Jewish particularism. And we did, in the course of our work, occasionally encounter people who have a clear ideological perspective that traces back to such early Reform understandings. Our sense of the matter, however, is that the specific, and more common, weakness of Reform in this connection is not with the way in which it proposes to resolve the tension, but rather that it often appears to deny that the tension exists at all. And, of course, by denying its existence, people are denied the opportunity to learn how to deal with it. But, since the tension is, if we are correct, an inevitable consequence of being Jewish, then the failure to prepare people for it is a failure of the first magnitude.

This is not, and does not try to be, an essay in theology. We do not say that the tensions which Judaism implies should be resolved in this way or in that. Basing our argument on a series of unusually open and extended encounters, we suggest that Reform Jews do, as a matter of fact, feel ill-equipped to cope with the perplexities of being Jewish, and still less well-equipped to help their children cope with them.

Having said all this, we should add that most of the people we met are coping, however ill-equipped they may be. We were dealing, after all, not only with members of Reform temples, but, in our workshops, with those members for whom the business of being Jewish was sufficiently interesting to warrant a serious investment of time. Nonetheless, by their own testimony, once serious discussion got under way, they were not satisfied with their success at sorting things out. We are persuaded that one powerful motive for the repeated effort to translate serious questions regarding personal behavior and intellectual belief into organizational issues—expanding the temple membership, reforming its committee structure—is the feeling, that however difficult the organizational questions, they are child's play compared to the difficulty of grappling with behavior and belief.

In short: the people we have dealt with call themselves Jews, and their Judaism matters to them. But they are vastly uncertain, in the main, regarding what calling oneself a Jew or caring about Judaism means or is supposed to mean; meanings seem rarely discussed, at least in ways that help. Consequently, the interest in meanings is repressed, sometimes lost entirely. And when, as in our experience, it is expressed, and the quest for meanings resumed, the paths that most people travel are unfamiliar, the maps they once were given of little use.

This strong impression is supported by our survey data as well. Those data show that Reform Jews, on the whole, no longer can be characterized as "partial" Jews, if ever they could be. Those who are most positively oriented toward Judaism-as-faith are generally also the most positively oriented toward Judaism-as-community. In this respect, Reform Judaism is clearly solidly in the mainstream of contemporary Jewish understandings and commitments. Nor are the responses of Reform Jews across a whole range of attitudes and beliefs markedly different from those of more diverse Jewish groupings, as comparison of our responses to those encountered in other studies of Jews shows. It is also the case, however, that this movement toward the mainstream is, evidently, a movement toward the confusions of the mainstream as well. As we note in our discussion of the survey data: "If there is an ideology of Reform Judaism, the evidence suggests that it is largely irrelevant as a shaper of the values and opinions of Reform Jews." Nor has a different ideology been substituted; there is commitment, intense commitment, but virtually no coherence, nor any substantial preparation or capacity to deal with the consequent ambiguity.

What makes the ideological ambiguity tolerable, as it is for most people, is the fact that it is not very salient. As we have already pointed out, most adult Jews of this generation have a rich enough set of Jewish memories that they can act out their Jewishness in a framework of memory and instinct, even where theory is wanting. For younger Jews, whose memories are less ample and whose instincts are more austere, the matter may be very different. This leads us to identify still another unmet need of Reform Jews, the need for affective stimulation.

We are concerned not only with a lack of capacity to deal with Judaism as serious intellectual inquiry, but also with the apparent lack of adequate opportunities for Judaism as expressive, even sensory, experience. Several of our experiential techniques dealt with early memories of Jewish experience, and the richness of those memories was in stark, and threatening, contrast to the present experiences our participants reported. . . . Even the most highly motivated of the participants report a peculiar inability to match their motives to their lives within the temple. If the most likely translation of Jewish commitment and interest is an invitation to serve on a temple committee, an imbalance between interest and opportunity exists. Yet that is precisely what we heard, and heard with disturbing frequency.

Some people, of course, try to go it alone, creating in their own homes, and, less often, within the temple, a corner that reflects their concern with Judaism, and not only with Jewish organization. More people, it seems, do not know where to begin, or are self-conscious about trying. They are, to be sure, not always aware that they are missing anything. It is perfectly possible to spend an extremely active Jewish life, going from meeting to meeting, from board to board, dealing with pressing matters of Jewish moment, without ever participating in a substantive Jewish experience, without ever relating oneself directly to the tradition, to the artifacts, to the sensations and the understandings that are the ostensible purpose of all the meetings and of all the boards.

There is, quite obviously, a limit to how long one can sustain a Judaism that cannot be expressed, whether because one does not know how to express it, or because the opportunity to express it is wanting, or because one is too busy with organizational needs to find time for expression. In one way or another, most of the people we met informed us that they had exceeded the limit, that they were themselves dissatisfied by the poverty of their Jewish experience. This was not an easy matter for many to acknowledge. Many of our participants were very active members of their temples, as well as of other Jewish organizations. For them to confess that something was wanting from their lives as Jews was no small thing. It was made still more difficult by the sense that most people had that little could be done about it, that the effort to create new capacities and new opportunities was not likely to succeed. Yet, withal, we report here not a wish of our own, but a clear conclusion of the five professionals who met with one or another of the temple groups. There was much holding back, and there were some who held back throughout; most came to speak of these matters, and, when they did, were often powerfully reassured that they were not alone in their concern. Indeed, it was precisely in this regard that the major support systems which the group process fostered were

Yet on the basis of our experience, we are not pessimistic about Reform Jews. Having said all that we have thus far said, this may appear a somewhat surprising conclusion, but, again, it is our unanimous judgment. We encountered far too many people of high motive and serious purpose to warrant a gloomy prognosis. To the degree to which motive and purpose normally tend to be suppressed, we believe, and our experience has shown, that intelligent professional intervention can encourage their expression, and can initiate the development of support systems which will forestall disappointment. Put differently: it is perfectly possible to initiate a revolution of rising Judaic aspirations. The question that arises is whether such a revolution is not bound to be, in the end, an experience in rising frustrations as well. The answer to this question begins with the provision of interpersonal support, which we think can be generated. But the ultimate answer, for most people, depends upon institutional capacities, and it is to an assessment of those capacities that we now turn.

The Reform Temple. In the preceding discussion, we noted three major needs of Reform Jews—the need for community, the need for an ideological foothold on Judaism, and the need for more direct Judaic experience. . . . The most glaring inadequacy of the temple is precisely in the area of greatest need of the congregant, the need for community. We have already reported that we were repeatedly told that new members are not made to feel welcome, and that old members relate to one another only superficially. Indeed, our own experience confirms this testimony, since, quite commonly, participants in our workshops would express surprise that others shared, or differed, with their own central beliefs about Judaism; although they had been worshiping or serving on committees together, sometimes for many years, issues such as these had rarely, if ever, been discussed.

Put most simply: the experience of temple membership is only rarely an experience in community. There are, as we see it, at least two major reasons why this should be so. The first is that few people, even among those who may actively pursue community, turn to the temple to find it. Our survey data, it will be recalled, show quite clearly that the temple is not based on close friendship among its members, nor, apparently, does it foster such friendship. The temple is, instead, a purveyor of services, the most important of which have to do with young people. A large number of our respondents state quite frankly that the temple is a relatively unimportant institution in their lives; while a still larger number count it as one among a number of important institutions, our sense of the matter is that even then, it is not the object of great psychological or emotional investment.

Most people, as we have said, do not invest great energy in the pursuit of community. If they sense its absence, they adjust to its absence, for most would scarcely know where to begin to look for it, or how. Thus it is not the case—and we believe this point to be critical—that the temple is seen as less promising a site for community to happen in than some other institution or agency. The gap is not filled by "competitors"; in the main, it is not filled at all. Which creates, of course, a most important opportunity for the temple. Insofar as it may develop a capability for meeting the widespread need for community, it may evoke a wholly new order of loyalty, of passion, of concern and commitment, than it has hitherto experienced.

This leads us to the second major reason why the temple has heretofore not been used by its members as a basis for the creation of community. The temple is, after all, an institution, an elaborate enterprise, and it takes very special skill to create community in an institutional setting. How can one, after all, infuse a necessarily bureaucratic structure with warmth, with joy, and with genuine human interaction? . . .

Anecdote: One of us, in the course of talking with a group of temple members in connection with the project, sought to illustrate the need for community by telling of a friend who had taken his own life. After the tragedy, a group who had known this poor man rather well came together, and tried to review his last weeks, to see whether there had been a hint that should have been noticed, some premonition that might have led his friends to offer help. There had been none, and, realizing this, the group realized as well how grotesque it is that a person in such massive distress does not find it possible to ask, somehow, for help, not from friends, not from family, not from professionals. And after this perception came the terrifying knowledge that among those who had come together, there was not one who felt that he would be able to ask for help were he in need.

To which a temple official replied that the story was interesting, but that no such problem existed in his temple, for it was blessed with a suicide prevention committee to deal with just such problems. A suicide prevention committee may, after all, be a very good thing, it may even be the best kind of thing a temple can do. It is a limited, bureaucratic response, and a decent, perhaps even helpful response. But it does not, for no committee can, help answer what it is about our lives that prevents us from asking for help, nor does it, for no committee can, offer love as its help.

This is hardly the place for a comprehensive critique of modern culture. We make the point, rather, in order to indicate that Reform Jews have very serious and very genuine needs which are, on the whole, unmet, and which it would be entirely appropriate for Reform temples to seek to meet. Insofar as temples find themselves able to provide the settings where such needs are met, it is entirely possible that they will move from the periphery of their members' consciousness and loyalty to the center. Save as they provide such settings, there is no reason whatever to suppose that they will have important meanings to more than a tiny minority. The only serious question, then, is whether the fulfillment of those needs is compatible with the necessarily institutional environment of the temple.

That, of course, must remain in some measure an open question. It will be difficult, to be sure, to break through the inhibitions of the members and the inertia of the institutions to create more vital and more humane interactions. But our judgment, based primarily on the workshop experience, is that though difficult, the task is not inherently undoable. . . . How, then, does one create a temple that is congenial to community, to which its members, therefore, turn for more important purposes than now attract them? The way to create community is not to set about to create community. The concept of community implies an organic relationship, rather than a contractual relationship. Let no committees be created that will "have charge" of fostering community; organic relationships grow out of organic experiences, or they do not grow.

In our judgment, the single best way for the temple to turn toward community would be for it to provide its members richer opportunities in the other two problem areas we earlier identified, the areas of intellectual, or cognitive, Judaism, and the area of experiential, or affective, Judaism. The process of sharing in intellectual and emotional growth is also, and inevitably, a process in community-building. Few, if any, people will respond if the temple announces as its goal for the next year the creation of a spirit of community; more will respond, and the spirit will follow, if more plausible, and more directly manageable goals, are announced.

That is a judgment which is based on our general professional experience, as well as on the specific experience of the workshops. It would be a mistake to exaggerate the significance of the workshops over the long haul; three weekends, or two, out of a person's time will have only marginal consequences for most, especially where there is no concerted follow-up activity that is encouraged within the temple. But it would also be a mistake to minimize their importance as the first step along the path to community, even though the creation of community was never the explicit goal. But when people come together in open search, and share in one another's search, the seeds of community are planted; if nurtured, they will grow. The search in which our participants joined was a search for Jewish meanings and for Jewish experiences. And that is exactly the search we propose be extended to include larger numbers, over a longer period of time. . . .

We view this as a central point. In the frenetic pursuit of community which some adults and many of the young seem now to be embarked upon, the rewards, such as they are, are typically ephemeral. The decision to "find" community is like the decision to fall in love; deciding doesn't make it so. Nor have the diverse matchmakers of community done much better; after the initial thrill, the real work begins, but by then the matchmaker is gone. Yet for Jews, as Jews, the problem should be simpler. The way into the affective living community, the community of shared emotion, shared experience, and shared support, that is needed may well be through more intensive exploration of the meanings of the historic, religious, sociological community that already exists. Jews are, after all, not strangers to one another; the task for them is not so much to create community as to extend its scope and to deepen its significance.

The experience of affective community is usually a small-group experience. The large temple, we suspect, cannot seek to become a single community; more likely, it must see itself as the place where a variety of communities are encouraged. In this regard, the fact that the large majority of our survey respondents thought that, ideally, their temples should be larger than they are is not necessarily distressing. It suggests what we have already observed, that most do not see community as one of the purposes of the temple. But the large temple is not necessarily the enemy of community, nor the small temple its friend. Indeed, the large temple, by permitting people of common interest to find each other, and to work together, may have an advantage. This follows from the fact that the threshold, beyond which a temple cannot expect to be a single affective community, is likely on the order of fifty families, at most. Once a temple grows beyond that number, it may well be better for it to grow a good deal beyond it, in order to enable each of its members to find a sufficient number of kindred spirits.

Now it might well be argued that the search for Jewish meanings and for Jewish experiences is precisely the search to which temples have traditionally been devoted, and which most members have traditionally been reluctant to join as active participants. If, as we have found, the temple is a peripheral institution to many of its members, perhaps that is because they want it kept at the periphery, and would resist its efforts to become more central. But it is also possible that the temple, by coming to devote so large a part of its and its members' attention to organizational ends, has trained its members to think of it as essentially an organization, and a set of services, rather than a set of interactions and experiences. We have found it possible to generate both interactions and experiences which quite diverse groups of people have, in large measure, found rewarding. While it is always somewhat hazardous to generalize from experimental results, the test of whether our experiments are, in fact, applicable on a larger and more institutionalized scale is easy enough to conduct.

What is wanted, we believe, is not so much a sudden transformation, as a gradual process of development of mutual confidence and testing of new roles. If the temple announces that it is anxious to promote interaction as well as to provide service, the announcement is likely to be greeted with initial skepticism, even by those who already acknowledge the desirability of interaction. Others will simply be perplexed, uncertain what this new departure is all about. And if people approach the temple as a home of interaction and humanity, those who have traditionally set the tone for the temple will find, with all the good will in the world, that this new demand is not easily met. Special skills may be required, skills not normally available, and exceptional tolerance, as people stumble to find a way, will surely be required. The process of reaching out is a fragile process; in the short run, it is surely safer to avoid it. In the short run, indeed, the temple is safer where it is, at the periphery. But the short run is very short, and, if the price of safety is irrelevance, that may be too high a price to pay even for a moment.

If there has been one central theme to our effort, it has been the direct involvement, in an open and supportive environment, of people themselves in the process of Judaic goal-setting. As we interpret the plea that the temple become more "relevant," relevance is not to be defined as related to current events, but rather as related to the real, if inarticulate, needs of people. The need for community cannot be satisfied by sitting as an audience to a religious service, much of which unfolds on a distant stage; active shared experience is required, and if a majority of our survey respondents find the level of participation in the present worship service adequate, it may well be because they do not expect the service to help create community. The need for intellectual understanding and ideological coherence cannot be met by an educational mode so superficial as the weekly sermon; more serious confrontation, and participation in the effort, are required, a level of participation beyond even that of the typical adult education program. And if a majority of our respondents hold sermonic ability to be among the most important qualifications a rabbi can have, that may be because they do not expect the temple to offer serious education. The need for stimulating Jewish experience cannot be satisfied by participation on a temple committee, nor the need for a richer Jewish idiom by an occasional visiting artist; more immediacy and intensity are wanted. In each case, the key is a more participatory mode. . . .

Temples, in their organizational parts, are sometimes fearful that to seek to deepen meanings and to broaden scope, to demand more of their members and of themselves as institutions, would drive people away. Large numbers of people, after all, seem to want no more (perhaps even less) than is currently offered; will a still more ambitious program attract, or further alienate? It is our judgment that people tailor their ambitions to fit their estimate of possibility. We cannot be sure that the potential constituency for a more intensive (i.e., more initimate, more inquisitive, more expressive) Judaism includes the large majority of present temple members, but we are convinced on the basis of our work, that there is at the very least a constituency of substantial size. That constituency, it appears to us, is not so much interested in "more" as it is interested in "different," in the development of congregational styles that touch them and challenge them in ways they do not now feel either touched or challenged. We suspect, moreover, that were that constituency to be encouraged, were its needs to find creative response, others, in large numbers, would begin to revise their expectations upward, and would begin to make the kinds of demands of their institutions—and of themselves—which alone can issue in genuine vitality.

THE CONSERVATIVE MOVEMENT /
ACHIEVEMENTS AND PROBLEMS
by MARSHALL SKLARE

INTRODUCTION

IN the last half of the nineteenth century it appeared indisputable
that the future Judaism of America's Jews would be Reform,
inasmuch as this was the religious movement most attuned to the
norms of American society. Many congregations composed of Jews
from Western and Central European countries abolished traditional
practices and evolved into Reform temples; others found themselves
split between those who wanted to retain traditional patterns and
those who wanted the congregation to join the Reform camp. In
instances of congregational division it was generally the Reform
element that was more powerful in numbers, status, and ideological
conviction. A handful of aristocratic Sephardic congregations
refused to join the trend to Reform, but the Sephardic group was
not only numerically insignificant but its synagogues had lost their
former importance. Furthermore, Sephardic Jews were generally
not Orthodox in their personal lives.

There were of course the new congregations founded by East
European Jews. While such congregations were Orthodox the
established element assumed this to be a temporary phenomenon,
believing that once the East Europeans loosened their ties to the old
country and became Americanized they would inevitably turn to
Reform Judaism. If the transition did not occur in the immigrant
generation it would certainly take place in the second.

This prediction has proved incorrect. As we have seen Orthodoxy did not die—indeed a new committed Orthodox group was eventually to appear on the American scene. But the prediction also did not take into account the emergence of Conservative Judaism.

In the first quarter of the twentieth century the Reform elite interpreted the newly developing Conservative movement as a halfway house, apparently necessitated by the unfamiliarity of the East European Jew with Reform thought and practice. From this perspective Conservatism was seen as helpful in assuring the eventual triumph of Reform; it would assist the East European in making the larger transition from Orthodoxy to Reform. The early proponents of Conservatism, on the other hand, maintained that while most East-European-derived Jews would desert Orthodoxy they could never accept the radical break with Jewish thought and practice that Reform involved. They further maintained that since Conservative Judaism sought to integrate the most meaningful and enduring practices of Jewish tradition with the best of American thought and practice, it would become the most significant force in the Jewish community. Nevertheless, the fact that the upper class and the established element were so solidly Reform left even Conservative leaders with lingering doubts about the permanence of their movement. And if Reform was the wave of the future, as it seemed, then possibly they were doing nothing more than preparing recruits for its ranks.

As American Reform gradually shifted from "Classical Reform" to "Neo-Reform" it did indeed attract a significant segment of second- and third-generation East European Jews. But Reform never succeeded in achieving primacy in the Jewish community; it was overtaken by Conservative Judaism after World War II. While some Conservative-trained young people did join Reform congregations, on the whole Conservatism managed the crucially important task of retaining the loyalties of the children of its founding generation. Furthermore, Conservatism made many new recruits from the ranks of uncommitted and residual Orthodox families.

Charles Liebman suggests that the reason for Conservatism's rapid growth was that it was closest to the folk religion of the East European Jew. There is no doubt that Conservatism was very open to the desire for ethnic continuity under the umbrella of religion. However its success may be explained, by the 1960's it was clear that Conservatism had triumphed—numerically it constituted the most powerful wing of American Judaism. There were even a handful of Jews of Reform lineage who had affiliated with Conservatism, highlighting the inaccuracy of the old supposition that Reform was the only form of Judaism acceptable to the American Jew.

The Conservative movement proved to be even more successful than its partisans had hoped. Fears about its durability evaporated as hundreds of new suburban synagogues were built after World War II. Many of the largest and most successful of such synagogues were Conservative. Indeed in some cities the new Conservative synagogues were so magnificent in architectural conception and execution, and the buildings of Reform so modest by comparison, that the very structures seemed to convey that the old predictions about the inevitability of Reform were not only unfulfilled but that they were in the process of reversal.

Conservatism, however, has never been able to take full satisfaction in its unexpected rise to primacy. As the following article points out there are members of the Conservative elite who look upon the rise of their movement with mixed feelings. Developments outside of Conservatism as well as the fact that certain problems within the movement have defied solution, have made committed Conservative Jews less satisfied with Conservatism's growth and less certain of its future than its present success would seem to warrant.

M. S.

ॐ

DURING RECENT YEARS more American Jews have come to consider themselves "Conservative" than either "Orthodox" or "Reform." The trend to Conservatism is particularly evident in cities of substantial Jewish population, especially cities located in the Northeast. For example, a survey conducted in 1965 in Boston found that 44 percent of the Jews of that community thought of themselves as Conservative, some 27 percent thought of themselves as Reform, and 14 percent as Orthodox.[1] In smaller cities in the same geographical area the triumph of Conservatism has been even more overwhelming. Thus a survey conducted in 1963 in Providence, Rhode Island, discovered that as many as 54 percent of the Jews of that community considered themselves Conservative, while only 21 percent thought of themselves as Reform and 20 percent as Orthodox.[2] Furthermore, Conservative strength has also become evident even in the Midwest, which has long been a center of Reform. In 1964 as many as 49 percent of Milwaukee Jews considered themselves Conservative, in contrast to only 24 percent who considered themselves Reform. . . .[3]

The new predominance of Conservatism is still imperfectly reflected in synagogal affiliation, for not every individual who describes himself as Conservative is affiliated with a synagogue. In Boston, for example, some 39 percent of those who describe themselves as Conservative are unaffiliated.[4] The problem of non-affiliation cuts across all groups; there are also unaffiliated Reform and, to a smaller degree, Orthodox Jews. But the presence of so many unaffiliated Conservative Jews is in one sense especially

[1]Morris Axelrod, Floyd J. Fowler, and Arnold Gurin, *A Community Survey for Long Range Planning* (Boston: Combined Jewish Philanthropies of Greater Boston, 1967), p. 119.

[2]Sidney Goldstein and Calvin Goldscheider, *Jewish Americans* (Englewood Cliffs, N.J.: Prentice-Hall, 1968), p. 177.

[3]Albert J. Mayer, *Milwaukee Jewish Population Study* (Milwaukee: Jewish Welfare Fund, 1965), p. 48.

[4]Axelrod *et al.*, *op. cit.*, p. 143.

advantageous to Conservatism—it means that there is a large pool of individuals to draw upon for future expansion.

Conservatism has made good use of its reservoir of potential recruits. Before the late 1960's there was a noticeable increase in the number of Conservative synagogues, as well as a sharp rise in the membership of those Conservative synagogues located in areas of expanding Jewish population. Furthermore, the type of synagogue that the Conservative movement pioneered—the "synagogue center" offering social and recreational activities in addition to the classical functions of prayer and religious study, and which conceives of itself as the central Jewish address in the geographic area it serves—has become predominant on the American Jewish scene. As a consequence, Reform and Orthodoxy have come to look to Conservative models in fashioning their own religious institutions.[5]

The rising influence of Conservatism can be traced, in part, to the suburbanization that has occurred during the past two decades among Jews living in the largest cities. Suburbanization brought with it the problem of the maintenance of Jewish identity, and it was to the synagogue that the new Jewish suburbanite tended to look for identity-maintenance. The result was that the synagogue emerged in the 1950's and 1960's as the crucial institution in Jewish life. And Conservatism exemplified the type of synagogue that was most appealing to the new suburban Jew. . . .

Prior to the 1950's, the emerging strength of Conservative Judaism on the local level was not reflected on the national scene. While the United Synagogue of America—the union of Conservative congregations—had been established as early as 1913, it remained a paper organization for many years. The only group that visualized Conservatism in national terms was the rabbis, organized as the Rabbinical Assembly of America. However, in the past two decades a sharp change has occurred: the laity has transmuted their loyalty to local congregations into attachment to a national movement.

The rapid development of the United Synagogue, which now has a membership of 832 congregations, is an index to the new sense of constituting a movement. During the 1950's and 1960's, the United Synagogue emerged as an important Jewish agency. In contrast to its older status as a paper organization, the United

[5]On the American synagogue see Marshall Sklare, *America's Jews* (New York: Random House, 1971), pp. 126–135.

Synagogue currently maintains some seventeen field offices in addition to its national headquarters. The conventions of the United Synagogue, held every two years at the Concord Hotel, have grown in size to the point where they tax the facilities of what is the largest kosher hotel in the country. The United Synagogue would long have surpassed its Reform counterpart—the Union of American Hebrew Congregations established in 1873—but for the fact that it has been under the control of the Jewish Theological Seminary of America. Fearful of the centrist and left-wing influence of the laity and of many congregational rabbis, seminary officials—all of whom belong to Conservatism's right wing—have discouraged aggressive growth. Their influence over the United Synagogue is symbolized by the fact that the agency makes its national headquarters in the buildings of the Seminary. . . .

In summary, the recent development of Conservative Judaism is characterized by: 1) the emergence of Conservatism as the favored religious self-designation of the American Jew and its consequent achievement of primacy on the American Jewish religious scene; 2) the emergence of Conservative synagogues, particularly in suburban areas in the East, as the leading congregations in their communities; 3) the emergence of national agencies that reflect the strength of Conservatism on the local level; and 4) the emergence of a sense of constituting a movement—a sense of a shared Conservatism on the part of the Conservative laity.

These developments appear to portend a brilliant future for Conservatism. The continued growth of Conservative Judaism seems assured: in the large metropolitan centers there are significant numbers of unaffiliated Jews who identify themselves as "Conservative." All that seems necessary to further augment the primacy of Conservatism is that such individuals be induced to activate a commitment they already hold.

THE PROBLEM OF CONSERVATIVE MORALE

Despite brilliant achievements and excellent prospects for future growth, the morale of the Conservative movement is on the decline.

Seemingly, present-day Conservative leaders are less satisfied with their movement than they have a right to be; they are less sanguine about its future than the facts would appear to indicate. Paradoxically, during the period when the movement was overshadowed by Reform and Orthodoxy, Conservatism's élan was high. But when Conservatism came into its own, morale began to sag.

Doubts about the movement are most frequently expressed by the rabbis. As religious professionals, they have a heightened interest in Conservatism, a special sensitivity to its problems, and a sophisticated set of standards by which to judge its success. The following statement illustrates the doubts felt by some Conservative rabbis:

> During these past decades we have grown, we have prospered, we have become a powerful religious establishment. I am, however, haunted by the fear that somewhere along the way we have become lost; our direction is not clear, and the many promises we made to ourselves and to our people have not been fulfilled. We are in danger of not having anything significant to say to our congregants, to the best of our youth, to all those who are seeking a dynamic adventurous faith that can elicit sacrifice and that can transform lives.[6]

This statement emanates from an esteemed leader of Conservatism, Max Routtenberg. As the rabbi of the Kesher Zion Synagogue in Reading, Pennsylvania, from 1932 to 1948, Routtenberg helped to establish Conservatism in eastern Pennsylvania. After a period during which he served as a leading official of the seminary and Rabbinical Assembly, Rabbi Routtenberg went on to become the spiritual leader of B'nai Sholom of Rockville Center, New York. He was instrumental in developing B'nai Sholom into an important suburban synagogue in the prime area of Long Island. In 1964 Routtenberg was elected to the presidency of the Rabbinical Assembly. He was viewed by his colleagues as a kind of ideal Conservative Jew: he succeeded in combining the scientific methodology he had encountered as a student at the seminary with the approach to learning he had assimilated during his earlier years at a yeshiva. Furthermore, Routtenberg was a man of the world—he sought in his person to combine Jewish and western culture.

[6]Max J. Routtenberg in R.A. [Rabbinical Assembly of America], *Proceedings*, XXIX (1965), 23.

However, in his presidential address to the Rabbinical Assembly from which we have quoted, Rabbi Routtenberg spoke in accents far different from those that characterize the man of success.

Why this disparity between achievement and satisfaction? Why the decline in morale among Conservative leaders? The proper starting point for an analysis of these questions is the world of Orthodoxy. More specifically, it is the attitude of Conservatism toward Orthodoxy.

The founders of Conservatism believed that Orthodoxy was fated to disappear. While some Orthodox Jews might persist, Conservatism held that such individuals would be relatively few in number and insignificant in social status. The founders of Conservatism did not relish the passing of Orthodoxy: they had strong sentimental ties with their Orthodox childhood, they had friends and relatives who had remained Orthodox, and they admired Orthodoxy's persistence in the face of seemingly over-whelming odds. However, while conceding Orthodoxy's historic contribution, they were convinced that it had run its course. As Rabbi Routtenberg put it:

> I think back to the period when my fellow students and I, at the yeshivah, decided to make the break and become Conservative rabbis . . . We were breaking with our past, in some cases with our families who had deep roots in Orthodoxy. We broke with beloved teachers who felt betrayed when we left the yeshivah. It was a great wrench . . . but we had to make it. . . . We loved the Jewish people and its heritage, and as we saw both threatened we set out to save them. We saw the future of Judaism in the Conservative movement.[7]

Orthodoxy, then, was viewed as a kind of *moshav z'kenim*—a home for the aged, and for those old in spirit. Accordingly, Conservatism was destined to supplant Orthodoxy, Furthermore, Conservatism was seen as a contemporary expression of what was most vital and creative in the Orthodoxy of old—that is, in the Orthodoxy of the pre-modern era:

> In spite of the claims made in other quarters it is we [Conservative Jews] who are the authentic Jews of rabbinic Judaism. . . . Many of those who attack our movement as "deviationist"—a term totally repugnant to the authentic Jewish tradition—and who demand

[7] *Ibid.*

unswerving adherence to the written letter of the Law are actually the Sadducees of the twentieth century. Had they lived in the days of Hillel, Rabbi Johanan ben Zakkai, Rabbi Akiba, Rabbi Meir, or Rabbi Judah Hanasi, they would have condemned every creative contribution that the Sages made to the living Judaism of their age.[8]

In a sense, then, Conservatism is conceived by its elite as twentieth-century Orthodoxy. Or, to put it another way, if Orthodoxy had retained the ability to change it would have evolved into Conservatism. . . .

In recent years it has become clear that Conservatism was incorrect in its diagnosis of Orthodoxy and especially in its prognosis of Orthodoxy's future. Unaccountably, Orthodoxy has refused to assume the role of invalid. Rather, it has transformed itself into a growing force in American Jewish life. It has reasserted its claim of being the authentic interpretation of Judaism.

Having achieved a new sense of élan, Orthodoxy has proceeded to implement a policy of strict non-cooperation with Conservatism. Orthodox policy has called for the rejection of all changes proposed by Conservatism—even changes that might be acceptable if they emanated from a different quarter. Furthermore, the tolerance of individual Orthodox rabbis toward Conservatism, characteristic of the 1920's and 1930's, has become only a dimming Conservative memory, especially on the Eastern seaboard. . . . Today's Orthodox leaders proceed on the assumption that Conservatism is a hollow shell—that its seemingly strong synagogues are peopled by weak Jews who are fated to assimilate. Only Orthodoxy will have the tenacity to survive the temptations of the open society.

The Orthodox offensive against Conservatism has been waged on two fronts simultaneously: Israel and the United States. Orthodox leaders in the United States have stimulated their colleagues in Israel to attack Conservatism. Inasmuch as Orthodox leaders in Israel are in firm control of their country's religious establishment, have considerable political leverage, and are not inhibited by a tradition of Church-State separation, they have been able to implement anti-Conservative policies inconceivable in the United States. Accordingly, Conservative rabbis have been disqualified from performing any rabbinic functions in Israel. The few Conservative institutions that have managed to gain a foothold in Israel are barely tolerated. The fugitive position occupied by

[8]Robert Gordis in R.A., *Proceedings*, XXIX (1965), 92–93.

Conservatism in Israel has been a particularly bitter blow for the American movement. To Conservative leaders it appears that, instead of being rewarded for its long history of support for the Zionist cause, Conservatism is being penalized. . . .

In summary, during the 1950's and 1960's the yeshivot multiplied in number, size, and fundamentalism; the Orthodox rabbis became ever more intransigent; the influence exercised by Orthodoxy in Israel became clearer; the Orthodox synagogues established themselves in upper-class and upper-middle-class areas. Even hasidism was transformed from an antediluvian curiosity into a movement which, it was said, had much to teach modern man. The net result was that the Conservative understanding of the American Jewish present, together with the Conservative expectation of the American Jewish future, became confounded. The ground was prepared for the development of a kind of Conservative anomie. The problem was particularly aggravated in the case of one segment of the Conservative elite—the rabbis. Many rabbis had a deep sympathy with Jewish traditionalism. Thus on the one hand they admired and identified with the Orthodox advance, but on the other hand, they were filled with dismay and hostility toward this totally unexpected development.

THE CRISIS IN CONSERVATIVE OBSERVANCE

While the renewal of Orthodoxy has been an important cause of the decline in Conservative morale, developments internal to the Conservative movement have also been an important influence. Conservatism is a religious movement. As such, it is subject to evaluation from the vantage point of suprasocial achievement. Thus, Conservative Jews may measure the progress of their movement in terms of its success in bringing man closer to God, or, as Rabbi Routtenberg phrases it, by its ability to "transform lives." Conservative Jews, if they are strong religionists, not only have this option but are impelled to embrace it. That is, they must give preference to suprasocial achievement and disregard, or even disvalue, such social achievements as monumental synagogue buildings and prosperous congregations.

All religious traditions have several yardsticks to measure suprasocial achievement, but each tends to stress a particular yardstick. The one that predominates in Judaism is that of the performance of the *mitzvot maasiyot*, the commandments of the Jewish sacred system. True to this thrust, Conservatism uses a ritualistic yardstick in gauging its effectiveness. While at times it has been attracted to the moralistic-ethical yardstick in measuring religious growth, it has nevertheless remained close to the sacramental approach of rabbinic Judaism.[9]

Conservative Judaism believes that it possesses a unique approach to the mitzvot, and especially to the problem of maintaining their observance. Conservatism holds that it is possible to advocate change in halakhah (Jewish law) and simultaneously to be loyal to halakhah. Change is seen as essential. From the Conservative standpoint, the maintenance of observance has been immensely complicated, if not rendered impossible, by what is regarded as Orthodoxy's ossification. While the modern Jew must be responsive to the requirements of halakhah, such loyalty cannot reasonably be expected unless halakhah is responsive to the needs of the modern Jew. Thus, in the Conservative view, Orthodox authorities who refuse to sanction change, much less to stimulate it, bear part of the responsibility for the lamentable decline of observance. As Rabbi Ralph Simon put it in a presidential address to the Rabbinical Assembly: "We have felt that Reform Judaism abandoned halakhah while Orthodoxy permitted halakhah to abandon us."[10]

As Conservatism sees it, certain mitzvot are outmoded or even offensive to the modern spirit. In the interest of promoting observance, as well as out of a desire for intellectual honesty, such mitzvot should be declared null and void. Furthermore, emphasis must be placed on the promotion of the essential requirements of the sacred system. Minutiae of the Jewish code can safely be disregarded. Mitzvot that are "fences around the Torah" rather than central to the Torah itself may be allowed to fall into disuse. Change can be effected by proper interpretation of the halakhic system, and, where necessary, by legislation.

The essence of the Conservative position, then, is liberaliza-

[9]On the problem such sacramentalism creates for the modern Jew, see Marshall Sklare and Joseph Greenblum, *Jewish Identity on the Suburban Frontier* (New York: Basic Books, 1967), pp. 45–48.

[10]R.A., *Proceedings*, XXXII (1968), 160.

tion. While Conservatism believes that liberalization is its own justification, it also holds that liberalization makes possible the promotion of observance. As religious authorities come to differentiate between major and minor—between what is required and what is elective, between what is in keeping with the modern temper and what is offensive to it, between what can be reinterpreted in the light of new needs and what is beyond rescue—the ground for a renewal of observance of the mitzvot is prepared. In addition to liberalization, the Conservative platform has two additional planks. One is "innovation," the development of new observances or procedures that are required when there is a need to substitute for, modify, or extend the traditional mitzvot. The other is "beautification," the requirement that the mitzvot be practiced in as esthetic a manner as possible—"the Jewish home beautiful." In sum, the Conservative position is that liberalization—in combination with innovation and beautification—will succeed in averting the evil decree of non-observance. . . .

The crucial aspect of the Conservative position on observance is . . . its success in promoting religious growth among the Conservative laity, and specifically in advancing their observance of the mitzvot. Judged from this vantage point, Conservatism has been an abysmal failure: there has been a steady erosion of observance among Conservative Jews. And despite a strong desire to encourage observance, Conservatism has not succeeded in arresting the decline in observance among its adherents, much less in increasing their level of conformity to the Jewish sacred system. The belief among Conservative leaders that the movement's approach to halakhah had the power to maintain observance, as well as to inspire its renewal, has proved illusory. . . .

Conservatism's defeat on the ritual front can be demonstrated in almost every area of Jewish observance. Sabbath observance is a case in point. After World War II there was a good deal of optimism in Conservatism with respect to Sabbath observance. The influences that seemed to portend a renewal included the rising prosperity of Conservative Jews and the increased popularity of the five-day workweek. The new life style of the suburban Jew, which stressed the building of a meaningful pattern of identity for one's children, constituted an additional factor. And the need for surcease from the increasingly hectic pace of life appeared to offer new justification for Judaism's stress on the sanctity of Sabbath rest.

Encouraged by these prospects, the Conservative rabbis

pushed for liberalization. In 1950 the Law Committee of the Rabbinical Assembly proceeded to make a daring innovation. On a split decision it voted to permit travel on the Sabbath—travel specifically for the purpose of attending services. It also voted to permit the use of electricity on the Sabbath.

What these decisions were saying was that the traditional concept of prohibited work was outmoded and counterproductive. Thus, driving an automobile was not intrinsically bad, and if the machine was employed to transport the individual from his home in the sprawl of suburbia to the synagogue on the Sabbath, it was a positive good. In any case the emphasis should be not on prohibitions as much as on positive acts that would promote the holiness of the seventh day: attending services, lighting candles, making *Kiddush,* reciting the blessing over bread, and serving special Sabbath meals. Furthermore, such an emphasis would inevitably lead the congregant to refrain from following his accustomed routine on the Sabbath. Thus the emphasis on positive acts constituted a more profitable approach to building Sabbath observance than would harping on a detailed list of prohibited activities.

In addition to the technique of liberalization, the Conservative approach to building Sabbath observance stressed the role of beautification. Thus the congregational gift shops conducted by the sisterhoods were stimulated to promote the sale of candlesticks, Kiddush cups, hallah covers, hallah knives, Sabbath napkins, and other such items. Finally, innovation was utilized. Innovation was in fact a long-standing Conservative tradition in respect to Sabbath observance—late Friday evening services had been one of the movement's most significant innovations.

The available evidence suggests that the Conservative strategy of liberalization, innovation, and beautification has been a failure; it underlies the fact that the majority of Conservative Jews do not follow even the most basic Sabbath observances. To cite the example of Conservative-dominated Providence, Rhode Island, only 12 percent of those who designate themselves as "Conservative" attend services once a week or more. And what is even more serious, attendance at Sabbath worship declines with each generation: while some 21 percent of the first generation attend, only 2 percent of the third do so.[11] The lighting of Sabbath candles

[11]Goldstein and Goldscheider, *op. cit.,* p. 194.

fares somewhat better, in part because the ritual is a female obligation. But despite the fact that lighting the candles is required of the Jewish woman, it is observed in only 40 percent of Conservative households. And while the ritual is observed in 52 percent of first-generation households, it is followed in only 32 percent of third-generation households.[12]

Kashrut is another area of observance that constitutes a problem for Conservative Jews. Only 37 percent of Conservative households in Providence buy kosher meat. Furthermore, in only 27 percent of the households are separate dishes utilized. And true to the pattern we have already encountered, observance declines in each generation: while 41 percent of the first generation maintain two sets of dishes, only 20 percent of the third generation do so. . . .[13]

For understandable reasons, the Conservative elite have avoided publicizing the painful evidence contained in congregational and communal surveys. Aware of how far its followers deviate from Conservative norms, the movement has felt in recent years that it can do little more than provide a source of information and inspiration for those who might somehow find their way back to the mitzvot.[14] While a "National Sabbath Observance Effort" was sponsored by the United Synagogue in the early 1950's when there was hope of a renewal of observance, the campaign has not been repeated.

In recent years it has become increasingly clear that the problem of observance constitutes a permanent crisis in Conservatism—that the religious derelictions of Conservative Jewry are much more than a temporary condition traceable to the trauma of

---

[12]*Ibid.*, p. 203. See Axelrod *et al.*, *op. cit.*, p. 131, for the somewhat higher figures in Boston.

[13]Second-generation Conservative Jews in Providence locate themselves between the relatively observant first generation and the highly unobservant third generation. However, the second generation tends to be positioned closer to the third generation than to the first.

[14]See, for example, the following publications of Conservatism's Burning Bush Press: Samuel H. Dresner, *The Jewish Dietary Laws*, and *The Sabbath* by the same author. Rabbi Dresner is singular in that he is a veteran Conservative leader of Reform background—he came to the seminary from Hebrew Union College, the Reform rabbinical school. Since he embraced the mitzvot by an act of will rather than by virtue of family inheritance, Dresner has been especially well qualified to provide information and inspiration to the exceptional individual in Conservatism who is interested in returning to the mitzvot.

removal from the closed society of the *shtetl* to the open society of the American metropolis. The elite are losing faith in their belief that through liberalization, innovation, and beautification the mass of Conservative Jews can be persuaded to return to the observance of the mitzvot. In lieu of a solution to the crisis, the movement has sought to insure the observance of the mitzvot in public: in the synagogue, at the Jewish Theological Seminary, at the Ramah camps, and during the tours and pilgrimages of the United Synagogue Youth. Although such conformity is gratifying to the elite—particularly to the older men who were reared in Orthodoxy and who have a strong need to justify their defection—it does not serve to erase the suspicion that the movement has been a failure. And Conservatism's failure in the area of the suprasocial is heightened by its brilliant achievements in the social arena: its success in building synagogues, in promoting organizational loyalty, and in achieving primacy on the American Jewish religious scene. . . .

THE NEXT CONSERVATIVE GENERATION

Although Conservative Judaism was not a creation of the young, its rise in the 1920–1950 era was closely connected with its appeal to young marrieds who were in the process of establishing independent households and developing a pattern of Jewish living that would be distinctive to their generation. Younger Jews who wished to retain continuity with their past and at the same time integrate with American middle-class culture found Conservative Judaism to be the perfect solution to their dilemma. Conservatism was traditional yet flexible, Jewish yet American. Its religious services were based on the Hebrew liturgy but also included prayers in English. Its rabbis appeared as authentic representatives of an age-old tradition yet were accepting of the culture of the larger environment. Conservatism stood for religious observance without rejecting the less observant.

The élan of Conservative Judaism during the period of its rise was in no small measure due to the fact that the elite of the movement felt their formula was precisely the one acceptable to younger age-groups in the Jewish population—groups whose connection with traditional Jewish culture was less firm than their own. In 1949 a leading Conservative layman in the Midwest, Julian Freeman, neatly summarized the appeal of Conservatism when he commented: "A generation ago the young architect, the young engineer, the young doctor, the young lawyer, the young businessman saw in Conservative Judaism a chance for religious self-expression integrated with the best of thinking in the world at large."[15]

The present-day Conservative elite, however, is no longer so confident that its formula will be attractive to the younger generation. There are two aspects to this crisis of confidence. One is the problem of Jewish continuity—the problem of whether the battle against assimilation can be won. This question, most commonly perceived in terms of the threat of intermarriage, began to preoccupy the Jewish community in the 1960's. . . .[16] It seemed to many that the very physical survival of the group was at stake. The threat inevitably spilled over into feelings about the prospects for Conservatism: if group continuity was in doubt, how much less was there a future for Conservative Judaism?

In addition to pessimism about whether the battle against intermarriage could be won, Conservatism in recent years has lost its older confidence of being in possession of a formula that can win the support of younger Jews. Despite interest in the shtetl and the East European milieu, many younger Jews—including those reared in Conservative congregations—have little connection with the Jewish culture of the immediate past. Inasmuch as Conservatism assumes some continuity with the East European past and some familiarity with Jewish culture generally, it has been deeply affected by such Jewish deculturation. If the mission of Conservatism has been to show how it was possible to practice selected aspects of Jewish culture in an American milieu, the result of Jewish deculturation has been that the movement no longer has its older foundation of Jewish culture on which to build its synagogual loyalties. . . .

Conservatism labors under the further doubt that it can prevail

---

[15]See *supra*, p. 90.

[16]On the rate of intermarriage and the Jewish response, see Sklare, *America's Jews, op. cit.*, pp. 180–206.

in its battle to win the loyalty of young people. The reason for
Conservative pessimism resides in the disjunction between its
cultural system and that of younger American Jews. Many
Conservative young people not only lack Jewish culture, but they
have been influenced by youth culture—some are card-carrying
members of the Woodstock Nation, others are fellow travelers, and
still others have inchoate sympathies with the counterculture.
While the problem of enlisting the loyalty of such young people is
encountered by all Jewish religious movements, the issue is a
particularly knotty one for Conservatism, with its stress on cultural
reconciliation and the blending of Jewish and general culture.
Despite the fact that the so-called *havurot* (communal fellowships)
originated among Conservative young people, Conservatism has
not been notably successful in enlisting the loyalties of those who
are part of the youth culture, who have little connection with East
European culture, or who are antagonistic to the type of American
culture on which the movement is based. . . .

Sensitive leaders in Conservatism are aware of how deeply the
movement is rooted in an older American middle-class culture
which is currently out of favor with a significant segment of
Conservative youth. The problem was presented to the Rabbinical
Assembly by Rabbi Edward Gershfield in an address which
celebrated the organization's seventieth anniversary. According to
Gershfield:

> Our services of readings in fine English, correct musical renditions by
> professional cantors and choirs, and decorous and dignified rabbis in
> elegant gowns arouse disdain and contempt in our young people. They
> want excitement and noise, improvisation and emotion, creativity and
> sensitivity, informality and spontaneity. On the other hand, they feel
> guilty about the spending of large sums of money for synagogue
> buildings rather than for social services (generally for non-Jews). And
> they are "turned off" by the very beauty and decorum which we have
> worked so hard to achieve.
>
> Of course, the youth do not wish to go into the reasons why these
> aspects of our life have been created. They are impatient with our
> explanations that most people are not dynamic and creative, and look
> to religious leaders for directions and instructions; that we who have
> managed to survive the rigors of youth appreciate regularity and
> stability in life, that we honestly want to endow our heritage with
> dignity and beauty, and that a congregation of a thousand persons
> cannot have a prayer service in a coffeehouse to the accompaniment

of a guitar . . . we seem to be doomed to having to watch as our youth relive the same self-destructive impulses that we have seen long ago, and have thought could not happen again. Our appeals to reason and history . . . go right past them and we are for the most part helpless.[17]

. . . in summary, the immediate reasons for the drop in Conservative morale at the very zenith of Conservative influence include the emergence of Orthodoxy, the problem of Conservative observance, and the widespread alienation among Conservative young people from the American culture to which their movement has been strongly attached. But on a deeper level the Conservative crisis—if that be the word—represents a questioning of whether the Jewish people and its "chain of tradition" can long endure on the American continent. Since Conservatism's future is predicated upon such survival, its fears are understandable. *Yisrael v'oraitha had hu*: the Jewish people and its tradition are indissolubly linked. There cannot be an authentic Jewish people without the continuity of Jewish tradition, even as there cannot be meaningful continuity of Jewish tradition without the maintenance of the integrity of the Jewish group. It is to this momentous issue that the Conservative movement, in its present mature phase, has been moved to address itself.

[17]R.A., *Proceedings*, XXXIV (1970), 90–91.

ORTHODOXY IN AMERICAN JEWISH LIFE
by CHARLES S. LIEBMAN

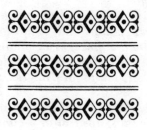

INTRODUCTION

ONE OF THE MOST surprising trends in American Jewish life
has been the emergence of Orthodoxy as a "third force" competing
with Reform and Conservative Judaism. In less than three decades
Orthodoxy has transformed its image from that of a dying
movement to one whose strength and opinions must be reckoned
with in any realistic appraisal of the Jewish community.

Behind this shift in image lies a sociological reality. Earlier
American Orthodoxy was pervaded with elements of folk religion *
and was dominated by what Charles Liebman has called the
"uncommitted Orthodox" and the "residual Orthodox"; in recent
decades this has given way to a new Orthodoxy dominated by what
Liebman calls the "committed Orthodox." The material which
follows is selected from Liebman's larger analysis of Orthodoxy and
centers on the committed group. As Liebman demonstrates,
committed Orthodoxy comprises an intricate network of organizations and institutions. Such institutions not only compete with each
other but also relate themselves to the Jewish community as a whole
and to the larger non-Jewish society.

*See Charles S. Liebman, "The Religion of American Jews," in Marshall Sklare, ed.,
The Jew in American Society (New York: Behrman House, Inc., 1974), pp. 223–252.

Understanding the Orthodox world is no simple task. A separate monograph would be required to comprehend just the Orthodox synagogue, although Liebman says enough about the institution to convey its infinite variety. But he focuses his analysis on the significant non-synagogal organizations and institutions in American Orthodoxy: the yeshivot, the rabbinical associations, the synagogal unions, the hasidic groups. Liebman also helps us understand the intricate leadership structure of American Orthodoxy.

The structure of Orthodoxy differs quite sharply from that of the Reform and Conservative movements. Instead of a comparatively well-integrated and coordinated structure, Orthodoxy's is highly proliferated and weakly coordinated. Part of the reason for this lies in the continuity Orthodoxy maintains with the European past (and in the case of some Sephardic Jews, with the Near-Eastern past). Furthermore, Orthodoxy's structure is not based exclusively on traditions and models generated on American soil. For example, instead of the Reform and Conservative model of a single institution serving as rabbinical school and source of Jewish learning, Orthodoxy preserves the European model of multiple yeshivot, each founded by an outstanding leader, independent of others, and free to emphasize a particular approach to Talmudic learning.

The study of Orthodox organizations and institutions presents formidable difficulties. As Liebman emphasizes, Orthodoxy has a strong sectarian element which is suspicious of outsiders. Even the "modern Orthodox," as Liebman designates them, are not particularly anxious to be studied by the social scientist. The world of modern Orthodoxy necessarily represents a delicate balance between the imperatives of Jewish tradition and the demands of the larger Jewish and Gentile worlds. Such a fine balance is not only inherently unstable but is especially vulnerable to attack by sectarians. Thus the modern Orthodox group fears that however fair-minded the social scientist may be, his findings may be used by sectarians for their own partisan purposes. The modern Orthodox group is in the difficult position of approving of research in principle but fearing that, in practice, research may work to its detriment.

The Orthodox sectarian can overcome his suspicion of the outsider by realizing that whether or not the outsider penetrates what he, the sectarian, feels is the essence of his religious perspective, publicity may be a positive good—it may serve the purpose of magnifying the importance of his sectarian group. The modern Orthodox group, having better access to the media of communication, looks for publicity on its own terms. It is dubious of the value of exposing differences in the Orthodox camp. Unlike the sectarians the modern Orthodox are concerned with building unity, and as they see it, the building of unity can only be harmed by public discussion.

In his analysis of the institutions and organizations of the committed Orthodox group Liebman, who is himself a committed Orthodox Jew, discusses both those who are close to him and those located at a greater remove. He relies on diverse concepts and different kinds of data, both in the general field of the sociology of religion and in the special area of the study of Jewish society. Convinced of the correctness of the Orthodox position and believing that it constitutes the only hope of American Jewry, Liebman succeeds in preventing his value judgments from working to the detriment of his analysis, as he critically evaluates each Orthodox institution, highlighting both its weaknesses as well as its strengths.

M. S.

. . . ORTHODOXY perceives itself as the only legitimate bearer of the Jewish tradition; to Orthodoxy this tradition is expressed almost exclusively in religious form (which is not to say that all elements of the tradition are necessarily religious in their essence). While Conservative and Reform see themselves as legitimate heirs to the Jewish tradition, neither claims to be its exclusive bearer. This distinction between Orthodoxy and the other denominations has analytically separable consequences which only seem to operate at cross-purposes. Since neither the Reform nor the Conservative lays claim to exclusive doctrinal "truth," they are free to cooperate with one another, with Orthodoxy, and even with secular Jewish groups; they risk only institutional losses. The doctrines of Orthodoxy, on the other hand, are more precise and are by definition beyond compromise or even the appearance of compromise. Hence Orthodoxy must be constantly on guard against appearing to surrender or water down its doctrine.

But there is a second consequence that flows from Orthodoxy's exclusive claim to the truth and its major tenet that it is the obligation of every Jew to observe the *mitzvot* (religious commandments). While Conservatives and Reformists are under no obligation to do anything about the matter, the Orthodox are doctrinally obligated to encourage the observance of Jewish law here and now. In addition, the doctrine of *ahavat Yisrael* (love of Israel), particularly as elaborated by the late Rabbi Abraham Isaac Kook, chief rabbi of Palestine until his death in 1935, impels Orthodoxy to extend itself to the non-Orthodox. If non-Orthodox Jews were unorganized, the consequences of Orthodoxy's doctrinal position would not be contradictory. It could simply undertake missions to the non-Orthodox. But when, in fact, about half of the non-Orthodox are organized in the Conservative and Reform movements, and the remainder are almost beyond reach of any religious group in Jewish life, then Orthodoxy is confronted with two mutually exclusive mandates—to promote faith and observance among non-Orthodox Jews, while giving no recognition and comfort to the only existing institutions which can reach those Jews.

In practice, different groups within Orthodoxy have emphasized one mandate or the other, and most of the divisions within Orthodoxy, in practice, reflect this division. But the point to be stressed is that, with the possible exception of the Satmar *hasidim*, all Orthodox groups consider both mandates as binding. (The Satmar probably do, too, but feel that the obligation to promote observance is simply impractical in this day among all but a handful of Jews and that their own piety is not so secure as to justify undertaking "missions" to other Jews.) Hence, no matter how zealous the right wing may be in its stress on religious continuity, maximal observance, and condemnation of the non-Orthodox, it hesitates to characterize the non-Orthodox as beyond hope of redemption. And no matter how outgoing and conciliatory the left wing may be toward the nonobservant and the institutions of the non-Orthodox, it is always restrained by its acceptance of the basic doctrinal principles as being beyond compromise.

Orthodoxy and the Demands of Society

The differences within Orthodoxy are best understood in the broad framework of the sociology of religion. While the concepts here developed are not directly applicable to Judaism, they are suggestive of differences among Jewish groups and serve heuristic purposes.

Students of religion, drawing their data primarily from the development of Christianity, have developed a typology of religions based on distinctions between church and sect. Following Yinger's refinement of Troeltsch,[1] church and sect are defined as ideal types, that is, end points on a continuum along which religious groups can be placed and compared with one another as they approach one end or the other.

The central problems to which the church-sect dichotomy is addressed are how a religious body confronts the secular world and how it provides a religious response to the personal needs of its adherents. The *church* "recognizes the strength of the secular world and rather than either deserting the attempt to influence it or losing its position by contradicting the secular powers directly, accepts the main elements in the social structure as proximate goods." The major function of the church is its effort to insure social cohesion and order and to do so it must extend its ministry to

[1]John Milton Yinger, *Religion, Society and the Individual* (New York: 1957).

everyone. As a result it must be willing to "compromise with the wide ranges of behavior that may be found in a society."[2]

The *sect* is a smaller group, arising from the inability of the church to meet some members' needs by virtue of its very flexibility and adaptability. The sect "repudiates the compromises of the church, preferring isolation to compromise."[3] Hence, unlike the church, it is hostile or indifferent to the secular order. It seeks primarily to satisfy individual religious needs rather than societal ones.

It is apparent that the church-sect dichotomy is not applicable in this form to Judaism today. The typology assumes a closed society in which the religious order is confronted only by the secular order and the individual needs of its members. When Judaism represented a basically closed society, before Emancipation, the dichotomy appears to have been more applicable. Where the definition of church or sect says "society," we can read "Judaism" or "Jews." Thus, the early development of hasidism appears to fit the definition of sectarian growth and development.

But religious groups within Judaism today are confronted with problems of the larger Jewish society—what we may call the secular (or non-religious) institutionalized Jewish order—as well as the non-Jewish society, and the problems of the religious denomination are not only to adapt to Jewish society and insure social cohesion and order within Judaism, but also to adapt to general society and insure cohesion and order within it. Furthermore, Judaism must meet not only the individual needs of members as they arise by virtue of Jewishness, but also those that arise by virtue of membership in the general society. An effort to solve one kind of problem frequently exacerbates another. To sum up—the Christian denomination plays a double role: vis-à-vis the social order or general society, and vis-à-vis the individual needs of its membership. To the extent that the Christian denomination stresses the solution to one order of problems it raises questions for the other. Judaism faces not two but four problems. It must meet the needs or demands of the broader society and of the narrower, Jewish society. It must meet the needs that arise from an individual's problems in the general society and those that arise from his problems in the Jewish society.

[2]*Ibid.*, p. 144.
[3]*Ibid.*, p. 146.

Let us be specific about the nature of these problems as they have emerged in the United States:

1) To meet the needs of the general society, it is necessary to affirm the democratic political structure and to develop a symbolism (transcendental or not) for its transmission; to affirm the unity of all Americans and the primacy of American national interests and needs.

2) To meet the needs of the Jewish society, it is necessary to achieve unity among Jews and to maintain Jewish identification in a permissive gentile society; to maintain defenses against prejudice and discrimination.

3) To meet the individual's needs in the general society, it is necessary to confront the problems of good and evil, of reward and punishment, and of alienation and anomie in an urban, heterogeneous society.

4) To meet the individual's needs in Jewish society, it is necessary to interpret traditional Jewish beliefs and practices in the light of the individual's present needs and problems.

Bearing in mind these four types of demands or needs, we can classify all Jewish organizations by the problem or combination of problems to which they have addressed themselves. Each of these classifications can, in turn, be refined according to the manner in which the problem is approached. Within any given organization there is bound to be some conflict or tension over which problem should assume priority. A general theory of Jewish organizational life would have to take account of the manner in which social status, education, accommodation to the American milieu, and other such factors cut across the leadership and constituent groups of each organization, determining the perspective in which problems are viewed and solutions chosen.

Our concern here is with Orthodoxy, but first we must look briefly into the Conservative and Reform groups, which today come closer than Orthodoxy to assuming the characteristics of church rather than sect. By and large, Conservatism and Reform address themselves to problems arising from societal demands. The application is made at an individual level and to individual problems, but the context out of which the problem emerges is generally societal—social cohesion and moral order—rather than individual. Until recently, Reform was more oriented toward general societal problems and Conservatism toward those of Jewish society. This is changing somewhat as Conservatism becomes more self-conscious about its role as a church and Reform, with a longer church experience, becomes more aware of the limitations of a church in reaching its membership directly. . . .

In contrast to Conservative and Reform Judaism, much of Orthodoxy's energy has been addressed to finding solutions within a halakhic framework for individual problems arising in contemporary life. Orthodoxy has been the least churchlike of all Jewish religious groups. In part this stems from the absence (until recently) of any self-consciousness. Only recently has Orthodoxy begun to define itself as a particular movement in the United States and been brought into contact with the broader society by the accelerated acculturation of its adherents and its own institutional growth. This new confrontation has raised problems that formerly did not exist for Orthodoxy or were overlooked. Thus, Orthodox leaders have been much slower than other Jewish leaders to define their attitude toward problems of civil rights or labor.

Since 1960 much of this has changed. In 1964, speaking to a Young Israel meeting in New York, Rabbi Aaron Soloveitchik, one of the leading Talmudic authorities in Jewish life, delivered a major address on civil rights from a halakhic perspective. In that same year a joint conference of the Industrial Union Department, AFL-CIO, and the Social Action Committee of the Rabbinical Council of America (RCA) heard a series of papers by young Orthodox rabbis on religion and labor. Such developments were a portent of serious stirrings within Orthodoxy. . . .

. . . some of the divisions within [Orthodoxy's] camp are best understood by analyzing the different positions of Orthodox leaders and institutions as they approach the church or sect ends of the continuum. The line between the left (or church) wing of Orthodoxy and the right wing of the Conservative movement is a very thin one. In fact, it is institutional loyalty far more than ideology which separates the two groups practically, though there are other, subtle distinctions, as well.

There are two alternative explanations for the differences among the Orthodox. The first argues that the two major categories of Orthodox—modern or church Orthodox and sectarian Orthodox—differ from one another in their degree of acculturation. It is true, as we shall show, that the sectarian Orthodox tend to be of lower income, poorer secular education, and more recent immigration than the modern Orthodox. (Sociologists of religion have noted that these tend to correlate with affinity to sect rather than church among Christians as well.) But the sectarians can boast their share of outwardly acculturated adherents; the leaders of the Association of Orthodox Jewish Scientists, to be discussed below, are far more sectarian than modern in terms of their concerns and orientations. And, most significantly, acculturation must be viewed as a dependent rather than an independent variable. The large number of American-born advanced yeshivah students who attend college at night to minimize interference with their Talmudic studies and value their secular education only for its vocational benefits have in a sense deliberately rejected acculturation because of their sectarian tendencies, rather than being sectarian because unacculturated.

A second explanation for the differences among the Orthodox distinguishes among them along a fundamentalism-liberalism scale. It argues that the sectarian Orthodox differ from the modern or church Orthodox by virtue of their beliefs concerning the Mosaic authorship of the Torah or the Sinaitic origin of the Oral Law. Although some modern Orthodox thinkers would consider Franz Rosenzweig's position,[4] for example, as within the framework of Orthodox belief, questions of actual dogma have not yet been broached among Orthodox leaders. When they are, as seems likely, there will be explosive consequences. Unquestionably there are Orthodox intellectuals who would like to raise the question, but with few exceptions neither they nor the fundamentalists have yet articulated exactly what they mean by Mosaic authorship or Sinaitic origin of the Oral Law.[5] It is fair to say that the entire belief

[4]Rosenzweig accepted the notion of a biblical Redactor, but saw the task of compiling the Bible as the human presentation of divine revelation. Rosenzweig's oft-quoted statement is that for him the symbol "R" does not stand for *Redactor* but for *Rabbenu* (our rabbi, our master).

[5]In one respect the argument that the written law (the Torah) and the oral law, which constitute the basis of halakhah, were given by God to Moses at Sinai requires no elaboration. It has always been an article of faith for the Orthodox Jew, and the meaning of the words and their historical referent seems simple enough. Biblical criticism has not challenged this belief; on the contrary, biblical criticism becomes meaningful only when this article of faith is denied. But it is this very article of faith in its plain meaning which has become "preposterous" to the modern mind. (This, of course, says nothing about the truth or falsity of the doctrine. A round world once also seemed preposterous.) That segment of American Orthodoxy which lives in the orbit of the *rashe yeshivot* does not find such a faith preposterous. It has no severe problem in reconciling its conception of God and human experience to its faith in the divine origin of Torah. That is not so for the more acculturated Orthodox Jew. The observer is perhaps forbidden to challenge a man's belief, but he is entitled to ask

structure of American Orthodoxy still finds verbal expression within the bounds of a rather narrow fundamentalism. Privately, the modern Orthodox admit that they simply interpret the same words to mean different things from what they mean to the sectarian Orthodox.[6] They have sought to keep the subject outside the area of controversy, making no serious effort, for example, to engage in biblical criticism, and thereby ruling out the development of any outstanding Orthodox biblical scholars in the United States. Modern Orthodoxy pays lip service to the notion that something ought to be done in this area and that aspects of biblical criticism can be incorporated into the Orthodox tradition, but no one is prepared to undertake or even encourage the work. It is sometimes acknowledged that some abandon Orthodoxy because their intellectual predispositions cannot be reconciled with traditional patterns of belief. But such losses, qualitatively important, are quantitatively insignificant. The main body of Orthodoxy in the United States appears at present to be doctrinally untroubled.

Institutions and Currents

Using the church-sect dichotomy, then, let us turn to a discussion of specific institutions and currents within Orthodoxy. . . . At one extreme are the *shtibl*-type synagogues. They meet in small rooms, where bearded men cover their heads with *tallitim* (prayer shawls) to pray, generally unheedful of the leader of the service, their bodies swaying. Women are separated from the men by a full-length wall in the rear, punctured by several peepholes through which a few can peer. At the other extreme are the modern edifices with spacious auditoriums. Here services are conducted by a cantor whose trained voice is carried to the ends of the hall by a microphone. Men and women are seated together, and the heart of the service is the rabbi's

whether the secularly acculturated Jew truly believes in *Torah min ha-shamayim* (Torah from heaven) when the entire structure of behavior and belief of that Jew seems inconsistent with this one article of faith. Inevitably efforts will be made to reinterpret the meaning of *Torah min ha-shamayim* in an effort to resolve the inconsistency. A variety of strategies are possible. One can begin by acknowledging this as a preposterous belief and proceed to a kind of Orthodox Jewish existentialism, with the events at Sinai being the object of some "leap of faith." One can maintain that the doctrine of *Torah min ha-shamayim* has metaphysical rather than physical referents and that we are dealing with two discrete levels of meaning. One can seek to reinterpret *Torah min ha-shamayim* as meaning something less than the entire written and oral law. These and other strategies of reinterpretation will undoubtedly be undertaken.

[6]The same is true of Conservative and Reform leaders among themselves with regard to the concept of revelation.

sermon. Although mixed seating and the use of a microphone on the Sabbath violate halakhah, the modern congregation considers itself as Orthodox and is in fact more likely to support many of the supracongregational institutions to be discussed below than the *shtibl*.

৪০৪

MODERN ORTHODOX

By modern Orthodox we mean those individuals and institutions among the committed Orthodox who tend toward the church end of the church-sect continuum. On the one hand, they seek to demonstrate the viability of the halakhah for contemporary life; on the other, they emphasize what they have in common with all other Jews rather than what separates them. Until recently they composed almost the entire upper-income, well-educated strata of the committed Orthodox. Many of the best-known Orthodox congregations in the United States, and most of the wealthy ones, are led by modern Orthodox rabbis.

Like the other groups within American Orthodoxy, the modern Orthodox have not produced any systematic statement of their ideology; in part, perhaps, because they shun the practical consequences of their philosophical or theological position, and in part because none has been sanctioned by eminent Talmudic scholars, still acknowledged as the arbiters of ideology. To the extent, however, that the modern Orthodox have produced an ideologist, it is probably Rabbi Emanuel Rackman, although his position is not representative of all modern Orthodox Jews. He is certainly the favorite target of the Orthodox right wing, notwithstanding the private concession of at least some of its members that he has brought more people into the Orthodox fold than any other person. Rackman has published widely on halakhah, Jewish values, and contemporary life.[7] His concern is with understanding the

[7]Essays from a variety of journals were reprinted in Emanuel Rackman, *Jewish Values for Modern Man* (New York: 1962). See also "Israel and God: Reflections on their Encounter," *Judaism*, Summer 1962, pp. 233–241; "Halachic Progress: Rabbi Moshe Feinstein's *Igrot Moshe* on *Even Ha-Ezer*," *Ibid.*, Summer 1964, pp. 366–373, and *Sabbaths and Festivals in the Modern Age*, in the "Studies in Torah Judaism" series (New York: 1961).

meaning of the halakhic injunctions in order to find contemporary applications. In the course of his efforts he has suggested what many feel to be a radical reinterpretation of the halakhah:

> The Halakhah is more than texts. It is life and experience. What made the Babylonian and not the Palestinian Talmud the great guide of Jewish life in the Diaspora was not a decree or a decision but *vox populi*. From Maimonides it would appear that it was the acceptance of the people who by custom and popular will constituted the authority. Can a Halakhic scholar lose himself in texts exclusively when the texts themselves bid him to see what practice "has become widespread among Jews," what is required socially "because of the precepts of peace," what will "keep the world aright," and many other social criteria? These standards are as much a part of the Torah as the texts themselves.[8]

Rackman is also prominently associated with the idea that Orthodox Jews, both individually and institutionally, must cooperate with the non-Orthodox. He is outspoken in his conviction that Orthodox rabbis should be free to associate with such groups as the New York Board of Rabbis (composed of Reform and Conservative as well as Orthodox rabbis) and that Orthodox groups should remain affiliated with the umbrella organization for all religious groups, the Synagogue Council of America.

Before considering the groups within which modern Orthodoxy is dominant, some comment on the sources of authority and unity within the Jewish community will be made. We will seek to demonstrate why the drive for unity, even within the organizations controlled by modern Orthodoxy, has been blunted in recent years, and what the Orthodox basis for unity has become.

Authority in the Jewish Community

There are four possible bases of authority within the Jewish community today: numbers, money, tradition, and person or charisma.

Authority of numbers is rarely exercised directly. Although organizations and institutions make some claim to authority on the basis of their numerical superiority, issues have rarely been resolved on this basis. There have been a few exceptions, the most noteworthy being the American Jewish Conference and particularly its 1943 meeting in which the sympathy of the masses of American

[8]Rackman, *Sabbaths and Festivals* . . ., p. 8.

Jews for the Zionist program was reflected in the division of votes. Today almost no Jewish organization lays claim to authority within the community by virtue of its size. In part this is because no organization has a generally accepted, trustworthy membership list. More significantly, it is because no mass organization in Jewish life can even pretend to be able to mobilize its membership behind one position or another.

The most potent claim for authority in Jewish life today is exercised by money. Perhaps this was always so, but until recently the claim was exercised in alliance with religious tradition. Tradition's loss of status has resulted in the dissolution of this alliance and today those who control the purse strings, alone, usually speak for the Jewish community and decide questions within it. Although the professionals and staff members of the various organizations generally initiate policy, their authority is often determined by their access to financial resources and particularly to the few big contributors. Orthodoxy cannot accept the authority of money because it contains neither a class of large contributors nor a group of professionals with access to large contributors. In this regard, the Conservative and Reform rabbinate are in a far better, though by no means ideal, position, as they confront the "secular" Jewish institutions. The potency of money in the rest of the community, therefore, has the effect of pressuring Orthodoxy to withdraw from the community. In other words, the rule of the game in the Jewish community is that "money talks the loudest." Because Orthodoxy only loses by these rules, there is a constant pressure from within for it to leave the game unless the rules are changed. Of course, the concessions and compromises made by the Orthodox in order to play the game become unnecessary when they withdraw from it and they then move to a more intransigent right-wing position.

Orthodoxy claims the right to preserve the unity of the Jewish community by invoking the authority of tradition and charisma. With regard to the first, it claims communal support for its essentially parochial schools on the ground that these are traditional schools which simply teach Judaism as it has always been taught (in terms of content, of course, not method). This claim to legitimacy has been challenged recently, most particularly by the Conservatives. The foregoing is not meant to imply that numbers or money have only recently become sources of authority, or that tradition has lost all its force. It does mean that the weight of the different bases of authority has changed, and that Orthodoxy's claim to its exclusive access to this authority has been challenged.

The fourth possible source of authority in the Jewish community is that of person, or charisma. Jews in the United States have never produced a charismatic leader for the entire community, although Louis Marshall, Judah Magnes, Stephen Wise, and Abba Hillel Silver came close to being such leaders.

The only group within Jewish life which lays claim to charismatic leaders today is the Orthodox. Preeminent among these for the modern Orthodox is Rabbi Joseph B. Soloveitchik. RCA's claim to leadership in the general Jewish community and its belief that it ought really to exercise this leadership rest almost entirely on the fact that Rabbi Soloveitchik is its leader. RCA members consider it enormously significant that the non-Orthodox Jewish community has accorded his opinions an increasing respect. Rabbi Soloveitchik, acknowledged by most Orthodox Jews as one of the world's leading Talmudic authorities, has become increasingly active in social and political life and is quite conscious of his role as a communal leader. As the descendant of the longest extant line of *gedolim*, rabbis who combined Talmudic and communal authority, this could hardly be otherwise.[9]

On the other hand, the more right-wing yeshivah world (to be discussed below) rests its claim to authority on the leadership of the outstanding *rashe yeshivot* who claim the mantle of traditional as well as charismatic authority.

We turn now to those organizations in which modern Orthodoxy holds a dominant position, stressing that in none of these groups is that position exclusive.

Rabbinical Council of America (RCA)

The Rabbinical Council of America is the largest and most influential Orthodox rabbinical body in the United States. It has 830

---

[9]His father, Rabbi Moses Soloveitchik, was one of the great Talmudic scholars in the United States in the last generation. His uncle, Reb Velvel Soloveitchik, was the *gedol ha-dor* ("the great man of his generation") of the last generation in Palestine. His grandfather, Reb Hayyim of Brisk, the famous Brisker Rav, was the leading Talmudic scholar of his time, and his great-grandfather, Rabbi Joseph Beer Soloveitchik, after whom he is named, was the *rosh yeshivah* of Volozhin, the greatest Talmudic academy of its time. For a biographical sketch of Rabbi Soloveitchik and a popularization of some elements of his thought see his son-in-law's article: Aaron Lichtenstein, "Joseph Soloveitchik," in Simon Noveck, ed., *Great Jewish Thinkers of the Twentieth Century* (Washington: 1963), pp. 281–297.

members, all ordained by recognized rabbinic authorities. About 600 are in the active rabbinate, and most of the rest are teachers and school administrators. About half of the active rabbis were ordained at Yeshiva University's Rabbi Isaac Elchanan Theological Seminary (RIETS), and another 15 percent at the Hebrew Theological College in Illinois. Both of these institutions represent a point of view different from that of other yeshivot in the United States which confer ordination. Another 20 to 25 percent of the RCA membership come from these other American yeshivot, and the remaining few are from Europe.

A major controversy within RCA has centered on the question of its relationship with non-Orthodox rabbinical groups, particularly the affiliation of its members with the New York Board of Rabbis. In 1955, 11 *rashe yeshivot,* the most influential leaders of all the large academies for advanced Talmudic study in the United States (except Yeshiva University and the Hebrew Theological College), issued an *issur* or prohibition against Orthodox rabbis joining organizations in which non-Orthodox rabbis were officially represented. Their position was phrased in halakhic terms as a *pesak din,* a juridical decision, but has been buttressed with the practical political argument that by officially recognizing the non-Orthodox rabbi as a rabbi, Orthodoxy accorded him a status to which he was not entitled under Jewish law and which cut the ground from under its own claim as the only legitimate bearer of the Torah tradition.

RCA referred the question to its own halakhah committee under the chairmanship of Rabbi Soloveitchik. At the end of 1964 the committee had not yet reported, and showed no disposition to do so as long as the *status quo* was maintained within the Jewish community.

Nevertheless, the political aspects of the question were raised on numerous occasions; in all instances the forces for separation in RCA, led by Rabbi David Hollander, were defeated, although there is a growing sympathy for the values which Hollander espouses. The opponents of separation have argued that by cooperating with the non-Orthodox they are able to restrain them from public violation of halakhah and are in a better position to help shape policy for the whole Jewish community. . . . Besides, they suspect that the vast majority of nominally Orthodox Jews do not see any sharp distinctions between Orthodoxy and other denominations, that a policy of separation would fail of general support, and that it would jeopardize the considerable support for Orthodox institutions that comes from non-Orthodox Jews.

Finally, and perhaps most importantly, they feel that RCA members do not view themselves as living in a community apart from the rest of American Jews. The Orthodox rabbi, particularly outside New York City, lives among and serves a non-observant constituency. In addition, he himself is likely to be American-born, a product of the American culture, which places a premium on compromise, sanctifies majority rule, and decries dogmatism. . . .

RCA looks for spiritual and, more recently, political leadership to Rabbi Soloveitchik, known affectionately to his followers as the Rov (Sephardi: Rav). One can almost distinguish a Jew's religious position by the manner in which he refers to Soloveitchik. The non-Orthodox are likely to call him Rabbi Soloveitchik; the RCA modern Orthodox call him the Rov; his own students, Rebbe; and the right wing, J.B., for the first two initials of his name.

RCA has moved to the right in recent years, though not as far to the right as its separatists would like. It has continued to concern itself with communal problems but has become increasingly outspoken and antagonistic toward other groups, both religious and secular, within Jewish life. This is a result of a number of factors. The younger rabbis, particularly those from Yeshiva University, are more right-wing today in both their practice and their communal outlook than their predecessors of a decade or more ago. Secondly, as the Orthodox community has grown in numbers and risen in income and status, the rabbi has attained greater personal security and confidence in the future of Orthodoxy and has become less compromising. Thirdly, the right wing within Orthodoxy has become more acculturated. This means that it is better able to communicate with the left wing and make an impact on it. . . .

RCA's move to the right has had the further effect of healing somewhat the breach between its modern Orthodox and sectarian elements on such questions as the development of halakhah, which is only indirectly related to the controversy over communal involvement. Rackman, as we have noted, is the leading advocate of radical halakhic development, but his viewpoint is almost totally isolated. Rackman elicits a sympathetic response from his colleagues when he demands that the rabbinic leaders grapple with contemporary problems and when he criticizes them for their "ivory tower" posture. But there is less sympathy with him on what the content of the response should be. As one observer put it, "The RCA rabbi doesn't want *hetterim* [lenient rulings], he only wants a good explanation for a *pesak* [a ruling]."

Union of Orthodox Jewish Congregations of America (UOJC)

Officially RCA is the rabbinical arm of the Union of Orthodox Jewish Congregations of America (UOJC), the major national congregational organization of Orthodox synagogues. . . .

The forum for the controversy over Orthodox participation in non-Orthodox roof organizations has shifted in the last two years from RCA, where the separatists have been defeated, to UOJC. At its 1964 convention a resolution by the separatists was defeated, but on the ground that withdrawal would be unwarranted unless a roof organization for all Orthodox groups was first established. Toward this end, Orthodox organizations like RCA, the Religious Zionists of America, the Rabbinical Alliance of America, and Agudath Israel were invited to submit position papers on their conditions for entering a unified Orthodox organization. Agudath Israel, whose position probably best reflects that of the sectarian Orthodox, stipulated two conditions for its participation: that all members of the proposed organization withdraw from anything more than *ad hoc* participation in non-Orthodox roof organizations, and that a council of Torah authorities, composed essentially of Agudath Israel leaders, be the arbiters of the new organization. It was unlikely that the modern Orthodox would meet either of these conditions.

For many years UOJC was led by a young, Americanized, modern Orthodox element without any real constituent base among the mass of Yiddish-speaking, immigrant synagogue members. In the past decade a closer relationship has developed between Orthodox synagogues and the parent synagogue body, and UOJC has grown considerably. This is because the synagogue leadership has become more acculturated; the UOJC leadership has moved to the right, away from modernism, and the success of Conservative and Reform parent congregational bodies, as well as of Young Israel, has shown the importance of a united Orthodox synagogue body. None the less, UOJC is still not as representative of Orthodox congregations as the United Synagogue is of Conservative, or UAHC [Union of American Hebrew Congregations] of Reform, congregations. . . .

UOJC congregations range from those with mixed seating to those which go beyond the letter of the law in observing halakhic standards. Individual members include Jews from all walks of life and with a variety of opinions. Conscious of its hybrid membership and anxious not to offend any group within it, UOJC has avoided policy formulation in areas of controversy affecting internal Orthodox Jewish life and has turned much of its attention toward the broader Jewish society and the general society. Thus its resolution of 1962, repudiating its long-standing opposition to Federal aid to education, can be taken to mean that the consensus that once existed in opposition to Federal aid is no longer present.

The changing temper within the Orthodox community—the increased emphasis on halakhic observance—is reflected within UOJC. Thus, whereas status once accrued to the leaders and rabbis of congregations without *mehitzot* (barriers separating the men's and women's sections of synagogues), and a certain contempt was evident toward those "old-fashioned" congregations which still had mehitzot or even separate seating for men and women, the situation today is reversed. Since 1955, according to a spokesman for UOJC, some 30 synagogues which formerly had mixed seating have installed mehitzot, the first break in a trend which had been moving in the opposite direction since the nineteenth century.

Association of Orthodox Jewish Scientists (AOJS)

Although affiliated with UOJC, the Association of Orthodox Jewish Scientists (AOJS) . . . does not belong under the rubric of modern Orthodox. It is far less oriented toward problems of Jewish society and hardly at all to problems of the general society. It is rather concerned with problems arising out of the individual Orthodox Jew's role in the secular and scientific world. In 1964 it claimed approximately 500 members and 12 local chapters in the United States and Canada. The overwhelming majority of its members, according to its 1962 directory, are natural scientists with universities or large corporations, rather than social scientists, whom the organization has also been anxious to attract.

AOJS is preoccupied with the problem of secular education. It has never thought it appropriate to adopt a position on some of the moral issues confronting American society or American scientists as a result of the new technology and its uses, but hardly a national meeting passes in which some discussion, and usually a major address, is not devoted to the subject of the study of science or secular education in the light of the halakhah. It is as if the membership has to keep reassuring itself or others that their vocation is a proper one for Orthodox Jews.

Members of AOJS include some distinguished intellects, but the organization has exhibited little critical concern with the nature of American or Jewish life. In general, the natural sciences have attracted more Orthodox Jewish graduate students than the social sciences or humanities. This may be because they offer preparation for more lucrative and prestigious professions today or because they raise fewer critical problems for Orthodox Jews. It is not difficult to dichotomize religious belief and scientific work, whereas the very assumptions of the social sciences are often thought to run counter to traditional Orthodox views. Whatever the reason, AOJS reflects the special concerns of the natural scientist and has failed to attract to its ranks the growing number of Orthodox Jews in the social sciences and the humanities who might be expected to adopt a broader and more critical approach to Jewish and general affairs.

Yavneh, National Religious Jewish Students' Association

In contrast to AOJS, Yavneh, one of the two national Orthodox collegiate bodies, exhibits great intellectual ferment and general communal concern. Founded in 1960, Yavneh had close to a thousand paid members in over 40 chapters in American colleges and universities by 1964. The founders of Yavneh were largely Yeshiva High School graduates who were dissatisfied with the complacency and lack of intellectual excitement in the Jewish community generally, and Orthodoxy particularly. A generation earlier most of them would no doubt have abandoned Orthodoxy completely. In the 1960's they chose instead to create a subcommunity within the Orthodox world that affirms the Jewish tradition but is concerned with its application to contemporary social and political problems.

Yavneh's founders were soon joined by a more conservative group of students who sought to move the organization along more traditional lines, both programmatically and organizationally; they favored, for example, abolishing mixed-swimming weekends. Yavneh chapters are usually dominated by one group or the other. All chapters, however, have attracted students from non-Orthodox homes who find in the high level of Yavneh's programs an alternative to accepting the deficiencies of the Jewish and general communities. On many campuses Yavneh has come into conflict with local Hillel groups because of its unwillingness to accept the latitudinarian *status quo*. . . .

Yavneh's attitude [toward halakhah] is that regardless of private individual practices, halakhah must continue to be the public standard at least. This halakhic commitment is interesting because it may portend a future direction for American Orthodoxy. Unlike left-wing Orthodoxy, it does not call for radical reinterpretation of halakhah. Unlike the right, it does not demand that every Jew live his life in accordance with the halakhic prescriptions of the rabbinical authorities. Rather, it calls for an understanding of what the halakhah is and then a decision by the individual. In many respects this is a revolutionary outlook for an Orthodox organization, Rosenzweigian in its implication that the ultimate criterion for an individual's observance is his own judgment. . . .

National Council of Young Israel

The Young Israel movement, with 95 synagogues and approximately 23,000 affiliated families, may be the largest single organization in American Orthodoxy. There are probably more families affiliated with the member synagogues of UOJC, but the relationship between UOJC's leadership and the members of its congregations is still so tenuous that it would be unreasonable to compare it with Young Israel, a large proportion of whose members identify closely with the movement and a few of whom are more intensely committed to the national movement than they are to their own synagogues. This is not to suggest that all or even most member families in the Young Israel are Orthodox in their personal behavior. But there is no question as to where the direction of the organization lies. In fact, only Sabbath observers are permitted to hold office in a Young Israel congregation, and synagogues remove their mehitzot only at the price of their charters.

Young Israel was formed in 1912 by a handful of Orthodox Americanized youth who felt themselves a part of American society, rejected many of the folkways and practices of their parents, but wished to remain Orthodox. . . . Until World War II, Young Israel was a lay movement, dominated by a lay leadership. It was led by native-born, middle-class, college-educated Orthodox Jews, who in their own rather disorganized fashion stood as a bridge between Orthodoxy and the rest of the Jewish community. With modern facilities, stress on decorum in worship, and an attractive social program, Young Israel brought thousands of Jewish young people into the synagogue, many of whom were encouraged to enroll in intensive study courses or to enter yeshivot. (Ironically, some of them emerged from yeshivot only to condemn Young Israel for not being sufficiently Orthodox.)

As late as World War II, Young Israel was looked upon as the least observant Orthodox group. This misconception was partly due to ignorance. In part, however, it reflected an awareness of Young Israel's deviations from Orthodoxy. In developing an attractive social program, for example, Young Israel had closed its eyes to such activities as mixed dancing, which few rabbinic authorities would sanction. Its lay leadership, which was not yeshivah-trained, refused to defer to an Orthodox rabbinate who, they felt, lacked secular training, sophistication, and community status comparable to theirs. Being church-oriented, it tended to lay less stress on matters of individual observance and more on Orthodoxy's role in the Jewish community. Young Israel was among the first Orthodox organizations to seek to raise the level and dignity of *kashrut* supervision, to work with the American chaplaincy, and to lend support to Zionism, youth, and collegiate work. . . .

Since World War II the nature of the Young Israel movement has changed. In the first place, the lay leadership has been challenged by the Council of Young Israel Rabbis, the rabbinical organization of Young Israel congregational rabbis. Native-born and acculturated, with increased sophistication and, most importantly, time and information, the postwar rabbi was able to compete with the lay leader. The very growth of the movement had created a need for greater professionalism. In addition, the expansion of membership brought a larger number of marginal affiliates, who recognized the rabbi, rather than the lay leader, as legitimate spokesman for Jewish religious values. With increasing power at the congregational level, the rabbis were in a position to determine the effectiveness of the national program, and their cooperation became essential. As the locus of money shifted to the congregation, the layman, who viewed himself as part of a national movement seeking a national impact, was replaced by the rabbi, whose interests were more local, and status accrued to the rabbi of the largest, wealthiest, and most observant synagogue.

Another factor accounting for the changes in Young Israel has been the general move to the right within Orthodoxy—the intensification of demands for halakhic observance, which means, almost by definition, the ascendancy of the Orthodox rabbi as the halakhic authority of the congregation. This has particular significance in the case of the Young Israel rabbi, who is not typical of most Orthodox American rabbis, either European-trained or the products of Yeshiva University. The European rabbi is often disadvantaged by his lack of acculturation, and even when he fancies himself as a communal or chief rabbi, he is conscious of his utter dependence on lay approval. Yeshiva University graduates are not all of the same mold; but at least until recently they tended to be church-oriented, communally involved, and very much aware of the necessity for compromise. Rabbis ordained by other American yeshivot, like Torah Vodaath, Rabbi Chaim Berlin, and Rabbi Jacob Joseph, on the other hand, reject the Yeshiva University model. These Americanized, non-Yeshiva University graduates tend to be more aggressive and less compromising. About half of Young Israel's congregational rabbis are just such men. . . .

Religious Zionists of America (RZA)

The Religious Zionists of America came into being as the result of a merger in 1957 of the two Orthodox Zionist adult male groups in the United States—Mizrachi and Hapoel Hamizrachi. The women's organization of each group, as well as their respective youth groups, Mizrachi Hatzair and Bnei Akiva, have remained separate. . . .

RZA attracts an Orthodox Jew similar to the Young Israel members, and there is a large overlapping membership. Its most active officers and members are themselves rabbis but they play little role in the organization as rabbis. Spiritually, RZA looks to Rabbi Soloveitchik for leadership, and, as in the RCA, his influence has increased in recent years as he has become more outspoken on contemporary issues. A measure of his influence in RZA is that although many of its leaders were embarrassed by his criticisms in 1963 of the State of Israel on the missionary question, none publicly expressed his misgivings. RZA gives political, social, and philanthropic support to Israel and to the Israeli National Religious party, with which it is affiliated. . . .

Yeshiva University

The one institution most prominently identified with modern Orthodoxy is Yeshiva University. Indeed, the very growth of the university bespeaks the increasing concern of Orthodoxy with problems of the non-Orthodox community, both Jewish and non-Jewish. Beginning as the Rabbi Isaac Elchanan Theological Seminary (RIETS), Yeshiva University has developed or acquired

17 schools and divisions including a new West Coast center in Los Angeles. This tremendous growth has occurred since 1940 under the leadership of its president, Samuel Belkin, who has remained singularly exempt from the public criticism directed against Yeshiva University by many in the Orthodox world. The university engages in a host of activities, including sponsorship of three Jewish periodicals and a semi-scholarly series of monographs in Judaica, "Studies in Torah Judaism." Among its other divisions are a Hebrew Teachers Institute for men and another for women, a liberal-arts college for men and one for women, graduate schools of education, social work and science, and a medical school. The relation of some of its division to Orthodoxy has, at best, become tenuous. Interestingly, however, the brunt of the right-wing Orthodox attack against the institution has not been against the secular divisions but rather against the college and the Jewish divisions associated with it.

Students at the all-male college (we are not discussing Stern College for Women) are required, in addition to their regular college program, to enroll in one of three Jewish study programs: RIETS, with almost exclusive stress on Talmud and preparation for entering the three-year *semikhah* (ordination) program upon completion of undergraduate studies; the Teachers Institute for Men, with heavy stress on Talmud but a varied curriculum of Bible, history, literature, etc., all taught in Hebrew; and a Jewish-studies program for students with little or no background in Jewish studies.

The last program has been the most dramatically successful. In 1964, in its ninth year, it admitted 100 freshman (the men's college has a total of about 750 students). The program is adapted to the needs of the students, most of whom are from non-Orthodox homes. It is led by a group of sympathetic and dedicated teachers, who produce, at the end of four years, reasonably well-educated (certainly by American Jewish standards), observant, committed Jews. Some graduates continue their studies in Hebrew and Talmud, transferring to RIETS or going on for further study in Israel. Even the severest critics of Yeshiva University have acclaimed the remarkable success of this program and are inclined to concede that no other institution within Orthodoxy is equipped to do a comparable job. The program's impact on American communities is only beginning to be felt, but inevitably its graduates will assume positions of responsibility. (In contrast to the Jewish-studies program is the Lubavitcher movement, which has also achieved a measure of success in winning youth to Orthodoxy but finds that these converts are often unable to reintegrate themselves effectively in the community from which they came.)

Contrary to popular opinion in the Orthodox world, neither the college nor RIETS espouses any particular philosophy or point of view within the Orthodox spectrum of opinion. RIETS, in particular, is almost a microcosm of the committed Orthodox world and includes among its instructors some who are out of sympathy with secular education. Both the strength and weakness of the institution, no doubt, derive from this eclectic philosophic attitude. Within its walls the whole constellation of Orthodox ideologies contend. . . .

As in RCA and RZA, the preeminent personality at Yeshiva University is Rabbi Soloveitchik, who teaches Talmud. At the university, however, his leadership in communal matters is not necessarily accepted by the other Talmud instructors, many of whom have also achieved eminence in the world of Talmud learning. Besides, President Belkin, a scholar in his own right, stands forth as an independent personality. Belkin, however, has been elevated above controversy in recent years and the students' image of him is somewhat hazy.

In addition to its purely educational functions, the university plays a major role in the Jewish community through its Community Service Division. The division is responsible for rabbinic and teacher placement, conducts adult-education and extension courses, provides educational services to many Talmud Torahs and youth groups, sponsors seminars for teenagers throughout the United States, and has had a hand, together with the Rabbinic Alumni Association, in sponsoring Camp Morasha, a summer camp which opened in 1964, patterned on the Conservative Ramah camps but with an Orthodox orientation. Powered by a large staff of experienced professionals, CSD has become increasingly important as a source of information and assistance for other Orthodox bodies. Its placement activities, in particular, have so strengthened the Rabbinic Alumni that rabbis from other Orthodox yeshivot have sought (and been granted) associate membership in that association. . . .

Sephardi Community

There are an estimated 25,000 Sephardim and 63 known Sephardi congregations—congregations which do not follow the Ashkenazi form of worship or are not of Ashkenazi descent—in the United States. They are largely of Spanish and Portuguese, Syrian, Greek, Egyptian, North African, and Yugoslav origin.

The Spanish and Portuguese, whose origin in the United States predates that of all other American Jews, are the most prestigious, and the leading Sephardi congregation is the famous Spanish and Portuguese Shearith Israel of New York. In 1963 the chief rabbi or *hakham* of the Sephardic community of the British Commonwealth, Rabbi Solomon Gaon, was also made a rabbi of Shearith Israel, and given the responsibility for the school and authority in all matters of religious law.

Unlike the members of the large Spanish and Portuguese congregations, like Shearith Israel and Mikveh Israel of Philadelphia, Pennsylvania, those of most other Sephardi congregations are predominantly first-generation Americans. All Sephardi congregations appear to share a strong sub-ethnic commitment to their form of worship (which differs from one group of congregations to the other), and a relative neglect of private ritual observance. (Thus, even the lay leadership of the Sephardi congregations tend to be quite lax in their religious practice. However, this has in no way affected the intensity of their desire to retain the traditional Sephardi public ritual.)

. . . as a minority within the American Jewish community, the Sephardi congregations face the problems of cultural dilution. Without facilities to train their own rabbis, and more importantly their own *hazzanim* (leaders of the religious service), they face danger of extinction. In 1962 they turned to Yeshiva University, which initiated a program (financed by the Sephardi community) to train religious leaders for them. . . . The Yeshiva University program is under the official direction of Rabbi Gaon. Its success depends to a large extent on its ability to recruit college-age students from within the Sephardi community.

SECTARIANS

Jewish sectarianism, unlike that of many Protestant groups, results not from the beliefs of the membership but mostly from a differing strategy as to the best way of maintaining the tradition. Thus, an organization such as Agudath Israel, which is essentially a sectarian group in the United States, was deeply involved in problems and activities of a Jewish and even a general political nature in Eastern Europe. In the United States, on the other hand, they have felt that communal participation with other Jewish groups would perforce involve a recognition of the legitimacy of non-Orthodox religious groups and institutions.

With few exceptions, the sectarian camp is of lower income, poorer education, and more recent immigration than the modern Orthodox.[10] The world of sectarian Orthodoxy is preeminently a yeshivah world, and its leaders are the *rashe yeshivot* and a few prominent hasidic rebbes. It is a mistake to think, as many even within Orthodoxy do, that the Orthodox world which has been created in this country is a replica of the European or even East European one. In fact, the *rashe yeshivot* have achieved a degree of authority in this country unparalleled in Eastern Europe, in good part because there is no counterweight to this authority here in the *shtot rov* or communal rabbi, as there was in Europe.

The years before and immediately after World War II brought to the United States an influx of Orthodox immigrants far more militant than those who had come earlier. They found in this country an Orthodox community largely composed of residual Orthodox and under the ostensible leadership of communal rabbis who seemed to be in despair about the future of Orthodoxy and convinced of the necessity for compromise. They found institutions such as *kashrut* in the hands of people whom they considered as unreliable or careless. They found a bare handful of day schools and a Yeshiva University or RCA ready to accommodate themselves to secular culture. They found almost no institutions with total

---

[10]There is a vast literature on the relationship between religious sectarianism and social class indicating that among religious groups low social class correlates with sectarianism. The classic study is H. Richard Niebuhr, *The Social Sources of Denominationalism* (New York: 1929; reprinted Hamden, Conn.: 1954). See also: Liston Pope, *Millhands and Preachers* (New Haven: 1942); Russell R. Dynes, "Church-Sect Typology and Socio-Economic Status," *American Sociological Review*, 1955, pp. 555–560; Donald O. Cowgill, "The Ecology of Religious Preference in Wichita," *Sociological Quarterly*, 1960, pp. 87–96; Nicholas J. Demerath, "Social Stratification and Church Involvement: The Church-Sect Distinction Applied to Individual Participation," *Review of Religious Research*, 1961, pp. 146–154, and Liston Pope, "Religion and Class Structure," *Annals of the American Academy of Political and Social Sciences*, 1948, pp. 84–91. Not all sects, however, are lower-class. Both Christian Science and the Oxford Movement were middle- and upper-class groups. See Yinger, *op. cit.*, p. 146.

commitment to the Torah life which had been their world.

They began by creating their own institutions or taking over the few existing ones which they found acceptable. The first step was the creation and expansion of yeshivot.

In 1941 Rabbi Aaron Kotler, *rosh yeshivah* of Kletzk in Polish Lithuania, famous as a Talmud scholar and Orthodox leader, arrived in the United States intending to spend a short time here and then move on to Palestine.[11] A handful of Orthodox Jews persuaded him to stay in the United States to build Torah institutions. Reb Aharon, as he was known in the Orthodox world, assembled 20 students, mostly graduates of American yeshivot, many already ordained as rabbis, and established the Beth Medrash Govoha of America, in Lakewood, New Jersey, now also known as the Rabbi Aaron Kotler Institute for Advanced Learning (the first *kolel* in the United States). His choice of site was a deliberate attempt to isolate his students from American life and facilitate total concentration on the study of Talmud. Within a few years he was joined by some former students from Europe; by 1946 registration had risen to 100, and by 1964 to over 200.

Reb Aharon's conviction was that Torah could grow and be "experienced" in America only through *lernen* ("learning"—in the parlance of the Orthodox world, studying Talmud). According to one of Reb Aharon's former students, only "sharing the experience of the halakhic process could enable the Jew to understand the heartbeat of Judaism." The student at Lakewood lived on a small subvention from the yeshivah and whatever other financial help he got from his family or wife. Students sat and learned for as long as they wished. When they felt ready to leave the yeshivah, they left. . . .

Reb Aharon, himself, did not confine his activity to Lakewood. He engaged in a multitude of activities where his point of view gained recognition. He served as a *rosh yeshivah* in Israel, became the head of Chinuch Atzmai (Hinnukh 'Atzmaï the independent, religious, Agudath Israel-oriented school system in Israel) upon its founding in 1952, leader of Agudath Israel in 1952, and chairman of the rabbinical administrative board of Torah Umesorah, the National Society for Hebrew Day Schools in the United States, in 1945. Though (interestingly enough) a poor fund raiser in contrast to some other *rashe yeshivot*, Reb Aharon elicited tremendous

[11]For a biographical sketch see Alex J. Goldman, *Giants of Faith; Great American Rabbis* (New York: 1964), pp. 257–273.

passion and dedication from those who came in contact with him. He brooked no compromise, nor did he ever question or seem to doubt his own path. He was a preeminently charismatic leader.

The influence of Reb Aharon and like thinkers extended to the higher yeshivot in the United States, except for Yeshiva University and the Hebrew Theological College. Thus, older institutions like Yeshivah Torah Vodaath, with its own famous *menahel* (principal) Shragai Mendlowitz,[12] or Yeshivah Rabbi Chaim Berlin under Rabbi Isaac Hutner, were caught up in the emphasis on *lernen* and separatism. In 1944 Rabbi Mendlowitz founded the Beth Medrosh Elyon in Monsey, New York, at first called *Esh Dat* ("Fire of Religion"), as a pilot institute for training Jewish educators to found and staff the day-school movement. Within a short period the original idea was abandoned and the institution was reorganized to make it similar to the one in Lakewood.

Advanced Yeshivot

At the heart of the sectarian Orthodox world are all the post-high-school yeshivot except Yeshiva University and the Hebrew Theological College. . . . Graduates of the sectarian yeshivot provide the major source of staff for the day-school movement. Many of these graduates, including those with ordination, avoid the rabbinate because they neither wish nor are able to serve predominantly non-observant Orthodox memberships. By choice and absence of alternative they enter the less prestigious and more poorly paid field of Jewish education. Students from Lakewood itself have established five institutions of intensive Jewish learning at the high-school level in different parts of the United States.

Yeshivah graduates who enter Jewish education frequently supplement their Talmudic training at college evening sessions, and some even take graduate courses in education. But contrary to their hopes and expectations, many of them are unprepared for the world they enter. Outside the walls of the yeshivah they meet new problems of both a secular and Jewish nature. Furthermore, there is no organization that speaks in their idiom, capable of providing help and direction for them. They continue to regard *lernen* as the

[12]Now known as Rabbi Mendlowitz, the former principal of Torah Vodaath used to refuse to use the title of Rav. His stress on the importance of Hebrew grammar and of pedagogy made him a unique figure in the yeshivah world.

highest end, but have no direction in living life short of that end. Of course this is a problem for all yeshivah graduates, not only those who choose Jewish education as their vocation. As true sectarians, they reject the communal Orthodox institutions surrounding them; their only source of leadership and guidance remains their *rosh yeshivah.*

Some yeshivah graduates do, of course, enter the rabbinate. This is a most dangerous course for a sectarian, and each has to make his own compromise with the world. A small proportion serve Reform congregations; more serve Conservative congregations, usually the smaller, less successful ones, which pay the smaller salaries. Of the majority who serve Orthodox congregations some make their peace with modern Orthodoxy, join RCA, associate themselves with the Yeshiva University Rabbinic Alumni, and are indistinguishable from Yeshiva University graduates. A few have chosen to remain isolated from the larger camp of Orthodox rabbis and are organized in the *Iggud Ha-rabbanim* (Rabbinical Alliance of America), to be discussed below.

We can consider now the institutions of the yeshivah or sectarian world, bearing in mind that the most sectarian (exclusive of the hasidim) are the least organized and simply continue to revolve in the orbit of their *rashe yeshivot.* We should also note that even the sectarian organizations' involvement in communal activity is not at all a reflection of the rank and file's interests or wishes.

K'hal Adath Jeshurun (Breuer Community)

Much of the preceding discussion does not apply to K'hal Adath Jeshurun. The Breuer community, in Washington Heights, named for its rabbinic leader, represents the continuation in the United States of the separatist Orthodox community in Frankfurt established in 1849 and led by Samson Raphael Hirsch after 1851. The establishment of Hirsch's separatist community is a fascinating story but not of direct concern here.[13] The New York community, established in 1940, now has over 700 affiliated families and 1,300 adult members, mostly of German origin, and provides a day school, high school, and advanced classes in Talmud for its graduates, who, in the German tradition, are encouraged to attend

[13]The best English-language account is Herman Schwab, *History of Orthodox Jewry in Germany,* trans. Irene R. Birnbaum (London: 1950).

college. The community sponsors a mikveh and provides rabbinical supervision for a host of butchers, bakers, and other food processors in the area. The leadership has maintained the strong anti-Zionism of the German period and is publicly identified with Agudath Israel.

Unlike the East Europeans, the German Orthodox separatists had already made a successful accommodation to western culture before emigrating to the new world; secular education was, indeed, a positive good in the Hirschian philosophy of Judaism. The leaders of the Breuer community might well have expected, that as the most acculturated and economically comfortable but also strictly observant and rigidly disciplined Orthodox institution in the United States, their point of view would sweep American Orthodoxy. Instead although the community has been quite successful in establishing its own institutions, it has won few converts to its particular ideological position of both communal separatism and a positive acceptance of secular culture. On the contrary, it is on the defensive against the more parochial elements of Orthodoxy.

In part, of course, this is a result of its own decision. As a tiny minority in this country it was faced with the choice of identifying itself communally with Yeshiva University, its neighbor in Washington Heights, and the world of modern Orthodoxy, or with the European yeshivah world with which it had been aligned in Europe. It chose the latter. But in Europe, boundaries and distances separated the followers of Hirsch from the world of the Mirrer or Telshe yeshivot where secular education was discouraged. Even so, there were signs just before the Nazi period that some of the best talent was attracted away from Germany by these and other Lithuanian-type yeshivot. In the United States this continues to be the problem. The Breuer community is forced to look outside its own ranks for educational staff, and some of its teachers and administrators have a negative attitude toward secular education. Its institutions are the envy of the Orthodox world, but its future as a doctrinal community is problematical. . . .

National Society for Hebrew Day Schools (Torah Umesorah)

Torah Umeshorah is the largest national body serving Orthodox day schools. . . . Although Torah Umesorah is staffed by one of the most competent groups of professionals in the Orthodox world, it is, nevertheless, a small body, which must operate within a framework created by rashe yeshivot who are somewhat disengaged from contemporary problems, a lay group of officials who tend to be rather uncritical, and a corps of teachers many of whom are untrained. A rabbinical administrative board, composed almost entirely of *rashe yeshivot,* officially dictates Torah Umesorah policy. . . .

[The number of day schools continues to grow but] a number of New York City schools are in neighborhoods of declining Jewish population. This has constricted enrollment and created severe financial problems. In many day schools outside New York, too, the financial problem is critical. Often this is the consequence of inadequate community support. Sometimes the Orthodox financial base is too narrow to support the schools independently, and the wider Jewish community, as represented by federations and non-Orthodox rabbis, often demands too great a voice in school policy to make its support acceptable. The situation differs from one community to another. In many areas, as long as the secular department of the day school functions well, community support is forthcoming.[14] But where the Orthodox base of a community is quite small, day schools find difficulty in pursuing a policy of intensive Orthodoxy within the institutions' walls while projecting the image of a broad Jewish communal institution deserving of non-Orthodox support from without. In addition, while the non-Orthodox parent may be indifferent to the ideological content of the day-school program, he is not indifferent to the general personality, characteristics, and attitudes of the day-school Hebrew teacher, who is himself often the product of an "other-worldly" environment and a yeshivah where secular education was downgraded.

Of course, not all Orthodox day schools are within the orbit of Torah Umesorah, nor are they all the same type. There are 28 hasidic day schools

. . . found mostly in the well populated areas of New York City—notably Williamsburg and Crown Heights and Boro Park to a lesser extent—now predominantly inhabited by followers of the

[14]This situation may change with the growing antagonism of Conservative leaders toward the ideology of the Orthodox day schools, but to date the Conservatives themselves have been handicapped by their own rabbis' unwillingness to undertake the arduous task of building day schools that are potential competitors to their own synagogues and Hebrew schools for money and pupils. Even Orthodox rabbis have often been lax in the actual support of day schools. The difference, however, is that Orthodoxy contains a more dedicated and Jewishly impassioned laity, who bear much of the day-school burden without rabbinical assistance.

leading Hassidic "Rebbeyim". . . . The major emphasis in these schools is upon preserving the distinct philosophy and way of living of the Hassidic group to which the pupils belong. Personal piety, with the particular and unique manner of observance of the Hassidic sect, is stressed. . . .Attention to general studies is secondary. Generally, these are studied only until the end of the compulsory school age.[15]

Within New York City, the language of instruction carries definite ideological overtones. Schools which stress Yiddish are primarily designed to prepare boys for advanced Talmud study, because Yiddish is generally the language of instruction in the advanced yeshivot. In addition, Rabbi Kotler is reported to have had particularly strong feelings for Yiddish and to have urged principals to abandon the use of Hebrew and substitute Yiddish instead. There are 31 elementary, non-hasidic, Yiddish-speaking schools in New York City and 19 such high schools, or a total of 50 Orthodox Yiddish day schools. The schools whose Jewish studies are in Hebrew are more likely to be of the modern Orthodox type, placing greater emphasis on Israel and some modern Hebrew literature. The current tendency is toward the use of the Sephardi (or rather, Israeli) pronunciation, although those traditional yeshivot which use Hebrew as a language of instruction, such as the Beth Jacob schools for girls, teach the Ashkenazi pronunciation. . . .

Rabbinical Alliance of America (RAA: Iggud Ha-rabbanim)

The Rabbinical Alliance of America, founded in 1944, is composed of graduates of sectarian American yeshivot who were unwilling to affiliate with the Yeshiva University-dominated RCA and either were excluded from membership in the Agudat Ha-rabbanim by its *semikhah* requirements, or themselves rejected the Agudat Ha-rab-banim image.* The first members of RAA were primarily from Torah Vodaath (with a few from Rabbi Jacob Joseph) and to this day placement for RAA rabbis is handled through Torah Vodaath under an arrangement reached in 1957–58, when RAA cut its formal ties with the yeshivah. . . .

---

[15]Joseph Kaminetsky, "Evaluating the Program and Effectiveness of the All-Day Jewish School," *Jewish Education*, Winter 1956–1957, p. 41. Part of the material in this section is drawn from the same article by Torah Umesorah's national director.

*Editor's Note: In an earlier section not reproduced here the author analyzes the Union of Orthodox Rabbis of the United States [Agudat Ha-rabbanim] at length. Pointing out that it is the oldest organization of Orthodox rabbis in the United States he stresses that its influence has declined during recent decades.

Agudath Israel

Agudath Israel was organized in the United States in 1939 as part of a worldwide movement, founded in Europe in 1912, which represented the largest organized force in the European Orthodox world before the Nazi period. . . .

In the light of its history, one might well ask why the organization has not become a more potent force among the Orthodox in the United States. The number of members is difficult to estimate, but undoubtedly falls below 20,000, many of whom are indifferent to Agudist ideology but become members automatically by virtue of their affiliation with Agudath Israel synagogues.

All observers are of the opinion that Agudah sympathizers and potential members outnumber those presently enrolled in the organization. There are a number of reasons why the organization has not been able to reach them. First of all, Agudah arrived relatively late in the United States. An effort to establish the organization in 1922 had failed. However, the Zeirei Agudath Israel (Agudah youth) predated the parent body. It was established in 1921, and by 1940 had seven flourishing chapters in New York City,[16] one in Philadelphia, and one in Baltimore. Much of the potential leadership talent did not join the parent organization until 1949, when the adult group forced a resolution requiring that no one above the age of 28 or married could remain affiliated with the youth organization. The adult body, however, was never able to develop the *élan* and social program that were so attractive to the youth.

A second and more important reason for Agudah's weakness stems from the depoliticalization and sectarianism of the yeshivot. Reb Aharon and the other *rashe yeshivot* who were leaders in Agudah trained a younger generation to value only one activity, *lernen*. The result was a devaluation of and contempt for political and societal activity in the Jewish community. Thus, the yeshivah students who might have formed the nucleus for a revitalized Agudah never joined the organization; nor has the organization ever become an active communal force. Its youth organization, now firmly under the control of the parent organization, avoids controversial topics of communal concern within the Orthodox community and confines its local activities to *lernen*. This, however, is hardly an attractive program to young people who spend

16For a discussion of the history of the Zeirei Agudath Israel chapter in Williamsburg and the growth of the national organization, see George Kranzler, *Williamsburg: A Jewish Community in Transition* (New York: 1961), pp. 248–286.

most of their time in a yeshivah where the level of *lernen* is likely to be as high if not higher. . . .

Hasidim

As noted above, the original hasidim represented a sectarian element in Jewish life. A variety of factors contributed to the rise of hasidism in the eighteenth century, but a discussion of its early period and its doctrines and religious expressions lies beyond the scope of this paper. We note only that the enmity between the hasidim and their traditionalist Lithuanian opponents—*mitnaggedim*—was quite bitter. The hasidim, with their particular doctrinal stresses and their original deemphasis on Talmudic learning, were considered by many to lie perilously close to the outer limits of normative Judaism.

The rise of the Enlightenment, Jewish socialism, and secular Zionism occasioned a reinterpretation by the mitnaggedim of hasidic behavior as an aspect of piety rather than rebellion. By the twentieth century there were strong ties between the hasidim and mitnaggedim which resulted, finally, in the joint participation of many of their leaders in Agudath Israel.

In the United States a further blurring of ideological differences between hasidim and mitnaggedim has occurred because most hasidim retain little that makes them doctrinally unique among ultra-pious Jews. Although they cling tenaciously to some of their special customs and generally retain their traditional European dress, with few exceptions they cannot be distinguished ideologically from the *rashe yeshivot*. The one constant that remains is the notion of the *rebbe* or hasidic leader, to whom the followers attribute extraordinary qualities and around whom they cluster.

Habad, the Lubavitcher Movement

The best-known hasidim are, of course, the followers of the Lubavitcher Rebbe.[17] It is impossible to estimate their number

[17]A sympathetic portrayal of the Lubavitcher movement and a description of their rebbe and his followers is presented by a Reform rabbi in two articles: Herbert Weiner, "The Lubavitcher Movement," *Commentary*, March and April 1957. Descriptions of other hasidic groups in the United States and Israel, which attempt to capture the essence of their religious meaning and attraction, are found in other articles by Weiner. See, for example, his "Dead Hasidim," ibid., March and May 1961 and "Braslav in Brooklyn," *Judaism*, Summer 1964. There is a vast literature on hasidism and the Lubavitcher movement in particular by both observers and followers. See for example publications of their former Rebbe, Joseph I. Schneersohn, *Some Aspects of Chabad Chassidism* (New York: 1944) and *Outlines of the Social and Communal Work of Chassidism* (New York: 1953).

because, unlike other hasidic groups, they are not concentrated in any one area, organized formally, or affiliated with any one institution. The Lubavitcher movement is in many respects the least sectarian of Orthodox groups although doctrinally it is among the most faithful of all hasidic groups to the tenets of its founders. (It is also the most doctrinally sophisticated and intellectually organized of all hasidic groups.) Its unique texts are taught in its advanced yeshivot or in private groups, together with the standard sacred religious texts shared by all Orthodox Jews.

The relationship of its followers to the Lubavitcher movement may best be described as one of concentric circles around the Lubavitcher Rebbe, Rabbi Menahem Mendel Schneersohn, with the inner circle located predominantly, but not exclusively, in the Crown Heights section of Brooklyn, where the Rebbe lives and the headquarters of the movement is located.

Unlike other hasidic groups, the Lubavitcher have friends and sympathizers, estimated by some members of the movement to be as many as 150,000, who far outnumber the immediate coterie of followers. The overwhelming majority are said to be non-Orthodox. Many Jews seek the Rebbe's advice on personal matters and accept him as a religious guide, and he sees an estimated 3,000 people a year for personal interviews averaging 10 to 15 minutes in length. . . .

The phenomenon of non-Orthodox hasidim (President Zalman Shazar of Israel is the outstanding example) is troublesome to many in the Orthodox camp. They wonder how a presumably ultra-Orthodox leader can find such affinity with and arouse such sympathy among unobservant Jews, and whether he has not in fact compromised some essential demands of Orthodoxy in order to attract this great following. The Lubavitcher movement, however, can only be understood on its own terms, and it does in fact stand outside the Orthodox camp in many respects. The movement does not recognize political or religious distinctions within Judaism. It has refused to cooperate formally with any identifiable organization or institution. It recognizes only two types of Jew, the fully observant and devout Lubavitcher Jew and the potentially devout and observant Lubavitcher Jew. This statement is often cited as a charming aphorism. In fact, it has tremendous social and political consequences. In every Jew, it is claimed, a spark of the holy can be found. The function of the Lubavitcher emissaries who are sent over the world is to find that spark in each Jew and kindle it. From the performance of even a minor *mitzvah*, they argue, greater observance may follow. Thus, every Jew is recognized as sacred, but no Jew and certainly no institution outside the Lubavitcher movement is totally pure. Consequently the Lubavitcher movement can make use of allies for particular purposes without compromising its position. It can follow a policy of expediency because it never confers legitimacy on those with whom it cooperates.

One result is that sympathy for the Lubavitcher movement generally declines the further along the continuum of Orthodoxy one moves. The militantly Orthodox are continually disappointed by the independent policy which the movement pursues. This is partly due to the fact that the *rashe yeshivot* are from the tradition of the *mitnaggedim* who once bitterly opposed hasidism and viewed its doctrines as heretical. Since the Lubavitcher are the most doctrinally faithful hasidim, they would naturally encounter the greatest opposition. But in larger part, the antagonism is a result of the fact that Lubavitcher sectarianism is very different from other Orthodox sectarianism.

Judgment as to the success of the Lubavitcher movement depends on one's vantage point. It is indisputable that many Jews, previously untouched by Judaism, received their first appreciation of their religious faith through the missionary activity of Lubavitcher emissaries. Almost every week students from colleges all over the United States, totally removed from Judaism, visit the Central Lubavitcher Yeshiva in New York City under the prompting of a Lubavitcher representative who visited their campus. But some Orthodox observers question how many of these students who thus visit the yeshivah or pray with an *etrog* and *lulav* at the urging of a Lubavitcher representative, whom they encounter by chance on the street, in school, or in a hospital, are genuinely affected by their experience. Despite pride in its intellectual foundation, the Lubavitcher appeal today is almost exclusively emotional. More than any group in Orthodox and Jewish life, the movement offers solutions to individual problems arising not only from the Jewish condition but from man's societal condition. . . .

Satmar Hasidim and Their Allies

The Satmar community is of Hungarian origin and is the most sectarian of all Orthodox groups in the United States. By the nineteenth century Hungarian Orthodox Jews had gained a reputation as the most zealous opponents of the non-Orthodox and as sponsors of a school system which introduced more intensive study of Talmud, and at an earlier age, than even the traditional Lithuanian-mitnagged yeshivot. The community is governed by the Satmar Rebbe, Rabbi Joel Teitelbaum, head of the Central Rabbinical Congress and leader of religious and political communities which are not identical.

As rov of the religious *kehillah* (community), Rabbi Teitelbaum is final arbiter in all matters of religious law. The kehillah numbers about 1,200 families, located primarily in Williamsburg, with smaller branches in Boro Park and Crown Heights (all in Brooklyn). Many of these families lost their rebbes to the Nazis and turned to the Satmar Rebbe when they came to the United States. The kehillah provides a full complement of religious and social services to its members, including welfare institutions, schools, mikvaot, bakeries, supervision over a variety of processed foods, and, informally, insurance and even pensions. It requires a high degree of religious conformity from its adherents, extending even to matters of dress. . . .

As rebbe, political or societal arbiter, the Satmar's influence extends to a number of smaller hasidic groups of Hungarian origin, each with its own rov. These include such groups as the Tzehlemer, Szegeder, and Puper. The total, together with the Satmar's own kehillah, is conservatively estimated at 5,000 families.[18] The Satmar Rebbe is also recognized as religious leader of the ultrasectarian Netore Karta of Jerusalem. . . .

The long-range impact of the Satmar community should not be minimized. Standing outside the mainstream of the communications network of even the Orthodox Jewish community, isolated from almost all Orthodox groups, it is easily ignored except when it erupts in some demonstration, such as picketing the Israeli consulate, which brings it to the public's attention. . . .

Although its attitude toward secular education is negative, some degree of acculturation is inevitable. The community has recently opened lines of communication with some personalities in Agudat Ha-rabbanim and invited Rabbi Moses Feinstein to a conference of its rabbinic body. The Satmar Rebbe was one of the

[18]The lowest figure was provided by a Satmar representative. Among those interviewed for this report the Satmar group was the only one whose own membership and school-enrollment estimates were lower than those hazarded by rival observers.

half-dozen prominent sectarian leaders who delivered a eulogy at the funeral of Rabbi Kotler, while Rabbi Soloveitchik, who also attended, was not asked to speak. . . . If the kehillah is successful in retaining the enthusiasm of its youth, it will inevitably play a more prominent role in Jewish life, and increasing numbers of Jewish leaders will have to reckon with the Satmar Rebbe.

LEADERSHIP

Orthodox institutions, as essentially religious organizations, "must rely predominantly on normative powers [as distinct from coercive or remunerative powers] to attain both acceptance of their directives and the means required for their operation."[19] Religious authority has been traditionally exercised charismatically. That is, the religious leader has been one able to "exercise diffuse and intense influence over the normative orientations of the actors."[20] But according to the value system and traditional expectations of Orthodox Jews, charisma can inhere only in a Talmud scholar. Talmud scholarship is a necessary but not sufficient condition for the exercise of maximum religious leadership or for becoming a *gadol* (plural, *gedolim*). The nature of the *gedolim* has been defined as follows:

> In Jewish life we rely completely on the collective conscience of the people that it will intuitively recognize its leaders and accept their teachings. There surely was no formal vote that thrust the Chofetz Chaim or Reb Chaim Ozer into world leadership. They emerged naturally. . . .
>
> There may be many [who] are recognized Torah scholars and yet they don't attain this wide acclaim. There is some ingredient, that transcends scholarship alone or piety alone—that makes one a Godol. Obviously, these qualities of knowledge, erudition, and piety are basic. But, over and above these there is another that is crucial and that is

---

[19]Amitai Etzioni, *A Comparative Analysis of Complex Organizations* (New York: 1961), p. 41.

[20]*Ibid.*, p. 203.

what we generally describe as "Daas Torah.". . . . It assumes a special endowment or capacity to penetrate objective reality, recognize the facts as they "really" are, and apply the pertinent Halachic principles. It is a form of "Ruach Hakodesh," as it were, which borders if only remotely on the periphery of prophecy. . . . More often than not, the astute and knowledgeable community workers will see things differently and stand aghast with bewilderment at the action proposed by the "Godol." It is at this point that one is confronted with demonstrating faith in "Gedolim" and subduing his own alleged acumen in behalf of the Godol's judgment of the facts.[21]

The notion of *gedolim* is, however, becoming increasingly institutionalized, at least for the sectarian Orthodox camp. Its first formal manifestation was in the establishment by Agudath Israel of its worldwide Mo'etset Gedole Ha-torah (Council of Torah Authorities). Rabbi Aaron Kotler, until he died in 1962, was the preeminent *gedol ha-dor* (*gadol* of the generation) for the yeshivah world. The fact that he also led the *Mo'etsah* did not add to his luster. Many, even in the Mizrahi camp or in the ultrasectarian hasidic camp to the right of Agudath Israel, recognized his eminence. Besides serving as chairman of the *Mo'etsah*, he was chairman of Torah Umesorah's rabbinical administrative board and head of Chinuch Atzmai.

With Reb Aharon's death, the vacant posts had to be filled, putting the unity of the right-wing Orthodox world to the test. In the absence of a personality comparable to Reb Aharon's, would the successors to his offices inherit authority equal to or approximating his? Would, in other words, Reb Aharon's charisma of person pass to charisma of office? Could there be "routinized charisma," so essential to organizational equilibrium, at least among religious groups?

There are three potential successors to Reb Aharon's authority among the American *rashe yeshivot*. (Only *rashe yeshivot* would be eligible since only they possess the necessary qualification of Talmud scholarship.) The most prominent candidate is Rabbi Moses Feinstein, *rosh yeshivah* of Mesifta Tifereth Jerusalem, who was elected chairman of the *Mo'etsah* and head of Chinuch Atzmai in 1962, but only vice-chairman of Torah Umesorah's rabbinical administrative board. He is also one of five members of the Agudat

[21]Bernard Weinberger, "The Role of the Gedolim," *Jewish Observer*, October 1963, p. 11.

Ha-rabbanim's presidium. Reb Mosheh is, as we noted, the leading *posek* (halakhic authority) of his generation. Within the world of authoritative *posekim* he is also the most lenient. His decisions, in fact, have bordered on the radical in departure from halakhic precedents to meet contemporary needs. However, greatness as a *posek* has never by itself entitled a scholar to the highest reverence in the traditional world. Reb Mosheh is a retiring, modest, unassuming person, who, while acknowledging his role as a leader of Orthodox Judaism, nonetheless, unlike Reb Aharon, seeks a strong consensus on political and social questions (in contrast to religious-ritual-ethical questions) before acting. . . .

The characteristics of leadership in the modern Orthodox camp are similar to those of the sectarian Orthodox. The modern Orthodox counterpart to Reb Aharon is Rabbi Joseph Soloveitchik (the Rov), and as long as the Rov remains active he will maintain his dominant positions in such organizations as RCA, RZA, Yeshiva University Rabbinic Alumni, and to a lesser extent UOJC. The future leader of the modern Orthodox world is likely to be Rabbi Soloveitchik's successor to the chairmanship of RCA's halakhah commission, an office which the rabbi is endowing with charismatic authority. At one time Rabbi Soloveitchik might have achieved a comparable role as spiritual mentor in Young Israel, but he rejected their overtures. (Significantly, his brother, Rabbi Aaron Soloveitchik, also a renowned Talmudic scholar, has come closer to the Young Israel recently and may possibly emerge as their religious authority. . . .)

Unlike Reb Aharon, the Rov assumed his leadership position only gradually. Indeed, the sectarians often charge that he never really became a leader, but is simply a front for the modern Orthodox. If that was true at one time, it certainly is no longer so, although he has been thought to change his mind on enough issues to introduce a measure of uncertainty among his own followers as to where he stands on a number of matters.

To call the Rov the leader of modern Orthodoxy is not to imply that he is always comfortable in that camp or happy with that designation. Nevertheless, his position is sharply differentiated from the sectarian *rashe yeshivot* by his positive affirmation of many elements in Western civilization (he holds a Ph.D. in philosophy from the University of Berlin) and his willingness to operate in a modern Orthodox framework. But the Rov is also part of the traditional yeshivah world. Indeed, in recent years he has moved to the right and has become more outspoken in his criticism of certain aspects of life in Israel, in his own halakhic interpretations, and in his attitude toward rabbis serving synagogues with mixed seating. The Rov may be the leader of modern Orthodoxy but he is not really modern Orthodox. Modern Orthodoxy has yet to produce a leader from its own ranks because it still continues to acknowledge mastery of the Talmud as a qualification for leadership and yet has refused to endorse, even at Yeshiva University, a restructuring of Talmudic education that would encourage bright, inquisitive minds which lack the fundamentalist position of the *rashe yeshivot* to undertake the many years of dedicated and arduous learning required to become a Talmudic authority.

Day-to-day leadership of Orthodox organizations has been assumed by professionals, almost all of whom are rabbis. The role of the professional is growing in importance, but the tremendous charismatic authority invested in the spiritual leader has contained the professional's image and often constrained his initiative.

The lay leader is left in a rather unfortunate position. He commands neither the prestige of the Talmudic scholar nor the time and information of the professional. No one within the Orthodox camp really regards him very highly or takes him very seriously. Even among laymen (that is, nonprofessionals), possession of rabbinic ordination, or at least extensive Jewish education, is increasingly becoming a ticket of admission to the councils of decision-making.

The only other premium is that placed on the money the layman contributes or raises, but any effort to dictate how the money should be used is resisted. However, as long as the Orthodox community contains only few men of really substantial wealth, it is inevitable that these will occupy positions of status and prestige.[22] On the other hand the growth of yeshivot means that Orthodoxy is producing a growing number of Jewishly educated laymen, many of whom acquire a good secular education and economically comfortable positions. This group is only beginning to make an

---

[22]One of the few Orthodox leaders who would augment the role of the laymen and argues that non-halakhic policy decisions should be made by the practicing rabbinate and lay leadership, together with the "masters of halakhah," is Yeshiva University's president: Samuel Belkin, *Essays in Traditional Jewish Thought* (New York: 1956), pp. 150–151.

impact on both the Orthodox and non-Orthodox Jewish community. It seems inevitable that they will play a more prominent role in
all aspects of Jewish life.

৪৹৪

DIRECTIONS AND TENDENCIES

In essence, contemporary American Orthodoxy or at least
committed Orthodoxy, whence springs the leadership and direction
of the community, is characterized by the growth of institutions
whose origins and spirit are sectarian and who are reacting against
the churchlike direction of Orthodoxy in its pre-World War II
period. Orthodoxy, in truth, might have been characterized in that
earlier period as simply lower-class Conservative Judaism. That this
is no longer the case is due to changes in both Conservatism and
Orthodoxy. Orthodoxy today is defining its role in particular and
differentiated terms and more than ever before sees itself as isolated
from other Jews. The result has been an increased sympathy for its
own sectarian wing. But the sectarians themselves have not
withstood all change. As one sociologist has written, if a sect is to
influence the world to change, "it must itself acquire or accept the
characteristics of this world to a degree sufficient to accomplish this
goal."[23] It must become "of this world" and in the process it changes
its definitions of what is or is not acceptable. Thus, the sectarian
institutions themselves are beginning to move in a churchlike
direction. Strident opposition to Israel among all but the Satmar
hasidim is a thing of the past. Coeducational day schools outside
New York are formally disapproved of and tacitly accepted even by
the rashe yeshivot. Yiddish, which Reb Aharon stressed as a vehicle
for maintaining tradition, has been deemphasized ever since his
death.

On the other hand, the entire community is more rigid in its
halakhic observance. Mixed dancing, once practiced even among
Agudath Israel youth, is a thing of the past in most committed
Orthodox groups. The formalistic requirements of "feminine
modesty," such as covering the hair, are stressed far more than ever

[23]Glenn M. Vernon, Sociology of Religion (New York: 1962), p. 167.

before. Observance of the laws of "family purity" and mikveh, which once seemed to be on the verge of total desuetude, is rising.[24] There are 177 public mikvaot in the United States—36 in the Greater New York area alone—and a number of private ones. There is even a Spero Foundation, which assists communities planning to build mikvaot with architectural plans, specifications, and suggestions. But if ritually the community is more observant, even the most sectarian groups are becoming churchlike or communally oriented in the problems they take cognizance of and their means of solution.[25]

Both camps, the modern Orthodox and sectarians, are growing, but the basic sources of their new-found strength are different. For the sectarians it is the young yeshivah graduates now at home in at least the superficial aspects of American culture and committed to tradition and the *rashe yeshivot*. They need not adjust completely to America because they are sufficiently well acquainted with it to be able to reject many of its manifestations. For the modern Orthodox it is the *ba'ale-teshuvah*, the penitents who were raised in nonobservant homes but find in Orthodoxy an emotional or intellectual fulfillment. The first group lacks the intellectual-philosophical perspective to broaden its appeal, but while it may not expand, it will survive. The second lacks halakhic leadership and sanction for much that it reads into Orthodoxy; it lives in a half-pagan, half-halakhic world, and the personal problems of its members are more serious.

A characteristic difference between religious life today and a few years ago, particularly among the modern Orthodox, is that problems have become far more personal. In other words, the personal significance of religion has assumed increased importance over its communal significance. This has fostered increased interest in sectarianism among the ostensibly modern Orthodox, as has the right wing's courage, conviction, and sincerity. Modern Or-

[24]The observance of mikveh, which requires that a married woman go to a lustral bath a week (generally) after menstruation, before which she is prohibited from having marital relations, is the best single measure for determining who is a committed Orthodox Jew. To the uncommitted, it is inconceivable that so personal a matter should be subject to ritual regulation. To the committed, it is inconceivable that an aspect of life so important as marital relations should not be subject to halakhic regulation.

[25]One example can be found in the pages of the *Jewish Press*, an Orthodox weekly whose editoral position is akin to the sectarian yeshivah world but whose pages devote an increasing proportion of space to news and features of general Jewish interest.

thodoxy's appeal is dulled by the lingering suspicion of its adherents that they themselves have suffered a loss for living in a half-pagan world. . . .

Whether the Orthodox community as such, however, can generate sufficient force to meet the intellectual stirrings and emotional quests in the American Jewish world remains to be seen. The non-Orthodox intellectual is not ready yet to embrace Torah and halakhah in their entirety. But two things have changed. First, the old antagonisms to the world of Orthodoxy are gone from many intellectuals furthest removed from Orthodox life. Second, there is a recognition and admiration for Orthodoxy as the only group which today contains within it a strength and will to live that may yet nourish all the Jewish world.

JEWISH EDUCATION
AND IDENTITY

JEWISH EDUCATION IN THE UNITED STATES

by LLOYD P. GARTNER

INTRODUCTION

LLOYD P. GARTNER'S *survey of Jewish education in the United States ranges from the earliest schools established by Spanish and Portuguese Jews to the recent growth of Jewish day-school education. Gartner's wide knowledge of American as well as of American Jewish history enables him to place the development of American Jewish schools in perspective and provide the reader with a new understanding of familiar institutions.*

The crucial development which determined the direction American Jewish education was to take was the acceptance by Jews of the public school as the basic educational institution for their children. Gartner points out that as soon as public education achieved a modicum of quality and, furthermore, eliminated the grossest forms of Protestant indoctrination, German Jews were quick to endorse the new system. It was a matter of principle to them that Jewish children be enrolled in the new public schools. This occurred despite the fact that the wealthiest German-Jewish families seldom practiced what they preached, preferring to send their own children to private schools.

German-Jewish enthusiasm for public education was shared by later arrivals—if anything the newly-settled East Europeans were more devoted to public education than were the established element. Yet Jewish zeal for public education is surprising—if any group should have insisted on the primacy of "parochial" education it was the Jews. As Gartner emphasizes at the beginning of his analysis, for millennia religious study was not only an obligation of Jewish males but was actually an integral part of the Jewish cultural pattern. While the precise attitude of Jews toward secular study differed from age to age and from region to region, the study of sacred literature was always considered to have priority.

The dynamics of the process by which Jews transformed themselves from a group which gave primacy to sacred learning into one which gave primacy to secular learning is still inadequately understood. Whether the process was initiated overseas and completed in the United States, or whether it was entirely a result of the encounter with American culture, remains a matter for debate. There is no question, however, that the transformation took place free of any demand by Jews that their support of public education be reciprocated by having the public schools assume the task of educating the Jewish child in his heritage. This was true even in places like the New York metropolitan area where by the 1930's Jewish teachers and administrators (and later Jewish union officials as well) were not only common but were qualifying for crucial positions in the educational system.

Gartner supplies the reason for Jewish apathy, if not antipathy, toward Jewish education under public auspices. He emphasizes that Jews viewed the public school ". . . as the symbol and guarantee of Jewish equality and full opportunity in America." In the Jewish mind equality and full opportunity meant that the public school would take no notice of the existence of religious or ethnic differences—any recognition of such differences raised the possibility of discord and ultimately the specter of discrimination, and would also inhibit the healthy mingling of children of diverse background. (In practice there were few non-Jews to mingle with in the large urban centers with concentrations of Jews in single school districts, and until Jews reached suburbia those who were available were seldom models that Jewish parents would want their children to emulate.)

It is clear that at times Jews were forced into positions that violated what they believed the public schools stood for. Thus in some cities they reluctantly participated in "released-time"—a plan whereby children who wished religious instruction were to be excused from school at an earlier hour. It was difficult to reject such a plan without appearing to be anti-religious. Jews also reluctantly agreed to Chanukah celebrations in the schools after it became evident that it was well-nigh impossible to implement a policy forbidding Christmas celebrations. In some cities Jewish communal bodies supported the request that high schools with large Jewish enrollments be permitted to introduce Hebrew language instruction. However, even today when ethnic studies are commonplace in public elementary and secondary schools, Jews are wary of encouraging the teaching of Jewish studies.

The Jewish view of the function of public education had as its correlate the following: that in the privacy of the ethnic and religious enclave any group had the freedom to make whatever institutional arrangement it deemed appropriate to induct its young into its culture. In practice this meant that it was the obligation of the Jewish parent to provide his child with a Jewish education. Indeed the history of Jewish education in America can be looked upon as the search for a viable arrangement whereby children whose prime learning experience was in the public sector could be afforded the benefit of an encounter with the culture of their group. Gartner analyzes the evolution of each of these arrangements: the Jewish Sunday School, copied from Protestant models; the engaging of melamdim (tutors) by parents and the opening of hedarim (elementary schools), both copied from European models; the communal Talmud Torah; the folkshul; the congregational Hebrew school.

All of these institutional arrangements began in high hope; each was thought by its protagonists to be the key to the educational needs of the hour as well as the true fulfillment of the injunction to raise up the child in the way of his fathers. And each form has proved to be a disappointment—frequently more of a disappointment to its supporters than to those outside. Since the last century a considerable literature has accumulated about the shortcomings of elementary Jewish education, the deplorable conditions of secondary Jewish education, and the meager accomplishments of adult Jewish education. Perhaps the most withering criticism has come from the educators themselves—knowing the shortcomings of the schools at firsthand they have been in the best position to expose their inadequacies.

The focus of the more sophisticated type of criticism of the American Jewish school has been the inadequacy of the school in attaining the very goals which it has set for itself. With the possible exception of radical folkshuln and melamdim who confined themselves to Bar Mitzvah preparation, all of the schools have sought in one way or another to continue the classical objective of Jewish education: to inculcate a knowledge of sacred texts. While their approach to the text may be untraditional, while they may prefer to focus on particular texts which they find congenial and neglect others no less sacred, and while they may introduce new subjects in the curriculum, at a minimum the schools have paid lip service to traditional ideals.

Among the many factors which have militated against the achievement of their objectives have been the scarce time and resources at the command of the schools and the attraction of students to the outside culture. Generally speaking the schools have been able to succeed only with outstanding students coming from above-average homes. The language problem has been a central difficulty. For many laymen and professionals connected with the schools the teaching of Hebrew has been essential—because it is the language of the sacred texts, because it is the language of prayer, or because it is the language of the Zionist movement and the State of Israel; whatever the motivation, the results have been seen as disappointing.

If the American Jewish school has not succeeded in producing literate Jews it has also been charged with failing to produce "identified" Jews. The charge is surprising in the sense that Jewish education has never pretended to create identification, proceeding instead on the assumption that the child comes to the school with a firm Jewish identity. The task of creating Jewish identification has been imposed upon the school by parents, who wish the school to create a countervailing force to the child's "Gentile" identity which emerges from his exposure to public education, to the mass media, to the general milieu, and most recently to what has come to be known as "youth culture."

The need for such a countervailing force has long been felt by American Jews, but in recent years it has taken on a new urgency. Forces as diverse as pride in the State of Israel, the threat of intermarriage, and fear of the consequences of suburbanization have all had a role in stimulating new support for Jewish education and new directions in the field. These changes have included informal education, especially summer camping; a shift in Hebrew-language teaching from classical to more up-to-date methods; study of Israel and summer programs including travel to the Jewish state; and a new attention to Jewish education for students of high-school age. As Gartner points out there has even been support in the Jewish community for the introduction of Jewish studies into the American university.

Gartner completes his analysis by pointing to what has indeed been a radical change in American Jewish education—the rapid growth of the Jewish day school. Crushed in the nineteenth century by the Jewish zeal for public education, in the past two decades the day school has undergone a remarkable resurrection and development. Some regard its growth as a function of socially conservative and anti-integrationist sentiment among Jews, while others see it as resulting from disillusionment with the achievements of public education in the 1960's and 1970's. From a Jewish perspective the rise of the day schools can also be seen as resulting from the determination of ultra-Orthodox elements in the Jewish community and from disillusionment with the accomplishments of the supplementary school—whether this be the Hebrew School, the Talmud Torah, the Sunday School, or some other arrangement. It is still too early to know whether the day school will succeed where other schools are said to have failed—whether it will produce both literate and "identified" Jews. But it has the distinction of viewing the problem of American Jewish education in radical terms—terms which are at once new and very old in the millennial history of Jewish education.

M. S.

SCRIPTURE commands the Jew to "impress upon your children" the revealed Divine teaching, and to think and speak of it day and night. In ancient times, the verses in Deuteronomy which contained this enjoinder became liturgy, to be pronounced daily with devotion by every worshiper. Actual education in biblical times had been conducted largely in priestly circles, but later, during the Second Commonwealth, universal schooling for all males became the ideal and, to a considerable extent, the rule. Every member of God's unique people had to be imbued with the Bible and with the oral traditions later committed to writing as the Talmud, which were also regarded as Divine in origin. Lifelong study and contemplation of the Torah became essential in the Jewish paideia. During Talmudic times and after, the Jew was enjoined to make a living which left him time not only for religious devotion but also for systematic study of the sacred literature. Honor and deference were due to the master student, even when he was poor or bashful. Social prestige and religious merit were thus intimately linked in Judaism with intellectual effort.

In Talmudic and medieval Jewry, and to the present day in some communities, scholarship was not only abstract erudition but a quite practical matter. Centuries of Jewish autonomous life were lived largely governed by this Divine law, which required legal responsa and judicial decisions.

Nowhere did the zeal for pious study exceed the intensity it attained in Poland and Lithuania, the areas from which the greatest masses of Jews came to America in the nineteenth and twentieth centuries. One law code widespread in Central and Eastern Europe summarizes the obligation to study:

> It is a positive commandment of the Torah to study the Torah . . . therefore every Jewish person is so obligated, whether rich or poor, healthy or sickly, youthful or venerable; even a door-to-door beggar or a husband and father. He must fix a time for Torah study, day or night . . . and one who is completely incapable of study shall assist others who do study and it will be reckoned for him as though he himself had studied.

> Until when is a man obligated to study? Until the day he
> dies. . . . (*Hayyey Adam*, Section 10, Parts 1 and 2.)

The main content of all this study was law, as discussed in the
tractates of the Talmud—civil, criminal, moral, ritual. The Talmud
seldom lays down the law, but discusses and disputes it back and
forth within accepted categories of reasoning along with a great deal
of seasoning: tales, aphorisms, biblical commentary, speculative
theology. It is not necessarily true, of course, that the techniques or
content of Torah study can be transferred to other realms of study.
In secular terms, however, the legacy from two millennia of
intellectuality is indeed imposing. Education as a universal lifelong
obligation, skill at critical and abstract thought, honor to the
intellectually distinguished, could outlast the environment in which
they first arose. From the onset of modern times in Jewish
history—approximately the eighteenth century in Central Europe
and the nineteenth century in Eastern Europe—the tradition of
intellectuality became diffused among many branches of the arts
and sciences. Our present interest, however, lies in the fate of the
tradition of Jewish education itself in the open, emancipated,
untraditional American society.

Educational ideals and intellectual tone were rather definite, but a
consistent Jewish school system was quite rare. The educational
institutions of the Jewish community as such were for advanced
students. The biblical obligation was understood as that of
overseeing the primary education which parents had to provide for
their children, and of directly educating only the indigent,
orphaned, or neglected. The parent, upon whom the obligation lay
in the first instance, generally hired a *melammed* (tutor) for his
child. This melammed was often a wandering student, an
impoverished tradesman, or some elderly factotum who kept a
heder (one-room school). His figure has come down to us in an
aura of pity and mockery, as one who failed in the main arenas of
life. However, the melammed who taught Talmud to an older boy
was a respected person. The Jewish community provided higher
studies for the talented after these parental responsibilities had been
fulfilled. Often it did so by engaging a renowned scholar as its rabbi,
providing stipends even for strangers who came to join the
townsmen in studying with him. A *bet midrash* (house of study) was
found everywhere in which young and old might occupy themselves

with individual or group study of the Talmud and other works of the sacred literature. Artisans and Jewish guilds might periodically study or hear learned discourses as part of their program. More than the synagogue, the bet midrash was the meeting place where pious study and social life could be carried on. The capstone was the yeshiva academy for advanced, nonprofessional study of Talmud. During the nineteenth century, the small, locally supported yeshivot were overshadowed by new, regional institutions, several of which—such as Volozhin, Mir, and Slobodka—became world famous. The heder, bet midrash, and yeshiva have all appeared in America.

These institutions of Central and Eastern European Jewry dealt exclusively with textual study and exposition. The culture and language of the surrounding society found no place, nor did any vocational or scientific or physical training. The aim was to produce religiously devout and learned men whose worldly requirements could be attended to by induction into a parental business or by an advantageous marriage.

The first major Jewish strain to arrive in America, the Sefardim —Jews of Spanish and Portuguese stock—came, to a considerable extent, from backgrounds quite different from those just described. Their glorious centuries on the Iberian peninsula had fostered an educational ideal of the cultivated Jewish gentleman, rather than the intense pietist of Northern and Eastern Europe. Sefardic education was given in Spanish and included loving attention to Bible, Hebrew language and poetry, and perhaps some rationalist Jewish philosophizing. During the tragic decline before the expulsion of Spanish Jewry in 1492, mystical and redemptionist thinking overshadowed but did not eradicate the earlier ideal. Most of the Sefardim who came to the New World were not cultivated persons, and their Marrano past did not prepare them for polite learning, much less for urbane skepticism. But they were modern in the limited but important sense that the Jewish and the secular managed to coexist within them.

The first Jewish children in America were born to these Sefardim. The education of the American Jewish child before 1800 was rather hit or miss. In the little colonial synagogues whose membership was pretty much coterminous with the local Jewish communities, the ministers' duties included the instruction of youngsters in the rudiments of the ancestral religion and necessary secular knowledge. Three to five years spent in learning to read Hebrew and more or less understand selected biblical and liturgical passages, and becoming acquainted with the main headings of practical Jewish observance like holidays, synagogue procedures, and customs, was the basic Jewish learning. The minister-teacher also drilled his pupils in English, reading, writing, arithmetic, and sometimes also in Spanish, which was still used in some homes and synagogues. Little more was expected by parents who were mostly small merchants and craftsmen. Only in Charleston, where a Jewish bourgeoisie became established at a relatively early period, were the graces of polite society inculcated. Some specimens of parental injunctions to children have survived, and they emphasize the maxims of diligence, honesty, and filial devotion.

It was the absence of schools other than Christian which compelled Jews thus to arrange for the entire education of their young. An agreement between Philadelphia Jews and Ezekiel Levy, dated July 18, 1776, requires that his services to the congregation include "to teach six children the art of Hebrew reading." These six were poor; others had to make private arrangements with Levy for pay. Such tutoring was rarely superseded by actual schools. One appears to have been founded in 1755 under the aegis of New York's Shearith Israel (the "Spanish and Portuguese") congregation and existed until 1776, when New York Jewry was disrupted by the British occupation. The curriculum resembled that of the private tutors—Hebrew and some Spanish, Bible, and the three R's. The same congregation opened a second school in 1808, known as the Polonies Talmud Torah, which lasted intermittently as a day school until 1821. (It still exists as the congregation's afternoon school.) In this and similar little schools maintained at various times in Philadelphia and Charleston, Jewish studies consisted for the most part of reading and translation of portions of the Bible and prayerbook, laws and customs of the religion, and perhaps some instruction in the Hebrew language and a smattering of rabbinic literature. They differed little from what a Jewish child would be taught in Western Europe. The novelty lay in instruction being given as a matter of course in general secular subjects during the eighteenth century. Such a practice was barely known in Central and Eastern Europe, and stirred bitter controversy wherever it was introduced.

During the first decades of the Federal Union, Jews still played little cultural or political role. Two changes faintly discernible during the 1820's became more noticeable during the 1830's and 1840's. At the Hebrew Sunday School of Philadelphia, founded by Rebecca Gratz in 1839 for children of the poor, the catechetical teaching of Judaism was introduced. Some of the very few educated native Jews, including Mordecai M. Noah, Daniel L. M. Peixotto, and Isaac Harby, began to think of the means to raise the pious, cultivated American Jewish gentleman. Their suggestive but rather nebulous ideas rapidly became antiquated, however, as a new immigration commenced, far greater than any earlier one. These were Jews from German lands. Few of the earlier German newcomers were of learned stock, and their Judaism was still essentially that of venerable tradition. (Later arrivals were fully Germanized.) They brought to America, or soon begot here, enough children to make large-scale Jewish schooling feasible and necessary. Some of the German Jews manifested dissatisfaction with the Jewish education they found, and from their midst came the numerous attempts between the 1830's and the 1850's to found Jewish day schools.

Mid-nineteenth-century Jewish immigrants stood out especially among the early settlers of the new cities of the Middle West—Chicago, Cleveland, Cincinnati, Milwaukee, St. Louis, and elsewhere. In these cities, extensive Jewish settlement preceded sometimes by decades the founding of a satisfactory public school system. Jewish parents in the early days founded private schools under synagogal sponsorship, such as Cincinnati's Talmid Yelodim Institute, and often collaborated with liberal local Germans in opening "German-English Academies."

The three decades during which Jewish day schools sprouted were not necessarily informed by zeal for Jewish education. Actually, their underlying *raison d'être* was the absence or poverty of public schools, or the Protestant sectarian tone of those which did exist. The definitive establishment of public schools without such sectarian features as prayers, Bible and especially New Testament readings and moralizing, and strongly Christian holiday observance, was the death knell of the Jewish schools. A new ideology regarded the tax-supported, religiously neutral, universal public school as the indispensable training ground for American citizenship. This outlook was enthusiastically adopted by the Jews. As they soon came to believe, Jewish children could best become loyal and fully accepted Americans by mingling freely in public school with children of all religions and social classes. Sectarian

Jewish education suggested undesirable, even dangerous separatism. Obviously also, Jews as taxpayers should use tax-supported institutions. Only here and there did Jewish voices question the view that Jewish children should on principle be enrolled in the new public schools. The Philadelphian, the Reverend Isaac Leeser, a traditionalist leader, stressed the inevitably Christian influence of public schooling where virtually all teachers and most pupils were Christians. Bernard Felsenthal, a Chicago Reform rabbi, urged the need for Jewish schools to raise an American Jewish intellectual class comparable to that of European Jewry. These views were little regarded and virtually forgotten. After 1860, scarcely any private Jewish schools remained in the United States. Wealthy Jewish families, however, often educated their children at private, non-Jewish institutions.

The triumphant growth of the public school and the spread of its ideology occurred when Reform Judaism was fast becoming the dominant mode of Judaism in America. Reform Judaism and the public school complemented each other admirably in American Jewish thinking. Fundamental to Reform Judaism was its conception of the Jews as fully integrated citizens of the modern secular state, differentiated only by religion. All rules of Jewish religious tradition to the contrary had to be discarded. State-sponsored, universal, religiously neutral schools were a blessing and a necessity, for they were a microcosm of the society in which Jewish children would find a place as adults. . . . The public school was viewed as the symbol and guarantee of Jewish equality and full opportunity in America. This deep American Jewish affinity for the public school lasted a full century, and turned to disenchantment only in places subjected to urban school crises in the 1950's and 1960's.

From the time the public school took over general education, Jewish education became solely Jewish in content. The millennial conception of a detailed, holy law as the object of meticulous observance was discarded, and also the ideal of its reverent study from childhood on. Judaism, interpreted by Reform mainly as a universal moral code, turned the content of Jewish education into moral didacticism derived from biblical exemplars. Study as such was no longer a paramount value. The Sunday School, derived from Protestant models, became the regnant institution for transmitting Judaism to Jewish children. Its curriculum included history (actually Bible stories) and religion taught catechistically, with a few Hebrew verses used in worship generally included. The Sunday School usually met on Saturday and Sunday mornings in rooms within the synagogue under the direction of the rabbi who served as "Superintendent," with volunteer teachers taking the classes. Textbooks appeared, written mainly by Superintendent rabbis, which were mostly manuals or catechisms of religious belief and of biblical history. The program was generally of three years' duration, and culminated in the newly introduced ceremony of Confirmation, when the graduating class of boys and girls were "confirmed" in their religion around the age of thirteen. In addition to Confirmation, some more traditional Reform congregations also permitted the old-style individual Bar Mitzvah for boys. . . .

The once- or twice-weekly schools "caught on" very quickly. By 1880, the Sunday School was almost synonymous with organized Jewish education, among traditionalists as well as Reformers. Families who belonged to Reform temples invariably sent their children to Sunday School, and many an unaffiliated family did likewise. To this day it remains the most widely attended form of Jewish schooling in America.

The year 1880 marks the great divide in the history of American Jewry, as unprecedented numbers of Jewish immigrants began to pour into the United States. With few exceptions they came from Eastern Europe. Thanks to these arrivals, the approximately 280,000 Jews of 1880 increased to about 1,000,000 in 1900, 3,500,000 in 1915, and were 4,500,000 when mass immigration was shut off in 1925. The Jews who had come earlier from German lands were possessed of some or at times a great deal of modern culture, usually in German garb, but those from Russia and Poland or Romania and Galicia were generally of traditional, fully Jewish culture, with little from the surrounding environment. However, the modern secular culture which was seeping into East European Jewish life overwhelmed the immigrant in America, where he indeed expected and wanted to enter the modern world while preserving something of the traditional culture. It is truly remarkable with what ease and alacrity immigrant Jewish children were despatched by their parents to the government's compulsory public schools. Attempts to require this in Eastern Europe had been bitterly resisted, but America was indeed different. The Jewish affinity to the American public school, which by the early twentieth century included the high school, was at its closest during these decades of East European Jewish mass immigration. The rapid social ascent of American Jews was in large measure owing to their zeal for education, for centuries the high road to honor and religious merit in the Jewish community.

During the first decades of this mass immigration, Jewish education among the immigrants expressed the determination, such as there was, to maintain the old ways rather than adapt to the new. Children were taught after public school hours in a heder kept by a melammed in his dwelling somewhere in the immigrant slums. *Hadarim* (pl.) existed in the hundreds. The content of their teaching, with rare exceptions, was rudimentary Hebrew reading and perhaps some Pentateuch and synagogal rules and customs. The melammed seldom taught a class but tutored each child in turn amid the clatter of the others. It was a poor system by any standard, whether that of the old learning or of the public schools the children had just come from. The heder, however, was familiar to immigrants, who came overwhelmingly from the poor, working classes of East European Jewry. To them it symbolized ethnic continuity in the ways of their fathers, especially yearned for when neither the fathers nor their ways were to be seen. The American heder also taught Yiddish, often giving the revealing reason of preparing children to "write a letter to grandparents." Only in terms of generational loyalty can the persistence of the heder in the 1940's be explained.

Surveys taken in various immigrant Jewish communities demonstrated that a majority of children attended no heder nor any other Jewish school. Not only the immigrant faithful but native Jews also were disturbed by these findings which seemed closely connected with the attractions of socialism and atheism, and the appearance of criminality in the immigrant districts. In most larger cities, native Jewish organizations like the National Council of Jewish Women established Sunday Schools and community houses for the children of immigrants. These educational institutions grew out of the prevalent desire to divest immigrants of their particular character and culture and remake them as "Americans." New York's Educational Alliance, founded as the Jewish People's Institute, for years typified this outlook. The persistent refusal to regard immigrants except as people to be made over into the philanthropic sponsors' conception of an American caused sharp intramural friction and limited the usefulness of these institutions. The combination of heder and settlement house Sunday School bestowed by "uptown" Jews set the Jewish educational pattern "downtown" until the turn of the twentieth century. Some immigrant synagogues or societies did maintain schools, but these were little more than several hadarim under one roof with the usual inadequate melamdim.

Higher Jewish studies began in America during the late nineteenth century as rabbinical training. After several unsuccessful beginnings, Isaac M. Wise, the Reform leader, founded the Hebrew Union College as a rabbinical school in Cincinnati in 1875. The traditionalist Jewish Theological Seminary and Yeshivath Etz Chaim both opened in New York in 1886. . . . [Etz Chaim] transplanted the East European Talmudic academy, and was the germ of today's Yeshiva University. Of these three schools only Hebrew Union College was firmly established by 1900. None then possessed the caliber either of major American colleges or of European Jewish models.

The major phase in American Jewish education began early in the twentieth century, when a theory and practice of Jewish education developed which has remained basic ever since. This new educational vigor owed much to the example of public education, which during the 1890's and 1900's underwent its most searching examination since the time of Horace Mann. The disciplinary severity and rigid rote learning, as well as the inadequacies of teachers and supervisors, came under sharp and well-informed criticism. The outlook of American philosophers of education during this period, above all John Dewey, became influential in finding American foundations for Jewish education. Two of their principles were especially important for Jewish education and invite further examination: cultural pluralism and the nexus between school and society.

The early goal in educating immigrant children had been "Americanization" in the native American mold. As seen above, native Jews fully concurred in this aim, which found room for Judaism as an American faith. The newer idea of the "melting pot" meant a modification of this doctrine; the term itself originated in a play by Israel Zangwill, an English-Jewish author and Zionist. In this view, the historic culture of the United States was to "melt" in the American social crucible along with the many immigrant strains, and ultimately a single, new American cultural amalgam would be produced. In its assumption that patriotic immigrants and natives should help a uniform American culture to emerge, the melting-pot idea did not really differ from the doctrine of Anglo-Saxonism. Much further-reaching was the doctrine of cultural pluralism, which came forth during the second decade of the century. It proposed the radically contrary view that Jews and all other groups best fulfilled their duty as Americans by fostering their distinctive ancestral heritage in all its forms—language, art, literature, and ethos in general. Cultural pluralists insisted that if the schools and other public institutions held the immigrant and his background in greater respect, and if children did not sense the constant disdain for parental ways, many a family fabric would remain unbroken and youth not go astray. Not only this psychological argument was employed. Cultural pluralists presented a critique of existing American culture as narrow and provincial, and prescribed a tonic of European immigrant inheritances to lend it depth and variety.

Cultural pluralism received its first full statement in Horace M. Kallen's essay of 1915, *Culture and Democracy in the United States.* The theory and particularly its implications for Jewish education were brilliantly expounded five years later in Isaac B. Berkson's *Theories of Americanization: A Critical Study with Special Reference to the Jewish Group.* It is probable that much of the basic thinking, which came from young American Jews, derived indirectly from the intellectual ferment of East European Jewry, especially the Hebraist intellectual Asher Ginzberg (pseud. Ahad Ha-Am, 1856–1927) and the historian Simon Dubnow (1860–1941). Ahad Ha-Am's cultural nationalism, focused on Palestine rebuilt, and Dubnow's doctrine of national minority rights were translated and adapted for America by the Polish-born Israel Friedlander (1876–1920), Professor of Bible at the Jewish Theological Seminary. Friedlander and several associates influential in Jewish public life proposed an American Jewish educational theory resting on the cultural pluralists' view of the duty of Jews as Americans to continue to be Jews. As scholars and Zionists, they envisioned Judaism modernized along the lines of Hebraic, humanistic, religious ethnic life. The Jewish school would be the laboratory where citizens of this new American Jewish community would be trained—a most interesting application of Deweyan thought.

Cultural pluralism began its career in Jewish education as new institutions were introducing far-reaching changes. In several dozen large new afternoon schools, the reviving Hebrew language became the vehicle of the "natural method," *Ivrit be-Ivrit.* Under this system, children first learned Hebrew and, having mastered its rudiments, proceeded to the study of Bible and other subjects, all taught in Hebrew. It is hard to overstress the meaning of the Hebrew tongue for the new educators. To them, the "natural method" was no mere pedagogical tool. Hebrew was the language and the symbol of the modern Jewish culture which they dreamed of implanting in newborn Palestine and fostering in America. As to the Yiddish of the immigrant plebs, it was considered culturally inferior and neither worthy nor likely to outlive the immigrant generation. The Hebraic modernists tended to shy away from religion as such. Among them were secularists who, like the mentors Ahad Ha-Am and Dubnow, viewed the Jewish religion as the shell, not the kernel, of Judaism. Most of the Hebraic modernists were quite Orthodox, however, and most Orthodox parents sent their children to the Hebraist afternoon schools. Parental and communal expectations ensured that whatever the private leanings of some Hebrew educators, their schools would be religious. One whose outlook was greatly influenced by association with the Hebraic modernists, Mordecai M. Kaplan (1881–   ), took Hebraism, Zionism, and cultural pluralism as bases for the new American Judaism which he promulgated, called Reconstructionism.

The new spirit in Jewish education of the early twentieth century became institutionalized in the Talmud Torah. This communal school was typically found in the densely settled working- and lower-middle-class Jewish neighborhoods in large cities. Talmud Torahs* were rarely found in more prosperous districts, where synagogue-affiliated schools tended to be the rule. In addition to tuition fees—$20 to $25 per annum seems to have been average during the 1920's—the school derived its support from synagogue and neighborhood appeals. Support in several cities also came from the federations of Jewish charities. To most of these federations, however, it was a controversial question whether the charity and social services they provided for needy Jews ought to be extended to hard-pressed Jewish schools. The choice before the Jewish charity federations was complicated not only by financial

---

*The grammatically correct Hebrew plural is Talmudei Torah, but the common usage is employed here.

considerations but by the qualms, ranging from polite reservations to disdainful antagonism, felt by federation directors toward the Hebrew, rather Orthodox, nationalistic schools.

The Talmud Torah usually offered a five-year course, seven to ten hours weekly. With Hebrew the principal medium and content of instruction, the pupils were led into Bible, Jewish history, literature, religious customs, and ceremonies. Even Mishnah and Talmud were studied in some of the best schools. The curriculum was rounded out by Hebrew songs, games, holiday parties, and a junior congregation. This was indeed an exacting course of study, made more so by coming after a full day at public school. The Talmud Torah's intellectual zeal and content were impressive on paper, but its realities were less appealing. For in fact, although the educators built Hebrew schools with burning devotion, they never really converted the mass of Jewish parents to their outlook. Hardly different from heder days, two or three years in Talmud Torah were considered quite sufficient. No Hebrew school really counted on boys attending beyond their Bar Mitzvah, and preparations for that event, so despised by the pedagogues, had to be provided to satisfy a virtually unanimous parental demand. On the other hand, girls were taken as pupils equally with boys. Because they had no Bar Mitzvah preoccupations, families were usually better motivated in sending their daughters, who therefore made better pupils.

The Talmud Torah was voluntary and depended directly upon parental support, while the Sunday School had the institutional force of the temple behind it. Indeed some advocates of the Sunday School argued that seven years of consistent attendance, which well-run Sunday Schools secured, equaled two to three years of indifferent enrollment at a Hebrew school and produced more positive Jewish attitudes. Two hours daily after school, and Sunday morning, was a large dose of schooling indeed. Not surprisingly, classroom discipline was a frequent Talmud Torah problem.

Talmud Torah education became the foundation of Jewish education as a profession. Its pioneer teachers arrived mostly in the decade preceding the outbreak of World War I, and were augmented by a still larger postbellum immigration. In intellectual attainment these teachers formed quite a notable group, differing radically from the rather motley teaching corps of the earlier Jewish schools. They included Hebrew essayists and poets, some of high standing, as well as scholars and modernist Orthodox rabbis. Many had taught in the modern, intensive Hebrew schools of Eastern

Europe and Palestine, and they turned to Hebraic education with missionary zeal. In 1911 they founded the Hebrew Teachers Union, which exhibited real power from the 1920's as a militant trade union. Their main struggle lay in establishing professional standards of Hebrew education, which in turn provided the basis for their own employment at the relatively high salaries of $1,000 and even $1,200 yearly. Until 1929, the Hebrew Teachers Union enjoyed modest success in establishing pedagogical professionalism and security of tenure and improved salaries.

From Hebraist educational circles also came the drive to establish local educational systems. The pioneer of the new pedagogy and educational structure was Dr. Samson Benderly (1876–1944), a Palestine-born physician who abandoned medicine for Jewish education during his internship at the Johns Hopkins Hospital. He became the first head of the Bureau of Jewish Education of the Kehillah (Jewish Community) of New York City, the city-wide communal organism founded in 1910. He was backed morally and financially, even if with reservations, by leading "uptown" Jews disturbed at some of the social ills of the immigrant East Side. Rejecting the hadarim as hopeless and the Sunday Schools as alien to its East European clientele, the Bureau of Jewish Education federated and supported the afternoon Hebrew schools, provided in-service training to acculturate their teachers, wrote the first modern textbooks, and vigorously recruited pupils. A corps of zealous young college students collected school tuition from house to house and educated parents in the process. Benderly and his staff had flair and inventiveness, and generated excitement never known before. "Benderly's boys" became the leaders in the field after Benderly's personal importance declined around 1920.

Other communities followed New York Jewry's lead. During the 1920's, men like A. H. Friedland in Cleveland, Bernard Isaacs in Detroit, Louis Hourwich in Boston, and Dr. George Gordon, a practicing physician in Minneapolis, led Hebrew schooling in their cities, federating the schools and raising standards. With far smaller and more cohesive Jewish communities than in New York, it was a good deal easier to found bureaus of Jewish education and adjust educational facilities to local needs. Moreover, the local federations of Jewish philanthropies proved somewhat more amenable to assisting Jewish education.

The intellectual movement which helped to create Hebrew education in America also produced a contrary movement—secularist, left-wing Yiddish education. The devotion of Yiddish socialists and laborites to Jewish education came late, for their movement which began in the 1880's originally had no such interest. For decades, it aimed to prepare Yiddish-speaking workers for absorption into the American labor movement in anticipation of the social revolution sooner or later to come. The use of Yiddish was merely regarded as an unavoidable expedient until linguistic assimilation was complete. Although many older leaders continued to hold this view, time brought its own changes. Around 1910, an impressive Yiddish social, cultural, and trade union environment existed, and the doctrine of absorption into the larger American entity was put aside. Indeed, as linguistic assimilation progressed speedily, especially among the young, the desire grew to preserve the Yiddish language and its new secular milieu. A considerable immigration of writers and intellectuals arrived who added depth and color to Yiddish, and a new outlook defined "the language of the Jewish masses," Yiddish, as the true Jewish tongue, rather than Hebrew with its implications of intellectual aristocracy and traditional religion. One major intellectual, Chaim Zhitlovsky (1865–1943), contributed to a Yiddish, secular reinterpretation of Judaism. The Yiddishists sought a Judaism divorced from its millennial religious anchorage, and like the Hebraists they regarded American cultural pluralism as the basis for their educational program. Unlike the Hebraist educators, however, the Yiddishists' educational efforts were ridden with political factionalism which split their school systems. From the founding of the first schools about 1910, there was a schism between the Socialist Zionists and the anti-Zionist majority which regarded the plans for Palestine as delusive or a diversion from the main business of building Yiddish and socialism throughout the world. After the Bolshevik revolution, the split between Communists and their opponents became a savage feud which reached into the schools.

By the mid-1920's, at the peak of Yiddish secular education, some 10,000 to 12,000 youngsters attended the folkshuln where the study of Yiddish was the main business. Modern Yiddish literature and songs held a place of prominence; Zionist folkshuln added some Hebrew. A "usable past" was fashioned by recasting the Bible and Jewish holidays in secular, humanistic terms, and the struggle for labor's rights and socialism had its part in the curriculum. An early influence came from contemporary "Socialist Sunday Schools," where children of socialist parents were taught socialism and labor brotherhood and inoculated against the biases implanted by the government's public schools. Yet even with the lively and inventive Yiddish curriculum, underlying problems remained. The Yiddish schools did not become part of the general Jewish educational scene, and tended to be somewhat sectarian. To the disgust of Yiddish secular educators, they had to accommodate themselves to the insistence on the Bar Mitzvah of parents who could not be satisfied by the "secular" Bar Mitzvah which the folkshuln contrived. Yiddish education's terms of reference remained Jewish, and the general socialist, humanistic elements were always secondary. Above all, the Yiddish language never succeeded in transcending its character as an immigrant tongue, discarded in the process of acculturation. Hebrew, although diffused in much smaller circles than Yiddish, had profound historic roots and its devotees with increasing frequency could cite the shining example of growing, Hebrew-speaking Palestine. Yiddish had the stamp of the Lower East Side, and this identification proved a crippling handicap.

Secondary and especially higher Jewish education slowly became significant after 1910 as the rabbinical schools expanded and schools for Hebrew educators were attached to them. The Jewish Theological Seminary in New York City was refounded as a modernist traditional institution, headed by Solomon Schechter (1847–1915), and quickly rose to prominence and scholarly eminence. Hebrew Union College, disadvantaged by its location in provincial Cincinnati while population and movements focused in the Northeast, grew at a slower pace and continued to be a religious and intellectual focus for Reform Jewry. Stephen S. Wise founded the Jewish Institute of Religion in 1925 as a rabbinical school of Zionist, Hebraic orientation, generally Reform in religion; in 1948 it united with Hebrew Union College. The Rabbi Isaac Elhanan Yeshiva was not a professional school resembling these, for it long continued in the East European manner as an institution for pure Talmudic learning, not formal rabbinic ordination. Gradually, however, it sponsored secular studies by opening a high school and, in 1929, the liberal arts Yeshiva College under the direction of Bernard Revel (1885–1940). The Orthodox institution's ambition, only slightly realized in practice, to synthesize Jewish sacred learning with the modern arts and sciences, was a fighting matter for many years. To some high Orthodox, a college alongside a yeshiva was religiously unacceptable. More revealing, however, was the widespread Jewish antagonism to a college under Jewish (especially Orthodox) auspices. This was viewed as a "return to the ghetto" and to "parochialism" opposed to true higher education which had to liberate young Jews. Hebrew Union College and the Jewish Theological Seminary were readily accepted and supported as professional schools, but the path of Yeshiva College (later University) was a hard one, intellectually and financially. Outside these schools, Jewish learning itself had no place in American universities save some chairs of Semitic languages and The Dropsie College, a small graduate school of Hebrew and Semitic studies in Philadelphia which opened in 1910.

The new Hebrew teachers institutes were an interesting genre. Aside from those linked with the rabbinical schools, there were independent institutions—Herzliah in New York City, and in Boston, Philadelphia, Baltimore, and Chicago. They were generally of high academic quality. Their hallmark, however, was less pedagogical preparation than whole-souled Hebraism and cultural Zionism. The Yiddish schools had the analogous Jewish Teachers Seminary and People's University, the latter title reflecting their populism.

Several after-school Hebrew high schools were established after 1910, as well as a Yiddish *mittelshul*. New York City's Marshalliah Hebrew High School network offered curricula which basically continued that of the Talmud Torahs. For several thousand willing young students an educational progression thus existed, from a Talmud Torah to Hebrew high school, to one of the Hebrew teachers institutes. Hebrew as a modern language could also be studied in many high schools in New York City and elsewhere, beginning in the 1930's.

At the close of the 1920's the Jewish educational picture included Hebraic, traditionalist Talmud Torahs and their Yiddish counterparts; Sunday Schools, typical of Reform and widespread among Conservatives and even some Orthodox; a few all-day schools, called yeshivot, whose growth lay ahead. Many larger cities had bureaus of Jewish education supported by Jewish communal philanthropies.

Jewish education was badly mauled by the Great Depression of the 1930's. The social class differences between the varieties of Jewish schools were glaringly revealed: it was the poorer Jewish population who tended to prefer the more costly forms of education. As incomes fell and unemployment and business failures rose steeply, tuition revenue in the Talmud Torahs—not to mention day schools where each pupil had two full-time teachers —plummeted. A very large proportion of children was carried on the rolls without charge. The local Jewish philanthropic federations, to whom Jewish education was usually of marginal interest, found their income severely pinched and had to devote it primarily to material relief. In many communities, federation support of schools was eliminated. Often, Talmud Torahs and day schools stayed open only because their hapless teachers allowed themselves to be owed months of pay. Sunday School staff were part time and usually taught in the public schools. On account of this, and thanks to the better financial condition of the Reform and Conservative temples, the 1930's proved hard but not catastrophic. The same may be said of the Jewish Theological Seminary and Hebrew Union College. On the other hand, Yeshiva College suffered even worse than the Talmud Torahs.

It is interesting to note that the great surge of American trade unionism late in the 1930's included militant activity in the miniscule sector of the Hebrew Teachers Union. The 1940's arrived before this proletarized intelligentsia again found steady work and money on pay day.

While the Depression still dominated Jewish education as it did American life, deep emotional forces were astir. Germany's turn to Nazism and its undreamed-of treatment of the Jews horrified and shook American Jews. Disturbing manifestations of anti-Semitism appeared throughout the world, even in America. Only the growth of Palestine radiated hope. During the 1930's Jewish self-identification and solidarity greatly increased and a new kind of Jewish bond began to be discernible, replacing that which had grown from the earlier common immigrant experience. As Yiddish faded and economic distinctiveness became blurred, and the Jewish neighborhood began to look like any other, a new unity was forged by concern over the fate of Jews overseas—the lot of the Jews under Nazi rule and then the founding of the State of Israel. A half-articulate search began for a Judaism removed from East European and immigrant ways, yet retaining something of the forbears' traditions and fervor. The profound educational consequences of all this were delayed, however, until World War II ended.

The effect of world Jewish events was emotionally overpowering, but American Jewish education was overtly shaped by the social and cultural development of American Jewry after 1945. Thus, extensive suburbanization focused Jewish communal life in the new synagogue buildings and weakened older organizational interests. The Hebrew schools which nearly all these synagogues sponsored kept shorter hours than the urban Talmud Torahs, meeting Sunday and twice weekly, and had less ambitious curricula. They were financially more stable, paying their teachers better and on time. Also, they generally managed to hold their pupils for four or five years by establishing this period as prerequisite for the still universally desired Bar Mitzvah. Most Talmud Torahs, situated in declining urban areas, diminished steadily. Some which boasted enrollments of 700 and even higher during the 1930's had to close during the 1950's. However, a number reestablished themselves in newer neighborhoods with congregational affiliation.

Of all demographic changes the birthrate proved the most influential. Like Americans generally, Jews had their "baby boom" during the late 1940's and 1950's which filled to overflowing Jewish school classrooms eight or nine years later. The form of school preferred by parents was that which functioned as an arm of a usually Conservative congregation. The advantage of a school within a congregational establishment was a ready flow of pupils, financial backing, and good facilities in the hundreds of new synagogues being built. Ideologists of the congregational school pointed out that since Judaism was above all a religion, it was fitting and necessary that Jewish education and the religious institution par excellence be linked. The real and alleged secularist tendencies of the earlier Hebraic Talmud Torah came under their sharp criticism. Congregational Jewish education was not by any means wholly advantageous, however. The widespread habit of tying children's schooling to parental synagogue membership and building fund contributions irritated many. The school was subordinate to the policies of the congregation, its board and rabbi, even though autonomy was usually extensive. The tendency could be noted in some schools to stress narrower synagogal concerns over broader Jewish interests.

Generally, their curriculum inherited the Talmud Torah's,

concentrating on Hebrew and Bible, and Jewish religious and synagogal practice. The Conservative approach to Judaism in terms of the historic, collective religious experience of the Jewish people justified all these elements of the modern Hebraic curriculum. However, Conservative educators sought increasingly to inculcate a religious synagogue-centered outlook. The teaching of religious observance was more latitudinarian than that of the Orthodox, since the Conservatives did not feel strictly bound to the full ritual in the tradition. On the other hand, the ideal of study was honored, albeit in modernized form and content, and some young people were inducted into it. At the elementary level, however, beyond which few students advanced, Hebrew become greatly attenuated. Time was too limited, and moreover, the reality of Hebrew as the actual language of the State of Israel proved a less alluring educational ideal than it had been when only a dream. The general decline of instruction in foreign languages in American schools probably affected Hebrew, which by the 1950's could count on little of the old piety toward the sacred tongue. Yet with all its weaknesses, the synagogue school produced some distinguished specimens in places as diverse as Milwaukee, Detroit, Brooklyn, Philadelphia, and Albany.

Vigorous efforts by congregations to retain adolescent youngsters attained some success. The social and cultural activities of synagogues drew many youths and "Hebrew High Schools" sprouted, but usually of a standard far beneath genuine secondary education. A contribution of utmost value came from the Hebraic summer camps operated by the Teachers Institute of the Jewish Theological Seminary, Massad Camps, and others. The link between Jewish education and the house of worship was no novelty in Reform Judaism, where the Sunday School was always connected with the temple. While the Conservatives virtually abolished Sunday Schools except for the youngest children, the Reformers tended to add one or sometimes two days of weekday instruction. The curriculum shifted away from the old moralizing Bible stories to a new concentration on Jewish existence in the non-Jewish world as a moral individual and as a Jew. Greater interest in Jewish tradition, widespread in Reform Judaism from the 1930's, also became manifest in the curriculum.

It was during the 1950's that the first adequate nation-wide statistical surveys were taken. They revealed that the number of children enrolled in Jewish schools, which stood at an estimated

200,000 in 1935 and 268,000 in 1950, skyrocketed to 488,000 in 1956 and 589,000 in 1962. Yiddish schooling and communal Talmud Torahs dwindled to insignificance as some 88 percent of total enrollment was to be found in synagogally affiliated schools (1958). A most suggestive statistic indicates the rise of day school enrollment from barely 10,000 in 1945 to above 50,000 in 1962. While the total for all schools has leveled off in the low 600,000's since the latter year, the day schools at the time of writing reach 80,000.

This large-scale growth of private institutions giving both Hebrew and general education is probably the most significant Jewish educational movement since the 1940's. Until Conservatives began entering the field in the 1960's the movers were almost all Orthodox Jews; there were also a few secularists. Day schools (widely called *yeshivot ketanot*—elementary academies) had actually existed since early in the twentieth century. Most of them were not only Orthodox but Hebrew and modernist. Their abundant hours of Jewish studies, from about 8:30 A.M. to noon daily, permitted the full implementation of what was only an ambition in the contemporary Talmud Torah. The day schools generally drew their pupils from pious and sometimes learned families. Several schools cultivated intensive piety and taught in Yiddish, opposing the modern trends. All shared the Orthodox conception that the totality of Jewish law was sacred and binding, and that the main function of Jewish education was to induct the child into this personal and communal religious life. The ideal of sacred study held an important place. Secular American culture was recognized and accepted more or less willingly, yet the Orthodox hoped also to raise up learned Jews of the traditional type.

The yeshiva day schools stirred more controversy then any form of Jewish education. Questions were raised regarding the adequacy of their secular studies, their lengthy hours, and physical facilities. The real issue, however, lay deeper: the day school contravened the venerable American Jewish alliance with the public school. As noted above, that was no marriage of convenience but the wholehearted acceptance of an ideology, which Jewish day schools now seemed by implication to question. When the issue was thus perceived, it was no wonder that feelings could run strong against these institutions. None of the Jewish philanthropic federations would grant them support, and regnant philosophies of Jewish education also regarded them dubiously.

That acculturated American Jews sent their children in sharply increasing proportions to Jewish day schools requires explanation. For many parents, prosperity made private schooling financially feasible and could betoken higher social status. Much more prevalent, however, were strong Jewish convictions and the desire to bestow upon children a comprehensive Jewish education, together with reluctance to send them to a second (and usually superficial) school after the public school day. The most menacing cause appeared around 1960—the decline of the urban public schools and the racial turmoil within them. In areas seriously affected by these problems, Jewish parents especially sought out Jewish and other private schools. Most of their doubts about the adequacy of secular studies were dispelled by the impressive performance of graduates in secondary and higher education. At the same time, spokesmen presented the day schools not only in simple terms of intensive Jewish education but also as an alternative to the educational bias of the public school. The yeshivot, as they saw them, inculcated esteem for intellectual achievement and moral responsibility, in both of which public schools failed. In terms of American Jewish communal needs, day school graduates were expected to become the sorely lacking educated leadership.

A significant feature of the day school movement was the rise not only of yeshiva high schools but of yeshivot for advanced students. Most of them were founded by refugee rabbinic scholars during and after World War II. The curriculum was exclusively Talmudic, and the general outlook was transplanted from nineteenth-century Eastern Europe. Several thousand young men, mostly of American birth, deferred or abandoned college study to enter into the yeshiva regimen of intense piety and Talmud study.

Jewish day schools suffered constant financial troubles, basically because each child required two teachers' services. Early in the 1960's tuition ranged between $500 and $1,000 yearly, a heavy burden for families with several children. Rarely was a teacher paid as much as $6,000 yearly; most of the staff also taught in afternoon congregational schools to make an adequate living. However, except for the day schools, the financial position of Jewish education as a whole measurably improved. This was a consequence not only of prosperity but also of increased communal support. Several dozen local Jewish communities added Jewish education as a beneficiary to their annual campaigns for hospitals and social services, community relations, overseas relief, and aid to

Israel. A superstructure of nationwide bodies was added during the 1940's— the American Association for Jewish Education, concerned with educational publicity, research, and statistics; the National Council for Jewish Education, consisting of upper-level professional educators; the National Society for Jewish Day Schools (Torah Umesorah), an Orthodox group; and denominational bodies like the United Synagogue (Conservative) Commission on Jewish Education.

Considerable improvement was thus to be seen in the enrollment, financial position, facilities, and regard for Jewish education. Yet the most serious problem, the shortage of teachers, showed no improvement. The European-trained generation of learned, profoundly committed pedagogues was dying out and new arrivals could not be expected. Young American Jews, with all professions open, were most unlikely to choose Jewish education as a career. The Hebrew teachers colleges had modest enrollments, and few in their graduating classes became—and remained—professional educators. A highly diverse group took up the slack—Israeli students, part-time rabbis, upper yeshiva students, and partially trained housewives. The salary and conditions of Hebrew teachers improved, but the professionally trained pedagogue on the staff of the Jewish school was the exception. Despite widespread awareness that the shortage was more serious than that in the public schools, it only grew worse.

Higher Jewish education also enjoyed an impressive growth from the 1940's. The Orthodox yeshivot have been mentioned, and the rabbinical schools enhanced their stature and renown. Yeshiva College remained firm in its Orthodoxy, and became a university granting degrees in many fields of the arts and sciences. A new institution, Brandeis University, was Jewish in sponsorship. A significant trend of the later 1950's and 1960's was the founding of chairs of Jewish studies at many universities, some of highest academic quality. This development was generally greeted in the Jewish community with enthusiasm, with little critical discussion whether one or two "Jewish courses" a Jewish student might take in college properly realized the goals of Jewish education.

The Jewish educational philosophy formulated after 1910, which reached its widest diffusion during the 1920's and 1930's, unquestionably exhibited signs of obsolescence. A tide of objection rose against the old Hebraism, arguing that Hebrew study in the stringently limited school hours required too much time and produced too meager results. Better, it was urged, use the few years to learn Bible, Jewish history, and religious principles and practices in English with a patina of Hebrew terms and verses. Orthodox day schools, which did not lack the class time, were for their part influenced by the sometimes anti-Hebraic pietistic surge of the 1950's and early 1960's. They tended to turn in many cases toward religious devotionalism. During these years, attempts were made to find a new educational vision, the most distinctive of which came from the Melton Research Center at the Jewish Theological Seminary, directed by Seymour Fox. Their ambitious, carefully articulated program proposed to combine modern behavioral science with the findings of contemporary biblical and historical scholarship to reach rather traditional Jewish educational goals. The end purpose, as the Melton group formulated it, was to produce a personally moral, socially responsible traditional Jew, in whom the synthesis between the secular and the Jewish had begun from the elementary level of his education. Similar curricular reexaminations were undertaken in other circles, but with less comprehensiveness and intellectual power.

Jewish education was better established and financed during the 1950's and 1960's than ever before. At the same time, the level of Jewish knowledge among American Jews lagged further and further beneath their general educational attainment as study, that ancient Jewish cynosure, inspired young Jews in almost every field except that in which it originated. By the standards of centuries, American Jews were indeed functionally illiterate as Jews. By the standards of American life, however, an ethno-religious community which founded and sustained a network of schools attended at some time by most of its youth possessed a great resource to assure its own future and enrich the fabric of American life.

THE INTERACTION OF
JEW AND GENTILE /
THE CASE OF
INTERMARRIAGE

LIVING WITH INTERMARRIAGE
by DAVID SINGER

INTRODUCTION

DETAILED STATISTICS ON *intermarriage are presented elsewhere in this volume, particularly in the article by Sidney Goldstein. While the present essay by David Singer reviews the statistical picture, in the main it is concerned with how American Jews respond to intermarriage.*

Singer's view is that the prevalence of intermarriage has given rise to what he terms an "accommodationist spirit" in many Jews. Accordingly, even if one is opposed to intermarriage the better part of wisdom is to make peace with the inevitable and seek to give the marriage the appearance of being unexceptionable. This type of response, Singer points out, is a distinct departure from the older pattern of seeking, by whatever means possible, to deter the Jewish partner from entering into an intermarriage.

One of the ways to make intermarriage seem unexceptionable is to have a rabbi officiate, thus replicating a wedding where both partners are Jewish. The desire for rabbinical approval has put the Reform rabbinate, in particular, under considerable pressure to conform with parental wishes. Singer notes that many Reform rabbis are now ready to accommodate anxious parents.

Singer believes that the motivations of such rabbis are not above suspicion, and he questions the claim that rabbis participating in intermarriage ceremonies are acting in the best interest of Jewish survival. He further believes that the accommodationist spirit has affected some social scientists as well as some rabbis, and addresses the work of those who seek to build scientific support for the view that the threat of intermarriage has been considerably overstated.

In theory the size of the Jewish community could be enlarged if the offspring of intermarriages regard themselves as Jewish even when, according to halachah, *they may not be. In actuality such a situation is fraught with danger. It is quite possible that the Jewish community could divide over the question of who is a Jew. Some who regard themselves as Jewish would not be accepted as such by other Jews. In past eras the Jewish community has been divided on many issues, but only under very exceptional circumstances have Jews questioned one another's credentials. From this vantage point, the accommodationist spirit, whatever its advantages, may have serious consequences not reckoned with by those who uphold a "dovish" response to one of the most serious problems confronting the Jewish community.*

M.S.

To NON-JEWS, the attitude of the American Jewish community toward intermarriage must appear puzzling. On the one hand, American Jews seem to want nothing more than to be fully integrated into American society. They take obvious pleasure in having found a place for themselves in the most exclusive neighborhoods, on the best college campuses, and in the highest councils of government, and are quick to label attempts to set up barriers against them as discriminatory. On the other hand, these same Jews, or at least the organized segment of the community, continue to oppose the ultimate step of the integration process—intermarriage. Several years ago, Jewish groups raised such a clamor over a CBS television series, *Bridget Loves Bernie*, which portrayed a marriage between a Jew and an Irish Catholic in a favorable light, that the program was eventually taken off the air. A non-Jew might well wonder, then, if American Jews are pleased or saddened by the recent Gallup Poll finding that fully 69 percent of Americans now approve of marriages between Jews and Christians.

The answer, of course, is that American Jews are both delighted by the Gallup finding and very worried about it—as one might expect, given the fact that their deepest commitment is to the twin goals of integration and survival. Organized Jewish life in the United States has always been predicated on the assumption that these two goals are fully compatible. But are they? The growing incidence of intermarriage has begun to raise grave doubts about the matter. For this reason, intermarriage has become the single most pressing problem confronting the organized Jewish community. But there is a gap between acknowledging a problem and dealing with it. Because the majority of American Jews are unwilling even to contemplate the possibility that they may have to choose between integration and survival, Jewish groups have been hard-pressed to cope with the burgeoning intermarriage crisis. If anything, there seems to be a growing sentiment within the community that attempts to halt the spread of intermarriage are doomed to failure and therefore the sensible course is to make the best of it.

II

Given the importance of the intermarriage issue, it is remarkable how little effort Jewish communal groups have made to obtain reliable information about it. Up to a point, this merely reflects a more general inertia: American Jews have never shown much interest in seriously examining their own institutions and mores. In this particular case, however, the lack of information probably also reflects what Marshall Sklare has called "avoidance behavior": American Jews have been reluctant to confront the issue of intermarriage because the dilemmas it poses are simply too painful. Most painful of all, of course, is the fact that, as Sklare puts it, intermarriage represents the "logical culmination of the quest for full equality," while at the same time striking "at the core of Jewish group existence." Then, too, Jews find it extremely unsettling that in opposing intermarriage they seem to be spurning that liberal creed of equality for all which they have always been so quick to embrace. Finally, taking a stand against intermarriage seems to imply a rejection of romantic love, and of the right of young people to choose their own marriage partners, and Jews feel uncomfortable being cast in such a role.

Small wonder, then, that the American Jewish community turned a blind eye to intermarriage for decades; the first symposium on the subject by a major national Jewish organization did not take place until 1963. Even now, when the intermarriage problem has reached critical proportions, Jewish groups have still not managed a systematic examination of the phenomenon.

The most reliable figures we have so far on intermarriage are almost ten years old. They derive from the National Jewish Population Study . . . carried out between late 1970 and early 1972. The data on intermarriage exist only in preliminary form, are based on sampling methods which have been challenged, and are subject to significant margins of error. Nonetheless, the NJPS statistics are the best guide currently available about marriages between Jews and non-Jews in the United States.

The most startling NJPS finding is that the rate of such marriages, which prior to 1960 had never reached 13 percent, more than doubled between 1961 and 1965 to a rate of 29 percent, and between 1966 and 1972 climbed to an astonishing 48 percent. It is important to note, however, that these figures deal with marriages and not individuals. Taking account of the fact, then, that there are two Jews involved in each endogamous marriage, and only one in each exogamous union, we find that 31 percent of the Jews who married between 1966 and 1972 married Gentiles.

Needless to say, the NJPS statistics, which indicated an intermarriage rate twice as high as had previously been assumed,[1] caused a great stir in Jewish communal circles. Some comfort could be found in the fact that the study, by defining intermarriage as a marriage of a Jew to someone who was not Jewish at the time the couple first met, also included converts to Judaism (19 percent of the initially non-Jewish spouses) among the intermarried. On the other hand, the study dealt only with intact marriages, thus ignoring divorced couples, among whom the intermarried may be disproportionately represented. All in all, the NJPS estimate of 48 percent for the 1966–1972 period is probably a rough approximation of reality. Since 1972, the rate has undoubtedly increased.

So much for the bad news. The good news, if one can call it that, according to the NJPS, is that intermarriage is not an automatic one-way ticket out of the Jewish community. On the contrary, the study found that nearly half of the initially non-Jewish spouses answered "yes" to the question, "Are you Jewish now?" Moreover, about three-quarters of intermarried couples who had children stated that they were rearing them as Jews, and 70 percent of the total number intended to provide their children with some form of Jewish education. That these affirmations of Jewishness had to be taken with a grain of salt, however, is indicated by the fact that something like three-quarters of intermarried couples were "not at all" active in a synagogue; the figure for those uninvolved in Jewish organizations of any kind was even more disappointing.

The National Jewish Population Study did not provide a statistical breakdown of differences in Jewish orientation between couples where a conversion had occurred and those where it had not. This is most unfortunate, since a study conducted by Bernard Lazerwitz in Chicago in 1966–1967, which was a kind of trial run for the NJPS, found the two groups to be strikingly different.[2] While non-

---

[1]Writing in 1970, Marshall Sklare estimated the rate of intermarriage to be around 25 percent. See "Intermarriage and Jewish Survival," *Commentary* (March, 1970).
[2]"Intermarriage and Conversion: A Guide for Future Research," *Jewish Journal of Sociology* (June, 1971).

converting Christians and their Jewish spouses were quite marginal
in their Jewish involvements, converts and spouses of converts rated
above-average in terms of synagogue and Jewish organizational activity. A new study carried out by the American Jewish Committee
confirms this pattern.[3] Reporting on a nationwide sample of intermarried couples, Egon Mayer and Carl Sheingold write:

> The level of Jewish content and practice in mixed marriages [inter-
> marriages where there is no conversion] is low; only about one-third
> of the Jewish partners in such marriages view their children as Jewish;
> and most such children are exposed to little by way of Jewish culture
> or religion. . . . Conversionary marriages compare favorably not
> only with mixed marriages but with endogamous marriages as well.
> In the conversionary marriage, Jewish identity is not merely asserted;
> it is acted upon, particularly with respect to religious affiliation and
> observance. Thus, in some ways, there is more reason for optimism
> about Jewish continuity in families where the born-Gentile spouse
> has converted to Judaism than there is in the typical endogamous
> family.

While the figures cited here provide a useful starting point,
they hardly begin to explain the phenomenon of intermarriage in
the U.S. today. We do not know, for example, what roles selective
migration and differing residential patterns play in determining intermarriage rates. We do not know what relation exists between
socioeconomic status (education, occupation, income) and intermarriage. We do not know whether Jewish background (education,
religious observance, organizational activity) plays a determining
role in intermarriage. We do not know why Jewish men tend to
intermarry more than Jewish women, and whether this situation is
changing as a result of the women's movement. We do not know
what factors lead non-Jewish spouses to convert, and whether conversions today are on the increase or the decrease. We do not know
if intermarried couples have a higher divorce rate than endogamous
couples, or what ultimately happens to the children of intermarried

---

[3]Egon Mayer and Carl Sheingold, *Intermarriage and the Jewish Future* (New York,
1979).

couples. In short, despite a general sense of urgency, we know very little.[4]

Yet whatever the gaps in our knowledge of the subject, one thing is clear: the ever-increasing number of Jews marrying non-Jews poses a threat both to Jewish group survival—particularly in view of the very low Jewish birth rate—and to the continuity of generations within the family and the ability of family members to identify with one another.

III

Prior to the 1960's, when the intermarriage rate was relatively low, the organized Jewish community, to the degree that it took cognizance of Jewish-Gentile marriages at all, felt confident that it could control the situation.[5] To be sure, intermarriage was regarded as a problem, but a problem of manageable proportions. Jewish groups did not hesitate to speak publicly about the need to prevent intermarriage, and there was no inhibition in speculating about the negative factors which led some Jews into it. Basically, intermarriage was regarded as a form of deviancy, attributable to such things as Jewish self-hatred, status seeking, a child's desire to inflict pain on his parents, and so forth. Within the family, the standard means of discouraging such marriages—so standard it has entered the folklore—was what Marshall Sklare has called the "discord approach": parents would dwell on the marital problems, frequently ending in divorce, which mixed marriages inevitably entailed. This pragmatic line of argument was particularly attractive to Jewish parents because it enabled them to oppose intermarriage in good conscience while avoiding the value conflicts that might otherwise have arisen.

Like so much else in American society, all this changed in the

---

[4]A point worth noting is that a high rate of intermarriage is hardly unknown to modern Jewish history. In Budapest and Vienna, for example, at the turn of the century, the rate was 20 to 30 percent, while in Berlin during the period of the Weimar Republic it was 25 percent. Even Warsaw in 1929 had a rate of 20 percent Arthur Hertzberg has argued that "intellectual secularization produces in the third generation everywhere, without exception, in the Diaspora, a 35- to 40-per-cent rate of intermarriage."

[5]The situation prior to the 1960's is excellently described in Marshall Sklare's "Intermarriage and the Jewish Future," Commentary (May, 1964).

1960's. As the intermarriage rate soared, there was a perceptible erosion within the Jewish community of all the old certainties. Marriages between Jews and Gentiles had become so commonplace that American Jews could no longer console themselves with the theory that intermarriage was a social or personal aberration. Nor could Jewish parents seriously expect their children to heed warnings about intermarriage leading to divorce, when the soaring divorce rate obviously affected Jewish couples no less than intermarried ones. Finally, as the rate of intermarriage increased, it generated—as is usual in cases of social change—a measure of approval for itself and began to look like the wave of the future. Thus, Marshall Sklare, writing in 1970, could point to an "erosion of confidence" among the more acculturated elements of American Jewry that the "battle against intermarriage [can] be won." He went on: "This is why the struggle is now viewed not as a matter of prevention, but increasingly . . . as a matter of accommodation to the inevitable." A decade later, it is clear that Sklare's analysis has been fully borne out. Everywhere, except in the Orthodox community, the spirit of accommodation is today in the ascendancy.

Since the rabbinate, and particularly the Reform rabbinate, is on the front line of the intermarriage issue, it is not surprising to find that accommodationist pressures have been most strongly felt here. Ironically, the best evidence for this is the fact that in June 1973, for the first time, the Central Conference of American Rabbis (the Reform rabbinic association), went on record as opposing the participation of CCAR members in "any ceremony which solemnizes a mixed marriage"—"mixed marriage" referring here to a marriage in which the non-Jewish partner does not convert.[6] Far from indicating a stiffening of resolution on the intermarriage question, as it might seem to do, the CCAR resolution actually represented a last-ditch effort to hold the line against the growing number of Reform rabbis who, under pressure from their congregants, had proved willing to officiate at mixed marriages. In 1972, such rabbis made up 41 percent of the CCAR membership; today they comprise more than half. The conditions under which Reform rabbis will agree to solemnize mixed marriages vary: some require the non-Jewish partner to sign up for a course of study on Judaism; some

---

[6]In the same month, the New York Board of Rabbis, representing all three branches of Judaism, voted to bar from membership rabbis who officiate at mixed marriages, or who make referrals to those who do.

require a pledge that the couple will raise their children as Jews; some have no requirements at all; and some will even officiate at a marriage ceremony in a church.

No sooner had the CCAR resolution been passed than it precipitated the formation of a counter group within the Reform rabbinate. The group, calling itself Concerned Members of the Conference, took issue with the resolution on grounds that, in the words of one of its spokesmen, Rabbi Irwin Fishbein, "rabbinic participation in mixed marriages is in the best tradition of Reform Judaism. It is an attempt to respond in a positive way to the increasing incidence of mixed marriage in a mobile and open society." Rabbi Fishbein, who directs the Rabbinic Center for Research and Counseling, argues that far from worsening the situation, participation by rabbis in mixed marriages actually improves it, for otherwise a "total sense of rejection would be transmitted to about one out of every three Jews who marry today, and would do irreparable harm to the cause of Jewish survival." He insists that he and his colleagues who perform mixed marriages are the true champions of Jewish survival since they seek to "maximize the Jewish potential [of such marriages] and thereby strengthen our historic tradition."

Rabbinic accommodation to intermarriage is, however, by no means confined to the Reform movement. As the Conservative laity has increasingly taken on the social complexion of its Reform counterpart, Conservative rabbis too have been faced with a rising tide of intermarriages within their congregations. They themselves are not willing, of course, to perform mixed marriages. However, many of them have become strong advocates of a liberalized approach to conversion, their aim being to make it easier for the non-Jewish partners in mixed unions to enter the Jewish fold. Thus, Robert Gordis, a leading Conservative spokesman, argues:

> On the theoretic level, the *halakhic* principle that the conversion must be free of ulterior motives is unquestionably sound. But it must not be approached in simplistic terms. Human motivation is always complex. When the non-Jewish partner is prepared to undertake a process of serious Jewish study and then finds that he can conscientiously accept the principles and practices of Judaism for himself, the fact that his original impetus was the desire to marry a Jew can hardly be described as "ulterior." . . . Nor can the desire to establish a home

that would not be religiously and spiritually divided against itself hardly be described as unworthy. For a non-Jew to abandon the advantage of being a member of the dominant majority and to throw in his lot with the Jewish community . . . is a substantial test of sincerity.

Rabbi Gordis is explicit as to his motivation here: "The Jewish community simply cannot afford to lose thousands upon thousands of its sons and daughters without making a yeoman effort to reduce . . . the defections from its ranks."

These arguments are not without weight. But there is another, more sordid, side to rabbinic involvement in the intermarriage issue which cannot be ignored. We must bear in mind that pressure upon rabbis to accommodate to intermarriage comes mainly from the Jewish parents within their congregations whose sons or daughters are about to marry non-Jews. As often as not, the couple itself is perfectly happy to settle for a civil marriage, while the Jewish parents insist on some kind of religious ceremony. If the Gentile partner (usually the bride, according to statistics) agrees to convert, there is of course no problem. If not, the search immediately gets under way for a rabbi willing to officiate at a mixed marriage. Unfortunately, this whole process lends itself to the most cynical exploitation—as Daniel Schwartz recently pointed out in an article titled "The Intermarriage Ripoff." The author, who is himself a Reform rabbi, surveyed 47 rabbis in New York State who officiate at mixed marriages and found the following:

> only ten as much as spoke to the [Jewish-Gentile] couples on the telephone prior to the ceremony, and of the ten, only three asked to see the couple before the wedding. Of the 37 who had no contact with the couple, 33 had their secretaries handle all the details; four had their secretaries ask the couple to come in for a meeting with the rabbi. . . . In every case the secretary was very careful to make sure that the caller understood what the rabbi's fee would be and what time the ceremony would begin and end. . . . The fees requested by all 47 ranged anywhere from $75 to $250, and in one particular case was $350. When asked why the last fee was so high, the secretary said indignantly, "Well, he's a national figure, you know." When the same rabbis were [approached by Jewish couples], the amounts plummeted to between $50 and $125, the highest charge being that of the "national figure."[7]

---

[7]Daniel Schwartz, "The Intermarriage Ripoff," *Moment* (August, 1979).

Rabbi Schwartz concludes: "If there is a principle involved here, it appears to be the principle of the fast buck."

But the corruption is not only of a financial kind, and it is not only Reform rabbis who are implicated. Many rabbis who do not themselves officiate at mixed marriages refer couples to rabbinic colleagues who do. Quite often, the referral is made by a Conservative or Orthodox rabbi who has a problem within his own congregation. Almost invariably, the rabbis who are recommended are the ones with the lowest standards, the ones who will, so to speak, make the "least trouble." They are the ones who get to wash the community's dirty laundry.

IV

Such is the prevalence of intermarriage, and the pressure to come to terms with it, that a new literary genre has come into being— "how-to" books for intermarried couples. Two examples of the genre, radically different in tone, are Samuel Sandmel's *When a Jews and Christian Marry*[8] and Samuel Silver's *Mixed Marriage: Between Jew and Christian.*[9]

Sandmel's book is a truly remarkable cultural artifact: a guide for perplexed Jewish-Gentile couples, written by a prominent Jewish scholar (the author is Distinguished Service Professor of Bible and Hellenistic Literature at Hebrew Union College) and presented to the public by a Catholic publishing house. In the foreword to the book, Sandmel makes it clear that he is not taking a position on intermarriage itself, but addressing "those who have already decided" to intermarry. Believing that "religious traditions exist to serve people, not people to serve religious traditions," he attempts to be helpful to couples of mixed religious background by dealing with a broad array of issues of concern to them: "How can they make a go of it? What are the possible pitfalls that can jeopardize such a marriage? How much does the religious difference mean? How much do family, history, and society intrude? What minimum ought the couple to know about Judaism and Christianity? In short, is such guidance possible as to insure a successful marriage?" As Sandmel tackles these questions, it is impossible, whatever one's

---

[8]*Fortress Press*, 1977.

[9]*Arco Publishing Company* (New York, 1977).

views about intermarriage, not to be impressed by his seriousness of purpose and genuine sympathy.

An altogether different venture is Samuel Silver's *Mixed Marriage: Between Jew and Christian*, which treats its subject with boundless high spirits. Writing as one who has officiated at countless Jewish-Gentile marriages—Rabbi Silver sets up no requirements for the couples involved, and often appears jointly with a Christian clergyman in a church ceremony—the author fairly bubbles with enthusiasm. To be sure, he points out that not everyone is suited for such a union and warns that intermarried couples can expect to "encounter complications galore." Those who do take the plunge, however, are reassured that they are the "harbingers of a new kind of world unity, in which not only couples but ideologies and theologies will "live happily ever after." Rabbi Silver rhapsodizes on the new dawn about to break over humanity: "The world . . . is undergoing a new '*briss*ening,' the emergence of people who are determined to transcend the limitations of adherence to one branch of the Judeo-Christian family." Small wonder, then, that, as he puts it, "families have 'schlepped' me long distances so that the Jewish moment in the weddings would be assured." His reward for all this, aside from the honorariums he receives, is the "satisfaction of being of service, and perhaps assuring the survival of my faith."

Sandmel and Silver address themselves to the actual couples involved, and may be said to be engaged in a species of pastoral counseling. But what about the Jewish community as a whole? When accommodation is the order of the day, it too must learn how to live with intermarriage. Here, it is social science which comes to the rescue with the argument that widespread intermarriage may not be such a bad thing—that, indeed, it may be a positive good. Two recent articles, which develop this theme are Samuel Lieberman's and Morton Weinfeld's "Demographic Trends and Jewish Survival"[10] and Fred Massarik's "Rethinking the Intermarriage Crisis."[11]

Lieberman, a statistician with the Population Council, and Weinfeld, a sociologist at McGill University, pull off a near-impossible feat: they manage to argue simultaneously for a low birth rate and a high intermarriage rate—and to do this, moreover, in the name of Jewish survival! Central to their "alternative, survivalist perspective on the Jewish future" is the assumption that de-

---

[10]*Midstream* (November, 1978).

[11]*Moment* (June, 1978).

mographic trends have to be assessed in the light of "specific community obligations and objectives." One vital objective of American Jewry is securing political support for the state of Israel, and intermarried couples, Lieberman and Weinfeld maintain, can play a crucial role in this regard:

> The successful exercise of influence is best achieved in a community with a large subset of members interacting with politicians and opinion leaders. Through intermarried Jews themselves, and certainly through their social networks involving Jewish family and friends . . . Jewish concerns, interests, and sensibilities can be articulated before a wider, more influential audience. In a recent interview, Presidential aide Robert Lipshutz traced the origin of Jimmy Carter's concern for Israel to his close friendship with a first cousin, an Orthodox Jew (Carter's aunt married a Jewish man, and their two children were raised as Jews).

This, then, is the "stratetic function" of intermarriage in contemporary American Jewish life.

Fred Massarik's article is of special interest because he served as scientific director of the National Jewish Population Study which first alerted Jewish communal circles to the existence of an "intermarriage crisis." Having been the bearer of sad tidings in 1973, Massarik now comes forward with a message of consolation: American Jews have suffered unduly because of "panic sowing" on the intermarriage issue; discussions of the subject have "overstate[d] considerably the danger we face." Has Massarik come into possession of new data? Not at all. He merely presents (selectively) the existing NJPS findings in such a way as to put the best possible face on the situation. Thus, he consistently focuses on attitudes—how many non-Jewish spouses identify as Jews; how many intermarried couples plan to give their children a Jewish education—rather than on behavior. He stresses the continued Jewish involvement of Jewish women who intermarry, while barely noting the fact that twice as many Jewish men marry non-Jews as do Jewish women. Most importantly, he never makes good on his promise to present data addressing the "issue of the quality of Jewish life as it is affected by intermarriage." Small wonder, since such data would hardly serve to buoy the accommodationist spirit.

V

American Jews, with the exception of the Orthodox, then, are clearly intent upon making peace with intermarriage. As the inter-marriage rate continues to rise, and it will almost certainly do so, pressures to accede to it will become even stronger within the community. The stronger these pressures become, the more they will encourage mixed unions which in turn will generate still further demands for concessions. The spiral is almost certainly bound to continue upward.

This does not mean that American Jewry is in danger of disappearing. No matter what, a sizable Jewish community will be maitained by the simple device of redefining Jewishness in such a way as to include all kinds of people whose *bona fides* would not previously have been acceptable. Just as non-Jews who have undergone conversions under Reform auspices which do not conform to *halakhic* practice are virtually accepted today as full-fledged members of American Jewry, so will other individuals also be accepted. Already, a number of Reform rabbis have begun to practice what they call "cultural" conversions, wherein the prospective convert is permitted to retain his Christian faith so long as he professes a sense of identification with the Jewish people. This is one area, we may be sure, where necessity will prove to be the mother of invention, whether among the clergy or elsewhere. This is certainly true of both the Lieberman-Weinfeld article and the one by Massarik, which actually speculate about a possible Jewish population *gain* as a result of intermarriage. Not surprisingly, the former writers are all in favor of "voluntaristic and subjective interpretations" of Jewishness, while the latter author stresses the importance of a "drift" toward Judaism on the current intermarriage scene.

If widespread intermarriage does not point to the inevitable demographic decline of American Jewry, it certainly poses the threat of a critical weakening of the quality of Jewish·life. It is one thing to call people Jews, but quite another to have them respond in a meaningful way to Jewish symbols and traditions. Where will these newly ordained "Jews" look for guidance when *The Jewish Catalog* is no less alien to them than the *Shulhan Arukh*? Can one realistically expect them to become consumers, let alone producers, of serious Jewish culture? Or, for that matter, to be staunch supporters of Israel simply because they have been dubbed "Jewish"?

Finally, what needs to be emphasized is that the intermarriage issue, for all its importance, is but one aspect—perhaps the most visible—of the larger problem facing American Jewry. A great deal of discussion is currently going on in Jewish communal circles about whether intermarriage leads to assimilation—or, as the new American Jewish Committee study puts it, whether Jewish-Gentile marriages "lead to a diminishing identification with Judaism and the Jewish community." But the real problem is exactly the reverse. It is not intermarriage which leads to assimilation, but assimilation which leads to intermarriage. The most telling NJPS findings are not those that deal with marriages between Jews and Gentiles, but rather those that deal with marriages between Jews. Is it surprising that intermarriage is so widespread when 57 percent of Jewish couples do not participate in any synagogue or Jewish organizational activity? Until the community comes to grips with this reality, the intermarriage crisis will continue to deepen.

THE HOMELAND/
AMERICAN JEWRY
AND ISRAEL

LAKEVILLE AND ISRAEL/
THE SIX-DAY WAR AND ITS AFTERMATH
by MARSHALL SKLARE

INTRODUCTION

THE RELATIONSHIP OF American Jews to Israel is one of the oldest and one of the newest topics in the sociology of American Jewry. Historically, most American Jews, and even many American Zionists, conceived of the relationship in terms of philanthropic aid, political assistance, or cultural reinforcement. American Jews would give financial assistance to the Jews of Palestine (and later of Israel) and would help by influencing American foreign policy in a pro-Israel direction. Such assistance would be reciprocated in two ways: 1) Israel would serve as a symbol of Jewish affirmation and achievement, and 2) Israel would constitute a center where Jewish culture could develop free of the limitations inherent in the Diaspora. While Israeli culture could never be transferred in toto to the United States, it would nonetheless provide American Jews with a significant source of enrichment that would, in turn, constitute a valuable resource in the fight against assimilation.

While there have been those who have been apathetic or even hostile to the idea of a Jewish state, the dominant tendency of American Jews has been to nourish and strengthen connections with Israel. Indeed, certain Zionist youth organizations have maintained that the relationship of American Jewry to Israel goes beyond philanthropy, political action, and cultural exchange—that there is a re-

*sponsibility for American Jews to participate personally in the up-
building of the land through aliya (migration). But this view, too,
has hardly been the dominant one, even among Zionists. While most
adult Zionist groups have approved of aliya in the abstract, they have
felt that America is an exceptional country and that there are no
grounds for expecting a significant immigration to Israel from the
United States.*

*A number of Israeli spokesmen have suggested that sooner or
later a Jewish problem will emerge in the United States, which will
disprove the doctrine of American exceptionalism. Other Israeli
spokesmen have conceded that anti-Semitism is unlikely to flourish
and motivate emigration, but have maintained that assimilation
will become rampant and that those who wish to retain their Jewish
identity will experience inner pressure to emigrate to Israel.*

*If aliya has not been the dominant response of American Jewry,
there is little question that the relationship with Israel is one of the
most significant aspects of the identity of the American Jew. The
following article analyzes the reaction of one Jewish community to
the Six-Day War of 1967. The assumption of the analysis is that this
event stimulated the acting out of feelings which in more placid times
would not rise to the surface.*

*It is difficult to say whether the feeling about Israel today is
different from the recent past. On the one hand the mass media are
not as favorably disposed to Israel as they were in 1967, and the issue
of oil complicates reactions. Also, the steady barage of anti-Israel
sentiment flowing from Arab and Soviet propaganda sources, international forums like the United Nations, and certain influential
sectors in American life, could conceivably take a toll upon Jewish, as
well as upon Gentile, opinion. On the other hand, feelings may be
more intense. Many more Jews have visited Israel in the intervening
period. It is also quite possible that anti-Israel sentiment has
boomeranged and created even stronger pro-Israel sentiment among
American Jewry. Whatever the current configuration of Jewish attitudes, the study of reactions to the Six-Day War provides valuable
insights into some of the enduring elements in the relationship of
American Jewry to Israel.*

M.S.

൧൦ൟ

The RESPONSE OF American Jewry to the Crisis in Israel in April–May of 1967, to the Six-Day War which followed, to the Israeli victory, and to the State of Israel from that time to the present, is as yet imperfectly understood. While a veritable flood of books has appeared about the War—the events which preceded it, the strategy on which it was based, and even the attitudes of Israeli soldiers engaged in the struggle—no comparable literature has emerged on events in the American Jewish community and on the attitudes of American Jews.[1]

In the early months of 1968 we returned to Lakeville—where field work had been conducted a decade earlier on the problem of Jewish identity—to learn something about the response to the Israel Crisis, to the War, and to its aftermath.

There have been no startling changes in Jewish institutional life in Lakeville since the community was originally studied. In the attitudinal area change has been slow as well: there is nothing to suggest that prior to May–June, 1967, feelings of Jewish identity were in strong movement, either in a positive or negative direction. People do feel that there has been a gradual increase in the frequency of intermarriage. But they also feel that there is greater interest in Jewish education both for adults as well as for the young.

The Crisis, and the Six-Day War which followed, altered the picture of orderly communal evolution and attitudinal change. All observers in Lakeville attest to the fact that no event during the past decade has had an impact upon feelings of Jewish identity comparable to that of the War. Yet there is no agreement about what the impact was, why it occurred, the extent of its duration, and its eventual result.

A definitive assessment of these challenging questions must await the mounting of a full-scale sociological assault. The present

---

[1] For details about the community and the findings of the original study see Marshall Sklare and Joseph Greenblum, *Jewish Identity on the Suburban Frontier: A Study of Group Survival in the Open Society*, 2nd ed., (Chicago, 1979).

effort is in the nature of a reconnaissance: a series of relatively unstructured interviews with seventeen Lakeville residents, eleven of whom were among the 432 persons interviewed in the original sample.

A reconnaissance effort, by definition, is only a beginning, although if successful it may contribute measurably to present understanding as well as to the strategy of future research. But first there is the problem of evaluation. Should Lakeville's response be considered on the high or the low side when we think in terms of the nation at large? In evaluating Lakeville's response we must bear in mind that the community does not have the reputation of being a hotbed of pro-Zionist sentiment. For example, in contrast to some less-statusful suburbs and inner-city Jewish neighborhoods where the most popular Jewish women's group is Hadassah, in Lakeville, Women's ORT occupies this position. Furthermore, there was a very small but recognizable segment of the community identified with the American Council for Judaism. This group was strong enough to establish a religious school in the community, and as an outgrowth of this school the David Einhorn Temple was established. While the connection between Einhorn and the ACJ is quite different today from what it once was (the Temple now belongs to the Union of American Hebrew Congregations), the fact that such an institution was established means that there was a group of residents whose family background included a non-Zionist or anti-Zionist tradition. Lakeville has its Zionists of course (including some who are leaders of Zionist organizations), as well as an extremely large group who are pro-Israel. Yet while there are Lakeville residents who have made large financial contributions to Israeli causes, Lakeville is not the type of community where one would look for a maximum response to the Six-Day War (unless of course one is prepared to argue that the maximum response occurred in precisely the wealthier, more acculturated Jewish communities). Thus if we find that a given impact occurred in Lakeville, it would be fair to infer that this impact was at least as strong in the country at large.

CONCERN AND INTEREST

Our respondents remember being very anxious during the days in April–May 1967 when the crisis was developing. Their anxiety was greatly heightened by the doubts which they had concerning the ability of Israel to withstand the might of the Arab armies. Such doubts can best be illustrated by the two respondents who found themselves under cross-pressures to shift from a feeling of anxiety to a feeling of confidence. In both cases the impetus was provided by Israelis. In the first instance the Israeli was a houseguest of one of our respondents who had come to the United States on a fund-raising mission for a specialized Israeli institution. In the other case the cross-pressure was provided by a neighbor, a *yored* (an emigrant from Israel) who had recently settled in Lakeville after reputedly having made a "killing" on the stock market.

Both of our respondents were more troubled than reassured by what these Israelis told them, namely, that there was nothing to worry about and that Israel would be able to take care of its enemies without much trouble. Our first respondent—the one with the houseguest—reported that in spite of his great esteem for his visitor he became hostile to him on the basis that he was so lacking in feeling as not to experience the anxiety the respondent himself felt. The respondent with the *yored* for a neighbor had other problems. While the *yored* lived in luxurious style, he had rebuffed our respondent when the latter had approached him for a donation to a Jewish charitable cause. Our respondent felt that his neighbor was an insincere person who was putting up a brave front since he refused to acknowledge how difficult was the situation of be-leaguered Israel and how much his help was needed.

If the two respondents who were under cross-pressures did not have their fears relieved, our respondents as a whole were left undis-turbed with their anxieties. If the optimism of the two Israelis was typical of the mood in Israel at the time—as we think it was—then our respondents' fears may in part be traced to their very distance from Israel and Israelis; were they more involved they would have been less worried. But even more must be at stake. The man on the fund-raising mission who told his host to stop aggravating himself was resented. Thus a psychological reaction probably occurred, namely, that if the Israelis are bearing the brunt of the struggle, the least that we comfortably situated American Jews can do is worry. Those who would deprive us of this function will make us feel like bad Jews whereas we wish to consider ourselves to be good Jews. However, in spite of their anxieties our respondents were able to carry on with their normal routines. Only one reported psycho-somatic symptoms.

The feeling of our respondents was unambiguously pro-Israel. There was no doubt in their minds as to which side was right. Support for Israel seems to have increased as the Crisis deepened, undoubtedly because it evoked unconscious feelings.

We shall have occasion to return to the problem of unconscious feelings; at this point we only wish to highlight the strength of pro-Israel sentiment. The depth of support for Israel during the Crisis and War can perhaps be gauged from the reactions of a respondent whom we shall call Robert Himmel. Himmel is a board member of the Einhorn Temple and a longtime member of the American Council for Judaism. He traces his lineage to pioneer German Reform stock. Himmel now considers himself "pro-Israel and anti-Zionist." His justification for supporting Israel during the Crisis and War was that: "It is the only democracy out there [in the Middle East]. It is important for the United States from a strategic point-of-view." When Rabbi Elmer Berger came out with a statement critical of Israel during the period of the Crisis and War, Himmel reacted strongly. He wrote Berger a long and blistering letter (he instantly put his hands on the correspondence). Himmel did not object to the content of Berger's statement: "What Berger said was right but it was bad timing. I hate negativism. If he couldn't say anything good about Israel why couldn't he have kept his big yap shut?"

Our respondents felt so highly involved that their appetite for news during the Crisis and the War was well-nigh insatiable. While they do not ordinarily listen to news broadcasts on transistor radios, such devices were pressed into service. One woman took her radio with her when she kept an appointment at her hairdresser. There was some radio-listening in business offices, a most unusual procedure for our respondents. One woman reported an almost insatiable hunger for news comparable to what she had experienced when President Kennedy was assassinated.

Many of our respondents watched the debates at the United Nations far into the night. As they saw it, the hero of the drama which unfolded there was Abba Eban. All were entranced by Eban. His presentation was felt to be both logical and stirring, his case airtight, his mind colossal, his oratory magnificent. One respondent feels that Eban far surpassed Churchill at his best. All felt Eban to be the perfect Israeli and the perfect representative of Israel. Their overwhelming enthusiasm for Eban would suggest that they saw him as their representative as well, and they were gratified that he provided them with a model they could so readily identify with. None of our respondents seem to be aware that their feeling that Eban is the perfect Israeli is not shared by all Israelis.

If Eban was judged to be a Jewish superman, the representatives of the Arab states were regarded with contempt. Their presentations were seen as fraudulent, their motives as sinister, their corruption complete. The speeches of the Arab representatives—and those of their Communist allies—only confirmed our respondents in their pro-Israel opinions.

AMERICAN LOYALTIES VS. SUPPORT FOR ISRAEL

Our respondents were not only united behind Israel but the Crisis and War was a case where they did not experience any strain between their national loyalties and their support for a foreign country. Or better, they strove not to perceive any such strain. The fact that Gentiles did not press for such a strain was very helpful to them.

The desire not to perceive any strain is exemplified by a respondent who was thrilled at the Jewish response to the Crisis and who was firm in his support of Israel. He then added "I'm a firm believer that what affects other countries affect us as well," as much as to say that any right-thinking American would have supported the Israeli cause out of the national interest.

In the present instance the possibility of a strain was provided not by anti-Semites, not by the general public, and not even by the American government, but, surprisingly, by the government of Israel when it made the decision to attack the U.S.S. Liberty. But even this incident did not, in most cases, affect the feeling of our respondents that good Americanism and good Jewishness were one and indivisible. Some interpreted the incident, in which thirty-four U.S. sailors died, as the type of accident which is inevitable in a fast-moving war. They suggested that if it had been known that the Liberty was an American ship there would not have been an attack. Others, however, viewed the attack as deliberate—as a move by the Israelis to preserve their sovereignty and security. These respondents felt that the Liberty had no right being where it was (some interpreted the Pueblo incident along much the same lines). Many of these respondents supported the Israelis in their action, while others showed understanding even if they did not support it. But whether the action was viewed as deliberate or accidental, there are those who remember being concerned at the time about the Gentile response. There is, for example, the man who recalls being ". . . concerned that bigoted people might fasten on the incident and try to make the most out of it."

The strongest criticism of Israeli actions in respect to the Liberty came from a respondent who considered himself a firm supporter of Israel rather than from a present or former member of the ACJ. This respondent felt that the action was deliberate. He recalls his sentiment at the time: the incident was a "catastrophe." The Israelis had no right to proceed as they did because it meant hurting their staunchest supporter, the U.S. government: ". . . the Israelis should remember you don't bite the hand that feeds you. . . ." But in actuality this respondent was much more concerned with the welfare of American Jews than with the relationship between the two governments: ". . . you don't complicate the position of American Jews who want to support Israel." In spite of his feelings against Israel for its action against the Liberty, there is no reason to suspect that this respondent shifted to a lower level of support. His strong reaction can be accounted for by the fact that, having considered himself pro-Israel for many years, he began to perceive a strain between his loyalties as an American and as a Jew.

ASSURING AN ISRAELI VICTORY

The story is told of an ultra-Orthodox Jew who, in the midst of the siege of Jerusalem during the War of Independence, went around the city proclaiming: "Jews, do not rely on miracles! Recite Psalms!" While prayers and Psalm-saying are traditional Jewish responses to impending catastrophe, there is little reason to suspect that they were much in evidence in Lakeville during the Crisis and War. We did not probe our respondents on this score but none volunteered information which would suggest any increase in personal devotions. (It is entirely possible, however, that prayers and Psalms were recited during the Crisis and War in various congregations during the course of their regularly scheduled services.)

If personal devotions were something which the Lakeville Jew was incapable of, he was able to perform a traditional act of another sort: the giving of money. In fact the giving of money is not only viewed as an act of solidarity with Israel but as having helped to assure an Israeli victory.

Strange as it may seem, our respondents even today connect their own actions with the Israeli victory. If the winning of any war ever depends upon superior financial means, the Six-Day War was not such a war: by the time the first public (if not private) fund-raising meetings could be convened, victory was a foregone conclusion. But sober businessmen long experienced in problems of procurement, of manufacturing and of transportation, acted as if the money they contributed one day could somehow miraculously be turned into the sinews of war the very next day. Because they wanted to believe in such a miracle, the emphasis was not upon pledges—the usual form of Jewish fund-raising—but on a different approach: the giving of cash. And when the imminence of the Israeli victory forced another justification for the fund-raising, and especially for the giving of cash, the following approach was articulated: "Since the costs of the War have been so great, Israeli resources have been completely depleted. Unless we help, Israel will become bankrupt and the victory will be in vain." American Jewish money, then, would keep Israel from losing the peace.

The agency charged with the responsibility of organizing the drive for contributions to Israel from Lakeville Jews is the United Jewish Welfare Federation and Council of Lake City (JWF). This organization sponsored a drive for the Israel Emergency Fund. However, since grassroots sentiment was so strong, drives were started on local initiative. Thus some of the religious institutions in Lakeville proceeded to organize campaigns; such campaigns, of course, were soon coordinated into the plans of the JWF. Nevertheless, the synagogue drives were more spontaneous than the JWF campaign and at the outset they were relatively free from professional control. Although the largest gifts were given through JWF channels, it was the synagogue drives where grassroots sentiment was apparent in its most pure and unsophisticated form. Thus, these drives hold a special interest for us.

Four of the five synagogues in the Lakeville area sponsored such drives. A detailed report on one of them—the drive sponsored by the Samuel Hirsch Temple—is presented below. This meeting eventuated from an extraordinary session of the Temple board which had been convened on the evening of June 5th in response to the news that war had just broken out that morning in Israel. The information below is from an interview with the congregation's spiritual leader, Rabbi Samuel Aaron:

At the meeting Monday night the immediate thought was to raise money. It was clear that the money would be for the Emergency Fund but there was some complication with the [Israel] Bonds people, who wanted in. However, it was the feeling that they should not be in and some compromise was arranged in that Bonds were not sold from the rostrum but the chairman announced that officials of the Bond campaign were in the audience, that they had blanks, and that if anybody wanted to purchase Bonds he should see these men and women in the audience.

The Monday night planning meeting was attended by Joe Cohen, who is on the staff of the JWF. Cohen came to the meeting late, tired from the many meetings that he had already attended. There was a decided lack of rapport between him and Rabbi Aaron and it was necessary for peace to be made between the two men. Apparently some people at the meeting lined up on the side of Cohen but more seemed to line up on the side of Rabbi Aaron. Cohen wanted to hold the Wednesday meeting in usual Jewish fund-raising style, to call cards, to announce donations in order of magnitude and to do all the things that go on at these affairs. Aaron felt that this was completely inappropriate and that Cohen did not understand the nature of the crisis and the mood of the people. Cohen wanted a big-name speaker. Rabbi Aaron burlesqued his approach as follows: "We'll even get you a guest speaker who died in the War." The people at the Monday night meeting who wanted to do it the Cohen way were those people who were old JWF people and not really active Temple people. It was finally decided there would be no calling of cards, that people could get up in any order in which they wished to, that they would not need to announce any amounts, and that they could say anything they wanted and not only announce a gift. It was also decided that no refreshments would be served. No guest speaker was to be invited.

Some 500 families belong to the congregation. It was decided to send a telegram to each. When these were ordered there was immediately a problem at the local Western Union office: there was not sufficient manpower to deliver the telegrams. The youth [of the Temple] helped out, although some were in school and Aaron is not quite sure how all the telegrams got delivered. There was some annoyance at the telegram approach. Some people resented being disturbed by deliveries made in the middle of the night. There were some people who were against the idea of the telegram itself, and perhaps some who objected to the expense connected with it.

About 500 showed up on Wednesday night. In trying to estimate what percentage of the families of the congregation were represented,

Aaron arrived at the figure of 55 percent. The people who had arranged the meeting had hoped for more. However, this was the largest meeting that had ever been held in the building. It attracted more people than on any other occasion in the history of the congregation except for the High Holidays.

The president of the congregation opened the meeting. Part of his job, he felt, was to justify the convoking of this extraordinary gathering. Aaron said "he is not a *farbrenter* Zionist" and therefore he had to put the meeting in context for the audience but even more for himself. The spirit at the meeting and the spirit during the week at the congregation was fantastic. More than on any other occasion the congregation was unified.

There was some problem at the Wednesday night meeting because the feeling of threat had been dissipated and by that time the Israeli victory was quite clear. Aaron took the approach at the meeting that even if the War would be won the disruption of the economy would be tremendous and that economic troubles might make Israel go down in the end. Money was therefore needed not so much to win the War but to keep the country alive.

Aaron is not sure how much money was actually raised at the meeting but it was an extremely large amount. The JWF was contacting people simultaneously and there was some confusion. They were also skimming off the cream by talking to the really big donors, so that from this point of view the meeting could be viewed as an anti-climax. It was not an anti-climax for any of the women, however, for they had not been contacted by the JWF.

The entire meeting was cash-oriented. A great many checks were handed in; people not only wanted to pledge money but they actually wanted to give cash at the meeting. Several people got up and said that they had arranged for a bank loan so that they could give the cash. Another man got up to say that Baron Rothschild in Paris had sold his race horses to raise cash. Aaron found this example of "privation" hardly inspiring.

The entire meeting on Wednesday night lasted only one hour and ten minutes. People stood around afterward. They were reluctant to go home. Everyone told Aaron, who was the principal speaker, that his presentation was wonderful. He felt it was not, that it wasn't as good as it should have been.

There are intimations in this interview that giving is seen as a religious act. Hence the criticism of those who would secularize or in some other way corrupt it. It is difficult to say whether other respondents feel the same way as Rabbi Aaron. What we do find in quite a number of interviews is the mention of heroic acts of giving—of individuals who could not afford to give what they did. Not all such acts are known personally to our respondents—some are the result of second or third-hand information. But some of those which are known at first hand may strike the observer as less than heroic. For example, one of our respondents who is in the banking business was amazed to find that individuals came in to his bank to arrange loans so that they might make their Emergency Fund donations in cash. However, while the loaning of money in order to give charity deviates widely from the philanthropic norms of our culture, it actually says little about what proportion of his wealth the individual is giving away.

We avoided probing the respondent too deeply about the size of his own donation to the Emergency Fund, lest rapport be interfered with. But in only a single case is there even a possibility that a family might have temporarily had to deny themselves something to which they were accustomed. There is also a case among our respondents of a family which thought it might be necessary to cancel their summer vacation because of their Emergency Fund contribution. However, they finally decided to go through with their plans.

All of our respondents who gave to the Emergency Fund had enough ready cash to cover their gifts. None say that they had to resort to bank loans or to the selling of securities in order to meet their obligations. Respondents did not claim that they personally gave in a heroic manner: few if any who participated in the Emergency Fund campaign claim that their giving was of such a magnitude as to make a noticeable dent in their personal assets.

Focussing exclusively on the question of the magnitude of the gift, however, creates the danger that we lose sight of the significance of gift-giving. This is particularly so in the case of first-time givers. One of the most interesting types of first-time givers is the kind whose previous non-giving is based on a lack of contact with Jewish life, rather than on ideological considerations or psychological makeup. An example of such a non-giver who became a first-time giver is Mrs. Mildred Fried. Of all of our respondents Mrs. Fried is closer to being assimilated than any of the others interviewed. Thus she lacks any of the points of contact which Mr. Himmel, the anti-Zionist, has with Jewish life. Mrs. Fried follows no religious practices in her home, does not belong to a synagogue or a Jewish organization, and has not given her children a Jewish education. A salaried professional woman, she has been criticized by Jewish and Gentile colleagues for working on Yom Kippur, but she feels that she would be perpetrating a fraud if she remained at home. In contrast to most of our other respondents, Mrs. Fried has a number of close friends who are Gentile. In spite of all this Mrs. Fried leads an underground Jewish life. While she has never disapproved of the idea of intermarriage, she was secretly pleased when her daughter married a Jewish boy. While she has never given her Gentile friends any reason to suspect she is ethnocentric, she feels that ". . . there is a certain 'ego' in being Jewish. Gentiles can't keep up with Jews."

Mrs. Fried was as emotionally involved as any of our respondents with the Crisis and the War. She was glued to the TV set, watching the UN debates far into the night and relishing each word of Abba Eban. She has saved the newspapers of June 6–11: "This is history, and this I wanted to keep." She made a contribution to the Emergency Fund. This is the first time she can remember doing anything for Israel. Giving a contribution was more complicated in her case than in others. Not appearing on any membership list of a synagogue or Jewish organization, she received no telegram summoning her to a meeting and she had to go out of her way to find out where contributions should be sent.

Mrs. Fried's desire to donate to the Emergency Fund was not an uncomplicated act of generosity but was intimately connected with the meaning which the struggle had for her. According to our record:

> The five days after the first day of the struggle Mrs. F. described as "pure ecstasy." Israel was performing miracles. She was deeply touched by what was happening. She felt that no more does the Jew march to the ovens. Now he has something to fight for.

Later in the interview Mrs. Fried told us about a letter she had received from her son who was at graduate school:

> "Bill wrote to me how proud he was to be a Jew at this time. He had told me before that he could not understand why the Jews walked to the gas chambers." Mrs. F. says that her boy believes in fighting back. He could not understand his grandfather and previous generations who lived by "backing away." Her implication was that while she had tried to explain this to Bill, she could not really understand it herself. Now no more explanations are needed.

The interview concludes on the following note:

> Mrs. F. emphasized that the Six-Day War was an enormous event in human history. "We have never fought back before. We always picked up our bundles and ran. Now we can fight back."

Mrs. Fried's donation, then, is intimately connected with her desire to assist those who, according to her understanding, were putting an end to Jewish behavior with which she could not identify—behavior which she had always been ashamed of.

Among the leaders of the David Einhorn Temple we find a different situation, for there we encounter cases where people have been approached year after year to contribute to Israel but have refused to do so, presumably because of ideological considerations. One of the leaders whom we interviewed persisted in non-giving, and refused to make a contribution to the Emergency Fund. But we also interviewed other leaders of the Temple who made a first-time contribution to Israel. Unlike Mrs. Fried, both non-givers as well as first-time givers seek to justify their respective actions. According to non-givers, money given to the Emergency Fund would continue the tradition of the United Jewish Appeal which draws no distinction between philanthropic and political purposes; it uses its funds for the illegitimate purpose of stimulating *aliyah* to Israel, including the *aliyah* of American Jews. Thus, according to one board member of the Einhorn Temple, the JWF utilized the Six-Day War to raise funds far beyond anything they had previously conceived of, the JWF was "hysterical" and played upon the emotions of Jews, and the JWF never specified how the funds being given to the Emergency Fund were going to be used.

While this particular non-giver was well-defended, he left us with the impression that he was not happy with his lack of giving. Two of his fellow board members—contributors to the Philanthropic Fund of the ACJ—had, on the other hand, donated to the Emergency Fund. These men were obviously happy that they made a decision for Israel. Their decision, however, was more a break with principles than a sacrifice of substance. While both are substantial businessmen, one stated that his contribution was $50 and the other did not reveal his gift. We infer it was also a pittance. Yet such token giving had deep significance for these men, for they were doing their bit to assure an Israeli victory. One man repeated his old resentments against the JWF: "They send the money to Israel and it comes back here for propaganda purposes." But he felt that money contributed to the Emergency Fund was different: "It is being used for economic needs in Israel."

The Einhorn Temple held no fund-raising meetings for the benefit of the Emergency Fund. Yet the question of how the group should respond to the Crisis agitated the leadership of the Temple. Some wished to do nothing while others went so far as to suggest that a fund-raising meeting be held. A compromise was arranged: a letter was sent out under the signature of the president and the rabbi, stating that if a member wished to make a donation he should contact the temple office where he would be supplied with a list of Israeli causes. One member resigned from the Temple as a result of the letter.

One board member of the Einhorn Temple remains staunch in his criticism of the philanthropic response of the Jewish community. He feels that people were exploited and as a consequence far too much money was made available to the Emergency Fund. On the whole, however, our respondents were thrilled at what was done. They have knowledge of some of the sums given by the big-givers and they highly approve of such generosity. Those who gave do know people who did not give and they also cite cases of friends, relatives, neighbors, or business associates who did not give enough. But in the main our respondents feel that the level of generosity was extraordinary. The most critical is Abraham Weinberg, a strong supporter of Israel and of all the laymen whom we interviewed the most devout, the most highly involved in Jewish life, and the most concerned with giving his children an intensive Jewish education. On his own initiative Weinberg organized a parlor meeting for the benefit of the Emergency Fund. About $5,000 was raised among his neighbors at this meeting but he told us: "They felt it was tremendous but I feel that the response was luke-warm. People were surprised and worried by their generosity."

One special aspect of this particular parlor meeting requires mention at this point. When the meeting was being organized there was a question concerning a Gentile who resided on the block. Since this man was particularly friendly with his Jewish neighbors he constituted a problem: if he was not invited he might feel insulted, but on the other hand, if invited he might feel compelled to give and thus be forced into participating in an act of Jewish solidarity. It was decided that he should be invited but that he be instructed that he was to come as a guest and thus was not to make a contribution. The man came but refused to act as instructed. He made a contribution of $100. He also gave an additional gift of $25 on behalf of his son.[2] He said he admired the Israelis and supported what he called their fight against the Arabs and against Communism.

Though money represented the dominant mode of response, there were other reactions as well. Little if anything was done by our respondents in terms of political activity, but one declared: "If it would have been necessary I would have contacted my Congressman." Others echoed the same sentiment. A further question was whether children should be encouraged to go to Israel to help. Our respondents were generally passive in this regard. There were one or two who had a problem, however, for their children took the initiative and said that they wanted to go during the Crisis. The tendency of these parents was to temporize. Thus Mr. Weinberg's oldest son wanted to go but he prevailed upon the boy to finish the term at college. In one family, however, there was an offer of support when a child indicated a desire to go to Israel. This is the Fried family—the most alienated among our respondents. But their youngster did not get to Israel: in spite of the approval of his parents, he was prevented from pursuing his objective of rendering personal assistance to Israel because of circumstances irrelevant to our present study.

THE MASS MEDIA AND ATTITUDES IN THE GENERAL SOCIETY

The problem presented by the Gentile on the block leads us to a consideration of the relationship between minority and majority. We have already discussed this problem in terms of the possible conflict between divergent loyalties, especially as these were highlighted by the Israeli attack on the U.S.S. Liberty. Here we shall be concerned about what the respondent perceived to be the attitude of Gentiles with whom he associated, of the mass media, and of society at large.

Most of our respondents report that they were happy, even delighted, with the coverage given to the conflict in the mass media.

---

[2] A number of our respondents did the same thing—wanting their children to participate, they made donations in their name.

Even media they expected to be hostile gave a fair presentation. The only critical reaction they can remember was to be found in letters-to-the-editor columns, where occasional anti-Israel sentiments could be encountered. While anti-Israel material was absent, the mass media contained considerable anti-Arab and anti-Russian comment. As one respondent put it: "It was clear that the Gentiles were with us against the Arabs."

If our respondents perceived the mass media as friendly, their contacts with Gentiles—on whatever level these occurred—reinforced the impression that the general community supported their position. *Most respondents reported an unambiguously positive reaction.* However, the wife of one respondent—a woman who works in an office where most of the employees are Gentile—reports that on the first day or two of the War the reaction was not too positive: "Then it abruptly changed for the better when the Israeli victory became apparent." Respondents were very pleasantly surprised to see the reaction of Gentiles. The respondent who appears to be the most surprised of all (he says he was "rather startled") is the board member of the Einhorn Temple whose negative comments about the Emergency Fund were quoted earlier.

Our respondents have different theories about why the Gentiles were sympathetic. One feels it was a case of Israeli cowboys against Arab Indians. Others introduce the theme that the anti-Soviet views of the public made them unusually receptive to a pro-Israel point of view. Yet another respondent says that while he feels Gentiles were basically pro-Israel, he suspects that Jews heard as much pro-Israel sentiment from Gentiles as they did because ". . . it was said for the benefit of the listener."

One respondent is thoroughly distrustful of the Gentile response. This is Rabbi Aaron, who ordinarily spends little time in interfaith work but who was drawn into such activities during the Crisis and War as well as during the months which followed:

> On June 7th Reverend James, the minister of a Presbyterian Church in the area (and one of the brightest and most pro-Jewish of the ministers in the area), had the idea of circulating a petition to support Israel. This petition was never published, however, because not enough signatures of other ministers could be gathered. If only some of the ministers signed, it was felt that the publishing of the petition would do more harm than good. At the time of the blockade the rabbis in the area sought to promote a petition supporting the

Israeli position, to be signed by ministers in the area. Aaron had been given about 15 names to call. He called all 15 and about eight or nine said yes. Other rabbis did not achieve such a high percent of assent. Since there was no clear consensus, this petition was dropped. Ministers who would not sign the petition generally responded by saying that the matter was a political one in which they could not interfere as ministers of the Gospel.

In addition to Reverend James, the other person who came to the fore during the blockade and crisis was the Unitarian minister in Lakeville. He sent a letter to his membership asking them to contribute to the Emergency Fund. It is Aaron's impression that this letter was signed by the president of the Unitarian Church as well as by the minister. This is the Church in which there are many Jewish-Gentile intermarriages and many people of Jewish lineage. The mood in the Church, as Aaron put it, was to show that "We Jewish Unitarians are doing our part."

The latest aspect of the Christian response is a gathering which had been held in the winter sponsored by the rabbis for the purpose of convincing Christian ministers that they had a long-range obligation to support Israel. It was first thought that the meeting should be held at the new sanctuary of the Isaac Mayer Wise Temple, but there was some question as to whether this was a good idea. The problem was whether the sanctuary was too showy and demonstrated too much wealth, and would therefore reinforce Gentile stereotypes.

Aaron is not quite sure how the meeting was financed, as this group has no treasury. He estimates the cost of the meeting was about $1,000. He wonders whether a Zionist group picked up the tab. The main speaker was the nationally-known Rabbi Jacob Benjamin of New York, who spoke on the theological commitment of Jews to the State of Israel. He was followed in the afternoon session by a local man, Rabbi David Rose, who spoke about the Christian reaction to the Crisis and the War. Rose put the cards very much on the table, stressing that there was much less support from Christian leaders than the Jewish community expected. He stressed the great disappointment and shock the Jews experienced when they found what the Christian reaction was. Most of the ministers sat on their hands. The specific purpose of the meeting was to light a fire under these ministers. It was quite obvious that none was lit.

The meeting was predominantly a Protestant meeting, for only three or four Catholic priests were present. Aaron summarized his reaction by saying that: "We Jews are dealing with a deep-seated and potentially very dangerous anti-Semitism in this ministerial group."

Except for Rabbi Aaron, then, our respondents perceive that Gentiles supported their own position toward the War. *Furthermore, our respondents feel the victory of the Israelis improved the status of American Jewry.* Perhaps the single deviant in this regard is the non-giver of the Einhorn Temple, quoted earlier. The most doctrinaire of the anti-Zionists whom we interviewed, this man stated: "Gentiles do not think that we American Jews are connected with Israel in any way." But other Einhorn board members took a very different view. One reported that: ". . . the stature of the Jew rose." A Gentile associate with whom this man has done business for many years told him over the long-distance phone with obvious approval: "You Hebes really taught those guys a lesson." Another board member, who had resigned from the ACJ because "they fight Zionism unintelligently," found that Gentile business associates considered the Israeli victory to be his victory. He became more respected in their eyes because of the Israelis' feat of arms. This was the general view: that the American Jew had achieved new respect in the eyes of the Gentile because of the Israeli victory.

THE PROBLEM OF LONG-RANGE IMPACT

Perhaps the most frequently-asked question about the Crisis and the War is its long-range impact on the attitudes of American Jews. Does it represent a decisive turning point in feelings about Jewish identity in the restricted area of attitudes toward Israel and/or in the more general area of attitudes toward self? Does it portend a renaissance in American Jewish life or will its impact—whatever it is estimated to be—gradually be dissipated by the inevitable march of other events which turn out to have greater meaning and relevance in the life of the individual?

These are difficult questions to answer on several counts—they require us not only to prognosticate but also to provide a definitive answer to the problem of what exactly it was that happened to American Jewry during the Crisis and War. In approaching this issue we shall first discuss the desire of our respondents to experience the victory at first-hand and to strengthen their ties to the country by visiting Israel in the aftermath of the Six-Day War.

1. *Visiting Israel*

In the original study, during the 1950's, we did not ask a question about visiting Israel since travel to Israel was still an exceptional experience. Asking in the 1960's about visiting, our assumption was that most of our respondents (particularly those who were over 40 and who were in the upper-middle or the upper class) would have visited Israel at least once during the intervening decade. But we were surprised at how few had done so. *We were particularly surprised that as late as February of 1968 not a single one of our respondents had visited Israel since the War.* Furthermore, with a single exception—a family we shall call the Melvin Whites—none had at the time any definite plans to visit Israel.

The lack of any compelling desire to go to Israel during the summer of 1967 or in subsequent months is highlighted by the case of Philip Green. Mr. Green, who is in his early sixties, is a wealthy owner of a wholesale electric supply house. He lives in a very comfortable ranch house situated on one of Lakeville's best streets. As is apparent from the following extract from his interview, Green experienced as strong a pro-Israeli reaction during the Crisis and War as any of our respondents. In respect to the Six-Day War, Green said:

> "I was never so vehement about anything in my life. I was practically ready to go over to fight." Green doesn't know why he reacted in the way he did but he knows that he had never felt anything like this before. He went to a fund-raising affair at the Isaac Mayer Wise Temple, where he is a long-time member. He gave more than he had ever given before. At the fund-raising affair he made a contribution in the name of each of his children. He wanted them to participate in some way.

Green—the only one of our respondents who spontaneously mentioned the phantasy of fighting for Israel—has never been to Israel and has no plans for going. When asked about travel plans he seized upon the President's recommendations against non-essential foreign travel:

> In respect to travel Green feels he is an American as well as a Jew and therefore the welfare of this country has to be considered. Thus, if travel to Israel has to be deferred because of the balance of payments, so be it.

Green's apathy about travel suggests that there was in his case, and by extension in others, a strong unconscious element in the reaction to the Crisis and the War. Like others, he could not explain why he reacted in the way he did.

The Melvin Whites are the exception—they are the only family which has made definite plans to visit Israel. This youngish family lives in a luxurious home on a heavily wooded site; it was once the estate of a member of the "400." Mr. and Mrs. White travel abroad regularly, sometimes with their three sons. Indeed they are the most fashionable people we interviewed in Lakeville: they travel more, play more, spend more, and seem to have better connections than any of our other respondents. Their style of life conveys a strong "JFK" image. To quote from the interview:

> The White family was in Israel two years ago for the first time, spending eleven "very full" days in the country. Mr. White, who has developed an important manufacturing business, was shown various projects in Israel. The family was apparently given the VIP treatment. However, to the best of Mrs. W's information her husband did not subsequently make any investment in Israel.
>
> The Whites were taken to S'de Boker to meet Ben-Gurion. He asked the boys when they were coming to live in Israel. The second thing he asked them was whether they spoke Hebrew. Receiving a negative response to both questions, he "bawled us out." Ben-Gurion told the Whites that the next time they would meet he wanted the boys to speak to him in Hebrew.
>
> They met "wonderful, wonderful people" in Israel. The study in their home has many framed color photos of their guide, people they had met at kibbutzim, officials of the Histadrut, factory managers, and prominent personalities: Eshkol, Ben Gurion, Teddy Kollek, Golda Meir. Mrs. W. emphasized again and again the wonderful, wonderful people they met and how very lucky the family was to have these connections. The boys were very impressed with Israel.
>
> From Israel they visited Greece and·Italy. They enjoyed these countries but there are very few pictures in the study about their visit there. The exception is a photo of Mr. and Mrs. W. with Pope Paul. Mr. W. is a generous contributor to a Catholic university located in Lake City.

Mr. and Mrs. White are going to Europe in March for a vacation. After sightseeing and winter sports they have made arrangements to spend several days in Israel. Thus, they will be the first of our respondents to see the country after the awesome events of June, 1967. But even they will not have planned a special trip to Israel—they will jet to Lydda after their European expedition is concluded. But the Whites do want to see what has happened since their first visit, and especially the changes which have occurred since the Six-Day War. Mrs. White looks forward to renewing her acquaintance with the people she met before. She experienced a quality with Israelis which she finds lacking in her friends and neighbors in Lakeville: ". . . they have been making great sacrifices for their country and it is a wonderful place because there is a strong feeling of nationalism and of giving oneself to a cause."

2. Shifts in the Level of Pro-Israel Support

In our original study a six-point scale was used to measure the level of pro-Israel support. Interviewees were asked to respond positively or negatively to the following types of support:

> raise money for Israel;
>
> seek to influence U.S. foreign policy in favor of Israel;
>
> belong to Zionist organizations;
>
> give Israeli financial needs priority over local Jewish causes;
>
> encourage their children to immigrate to Israel;
>
> participate personally in the building of Israel through becoming a citizen of Israel.

Some 93 percent approved of raising money, 63 percent of influencing foreign policy, 31 percent to belonging to Zionist organizations, 14 percent to giving Israeli needs priority, and 1 percent to both of the items on *aliyah*.

This scale was administered to ten of the eleven respondents who were part of the original sample, with the following results:

Same response	5
One-step increase	2
Two-step increase	1
One-step decrease	2

Half of our former respondents, then, would extend the same level of support today as a decade ago. These five individuals include two who only go so far as raising money, two who approve raising money and also influencing U.S. foreign policy, and one who approves of belonging to a Zionist organization and giving Israeli needs priority as well. The two individuals who increased by one step were both money-approvers who moved up to the influence-foreign-policy

level. The single individual who increased by two steps moved from
a zero score to approving money and influence. The two individuals
who experienced a two-step decline formerly approved of money,
influence, and belonging to Zionist organizations; they no longer
approve of Zionist organizations.

Very surprisingly, then, the Crisis and War do not appear to have
made any real impact on levels of pro-Israel support. Our respondents are not ready to go farther today than they were a decade ago.
There are those who have moved up a step but their example has
been balanced by those who have moved down.[3] Finally, the single
case of a two-step increase does not represent a conversion from a
medium level of support to a high level. Rather, this individual
started out at the zero level and is now at a level which is very close
to the average for the community. His life history reveals the story
behind this shift. George Mandel was born and raised in a small
Iowa town where Jewish influences were minimal. His origins are
still manifest in his quiet speech and his reticent manner. Since his
marriage to a Jewish woman and his settlement in Lakeville, Mandel has gradually acculturated. This has meant that he has become
more "Jewish," including the adoption of normative attitudes toward Israel.

3. Shifts in Feeling about Jewishness

If we cannot discern any real increase in the types of support which
Lakeville Jews feel compelled to render to Israel, it is possible that
there have been subtle shifts in feeling about Jewishness—shifts
which have long-range implications of a positive kind for Jewish
survival. What these shifts might be we cannot say. But our interview with Rabbi Aaron contains some relevant hints:

> Asked about the High Holidays, Aaron said that they were better
> attended this year than previously. The services were also the best
> services. He does not know whether this is directly because of Israel
> but in his opinion it helped. In general, the Israeli crisis served to
> bring the congregation closer together. There was an impending crisis
> in the congregation over Vietnam, but the Israel victory averted any
> such confrontation. His first sermon for the High Holidays was on

---

[3] It might be claimed that the meaning of the item "belong to Zionist organizations"
is not the same today as it was a decade ago.

Israel. He imagines that every rabbi in the country did the same. The people who were with Aaron on Vietnam (he is a dove) he describes as the better Jews in the congregation. Peculiarly enough, people who followed him on Vietnam were more Zionist-minded than the hawks in the congregation. He thinks that because Vietnam, Jewish identity, Israel, and Hebrew had been presented by him as a package, those who wished to emulate him bought both his Jewish attitudes as well as his general social attitudes. He feels there has been and continues to be a conflict with some over supporting Israel and being against Vietnam. The conflict is sometimes a very subtle one, and in some people there is a conflict but they are not aware of it. He personally is worried about Moshe Dayan and his image, and there are some people in the congregation who are also worried about Dayan. Aaron is more comfortable with the "Buber image" than with the Dayan image and he said that for himself and those who follow him in the congregation: "Eshkol is for us a better image than Dayan."

Asked about what residue the Crisis and War have left or what it has meant in addition to the High Holidays, he said that the congregation is in favor of extending its program of sending youngsters to Israel for the summer. This would involve increasing the amount of money they make available—the program now costs the congregation about $3,000 a year. It will escalate and he feels there is no question but that the congregation will continue to pay for it. The congregation is very proud of its subsidy program in sending some of its young people to Israel each summer. It represents a kind of commitment to Israel. The Reform appeal for Israel, on the other hand, is not attractive; the congregation is not excited about raising money to establish a Reform presence in Israel.

The Israeli Bond dinner that the congregation sponsored raised more money this year than before and almost everything in the congregation this year has gone somewhat better than before. There is more attendance at Hebrew classes this year.

The impact of the Israeli crisis may be involved perhaps in the new high school department which the congregation has embarked on. Aaron feels the congregation will spend more per pupil in the high school department than any Reform congregation in the country, and that while the groundwork was prepared for this in past years, the issue had to be voted on during the time of the Crisis. He expected much more opposition to the new program than developed. He wonders whether the program received such firm support because of the mood induced by the Crisis.

Aaron finds that Jewish life at the Temple isn't *all* that different this year, however. He expected the change to be sharper than it actually has been.

THE MEANING OF THE CRISIS AND THE WAR

We are now prepared to confront the question of what exactly happened to American Jewry during the Israeli Crisis and War. We know that our respondents were shaken by the threat posed by the Crisis, were unambiguously pro-Israel, were tremendously stirred by the victory, felt that they did their duty to bring such victory about through their financial contributions, have not shifted in their level of pro-Israel support, and have not evinced any extraordinary eagerness to visit Israel. We also know that central participants in Lakeville Jewish life, such as Rabbi Aaron, expected ". . . the change to be sharper than it actually has been." And it has occurred to one of our respondents who occupies a much more marginal position in Jewish life, George Mandel, that he no longer feels about Israel the way he did. He recalls how he felt last June:

> "If anything had happened to Israel it would have been a catastrophe. People wouldn't have had any place to go. Israel was a symbol of what modern Jews can do." While Mandel did not take any political action, if the war had taken another turn he would have contacted his Congressman and asked for U.S. support. He remembers having a feeling of great pride in what the Israelis had done.

The following excerpt from his interview records his contrasting feelings at the present time:

> Mandel does not have as much feeling about Israel at the present time as he thought he would based on his feeling in June. If he was going on a foreign trip, Israel would not be the first place he would visit. He has seen slides taken by one of the people who works at his office. This person brought back an extensive collection and showed them to a group for a whole evening. "When I saw the people and the countryside I didn't relate to it as much as I thought I would. I don't know why but the people looked very foreign to me." He has no urgent feeling about visiting Israel. He does not know anyone who has changed decidedly in his feelings and his actions about Israel as a result of the Crisis. Since the situation has cooled off he doesn't see much difference. People feel about the same way as they did before.

How then may we explain the sharp difference between present emotions and those of the immediate past, as well as the absence of a revolutionary change in Jewish life?

It seems to us that the response of May–June was not a response to Israel in the conventional sense but rather a response to the events of Jewish history from the 1930's onward. The response in Lakeville must be understood in light of the fact that American Jews, by fortunate circumstance, have been exempt from this cataclysmic history. The Crisis brought to the forefront of consciousness the possibility of a repetition of that history—the possibility of another holocaust. Like the first holocaust—in which American Jewry was exempt not by virtue of any special nobility of its own but rather by pure happenstance—another holocaust would have meant that again the American Jew would miraculously escape harm.

It is suggested that the Jewish reaction proceeded along the following lines. If we have the problem of justifying our escape from the first holocaust, the least that we can do is make the gesture of helping to prevent a second one; at the very minimum such a gesture will indicate that some good purpose was served in our being spared. (And the possibility of a second holocaust presents us with an opportunity to cleanse the record of the 1930's and 1940's— perhaps we are not entirely sure that we did all we could to avert that holocaust and to succor its victims.) Thus, our support of Israel is intimately connected with our desire to preserve a feeling of our worth as human beings.

Furthermore, we support Israel to protect our sense of meaning. Israel created meaning, for it meant that out of the destruction of the holocaust something new, clean, and good was born. Thus, Israel protected our sense of meaning in a world which assaulted any sense of meaning which the Jew might have. Israel's destruction, then, would involve the destruction of meaning. Hitler, whom we thought to be dead and conquered, would be alive again; the final victory would be his. By upsetting our sense of meaning, a new holocaust would have plunged American Jewry into total *anomie*. From this perspective, Israel *had* to be supported as never before. Her destruction would have meant our end as an American Jewry, for we could not survive such a complete loss of meaning.

These perspectives, tenuous as they are, help us to understand why Mr. Green, who fantasied going to Israel as a soldier, has not taken the first plane and gone there as a tourist; why Mr. Mandel, with his lack of any contact with a meaningful Jewish culture, cannot recapture the enthusiasm of the immediate past; why Mrs. Fried is still as marginal a Jew as before; and why Rabbi Aaron is surprised that

Jewish life in Lakeville, although characterized by an aura of good feeling, has seemingly resumed its accustomed tempo.

Those who are disappointed, who feel that an *immediate* and *revolutionary* change in Jewish feeling and behavior should have occurred in Lakeville and throughout the land, might consider that only if events in Israel during May–June 1967 had taken an unfavorable turn might we have expected such a rapid change of values. But such a change would necessarily have been in a negative, rather than a positive, direction; instead of optimism such a change would have induced the blackest kind of pessimism about the future of being Jewish. Thus, for those who are disappointed there is a kind of ironic consolation in the fact that no immediate revolution in Jewish life took place in Lakeville during the aftermath of the Six-Day War. Finally, for students of ethnicity in general and of Jewish life in particular, the response in Lakeville demonstrates that feelings of Jewish identity—albeit on the unconscious level—are more abiding than we had any reason to suspect previously.

SOURCES

Lloyd P. Gartner, "Immigration and the Formation of American Jewry, 1840–1925," *Journal of World History*, Vol. XI, No. 1–2, 1968, pp. 297–312.

Ben Halpern, "America is Different," from *The American Jew* by Ben Halpern (New York: Theodor Herzl Foundation, 1956), pp. 12–33.

Sidney Goldstein, "Jews in the United States: Perspectives from Demography," in *American Jewish Year Book 1981*, Vol. 81 (New York and Philadelphia: American Jewish Committee and the Jewish Publication Society of America, 1980), pp. 3–59.

Chaim I. Waxman, "The Threadbare Canopy: The Vicissitudes of the Jewish Family in Modern American Society," *American Behavioral Scientist*, Vol. 23, No. 4 (March–April 1980), pp. 467–486.

Herbert J. Gans, "The Origin of a Jewish Community in the Suburbs," in *The Jews: Social Patterns of an American Group*, edited by Marshall Sklare (Westport: Greenwood Press, 1977), pp. 205–248.

Marshall Sklare and Joseph Greenblum, "The Friendship Pattern of the Lakeville Jew" in *Jewish Identity on the Suburban Frontier* by Marshall Sklare and Joseph Greenblum (Chicago: University of Chicago Press, 1979), pp. 269–290.

Daniel J. Elazar, "Decision-Making in the American Jewish Community," in *The Future of the Jewish Community in America*, edited by David Sidorsky (New York: Basic Books, 1973), pp. 271–315.

Charles S. Liebman, "The Religion of American Jews," from *The Ambivalent American Jew* by Charles S. Liebman (Philadelphia: Jewish Publication Society of America, 1973), pp. 46–87.

Leonard J. Fein, Robert Chin, Jack Dauber, Bernard Reisman, and Herzl Spiro, "Reform is a Verb," from *Reform is a Verb: Notes on Reform and Reforming Jews* by Leonard J. Fein, Robert Chin, Jack Dauber, Bernard Reisman, and Herzl Spiro (New York: Union of American Hebrew Congregations, 1972), pp. 135–151.

Marshall Sklare, "The Conservative Movement/Achievements and Problems," from *Conservative Judaism: An American Religious Movement* by Marshall Sklare (New York: Schocken Books, 1972), pp. 254–282.

Charles S. Liebman, "Orthodoxy in American Jewish Life," in *American Jewish Year Book 1965*, Vol. 66 (New York and Philadelphia: American Jewish Committee and the Jewish Publication Society of America, 1965), pp. 21–92.

Lloyd P. Gartner, "Jewish Education in the United States," in *Jewish Education in the United States: A Documentary History*, edited by Lloyd P. Gartner (New York: Teachers College Press, 1969), pp. 1–33.

David Singer, "Living with Intermarriage," *Commentary* (July 1979), pp 4–53.

Marshall Sklare, "Lakeville and Israel/The Six-Day War and its Aftermath," *Midstream* (October 1968), pp. 3–21.

INDEX

Aaron, Samuel, 422–423, 429–430, 435–439
Accommodation to intermarriage, *see* Intermarriage, accommodation to
"Actual Jew: A Research Report on Reform Jews and Their Temples, The" (report), 281
Adolescents
  friendship patterns of, 184–190, 192
  See also College students
Advanced yeshivot, 345–347, 390, 391
  See also specific advanced yeshivot
Age
  of Jewish population, 25–26, 50, 60, 74
  age composition, 101–105, 118
  age-specific death rates, 62
  fertility levels by, 65–66
  of marriage, 65, 66, 73, 116, 124, 130
  migrations and, 94–96
  of Park Forest residents, 154–155
Agudat Ha-rabbanim (Union of Orthodox Rabbis of the United States), 255, 258, 355, 357–358, 359n
Agudath Israel, 335, 344, 345, 348, 351–353, 357, 360
Ahavat Yisrael doctrine, 322, 323
Aharon, Reb (Aaron Kotler), 345–346, 350, 351, 356–358, 360
AJYB (*American Jewish Year Book*; 1973), 54, 56, 57, 85, 89, 134
Alienated Jews, friendship circles of, 193–199
"Ambassadorial" role of Lakeville residents, 197–199
American Association for Jewish Education, 211, 219, 391
American-born Jews
  divorce among, 131
  foreign-born as percentage of, 99, 100
  marriage among, 124
  See also Generation status; Generational status; German Jews

American Council for Judaism, 26–27, 416
American Federation of Labor-Congress of Industrial Organizations (AFL-CIO), Industrial Department of, 320
American Jewish Committee, 79–80, 212, 220, 221, 409
American Jewish Conference, 330–331
American Jewish Congress, 212, 220, 221, 267, 269
American Jewish Historical Society, 220
"American Jewish Population Erosion, The" (Bergman), 133
American Jewish Year Book (*AJYB*; 1973), American Revolution, 5, 28, 35
American Zionist Federation, 224, 240
Americanization
  as goal of public-education, 366, 378–379
  World War I as Americanizing experience for Eastern European Jews, 21, 22
  See also Assimilation
Annual Report on Charleston's Jewish Population (1977), 91–92
Anti-Defamation League, 220, 221
Anti-Semitism
  assimilation and, 27–36
    See also Assimilation
  and attitudes of German Jews toward Eastern European immigrants, 4
  character of U.S., 23–24, 28–30
  in Colonial Period, 6–7
  defense against, as organizational task, 235
  early 20th-century, 259
  effects of, on fertility levels, 72
  European, *see* European Jewry, anti-Semitism against
  friendship patterns and, 166
  Holocaust and, 22, 45, 83, 255
  1930s, 386
  possibility of, as viewed by Reform Jews, 283
  self-consciousness rooted in, 198–199

DATE DUE

	DEC 1 8 2008		
	JAN 1 0 2009		
	MAY 2 7 2013		

Demco, Inc. 38-293